Greenhouse Operation and Management

Paul V. Nelson
Department of Horticultural Science
North Carolina State University

Reston Publishing Company, Inc.
A Prentice-Hall Company
Reston, Virginia

Library of Congress Cataloging in Publication Data

Nelson, Paul V
  Greenhouse operation and management.

  Includes bibliographies and index.
  1. Greenhouse management. 2. Floriculture.
I. Title.
SB415.N44   635.9'82   77-27997
ISBN 0-87909-319-6

The use of trade names in this book implies neither endorsement by the author of the products named nor criticism of similar products not mentioned

© 1978 by Reston Publishing Company, Inc.
A Prentice-Hall Company
Reston, Virginia 22090

10 9 8 7 6 5

Printed in the United States of America

To my wife, Jeanne,
and my children,
Scott, Christopher, and Nancy,
for their support and perseverence

Contents

Preface

Congratulations! You have selected an industry with an astronomical potential. Floriculture is an industry in the early throes of revolution: a revolution in consumer demand for its products, in marketing channels, in crops grown, and in methods of culture.

The American floriculture revolution has not gone unheeded in other parts of the world. Latin America has become a sizable competitor for the North American fresh flower market. This has had a competitive and disruptive effect on the domestic cut flower industry. In the long run it will have a beneficial effect in fostering consumer demand for floral products by holding down prices and stimulating new products. With all change, harmful and beneficial effects are to be found. The person who can recognize change and prepare for it is invariably the one who benefits because he directs change. Many steadfast flower growers will perish in this period of escalating floricultural change, only to be replaced by others with a vision to the future who will find the next decade one of the most profitable eras in floricultural history.

It would be a fallacy to prepare for a career in floricultural production by merely learning how to grow crops. Whether you own your own business or work for someone else, your well-being will depend upon your ability to manage materials, money, and the time of yourself and others. Without this ability the application of your technical knowledge of growing crops will not be ultimately profitable and rewarding. You must become knowledgeable in cost accounting, business management, and marketing. Recognizing that an appreciation of these areas is not common in the young student entering the floriculture field, this book is written in such a way that these principles are developed and presented in context with cultural instructions.

The outline for this book anticipates the decisions in the order in which they occur for a person entering the floricultural production business. Initially, the decision to enter the floriculture field is dealt with in a chapter on the worldwide perspective of floriculture. Decisions involving the physical arrangement of a greenhouse business are taken up in successive chapters considering site selection, greenhouse types, and heating and cooling systems. Upon completion of the greenhouse range, considerations turn toward the type of root media in which the crops are to be grown, pasteurization of the root media, maintenance of disease-free conditions in the greenhouse, watering principles and automated systems, fertilizer formulations and methods of application, injection of carbon dioxide gas into the greenhouse atmosphere, light, temperature, chemical growth regulation, pest control, post-harvest handling of crops, and cost accounting. These are the main categories of decisions with which you will be faced as you design, build, and operate a greenhouse business.

Special appreciation is offered to Dr. Jay S. Koths of the University of Connecticut for his invaluable, meticulous role in reviewing this book.

Chapter 1

Floriculture–
A Dynamic Industry

LOCATION

Flowers are grown wherever man has established himself. In the tropical climates they are grown out of doors and limited quantities grown by amateurs and businessmen alike enter the local sales channels there. The compulsion to purchase floral products is greater in temperate and frigid climates where natural floral plants are not so abundant and where there is a need to establish ties with nature during the dormant winter season. A few tropical regions have recognized this need and have developed impressive export businesses. In nontropical areas, vast quantities of floral products are produced under protected environments.

The leading centers of production are in the more northern countries of Western Europe, Japan, and America (referring to Canada and the United States collectively in this book). Limited quantities are also produced in Russia, the Eastern European countries, and Australia. More recently, tropical countries in Central America, as well as the countries of Colombia, Israel, and South Africa, have become important production areas sending most of their products to the markets of Western Europe and America.

ORIGIN OF GREENHOUSE INDUSTRY

The greenhouse industry as we know it today probably originated under circumstances similar to those which existed in Holland durings its *Golden Age,* the 1600s. During the first half of the seventeenth century, The Netherlands became the world's foremost sea power. Its merchant fleet tripled to the point where The Netherlands provided half of the world's shipping and Amsterdam became the world's leading commercial city. The

Dutch standard of living was the highest in the world. In 1602 the Dutch East India Company, and in 1621 the Dutch West India Company, were founded, expanding trade throughout a vast colonial empire. Conflict existed also throughout part of this period beginning in 1581 with the Declaration of Independence from Spain and continuing through the Thirty Years War (1618-1648), which involved most of Europe. At the culmination of the Thirty Years War, The Netherlands won its cause and became an independent nation.

The royal courts of Europe had a taste for elegance and the means to afford it. Spring flowers in the winter and fruit out of season were very enticing. The productive capacity of the large middle class and the trade channels of the merchant segment soon gave birth in The Netherlands to what is today the largest greenhouse industry in the world. Grapes were grown along rock walls in western Holland under glass enclosures constructed in a lean-to fashion. These greenhouses conserved the energy of the sun during winter and permitted early crops of grapes. Today a vast greenhouse vegetable and cut flower industry exists, with its center in the Westland area, as a direct descendent of this initial business.

In the region near Amsterdam, field-grown lilac bushes were dug in late fall prior to freezing of the ground and were stored outside. Periodically during the winter, bushes were moved into greenhouses where they broke dormancy and flowered (Figure 1-1). The cut blooms graced the palaces of seventeenth century royalty in Great Britain, France, Germany and other countries. Even today this industry persists although much of this region, centered around Aalsmeer, is involved in pot plant culture in general.

(a)   (b)

Figure 1-1. Lilacs were one of the first floral crops grown in The Netherlands and they are still grown today. Dormant bushes are dug in the late fall and stored (*left*). Periodically during the winter, bushes are brought into the greenhouse for forcing (*right*).

AMERICAN DEVELOPMENT

Development of the greenhouse industry in America followed much later due to its dependence on the economic growth of the new land. Greenhouse technology brought in by immigrants from Europe was used to establish an industry which began to flourish during the nineteenth century. Floriculture first started around the population centers of Boston, New York, Philadelphia and, later, Chicago. In those days, modes of transportation necessitated production in close proximity to the markets.

Transportation posed less of a problem as trucks became commonplace in the early part of the twentieth century. The populated areas of eastern Massachusetts, Connecticut, and the New York City region, particularly Long Island, became major centers for carnation production. Rose production became particularly important in the northeastern urban areas as well as Chicago. Pot plant production continued to spread across America following population growth.

These trends were shaken during the 1950s. Air transportation had developed to the point where it was possible to ship cut flowers to any point in America. The potential for growing cut flowers outdoors in warm climates became a possibility. Production of cut chrysanthemums expanded at a startling rate in Florida, southern California and, to a lesser extent, Texas. Crops were (and are still) grown the year round under shade cloth fabric supported on inexpensive frames (Figure 1-2). No heating or cooling was required. The increased cost of transportation was more than offset by lower production costs—cheaper growing facilities, no heating expense, and less expensive labor.

The production of *stock* (a cut flower crop of secondary importance) essentially came to a halt in northern greenhouses with nearly all of the demand being met by southern California growers (Figure 1-3). Northern chrysanthemum growers feared that they too would soon be a relic of the past. Interestingly, chrysanthemum production in the field plateaued during the 1960s and came into balance with the rest of America. Field-grown chrysanthemums continue to represent a significant proportion of the total American crop today. The attainment of this position caused many greenhouse growers to turn away from the production of this crop.

Those northern growers who foresaw the trends improved the quality of their product to give themselves a competitive edge over poorer quality flowers grown during periods of harsh weather conditions in the fields. Particularly in the more northern areas, near the ends of the distribution lines from the southern fields, chrysanthemum growers established year-round production schedules to guarantee a steady 52-week supply of flowers. Where it was not possible to meet the competition of southern spray-type chrysanthemums during the winter months, astute growers switched to

Figure 1-2. A large area of crops, particularly fresh flowers such as this chrysanthemum crop in Florida, are grown outdoors under shade fabric in Florida and California.

standard chrysanthemums which were not well-grown at that period in the fields.

The equilibrium between field- and greenhouse-grown chrysanthemums has been further supported by the lack of control over natural factors in the weather-dependent field environment. Frosts, tropical storms, winds, periods of excessive moisture, and sudden infestations of insects are all very difficult and sometimes impossible to control in the field. When these forces come into play, the market demands for quantity and quality are not met and the door is opened for controlled environment (greenhouse) crops. Roses are a good example of this point. Their production continues to date to be in the heavy population centers with the northern cities predominating over the more southern cities. Field injuries to the rose cannot be tolerated because of the more delicate nature of this flower and its inherent short vase life. The quality of field-grown roses has not been sufficient to support such an industry.

Based on the value of a controlled environment coupled with the need to minimize production costs, a mammoth fresh flower greenhouse industry has developed in California over the past twenty years (Figure 1-4). According to the Statistical Reporting Service of the U.S. Department of Agriculture, in 1976, California produced the following percentages of the total number of fresh flowers sold out of twenty-seven leading states in the United

Figure 1-3. A crop of field-grown stock in California. Relatively inexpensive field culture such as this replaced greenhouse crops in the northern states. *(Photo courtesy of R. A. Larson, Department of Horticultural Science, North Carolina State University, Raleigh, NC 27607)*

States: 52 percent pompon chrysanthemum, 71 percent standard chrysanthemum, 69 percent carnation, 48 percent tea rose. The twenty-seven states accounted for more than ninety percent of the U.S. production. They include: Alabama, Arkansas, California, Colorado, Connecticut, Florida, Georgia, Illinois, Indiana, Iowa, Kansas, Maryland, Massachusetts, Michigan, Minnesota, Missouri, New Jersey, New York, North Carolina, Ohio, Oregon, Pennsylvania, Tennessee, Texas, Virginia, Washington, and Wisconsin.

The predominance of California is due to several factors: Heating costs are low in that mild climate, there is a large market at hand, and of great importance at the time the movement got underway was the favorable air freight rates to the east. The predominant movement of air cargo in 1950 was westward, resulting in partially empty planes returning eastward. To fill these planes lower rates were offered for eastward transport. This effectively opened the eastern markets to the western growers and at the same time protected the western markets against competition from eastern growers.

It is interesting to compare air freight rates from San Francisco to Chicago between 1950 and 1972 (see Table 1-1). The influence of these rates on floricultural development in the southwest is immediately evident. A reduction from $21.47 per thousand cut carnation flowers in 1950 to $12.65 in 1965 constituted a strong motivation. Nothing is static in our existence,

Figure 1-4. The past two decades have seen a dynamic expansion in green-house-grown fresh flowers in California. *(Photo courtesy of Hall-Manatee Greenhouses, Encinitas, CA)*

however, and by 1972 the rate had risen to $15.15. Although this is not as high as the 1950 rate, it was serious because it occurred at a time when imported carnations from Latin America began to constitute serious competition for the San Francisco and Denver production areas. Today, transportation costs are a serious problem rather than an advantage for southwestern growers.

A very interesting chapter of American floriculture is seen in the carnation industry. Production centers prior to 1950 were located in New England

Table 1-1
Air Freight Rates From San Francisco to Chicago*

YEAR	RATE
1950	$21.47
1957	13.03
1965	12.65
1969	13.40
1972	15.15

*Per 1000 cut carnation flowers.

and New York. Through the efforts of forward-thinking individuals, among them Professor W. D. Holley of Colorado State University, more satisfactory environments were identified which came closer to fitting the requirements of this crop which calls for 52°F (11°C) night and 75°F (23°C) day temperatures, high light intensity, and 12-hour day-lengths. The Denver, Colorado region offered more temperate summer temperatures and a high light intensity owing to its high elevation. From an essentially nonexistent floral industry in 1950, an impressive carnation industry grew, which accounted in 1976 for 34 percent of the value of blooms sold in the leading 27 states (26 percent of the number of blooms sold).

Carnation production soon spread to the San Francisco Bay area. The poorer light intensity of this area has been offset by more temperate winter and summer temperatures and a greater availability of labor. Fifty-five percent of the total U.S. carnation plants were grown in California in 1975. Obviously the phenominal expansion in Colorado and California had a devastating effect upon the eastern production areas.

IMPORTED FLOWERS

The carnation story goes one step further. Two carnation ranges begun in 1966 in Bogota, Colombia, in South America, were producing quality carnations at an incredibly low price. They were joined in 1969 by an American and others followed until today there are over fifty firms. More than 500 acres of plastic greenhouses are in operation for carnations alone. That region enjoys a day-length close to 12 hours year round because of its location near the equator. Evening temperatures are in the 40s or 50s and day temperatures in the 60s and 70s, in all seasons, coupled with high light intensity as a result of the high altitude. All these factors contribute to high quality. Added to them are the low cost of labor and the absence of heating bills because flowers are produced in unheated plastic houses in Colombia (Figure 1-5).

Colombian carnations constituted a modest 0.5 percent of all carnations sold in the U.S. market in 1970 but by the end of 1974 the figure was a stunning twenty-five percent. While the level waned a bit in 1975 due to a politically motivated shift of emphasis to the European market, it regained its strength in 1976, making up about twenty-seven percent of total sales. This new competitor has necessitated an increase in efficiency in California and Colorado and, together with these states, has all but annihilated the carnation growing industry in the rest of the U.S.

U.S. floral imports are primarily in the fresh flower category. Besides carnations, twenty-eight percent of the pompon chrysanthemums, and 10 percent of the standard chrysanthemums sold in the U.S. in 1976 were imported. Orchid blooms were imported to the extent of 3/4 million blooms in 1975. Much of the former domestic production has ceased. Several other

(a)

(b)

Figure 1-5. Carnation production in the Bogota area of Colombia, South America.

crops are imported including cut tulips from Holland, statice, daisies from Colombia, protea from tropical regions, and cut palms for floral arrangements from Mexico and Guatemala. These have not been produced in sizeable quantities in the U.S. in prior times.

PRODUCTION AREA DETERMINANTS

It should be obvious to you by now that the floral production industry is far from static. There are three forces which govern its location: (1) cost of production, (2) quality, and (3) cost of transportation (Figure 1-6). Prior to 1950 carnations were grown near large markets in spite of poor quality achieved during dark winter months in the north. When transportation became reasonable carnation production shifted to Colorado where high quality could be achieved. The shift in chrysanthemum production to the fields of Florida and California was in response to lower costs of production in those areas. The savings in production costs was greater than the added transportation cost, thus the shift occurred. Colombian production has become a stable situation because production costs are lower than in Colorado, quality is reasonable high, and transportation costs are modest. Under present technology it would be very difficult to cause a further shift in carnation production.

Roses continue to be produced in close proximity to their markets because of the quality factor. Any attempts thus far to reduce production costs by abandoning the controlled greenhouse environment have resulted in an

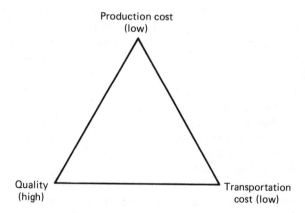

Figure 1-6. Crop production areas often can be explained on the basis of three factors: production cost, quality, and transportation cost. If all three factors are ideal, then the area is safe from competition. If conditions are less than ideal, as is usually the case, the weakness of any one factor must be offset by the strengthening of one or both of the others in order for the production area to meet outside competition.

unacceptable reduction in quality. Pot plants are also produced near their markets due to quality and cost consideration in shipping. The triangle in Figure 1-6 should be fixed in your mind as you read the remainder of this book. It will have a great bearing on the location and greenhouse types you select for your business from Chapter 2 and on the degree of automation and type of production systems which you decide upon in the remainder of the chapters. Keep in mind that a "love of flowers" alone does not justify your business involvement; you must bring home a paycheck as well.

FRESH FLOWER PICTURE IN AMERICA

An effort is underway to categorize greenhouse crops under the headings:

1. Fresh flowers–flowers which are cut from the plant prior to sale

2. Flowering plants–plants bearing flowers which are sold in a pot

3. Green plants–plants sold in a pot and valued more for their foliage than their flowers.

4. Bedding plants–young plants sold for planting around the home (including vegetable seedlings)

5. Vegetables–grown to maturity

The situation with fresh flowers from 1970 through 1977 has been bleak. It has been a no-growth period for U.S. growers. The modest expansion in retail sales has been supplied by imported flowers. Note in Figure 1-7 that U.S. production of pompon chrysanthemums and standard chrysanthemums is nearly static, while the production of carnations and roses is dropping.

The pressure of imported chrysanthemums and carnations has reduced the profitability of producing these crops for many growers in America and consequently they have switched to the production of potted plants where competition is generally localized. Notice in Table 1-2 the significant drop in number of growers of various floral crops in the U.S.

The rose decline has not been the result of imports since they account for less than 2 percent of the domestic market. High pricing, which automatically limits the size of the market, and the condition of the flowers by the time they reach the consumer have been responsible for the decline. Ohio State University sponsored a National Floricultural Conference on Commodity Handling which examined handling of fresh flowers (particularly after harvest) and what could be done to improve the situation. The findings were that 5 percent of fresh flower crops are not harvested and that 20 percent of those flowers which are harvested end up unsuitable for final sale. The twenty

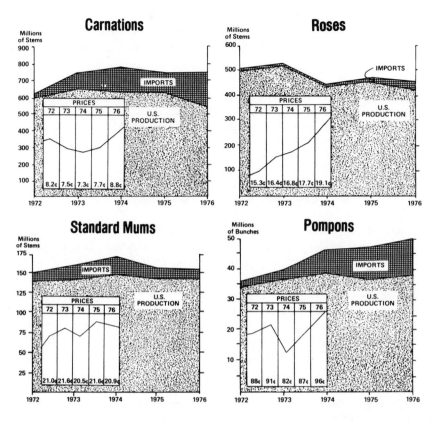

Figure 1-7. Number of blooms of various fresh flowers sold in the United States per year from 1972 through 1976 and their sources. (*Reprinted from Grower Talks, 1977, George J. Ball, Inc., West Chicago, IL 60185*)

percent post-harvest loss alone in 1975 in the U.S. had an economic value of $134 million which had to be added to the price of those flowers sold. This greatly weakens the case for fresh flower production, particularly for roses which already have a short vase life expectancy of about five days. Roses, or for that matter any flowers, which die one or two days after they are purchased are not a stimulus for repeat sales.

FLOWERING PLANTS AND GREEN PLANTS

Fresh flowers constitute a no-growth industry for the producer while the demand is rising rapidly for flowering and green plants. Notable among the flowering plants is the pot mum (chrysanthemum). Production increased in the U.S. by nearly 40 percent from 1972 through 1976 (Figure 1-8).

Table 1-2
Total Number of Growers of Each of Five Floral Crops in 22 Leading
States Accounting for Perhaps 90% or More of the U.S. Production

	NUMBER OF GROWERS		
CROP	1971	1976	Percent of Change
Pompon chrysanthemum	2168	1126	−48
Standard chrysanthemum	2134	1029	−52
Carnation	1525	539	−65
Rose	323	230	−29
Pot chrysanthemum	1394	1339	− 4

During this same time the market has seen the reappearance of several flowering plants which lost popularity in the marketplace during the first half of this century. Kalanchoe, calceolaria, cinneraria, and cyclamen are some examples. There also have been new crops introduced including Rieger begonia and clerodendron. These crops are not new to Europe where a much wider variety of plants is grown commercially.

A unique group of plants is the bedding plants. Fifty plant species or more are grown ranging from vegetables such as tomato, eggplant, and cabbage to flowers such as petunia, marigold, and impatiens. These plants are established in small containers and sold for use in home gardens, window boxes, displays, etc. Sales have increased by 10 to 12 percent per annum in recent years. The wholesale value of this crop in the U.S. was near $200 million in 1977.

Green plants, also commonly referred to as foliage plants, constitute the most phenomenal success story today. A stable crop between 1959 and 1970 when it increased modestly from $24 million to $27 million in wholesale value in the U.S., it commanded a wholesale value of over $235 million in 1976 (Table 1-3). The area in production expanded 269 percent from 1969 through 1976 while the wholesale value increased 770 percent!

Again, numerous plant species make up this group including philodendrons, dracaena, ficus, croton, a wide range of hanging basket plants, and many others. Forty-seven percent of the U.S. production of green plants was in Florida, 26 percent in California, and 5.8 percent in Ohio in 1976. Except for hanging basket plants only a modest number of green plants are grown in other states. Many of these plants are of tropical origin and can be produced more economically in subtropical areas.

More northern areas, where heated greenhouses are required, have found a future in green plants, although more modest than that of the subtropical regions. Premium hanging basket plants being large in volume and cumbersome to handle are expensive to ship. These are best grown close to

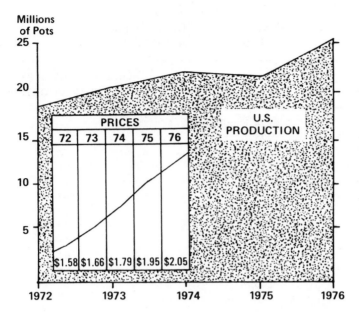

Figure 1-8. Number of pots of pot mums sold in the United States per year from 1972 through 1976 and the average price per pot. (*Reprinted from Grower Talks, 1977, George J. Ball, Inc., West Chicago, IL 60185*)

the terminal markets. The cost of production of hanging baskets is low since many of the fixed costs such as greenhouse depreciation and heat are shared with another crop on the benches or ground below. Hanging baskets offer a means for utilizing nearly 100 percent of the equivalent floor space of a greenhouse (Figure 1-9).

Many greenhouse enterprises in temperate regions purchase finished green plants from the tropical regions and hold these in their greenhouses until they can sell them to a network of retail outlets they service. Other green plant crops are purchased in various intermediate stages of development and are finished in the temperate region greenhouses.

THE GROWING DEMAND FOR FLORAL PRODUCTS

Anyone who has traveled in Europe is awestruck by the extensive use of flowers. In several of these countries where apartment dwellings abound over single family homes, the occupants have literally taken to indoor gardening. The apartments are constructed with plants in mind, making use of large windows and deep sills on the high light intensity sides. A veritable plant

Table 1-3
Wholesale Value of Green (Foliage) Plants
in the U.S. From 1959 to 1976

YEAR	VALUE	CHANGE (%) OVER PREVIOUS YEAR REPORTED
1959	$24.1 million	—
1966	25.2	5
1967	26.1	4
1968	26.4	1
1969	29.2	11
1970	27.1	-7
1971	37.6	39
1972	48.4	29
1973	68.0	41
1974	113.5	67
1975	187.2	65
1976	235.8	21

Figure 1-9.   The expense involved in producing hanging basket plants is shared with other crops since the baskets occupy space over the walks not formerly used. It is possible to achieve 100 percent utilization of the equivalent floor area of a greenhouse with such a production program.

paradise exists within most dwellings. Numerous customs enhance the use of flowers. It is generally an offense to arrive at the home of your host without a gift, most often a plant or flowers. Floral products are exchanged between loved ones on a regular basis; in Holland quite often on a weekly basis. Flowers are a part of daily life from decoration in a street intersection, a vacant lot, or on a light pole to vases in a wedding coach or on the dashboard of an automobile.

Many would say that Americans are not of the same inclination; however, the past ten years have proven this wrong. Dormitories on American campuses abound with plants regardless of whether the occupant is male or female. Flowers and plant sales have made their appearance in drug, food chain, and discount stores from coast to coast. People never before reached are becoming repeat customers. Americans, given the proper exposure, can be as ardent about floral products as Europeans.

The wholesale value of floral crops produced in the U.S. in 1976 was about $900 million. This was a 100 percent increase over the value six years earlier in 1970. Social changes of many extremes have all been kind to the floral industry. The environmental movement nurtured an awareness of nature and a desire to bring plants into personal lives. The recession of the early half of the '70s would certainly have been thought to be injurious to the floral industry as it was to so many others. Instead, people diverted from their former expensive pastimes, took to gardening, both indoor and outdoor, in great numbers. The oil embargo, while reducing the number of people along pleasure routes, swelled the ranks of plant hobbyists. The continued urbanization of America threatens man's biological roots and causes him to hold more tenaciously to them. These forces and many others have had effects seen in the escalation of horticulture courses taught in high schools, in adult education courses, and in the four-fold or better increase in college level horticulture students. While not all of these people will find their employment in floriculture, they will for the most part be zealous consumers of floral products and will spread their enthusiasm to other people.

CHANGING MARKET CHANNELS

The Conventional Florist

Traditionally Americans have purchased their floral products at full-service retail flower shops. These shops were characterized in the past by non-spontaneous purchases. Eighty-five percent of fresh flower sales went into funeral and wedding orders in the early 1950s. Traditional holiday sales accounted for another heavy proportion of fresh flower and pot plant sales including such demands as Easter lilies at Easter, poinsettias at Christmas, and roses for Valentine's day. Aside from weddings, funerals, and the strongly motivated floral holidays just mentioned, routine customers represented a small percentage of the American public, about 25 percent.

Full-service retail flower shops generally purchase fresh flowers from wholesalers who in turn purchase them from the growers. The wholesaler retains an average 25 percent of the wholesale price which he charges the retail florist and returns 75 percent to the grower. Pot plants are customarily delivered directly to the retail florist by the grower. The grower does not pay a sales commission, but he must meet the expenses of transportation and sales himself.

The full-service retail florist in addition to selling floral products is selling service. The fresh flowers are professionally arranged beyond the competence of the average consumer. Pot plants are wrapped in foil and tied with a bow. These products carry the prestige of the flower shop's name. The convenience of home delivery is an important part of the service. Through the services of organizations referred to as wire houses such as *American Floral Services, Florafax, Florists Clearing Network, Florist's Transworld Delivery, Gold Medal Florists, Sears Flowers by Wire,* and *Teleflorist,* a customer is able to telephone his local florist and place an order for flowers or plants which will be arranged and delivered nearly anywhere in the world by a florist in that locality.

Services cost the retail florist dearly in trained personnel and in physical overhead such as buildings and trucks. These costs must be passed on to the consumer. It is not uncommon for floral products to be marked up to a retail price three and four times the wholesale price paid for them. At first sight this may seem exorbitant, but it is not. This markup is fair in light of the overhead expenses of the flower shop and is acceptable to the customers who frequent these outlets. The emotional effect of a gift of flowers sent by a son to his mother some 3000 miles away on her birthday is very significant. The impact of a florist delivery van pulling up to the home of your hostess for an elegant gathering that evening is as great as that of the flowers alone.

The Mass Market

Not everyone places this emphasis on prestige and service, nor can everyone afford the prices a full-service florist must charge. As is the case of so many other commodities in our American society, methods have been found to increase the availability and decrease the retail price of floral products making repeat purchases possible for a larger proportion of the American public—the 75 percent of the population who have not been reached in the past. Such development could increase the wholesale value of floral crops sold in the U.S. from today's $900 million to a future $3.6 billion. Mass marketing is the strongest recourse at hand today for realizing such a potential.

Mass marketing refers to marketing in high traffic locations such as supermarkets, large discount stores, shopping center malls, busy street corners, airport terminals, etc. (Figure 1-10). The objective is a high volume business. Purchases are usually spontaneous so prices must be sufficiently low to attract the discretionary dollars (money remaining after the necessities of life are purchased) of the customer. This is achieved by avoiding services such as floral arranging and delivery. Such businesses are generally cash-and-carry.

Floral mass marketing was developed long ago in Europe and is highly perfected. It has only begun to develop in the past fifteen years in the U.S. The potential of mass marketing, however, was recognized well before that time. The results of the Northeast Regional Marketing Project NEM-8 conducted in the 1950s indicated optimistic prospects for mass marketing of fresh flowers through nonfloral outlets regularly patronized by consumers.

Initial development was slow to come partly because of the initiative and resources needed to bring about such a change in production and marketing and partly due to resistance within the industry. Taken at face value, mass marketing appeared as a great threat to the continued existence of the conventional florist market system. Lower prices and high volume struck a chord of fear in spite of optimistic predictions coming out of market studies.

Figure 1-10. A street-side outlet for fresh flowers in San Francisco. This is one of the forms mass marketing has taken in recent years. Others include no-service cash-and-carry shops in supermarkets, airports, and shopping malls. (*Courtesy of J. C. Raulston, Department of Horticultural Science, North Carolina State University, Raleigh, NC 27607*)

Such studies indicated that flowers purchased from mass market outlets would be for a different purpose than those purchased through the already established florists' outlets. These studies further indicated that mass market sales would help to create a greater appreciation and desire for flowers in America and thereby enhance sales in the conventional florists channel.

Many conventional florists in the 1950s and 1960s boycotted growers who sold in mass channels. This slowed, but could not stop the change that was and is destined to come. In 1962 Kiplinger and Sherman of Ohio State University reported on a mass marketing study conducted in four Columbus, Ohio supermarkets. Sales of fresh flowers and plants were very optimistic and prompted the researchers to state that

> based on sales in the four Columbus, Ohio supermarkets, the sales potential would be at least $135 million if offered in all supermarkets with weekly volume of $20,000 or higher in the U.S.

Some estimated that $450 million worth of floral products at the wholesale level were marketed through mass outlets in the U.S. in 1976. This was half of the 1976 production. Development has been more rapid in California than other areas. Better than $35 million in sales were made in the Los Angeles area through mass outlets in 1976 at the retail level. One large chain store which is a leader in mass marketing of floral crops in that area estimates that it is selling floral products to only 10 percent of its customers. They are optimistic that they will eventually market these products to most of their customers.

Mass outlets customarily mark up floral products by an amount constituting 25 to 40 percent of the retail sales price. In other words they increase the wholesale price by 33 to 67 percent. This is a modest increase compared to the 200 to 400 percent figure in full-service flower shops. On the other hand, it is a very large markup for a chain store. Floral products are therefore very profitable; a point which has given impetus to the stores to develop this business. Besides supermarkets, discount stores and the like, mass floral outlets are to be found as plant boutique shops in the middle of the malls of shopping centers, in airport lobbies, and on carts along the side of city streets. An interesting concept is that of plant parties hosted in the homes of customers or in the meeting rooms of apartment complexes.

The interesting point is that the industry is not bound by traditionalism. New customers are purchasing new crops along with old, accepting new colors, forms, and sizes, and are eager to do so through new outlets. You as a grower or marketer are free to set your imagination to work and your chances of success are great.

During this past decade of mass market development the full-service florist channel has grown handsomely as well, proving the original assertion that one would benefit the other. As a matter of fact, a number of full-service retail florists now operate nonservice plant boutiques. The line of demarcation is becoming less clear between the "conventional" full-service florist and the mass marketer. This is not to say that the demand for floral products with service is diminishing. This demand is growing and remains distinctly different from the demand of spontaneous purchases and of personal consumption which is satisfied at the mass outlet.

The overall expansion of floral sales has been educational to the public, showing them ways to enhance their personal lives. It has generated yet other uses for our products and will continue to do so. An interesting business of the recent past is that of plant rentals. This is an enterprise partly involved in growing and partly in merchandising. Such firms decorate commercial buildings, malls, etc., providing plants on a rental basis. In time, these plants are returned to greenhouses for rejuvenation and new plants take their place.

FUTURE DIRECTION OF PRODUCTION

Increased Production and a Lower Sales Price at a Reasonable Profit

The future holds much optimism for American production. The market will continue to expand rapidly, bringing an even greater demand for floral production. Systems are currently available which will lend efficiency to production and post-harvest handling to insure America's place in production and at the same time guarantee a respectable profit. Three factors attest to this potential.

1. The current consumer demand exceeds production in spite of the fact that only a modest effort has been made to truly market floral products. The Society of American Florists (SAF), serving as a parent organization to all segments of the industry, including growing, transportation, wholesaling, and retailing, has made great efforts through the American Florists' Marketing Council (AFMC) to collect voluntary contributions from all segments for the purpose of promoting floral products nationally. Their budget for fiscal year 1975-76 was $1,660,000. This investment represents only 0.045 percent of the total retail industry worth of $3.65 billion and is grossly inadequate. No other viable industry would attempt to promote itself on such a weak basis. Of course the wire houses are advertising and are actually investing better than six times the amount of the AFMC to promote the full-service florist channel. In addition retail florists and mass outlets advertise on a local basis, but more must be done nationally. Fortunately, this need is recognized and is being pursued. Undoubtedly the market for floral products will expand even more rapidly and bring with it a tremendous opportunity for growers.

2. Current production is profitable, but is still not highly efficient. Systems exist for further increasing efficiency and profit. Inefficient greenhouse ranges comprised of several free-standing small greenhouses which cannot be properly automated or managed are giving way to newer reasonably priced ridge-and-furrow type designs. The newer designs can take advantage of the many systems of automation discussed in this book. Systems for growing pot plants directly on specially prepared floors rather than in benches permit more efficient handling of plants and a growing area of 85 percent rather than the traditional 67 percent of the heated greenhouse area. Perhaps most important, the motivating mentality, *a love for plants,* which has accounted for many floral growers is now expanding to include the satisfaction of sound business management.

3. Post-harvest handling of floral crops has considerable room for improvement. As mentioned earlier, 20 percent of harvested fresh flowers are lost to the market. Technology exists to reduce this level significantly.

Standard chrysanthemums and carnations can be harvested in the bud stage, shipped and opened at the wholesale market. The net result is increased profit. The cost of opening the buds is more than offset by increased production at the growers' level and reduced shipping costs. Some growers are using this technique but must open the buds on their own premises, generally in a heated work building, since the cooperation of the wholesale market has not been fully obtained. Even operated in this limited way the system is profitable, although the benefits of reduced shipping cost are not realized. Cooperation among grower, wholesaler, and retailer will undoubtedly come. Growers in concentrated production areas of the U.S. and Colombia will very likely establish such markets themselves throughout America.

Great horizons exist for prepackaging of floral products which would improve sales and increase shelf life. Pot plants in transparent packages continue to receive light but remain in a moist atmosphere where they are not injured by drying and do not require watering during the normal period of sales. The package carries information for the consumer, including instructions for the care of the plant, along with further enticement to purchase the product. Fresh flowers sell much better in the mass outlets if a mixture of flowers is offered including a stem of greenery. When the package is opened one has an instant bouquet. Packaging of such combinations permits handling by the customer in self-service outlets and affords a place to present a brand name, information and price. A stated price and accessibility to the customer are important sales incentives.

The improvements just mentioned in these three areas will go a long way toward improving sales demand and profit for the grower. Just as plant roots will develop in the soil zone where moisture and nutrients are plentiful, business will develop wherever profit is rendered for a just service. There is no doubt that a vast American floral industry has begun to develop. The question to be answered is, who will earn this business?

Competition from other parts of the world will continue to grow as political and geographical boundaries continue to dissolve. Today we are in a communications revolution. Technical information, including cultural crop programs, can be obtained in most any part of the developed world in a matter of hours. Multinational cooperations form a network around the globe insuring manufactured goods to any society which can develop the financial basis for exchange. More and more the world moves toward the model situation described by the Dutch Nobel prize winner Jan Tinbergen in 1969, which calls for production of each product in the location and by the society in which it can be produced the most efficiently at the required quality level.

This competition will be the driving force bringing about efficiency in production and marketing in America. Many growers who are unable to accept change will perish while the others will prosper. We are in a period similar to the revolution in the poultry industry in the 1950s when massive production operations replaced family businesses and the prices of poultry and eggs came down. As in that industry, numerous large nonhorticultural firms can be expected to enter our industry bringing with them sound principles of management and marketing in order to develop and enjoy the great profit potential we have. This has already begun to happen.

Profile of Growers to Come

What form will production take from here on? This is perhaps easiest to discuss under three headings: production for full-service florists' shops, production for mass outlets, and new production businesses.

Production for full-service florists' shops will continue in its current trends. Fresh flowers will be produced for the most part in specific areas where satisfactory quality can be achieved at a low production cost. Transportation costs will continue to play a relatively small role as shipping of some crops in the bud stage reduces this cost. American production will continue to have competition and will depend upon increased efficiency of production and post-harvest handling.

Flowering plant production for full-service retail florists will remain for awhile near the markets throughout America due to the high costs of transportation for heavy pot plants and the need for a controlled environment to produce the quality level required for these outlets.

Green plants of tropical origin are well adapted to our subtropical field conditions and can be produced cheaply and at high quality in these regions. Increased competition will come from other subtropical and tropical countries. The key to success here will lie in freedom from diseases and insects, a high level of quality, and a plant which has gone through a special period of acclimatization to the low-light, slow-growth conditions it will face in the final consumer's environment. Such plants will offer a greater assurance of success to the consumer, thus encouraging success in the marketplace. The increased efforts of production and acclimatization will have to be absorbed by production efficiency and sound merchandising. The demand for poor quality will always be small.

The second category of production, for the mass market, comprises about half of our floral output now. Eventually it will probably encompass eighty percent of total production. This will not be achieved at the expense of retail florist outlets since their sales will continue to increase as the population expands and the economy improves. The mass market increases will be supported by large segments of our public who have not before been steady floral customers.

Fresh flower production for the mass market will change considerably. Long flower stems, as currently produced, are for the most part a detriment. They raise the production cost because of the longer time it takes to grow them. Transportation costs are greater to cover the large volume and weight. In the end the excess stem is cut and discarded because it is inappropriate for home decoration.

The smaller sweetheart roses are more appropriate than the large hybrid teas. Miniature spray-type carnations and miniature gladioli have great versatility in the mass market. Schedules already exist for producing short-stem chrysanthemums. Other fresh flowers not common to American floral production are needed such as margarita daisy, and alstroemeria. Garden flowers including marigold, daisy, zinnia, dahlia, and others should be grown. Minor crops need to be produced in greater quantities, e.g., aster, stock, tulip, daffodil, iris, and peony. There is a large market for dried plant materials sold in arrangements or separately.

While some of these crops will best lend themselves to subtropical field conditions, many with their short schedules will be profitably grown in more northern locations close to the markets. Dried plant materials can be produced outdoors in the northern areas, processed and sold throughout the year.

The most important aspects of mass market fresh flower production will be (1) a steady 52-week supply of fresh flowers of high keeping quality, (2) the capability to expand production for periods of peak demand, (3) modest prices, and (4) prepackaging and distribution systems to minimize labor and maintain a full inventory at the retail outlet. This latter requirement may be accomplished singlehandedly by large producers or by cooperatives of smaller growers. Fresh flowers would be delivered to a central facility where they would be assembled in combinations. Mixed colors, flower types, and sufficient greenery to insure a pleasing arrangement would be included.

A tasteful balance of garden flowers with more impressive greenhouse flowers might enable pricing low enough to attract more discretionary spending during warmer months. Undoubtedly some flowers will be purchased from distant areas where they are produced cheaper. The bouquets would be packaged in a transparent film permitting customer handling on self-service shelves in retail outlets and would bear instructions for home display, prolongation of vase life, and, most important, a trade name attesting to guaranteed quality to which the customer can relate in subsequent purchases. Packaged flowers would then be distributed on a daily basis to the outlets. It is very important in spontaneous marketing that a full, massed offering be maintained to attract the desire of the potential customer.

Potted plant production for mass markets also will deviate from retail florist production. Many smaller size pots will be grown along with the larger premium pots. A much wider range of crops will be grown. Many crops important in Europe will be developed in America. The mass market chains will encourage the growth of large greenhouse production ranges which can fill the contract for a large number of outlets. The large ranges in turn will be able to produce efficiently and sell at a low price. This evolution will make it difficult for small growers to produce the major pot plant crops unless they are producing exceptional quality, an unusual size of the product, or are able to provide delivery to rather remote outlets.

The third category of growers is the new growers. Today the greatest opportunity to enter floral production lies in pot plant crops. The return per square foot is generally too low for fresh flowers to justify a small range. Bedding plants afford a particularly good avenue for entry. This is a labor-intensive crop but that can be provided by the person starting the business while it is still small. Three crops or better can be turned over within the season of January through May in some parts of the country. This brings in income before the season ends. At the same time the initial cash outlay is not great. Cold frames can be used later in the season to supplement the greenhouse and bring the overhead costs down, but they require more labor and are seldom used in northern areas.

When pot plant production becomes more efficient in the future it may become difficult to enter the business by growing any of the major crops. The margin of profit will be too low for a small range to compete when it is unable to hold the cost of production down through automation.

Such a producer will find his opportunity in the low-demand specialty crops. Since the production of these crops will not have been worked out on a production line basis, the margin of profit will be respectable for smaller, less automated growers. New crop introductions and plants with regional appeal will fit this category.

Labor-intensive crops will be a good possibility as well. Such crops are difficult to mass produce. Terrarium plants, for instance, involve numerous types of plants, each with a different cultural program. The volume of any one is not great.

A combination grower–retailer will likely be an avenue of entry for a beginner. This is actually two separate businesses and eventually as the business grows, it should be treated as such to determine where the profits lie. Until the business grows to that size, this combination can provide the profits necessary to keep going. People have a natural inclination to browse about in greenhouses and pick their own plants. Even in a small town there are sufficient customers to support such a business. After a period of time, volume of sales would become large enough to profitably enter the wholesale market channel.

YOUR PROSPECTS IN FLORAL PRODUCTION

The situation today and prospects for tomorrow indicate that this is a great time to be in the floral business. The 300 percent growth potential of the U.S. floral market which may well be realized by the end of this century could raise the wholesale production figure of $900 million to $3.6 billion. Since much of the additional production will pass through the mass market where modest markups of perhaps a future average of 100 percent will be applied, the current retail floral value of $3.65 billion will rise to $9 billion by today's monetary standard. The profits ahead of us which lie within this $5.4 billion increase are indeed enticing.

It cannot be emphasized too strongly that a technical knowledge in floriculture is only half of what it takes to succeed in the floral production business. You must become equally well-versed in principles of business management and marketing. The foundation for this can be laid in formal courses, but ideally it is an educational process which you will maintain throughout your career. You can do this by reading books on the subject, subscribing to business periodicals, and, most important, by establishing communications with people in other phases of the floral industry. Knowledge of the responsibilities of these people is your responsibility even though you are not directly involved in their work. In addition to attending your local flower grower association's meetings and short courses, get accustomed to participating in conferences held by floral associations representing other areas such as transportation, wholesaling, and retailing. The Society of American Florists is such an organization.

No knowledge is of value unless there is a human mind to assemble it into a plan and a spirit to activate it. If you feel a glow when you handle a plant, or a thrill when you walk into a greenhouse, then you are in the right field. Make your mind up now that this is your field and that you will suceed. Don't waste further energy doubting yourself. Invest your efforts in learning how to succeed and in formulating a plan. Sit down now and write on paper what it is you want to achieve in life. This book will take you through many of the decisions you face ahead. As you study the facts, reflect on how these can fit into your plan. Seek further knowledge to fill in your plan by perusing the suggested readings at the end of each chapter, by attending local growers' short courses, by establishing a relationship with commercial people, and, best of all, by taking a job in the area of your choice—perhaps part time during your school year or during the summers. Sooner or later you must gain practical experience to supplement your book learning if you are going to be able to apply it. It is not your background or your current aptitude that will bring you success, but rather your knowledge of what you want out of life, your belief in yourself, and the persistent effort you're willing to put forth to achieve your goal.

SUGGESTED READINGS

Ball, V. "Crop Trends in '76," *Grower Talks* 41(2):1–11. 1977.

Ball, V. "Early American Horticulture," *Grower Talks* 40(3):1–56. 1976.

Kaplan, P. "Origins of Commercial Floriculture in U.S. Found to Predate Declaration of Independence," *Florist* 10(2):39–46. 1976.

Kiplinger, D. C. and R. W. Sherman. "Florist Crops for Mass Market Outlets," Ohio Agricultural Experiment Station Res. Bulletin 928, 1962.

Staby, G. L., J. L. Robertson, D. C. Kiplinger, and C. A. Conover. "Procedures of National Floricultural Conference on Commodity Handling," Ohio Florists' Association, 2001 Fyffe Ct., Columbus, Oh. 43210. 1976.

Statistical Reporting Service. "Flowers and Foliage Plants. Production and Sales, 1975 and 1976, Intentions for 1977." *Statistical Reporting Service*, U.S. Department Agriculture, Washington, D.C. Sp. Cr. 6–1(77). 1977 (available annually).

Chapter 2

Greenhouse Construction

The term *greenhouse* refers in the United States to a structure covered with a transparent material for the purpose of admitting natural light for plant growth. These structures are usually heated artificially and differ from other growing structures, such as cold frames and hot beds, in that they are sufficiently high to permit a person to work from within. The European definition of greenhouse differs in that the structure receives little or no artificial heat. The term *glasshouse* is used in Europe for an artificially heated structure. Quite frequently two or more greenhouses in one location are referred to as a *greenhouse range*.

Greenhouses are to be found in many designs including the conventional A-shape frame, quonset shapes, and vertical towers. The transparent coverings are highly variable as well. Originally glass was used, but now plastic films and fiberglass reinforced plastic (FRP) are used as well. The future holds promise of new covering materials which will reduce the burden of heating and cooling, and new frame designs which will be more economical.

LOCATION

The first consideration in establishing a greenhouse range is that of location. Several factors to be considered are listed in the following text. Usually it will be necessary to make certain compromises dictated by the crop to be grown, the anticipated size of the business, and the degree of automation desired. Common forms of automation include thermostatically integrated heating and cooling, mechanized watering and fertilization, motorized shading of photoperiodic crops, automatic potting, and conveyor movement of potted plants.

Room for Expansion

A parcel of land larger than the immediate needs should be acquired. The ultimate size of the range should be predicted. Area should then be added to this figure to accommodate service buildings, storage, and access drives. Doubling the area covered by greenhouses would not be too much. Finally, an extra allotment of space is desirable to cover the unforeseen. For instance, it may become necessary to engage in stock-piling of supplies as fostered in recent years by shortages of materials, or the future may call for holding ponds for water effluent from the range in order to reduce the nutrient content before releasing it into streams or the ground water table.

Topography

The building site should be as level as possible to reduce the cost of grading. A level site also permits the construction of large greenhouses which can be easily automated. The site should be well drained. Due to the extensive use of water in greenhouse operations it is always advisable to provide a drainage system. Try to select a site with deep, well-drained loam or sandy loam soil. Where drainage is a problem, it is wise to install tiles below the surface prior to constructing the greenhouses. It is advisable to select a site with a natural wind-break on the north and northwest sides, such as a tree line or hill. In regions where snow is expected, trees should be 100 feet away in order to keep drifts back from the greenhouses. Obstructions which would cast shadows should be avoided on the south side.

Land Use Prediction

Local zoning and tax laws are subject to changes brought on by development pressures. Such changes have brought about the termination of many greenhouse businesses. One should carefully study the past development of the location in question in order to assess its future direction. Some local governments have made provisions to protect agricultural businesses from prohibitive taxation due to zoning shifts. Others have not, as witnessed by the extensive disbandment of the once vast greenhouse industry immediately east of New York City.

Climate

As indicated earlier, climatic conditions have dictated world-wide geographical shifts in floriculture. Such forces are also at work within local regions. Areas of frequent fog or inclement weather are poor for crops in general. The better light intensity of higher altitudes is particularly advantageous for the carnation crop but would have little benefit for crops with a low light intensity requirement such as African violet, begonia, gloxinia, and most green plants. The greenhouse site should be selected with specific crops in mind. The greenhouses of one carnation range forced to terminate operations on Long Island, New York were disassembled and trucked to carefully selected high elevation sites in the Appalachian Mountains in the southeastern United States and then reconstructed. These sites were located well above the customary morning fog layer of this region and enjoyed high light intensity and cool summer temperatures, conditions ideal for carnation growth. Subsequent production records testified to the successful selection of these sites.

Labor Supply

Present and future labor needs should be assessed and should be in accord with the labor supply of the area. Procurement of a labor supply has been a perennial problem in the floriculture industry. While the solution has appeared to rest in locating close to an urban area, this has not always worked. Traditionally greenhouse wages have been low, which has given the labor recruitment advantage to the more unionized industries. The solution appears to lie in meeting the competition directly through higher wages. Higher wages can be compensated by increased productivity of the individual brought about through automation.

Accessibility

A site should be selected which has easily accessible shipping routes. Marketing of floral crops costs approximately one-quarter of the gross wholesale return. Minimization of shipping costs by close proximity to markets for the earlier stages of business development as well as to long distance shipping routes such as bus, truck, or air terminals for the later, more successful stages of development will go a long way toward alleviating this burden. At the same time this will reduce local carrier costs for goods received.

Site location has often been the deciding factor in the type of fuel used. In some regions natural gas has been a cheaper source of energy than other fuels. Some greenhouse ranges have not been able to take advantage of this factor due to their location at a prohibitive distance from the gas line while the competition located near the line has enjoyed this advantage. In one situation where a greenhouse range was built at a high altitude to take advantage of light conditions, the remoteness of the location necessitated the transfer of oil from large tank trucks to smaller trucks during delivery thus raising the cost of the oil.

Water

Water is one of the most frequently overlooked commodities in the establishment of a greenhouse business. The quality and method of application of water, however, is perhaps the most troublesome cultural problem in the growth of plants. Before purchasing a site, the available water source should be tested for quality and quantity. There are several cases where businesses located in coastal and river bottom regions have been compelled to move to new locations to obtain water of suitable quality. The cost of removing ions such as sodium and chloride can be prohibitive, but failure to do so results in plant injury. Water quantity is equally important since as much as two quarts of water can be applied to one square foot of growing area in a single application.

Orientation

Shadows are cast by the greenhouse frame. The magnitude of the shadows depends upon the season of the year because of the changing angle of the sun. The effect can be most detrimental to growth in the winter when light is often a limiting factor.

Single greenhouses, located above 40°N latitude in the Northern Hemisphere should be built with the ridge running east to west so that low angle light of the winter can enter along a side rather than from an end. Below 40° N latitude, the ridge of single greenhouses should be oriented from north to south since the angle of the sun is much higher. Ridge and furrow greenhouses (greenhouses connected to one another along their length) at all latitudes should be oriented north to south in order to compensate for a shadow which occurs from the north roof and gutter of each adjacent greenhouse. The north–south orientation permits this shadow to move across the floor during the day, whereas the east–west orientation does not.

GLASS GREENHOUSES

Only the glass greenhouse existed prior to 1950. It is one of the more expensive types today. Although they have been known to last 100 years and longer when properly maintained, the average cost per year is still more than that of the film plastic greenhouse.

There are several styles of glass greenhouses designed to meet specific needs. A *lean-to* design is used when a greenhouse is placed against the side of an existing building (Figure 2–1a). This design makes best use of sunlight and minimizes the requirements for roof supports. An *even-span* greenhouse is one in which the two roof slopes are of equal pitch and width (Figure 2–1b).

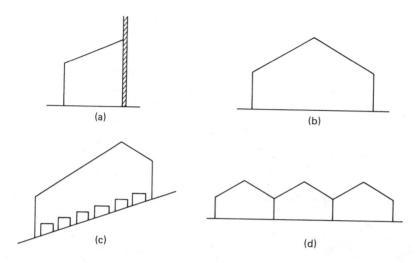

Figure 2-1. Four basic greenhouse styles: (a) lean-to, (b) even span, (c) uneven span, and (d) ridge-and-furrow.

By comparison, an *uneven-span* greenhouse has roofs of unequal width which make the structure adaptable to the side of a hill (Figure 2-1c). This style is seldom used today because they are not adaptable to automation. Individual greenhouses standing free of one another are well adapted to cold climates since snow easily slides from the roof. *Ridge-and-furrow* refers to two or more greenhouses connected to one another along the length of the eave (Figure 2-1d). The eave serves as a furrow or gutter to carry rain and melted snow away. The side wall is eliminated between greenhouses which results in a structure with a single large interior. Consolidation of interior space reduces the cost of automation and thus fosters it. A second advantage over individual free-standing greenhouses is the economy of heating a ridge and furrow range. Heat is lost through the exterior walls. Since there are fewer exterior walls in a ridge-and-furrow range, heat loss is reduced. The snow load must be taken into account in the frame specifications of these greenhouses. Snow cannot slide off the roofs, as in the case of individual free-standing greenhouses, but must melt away. Heating pipes are generally located beneath the gutters for this purpose. In spite of the susceptibility to snow stress, ridge and furrow greenhouses are effectively used in the northern countries of Europe and in Canada.

The frames of glass greenhouses have been constructed from various materials depending upon the width of the structure (Figure 2-2). Basically three frame types were used, but there were many combinations of these types. Wood frames were used for narrow greenhouses, generally under

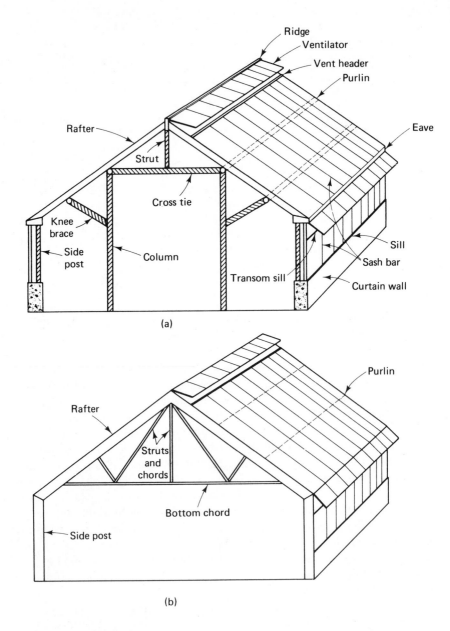

Figure 2-2. Structural components of (a) a pipe frame greenhouse, and (b) an iron frame greenhouse. In the house in part (b), the side posts, rafter, chords, and struts are one unit known as a *truss*.

20 feet in width. Side posts and columns were constructed of wood without the use of a truss. A truss consists of a single prefabricated unit consisting of rafters, chords, and struts. Wider houses required sturdier frames. Pipe frames served well up to a width of about 40 feet (Figure 2-2a). The side posts, columns, cross ties, and purlins were constructed from pipe. Again, a truss was not used. The pipe components did not all interconnect, but depended on attachment to the sash bars for support. Some greenhouses under 50 feet in width and most over this width were built on an iron frame (Figures 2-2b, 2-3). Flat steel, tubular steel, or angle iron were welded together to form a truss encompassing the rafters, chords, and struts. Angle iron purlins running the length of the greenhouse were bolted to each truss. The frame thus constructed could stand without support of sash bars. Columns were used only in the very wide iron frame houses of about 70 feet and wider.

Today glass greenhouses are primarily of the iron frame type. Iron frame greenhouses are best suited to prefabrication which has made the construction of greenhouses more economical over the years. Automation has also fostered wider houses which require the strength of an iron frame.

The glass on the greenhouse is attached to members called sash bars. Sash bars were made exclusively of wood in earlier days, primarily cypress and redwood. Wood required periodic painting to protect it against rot. Ideally, exteriors were painted every two years and interiors every five to seven years. This was a costly procedure. Aluminum sash bars and ventilators

Figure 2-3. An iron frame greenhouse.

were introduced in the early 1950s. The resultant all-metal greenhouses were very expensive at the outset, but quickly became competitive with wood sash bar houses. These greenhouses are cheaper to maintain since they require no painting. Virtually all glass greenhouse construction is of the metal type today.

Application was also found for aluminum on the existing wooden sash-bar greenhouses. Aluminum barcaps were developed which covered the portion of the sash bar exterior to the glass, thus eliminating most of the exterior painting needs (Figure 2-4). A considerable effort is required to cover a greenhouse with barcaps, but the advantages make it well worthwhile. Prior to the use of barcaps, lites of glass were usually installed in a staggered rather than parallel fashion to increase the greenhouse strength. The lower end of each barcap is crimped downward to hold the lower edge of the glass lites on either side of the sash bar from sliding. For this reason the glass must be in parallel rows and only full lites can be used. It has been necessary to reglaze many greenhouses prior to installing barcaps.

The structural members of the greenhouse cast shadows which reduce plant growth during the darker months of the year. Aluminum sash bars can be made stronger than wood and thus wider panes of glass are used with the aluminum bars. The original 16-inch wide by 18-inch long panes were replaced by 20-inch wide panes and finally by 24-inch wide panes ranging in

Figure 2-4. Aluminum barcaps installed on wooden sash bars to protect them from the elements and eliminate the need for painting. Shading compound on the glass reduces the interior light intensity during the summer.

length up to 36 inches. The reduction in structural material plus the reflec-
tance of aluminum has given these metal greenhouses a great advantage over
wooden greenhouses in terms of interior light intensity.

FILM PLASTIC GREENHOUSES

Role

Flexible films of plastic including mylar, vinyl, and polyethylene have
been used for greenhouse coverings. Polyethylene is principally used today.
The low cost of polyethylene film compared to glass and FRP, its lighter
weight, and the ease with which it can be adapted to a wide range of frame
designs makes this covering suitable for inexpensive greenhouse frames.
Film plastic greenhouses are the most desirable type to operate under certain
situations. Many bedding plant growers, for example, operate their greenhouse for the limited period of January through May. The heavy investment
required for a glass greenhouse is not justified. In some municipalities, structures which are covered for six months or less are not classified as buildings
for tax purposes. Film plastic houses used for a crop such as bedding plants
fit this tax advantage very well. Film plastic greenhouses also fit well into the
plans of a new greenhouse investor with limited funds since it affords the
least expensive means for entering the business.

Polyethylene film was developed in the late 1930s in England and its
use as a greenhouse covering was pioneered about the middle of this century.
The expanded use of polyethylene for greenhouses has been very rapid and
continues to be so at the present. In the United States alone, about 40 acres
of plastic greenhouses were in use in the middle 1950s, about 2,300 acres
by the mid-1960s, and 4,800 acres in 1977.

There are disadvantages which go along with the advantages of film
plastic. The covering material is short-lived. The highest quality 6 mils thick
(6 one-thousandths of an inch) polyethylene films can last, at best, two
winter seasons including one interim summer. Only one year is obtained in
many cases where the frame design or means of attachment subjects the film
to unnecessary stress. While the time required to cover a 30 by 100 foot
quonset design house is minimal, about eight man hours, the task is never-
ending.

Types of Film Plastic

Polyethylene has always been the principal choice of film plastic for
greenhouses. Mylar brand polyester film for a time offered the strong advantage of durability. Films of 5 mil thickness were used for the roof and lasted

four years while 3 mil films were used on the vertical walls and had a life expectancy of seven years. Although the cost of mylar was higher than polyethylene, it was offset by the extra life expectancy. Mylar was produced in widths up to 51 inches. It was applied to the greenhouse in strips running the length of the house with each strip overlapping the other by three inches. Other advantages included a level of light transmittance equal to glass and freedom from static electrical charge which collects dust. Other industrial uses were found for mylar along about the mid-1960s and soon its price increased out of the realm of floriculture.

Vinyl films (polyvinyl chloride) also outlast polyethylene. Ultraviolet (UV) light-resistant vinyl films of 8 and 12 mil thickness are guaranteed for four and five years, respectively. The cost of vinyl is three to four times that of 6-mil polyethylene but again this is partially compensated by its long life expectancy. Although the film is produced in rolls up to 50 inches wide, any width can be purchased since the supplier can seal strips of vinyl together. The vinyl films have tended to hold a static electrical charge which attracts and holds dust. This in turn reduces light transmittance until it is washed off. Vinyl films are not used to a large extent in America.

The principal advantage of polyethylene is its low price compared to vinyl film, FRP, or glass. Polyethylene transmits 88 percent of the visible light of the sun when one layer is used and 81 percent when two layers are used (Table 2-1). This is less than glass which transmits 90 percent of visible light, but is sufficiently high to promote favorable growth. Conventionally, polyethylene was used for one year only. It was applied in the fall and generally by the following summer UV light had caused the film to darken and become brittle. It quickly disintegrated after that. UV-resistant polyethylene is now available which can last two heating seasons and the interim summer. Most deterioration takes place during the summer when the UV light intensity is highest. For this reason the film is applied in the fall. A double layer of polyethylene is almost always used. The second layer cuts the heating load by nearly 40 percent. The outer layer of polyethylene is 6 mils and the

Table 2-1
Light Transmission Values (%)
for Various Greenhouse Coverings

COVERING	LIGHT TRANSMISSION (%)
Glass	90
FRP	89–95
Polyethylene	
1 layer	88
2 layers	81
With 3/16″ air cells	85

Air is taken to have a transmission value of 100%.

inner 4 mils in thickness. The outer film absorbs some UV light, lessening the burden on the inner film and reducing its strength requirement.

Film Plastic Greenhouse Designs

Numerous frame types have been used for film plastic houses, all with the common denominator of economy. An A-frame greenhouse was designed at the University of Kentucky in the early 1950s. Many variations of it have appeared, with and without columns, depending upon snow load and width (Figure 2-5). Widths of 20 to 30 feet were commonly seen with these designs. Side posts and columns usually consist of 4″ X 4″ lumber while rafters, spaced on 30- to 36-inch centers, consist of 2″ X 3″ or 2″ X 4″ alternated with 1″ X 4″ members. The scissors truss greenhouse developed by the Virginia Polytechnic Institute (Figure 2-6) was a particularly strong design constructed from 2″ X 3″ rafters and had a width of 21 feet. Rigid frame houses deriving strength from exterior gussets have been developed at Cornell and Rutgers Universities. A desirable feature of these houses is the absence of internal support members. In spite of this, these houses can be constructed up to 40 feet in width. The gothic-arch greenhouse (Figure 2-7) was developed at the Virginia Polytechnic Institute. Again, it is a design devoid of internal support thus maximizing the space for work operations and features of automation. The trusses are prefabricated on the site from 6-inch lengths of 2″ X 4″ lumber enclosed in a double bead of ½″ X 2″ wood on either side. The trusses are spaced 48 inches apart. The house can be constructed

Figure 2-5. An inexpensive but temporary A-frame film plastic greenhouse very popular in the early days of film plastic greenhouses.

Figure 2-6. A scissors truss film plastic greenhouse designed at Virginia Polytechnic Institute. This is a particularly strong design.

Figure 2-7. A gothic arch greenhouse of the type designed at Virginia Polytechnic Institute. Trusses used in this greenhouse are fabricated during the construction of the greenhouse. This greenhouse offers a pleasing appearance and is devoid of internal columns.

up to 30 feet in width. The Trox house developed by the Trox Manufacturing Co. makes use of trusses of laminated wood. No internal supports are used. This house is available in 23- and 30-foot widths.

The structures thus far described are constructed from inexpensive soft woods, primarily pine. They require continual painting for protection against rot and for the purpose of reflecting light which would otherwise be absorbed by this massive structure. White is a very suitable color. Care must be taken to avoid the use of a paint with a mercury base. Mercury will volatize from the paint for a considerable length of time causing damage to the crop. Paints sold as greenhouse paints are safe; however, other paints may be used as well if those with a mercury base are avoided. If mercury base paint is used by mistake, injury can be avoided by painting over it with a mixture of 5 parts of lime-sulfur fungicide and 10 parts wheat flour in 100 parts water.

Posts and other wood in contact with the ground should be treated with a wood preservative.Treated wood may be purchased for this purpose, or the wood may be treated at the time of use. There are several treatments, but not all are safe. Pentachlorophenol and creosote should *not* be used. They produce fumes for better than a year which are toxic to plants. Entire crops can be killed by moving them into a new house with treated posts. A single treated board can cause abnormal growth throughout the house. A very suitable wood preservative is copper naphthenate which is sold under several trade names. It is generally used as a 2 percent solution of copper naphthenate. It can be sprayed, dipped or applied with a brush and is an excellent preservative for frame members as well as wooden benches and flats.

In spite of a protective coat of paint, eventual replacement of rotted portions of the frame is necessary. The high cost of wood coupled with the maintenance costs has caused a shift toward metal frame houses for film plastic. Two designs constitute most of the film plastic construction today. Quonset houses (Figure 2-8) can be purchased prefabricated or can be fabricated on the site. Often the trusses are constructed from pipe which is bent to fit a 180° arc modified for somewhat more vertical sides. Slightly larger pipe is driven into the ground into which the pipe arches are inserted for support. A 2″ X 8″ wooden plank is attached to the base of the pipe arches such that it runs along the ground partially buried. This provides a basal point of attachment for the film plastic. The pipe arches, or trusses, are supported by either pipe purlins running the length of the house or by 12½-gauge reinforcing wire of 4-inch mesh and 8-foot width laid from ground to ground over the trusses. In the former case trusses are spaced 30 to 36 inches apart, and in the latter case they may be up to 4 feet apart to conform to the width of the reinforcing wire. Quonset houses are constructed in a free-standing style or may be arranged in an interlocking ridge-and-furrow manner as depicted in Figure 2-9. The trusses overlap sufficiently to place a bed of

Figure 2-8. A metal frame, Quonset style greenhouse very popular today with users of film plastic. This greenhouse is very inexpensive, does not require painting, and is well suited to a double covering of film plastic.

Figure 2-9. An interconnecting arrangement of Quonset greenhouses offering a single large interior for several greenhouses. This greenhouse arrangement is in harmony with the current needs for automation and efficiency of movement.

Figure 2-10. Exterior and interior view of the gutter-connected polyethylene greenhouse range of Mr. Aart van Wingerden in Horse Shoe, North Carolina.

plants between the overlapping portions of adjacent houses. A single interior exists for a set of houses which is better adapted to the movement of labor and to automation.

The straight-sided, gutter-connected house is the other currently popular film plastic greenhouse design (Figure 2-10). The gutters can be placed at greater heights than in the ridge-and-furrow quonset ranges. This permits a roadway in either direction within the greenhouse which will accommodate tractors as well as trucks. Gutters, depending upon the manufacturer, occur at approximately 12 to 25 foot intervals. Columns can be placed in the greenhouse with gutters spaced 12 feet apart under each, every other, or every third gutter. A 36-foot spacing between rows of columns, while more expensive, does greatly enhance the ease with which the shading of plants with black cloth can be accomplished. These greenhouses greatly minimize the exposed surface area and consequently the heating bill. Only 13 feet of film plastic is required to span a 12-foot bay. When additions are made, the film plastic can be removed from an existing side wall and the new houses connected at that point without any resulting discontinuity. In this way a modest initial investment, unadaptable to automation, can be developed through expansions into a structure well-suited to automation.

Double Layer Covering

When the first film plastic greenhouses were designed, a single layer of covering was commonly used. The advantage of saving at least one third of the heating cost by applying a second layer was quickly recognized and much effort was put into developing frame types to accommodate this.

Ideally the dead air space should be 1-1/2 inches thick. When it exceeds 8 inches, air currents can become established inside which reduce the insulating property of this space. Below 3/4 inch the insulating property again diminishes, and when the two layers touch, the insulation value is totally lost.

Many of the earlier A-frame greenhouses had support columns. This made the application of a second layer of plastic within the greenhouse a very tedious and expensive proposition. Invariably the inner layer of plastic was left with unsealed cuts or gaps where sheets were not fitted well together. Such holes reduced the insulating effectiveness of the double-layer system. The insulating property depends upon a dead air space. If circulating currents set up in this space, heat will be carried from the warm inner layer of plastic to the cold outer layer where it is rapidly lost to the outside. Holes in the inner layer of plastic permit the entry of warm air into the dead air space. Once inside, the warm air continues to rise, setting up air currents.

Stronger trusses were designed to avoid the use of columns. The scissors truss design lent strength to the truss and reduced the volume of the dead air space overhead. The V. P. I. (Virginia Polytechnic Institute) gothic arch greenhouse reduced the dead air space to a uniform 4.5-inch thickness over the entire greenhouse and also eliminated support columns. Quonset greenhouses constructed from pipe frames presented a situation similar to the gothic arch greenhouse. Pieces of wire were tied to the pipe trusses at intervals of two to three feet in such a way that the ends of the wire projected toward the inside of the greenhouse. When the inner layer of plastic was applied, it was pushed against the wire ends so that they punctured the plastic. The wire ends were twisted around a supporting string running from end to end beneath the plastic inside the greenhouse (Figure 2-11).

The difficulty of applying an inner layer of plastic led to plans for applying both layers from the outside. For a time some growers applied one layer to the outside in normal fashion, then attached 2-inch thick pieces of wood to the trusses over the film plastic, and finally added a second layer of plastic to these 2-inch wooden members. In many cases it was easier than the method of applying an inner layer of plastic. This method of two externally applied layers required a considerable outlay in wood and occasionally the plastic sheets contacted each other at several points. Where the plastic layers came into contact, the insulating effect of the double layer was lost.

(a)   (b)

Figure 2-11. Method of attachment of the inner layer of film plastic in a metal frame Quonset greenhouse. (a) The inward projecting ends of wire tied to the truss puncture the inner plastic layer and are tied to a piece of string which supports the plastic film from beneath. (b) Several strings or wires running the length of the greenhouse are used to support the inner layer.

Today, virtually all film plastic greenhouses make use of the air-inflated system. Two layers of film plastic, one applied directly on top of the other from the outside, are held apart by a cushion of air maintained at a low positive pressure. Single sheets of plastic, wide enough to span the entire truss from ground to ground, are rolled out the length of the greenhouse and are attached to the greenhouse at the ground level on either side along the length of the greenhouse. The ends of the sheet overlap the greenhouse ends by a few inches and are attached at that point. No attachment is made to the trusses. Two sheets of plastic are attached to each end of the greenhouse as well. The plastic is attached by placing a batten strip over it and nailing or stapling through it. Some growers use thick plastic strips about 1-inch wide obtained from greenhouse jobbers while others use strips of wood ¼-inch thick and 1 to 2 inches wide. Many of the newer greenhouses are equipped with metal channel locks. The plastic is laid over the channel and then a metal rod is placed over the plastic and pushed into the channel locking the plastic in place. Plastic channel lock systems are available for installation on greenhouses which were not originally equipped with such a system.

The tension under which the plastic is installed is important since film plastics contract and expand to a considerable degree, depending upon the outside temperature at the time of installation. If applied on a cold winter day the film should be pulled taut. On a warm day, with temperatures near 80°F (27°C), about 2-3 inches of slack should be left in the covering along the length of the greenhouse to permit contraction over the truss when cold weather comes. If this slack is not allowed, the film will tear loose from the points of attachment when it contracts during cold weather. Conversely, if it is not pulled taut when applied on a cold day, excess slack will occur during warm weather resulting in an excessive air space between the two layers.

A small squirrel cage fan is installed inside the greenhouse to inflate the space between the two film plastic layers (Figure 2-12). Air is maintained between 0.2 and 0.3 inches of water-column pressure. Even higher pressures have been used, up to 0.5 inches, under conditions of heavy wind. They should not be maintained because of stretching of the plastic. The fan should have an adjustable door on the air inlet for adjusting the pressure between the two films. For a greenhouse measuring 26 X 96 feet, a fan delivering air at 200 to 400 CFM at a static pressure of 0.5 inch of water is sufficient.

Sheets of wood with a hole in the center of each can be placed on either side of the inner layer of polyethylene and the fan bolted to these. Another arrangement calls for cutting a +-shaped cut in the inner layer of plastic and inserting a 4-inch flexible clothes dryer tube through it. The four points of plastic resulting from the cut are pulled out over the tube and taped to the tube to make an airtight seal. Air is conducted from the fan to the inner space through this tube. This system is sufficient to inflate the entire roof of a Quonset style greenhouse. Generally the two layers of plastic pull tight at the ridge of an A-frame greenhouse, separating the roof into two inflatable portions. In this case, air from the fan can be divided in a 4-inch stove pipe tee and introduced to each side of the roof through flexible tubing

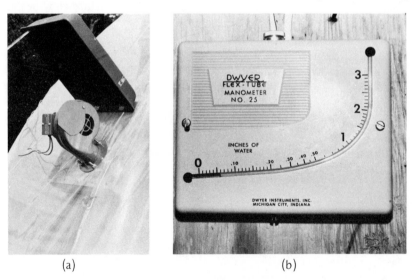

(a)   (b)

Figure 2-12. (a) A squirrel cage fan used to inflate the space between two layers of plastic. The plate on the side can be moved to adjust the air supply to the fan and, consequently, the pressure between the two coverings on the greenhouse. (b) A manometer used to measure the air pressure between the two plastic covers.

immediately below the ridge. Side or end walls can be inflated as well without adding additional fans. Pieces of garden hose can be inserted between the layers of plastic to connect the roof cavity to the end or side wall cavities.

The pressure between the layers of plastic should be sufficient to hold the layers apart under conditions of wind and yet low enough to avoid tearing of the sheets. A manometer can be purchased from greenhouse supply houses for measuring this pressure. The manometer is a simple device and can be easily fabricated by the grower. Bend a 2-foot long piece of clear plastic tube into the shape of a U and attach it to a board. Make a +-shape cut in the inner layer of plastic and insert one end of the plastic tube. Seal the tube to the plastic film with plastic tape. Put about 8 inches of water in the tube such that it settles at the bottom of the U. Leave one end of the tube open inside the greenhouse. Pressure between the layers of plastic will push the water down on the film plastic side of the U and up on the opposite side of the U. A rise in water level of 0.2 to 0.3 inches indicates the desired pressure. Coloring the water helps to see it more easily. A ruler is attached to the board behind or alongside the plastic tube.

The air-inflated system offers the easiest method for covering a greenhouse with two layers of film plastic. It has another very decided advantage because the outer layer of plastic rests on a cushion of air which adds greatly to its term of usefulness. Plastic applied by techniques other than the air-inflated system is constantly chafed against the trusses by the lifting and dropping action of the wind. This reduces its life expectancy in many cases to one heating season.

RIGID PANEL GREENHOUSES

PVC

Two types of rigid panels have been used for greenhouse coverings, PVC (polyvinylchloride) and fiberglass reinforced plastic (FRP). PVC panels have for the most part been dropped from use. Initially they showed promise as an inexpensive covering (about 40 percent of the cost of long-lasting FRP), and had a life expectancy of five years or better. Commercial use of these panels soon indicated that this life expectancy was much shorter, sometimes as little as two years. This was unacceptable because the cost of PVC panels was four to five times that of polyethylene film and was much more time-consuming to install. Rigid PVC, like its film plastic counterparts, is subject to the deteriorating effect of ultra-violet light which causes it to turn dark in color and become brittle. At first, light transmission is reduced and later the panels break apart. Rigid PVC was purchased in corrugated panels 26 or 28 inches wide and 8, 10, or 12 feet long. The panels were available in various colors; however, clear panels were used for general greenhouse culture.

Fiberglass Reinforced Plastic (FRP)

Role—FRP is popular as a greenhouse covering today. As in the former case of PVC, corrugated panels are used, although flat panels are occasionally used on the end and side walls of temporary frame greenhouses. Panels are available in 51½-inch widths, lengths up to 24 feet, and a variety of colors. The panels are flexible enough to conform to the shape of quonset greenhouses which makes FRP a very versatile covering material.

FRP can be applied to the inexpensive frames of the film plastic greenhouses (Figure 2-13) or to the more elaborate frames of the glass type greenhouses (Figure 2-14). In the former case the price of the FRP greenhouse lies between that of a film plastic greenhouse and a glass greenhouse but is compensated by elimination of the need for biennial replacement of film plastic. In the latter case the FRP greenhouse costs about the same as the glass greenhouse. FRP and glass greenhouses each have advantages and disadvantages and growers are found to be divided as to their preference. FRP is more resistant to breakage by such factors as hail or vandals. Sunlight when passing through FRP is scattered by the fibers in the panels with resulting light intensity rather uniform throughout the greenhouse by comparison with a glass covering. Plants on the north sides of beds, and particularly in the north beds, as a whole grow much better. But there are disadvantages as well.

Figure 2-13. A Quonset greenhouse being covered with sheets of corrugated FRP.

Figure 2-14. A permanent iron frame greenhouse with FRP covering.

The acrylic surface of FRP panels is subject to etching and pitting by dust abrasion and chemical pollution. This permits glass fibers to be exposed and subject to fraying and they begin to collect dust as well as harbor algae. The resultant effect is darkening of the panels and a subsequent reduction in light transmission. The situation can be corrected by scrubbing the FRP surface clean with a stiff brush or steel wool and then painting on a new surface of acrylic resin. The material is inexpensive, but the labor is extensive. The need for refinishing varies with the grade of FRP purchased. Some grades do not carry a guarantee and may last only five years or so. Other grades carry guarantees of various lengths of time up to 25 years. Those with an ultraviolet light-resistant coating of polyvinylfluoride hold the longest life expectancy. The guarantee generally protects the level of light transmission and compensates for the unused portion of the term of the guarantee. By contrast, glass can exceed a grower's life expectancy, while FRP is guaranteed to cover about half of the period. The decision between glass and FRP is not clear-cut. Some northern growers have been known to cover only the north slope of a glass greenhouse with FRP to increase the light intensity within. A portion of the sunrays impinging upon the north roof are transmitted inward rather than being deflected off.

Light transmission—the total quantity of light transmitted through clear FRP is roughly equivalent to that transmitted through glass (Table 2-2), but diminishes in relation to its color. For greenhouse crops in general only the clear FRP permits a satisfactory level of light transmission. Colored FRP

Table 2-2
Light and Heat Transmission Levels Through Glass and Various Shades
of One Brand of FRP Relative to Transmission Through Air

COVERING MATERIAL	LIGHT TRANSMISSION (%)	HEAT TRANSMISSION (%)
Air	100	100
Glass (double strength)	90	88
Fiberglass		
Clear	92–95	63–68
Jade	81	61–68
Yellow	64	37–43
Snow	63	30–34
Green	62	60–68
Coral	61	57–66
Canary	25	20–23

has found a limited use in greenhouses used for growing some house plants which require low-light intensity and for display greenhouses used for holding plants during the sales period.

Heat transmission—as shown in Table 2-2, FRP has a distinct advantage over glass because it does not transmit heat as well. During the summer when the source of heat, the sun, is external less heat penetrates the greenhouse, thus reducing the cooling load. In an experiment conducted at Colorado State University with two greenhouses of identical size and style, one was covered with clear FRP and the other with glass. The length of time that the cooling fans operated in each greenhouse was recorded for the period June 4, 1961 through June 14, 1962. Less hours of cooling were required in the FRP greenhouse month by month. At the end of the 13-month period, a total of 2066 hours of cooling had been required in the glass greenhouse versus only 1668 hours in the FRP greenhouse (Table 2-3). This represented a reduction of 19 percent. The advantage of reduced heat transmission through FRP also shows up in the winter. The heat source of concern during that season is the heating system within the greenhouse. The greenhouse covering serves to trap the heat in the plant zone. Reduced heat transmission, due to less air infiltration than glass, leads to conservation and ultimately to a lower heating bill for the FRP greenhouse. The reduction in heat requirement, however, is not nearly as great as that achieved by covering a greenhouse with a double layer of polyethylene.

Construction—FRP greenhouses require fewer structural members than glass greenhouses since sash bars are not needed. The construction labor input is somewhat lower for an FRP greenhouse, but these savings are offset by the

Table 2-3
Hours of Cooling Required in Two Similar Greenhouses,
One Covered With Glass and the Other With Clear FRP,
During a 13-Month Period

MONTH	GLASS	FRP
June	230	223
July	332	293
August	291	265
September	132	104
October	156	98
November	70	68
December	25	16
January	48	25
February	81	57
March	153	100
April	209	156
May	231	174
June	113	87
Total	2066	1668

higher cost of the FRP covering material and closures. High quality FRP costs about 50¢ per square foot versus 40¢ for glass. FRP panels are 51.5 inches wide, but due to overlap have an effective covering width of only 48 inches. The thickness of FRP is measured in terms of weight per square foot. Where a snow load is expected, 5-ounce weights are used on the roof, otherwise a 4-ounce weight is used. The 4-ounce weight is common on vertical walls. Trusses are spaced 8 to 10 feet apart and purlins 4 feet apart.

The greenhouse must be constructed as airtight as possible. Plastic corrugated closures (Figure 2-15) are available for insertion between the FRP panel and such frame components as the eave and the sill to seal off outer air. Flashing is used at the ridge to cover the exposed ends of the FRP panels for the purpose of preventing water entry. The flashing can be constructed from aluminum or corrugated FRP. The FRP panels are attached to the purlins by aluminum screw nails or by aluminum wood screws. These nails and screws have a rubber washer immediately beneath the head to seal the hole made by the shaft.

FRP as well as film plastic has a water-repellent surface. Condensation forming on this surface collects in droplets. These in turn drop when a sudden breeze blows up or a door is closed. The result is wet foliage which fosters disease development. If the FRP surface were not as water-repellent, the condensing water could flow over the surface to the ground. Spraying with

Figure 2-15. A corrugated plastic closure strip in place, sealing off the outer air at the point of attachment of a corrugated FRP panel to the frame member.

detergent will stop droplet formation but the detergent washes off quickly. There is a liquid (Sun Clear®) on the market which is diluted with water and sprayed on the inner surface of FRP and film plastic greenhouses that will persist. This material costs 0.35¢ per square foot of surface treated. Another benefit derived from this treatment is that of reducing the barrier to light transmission which is caused by the layer of condensation on the plastic surface.

When condensation flows along the inner surface of FRP, it does so along the corrugation valleys. If the FRP panels are attached directly to the

Figure 2-16. U-shaped metal supports are placed between the purlin and FRP panel to provide a space so that condensation water can flow along the inner surface of the panel to the ground or to a gutter.

purlins, the corrugation valleys are in contact with the purlins. Condensation upon reaching this point flows onto the purlin and drips from its lower edge, thus causing harm to plants beneath. The FRP panel must be elevated away from the purlin. Metal U-shaped supports are placed between the purlin and the corrugation ridges of the FRP panel. The nail or screw attaching the panel to the purlin passes through the support (Figure 2-16).

FIRE HAZARD: Many greenhouse structures are insured. One cause of destruction is fire, which is not a significant danger in glass greenhouses, but is a very definite concern in FRP greenhouses. The glass fibers themselves do not burn but the polyester and acrylic resins binding them together do. A few years ago a fire believed to have originated from a faulty electrical wire beneath a sheet of black shade cloth spread to the FRP covering of a ridge-and-furrow range on a windy night. More than one acre of greenhouses was consumed within 20 minutes. Insurance rates are assessed according to the risk involved, which is greater for FRP greenhouses. Fire-retardant FRP panels are available which carry the best rating for building materials, Class I. These panels offer no support or sustainment to flame even when directly attacked. Benefits associated with standard greenhouse FRP are not associated with fire-retardant FRP by manufacturers.

NEW AND EXPERIMENTAL DESIGNS

Tower greenhouses

Greenhouses have traditionally been located close to metropolitan markets. Encroachment of residential and commercial buildings has placed a premium value on greenhouse property. One answer to the problem was introduced by an Austrian, Diplom Ingeneur O. Ruthner, at the international garden show in Vienna in 1964. He introduced the concept of a high-rise greenhouse as pictured in Figure 2-17. It has the growing area equivalent to that of a 3000-square foot conventional greenhouse, but only occupies 400 square feet of ground. The greenhouse is 75 feet high and inside it has 125 platforms 20 inches wide and 8 feet long riding slowly up one side and down the other on a chain. Plants growing on these platforms make the round trip from the bottom to the top and back to the bottom of the tower in about one hour. En route plants are exposed to light from all sides and at all locations in the greenhouse. This results in very uniform plants. Since all plants share both light and shade, high light requiring crops may need supplemental illumination.

Many of the cultural procedures are carried out at the bottom of the greenhouse. Plants can be sprayed by fixed nozzles as they pass through the

Figure 2-17. View of a tower greenhouse designed by the Austrian firm, Ruthner Industrieanlagen fur Pflanzenbau Gesellschaft m.b.h. and displayed at the International Horticultural Exhibition in Vienna in 1974.

bottom. The chain may be stopped as each platform reaches the bottom to permit watering, fertilization, disbudding, etc. There is an economy of space in this design which permits the culture of twice as many plants as in an equivalent volume of space in a conventional greenhouse.

A limited number of these greenhouses have been built in countries including Austria, Germany, Norway, Poland, Sweden, Switzerland, and Canada. The economic advantages of land conservation are certainly sizeable and the efficiency of space and operations within are attractive.

Air-Supported Greenhouses

Various designs have been tried for air-supported greenhouses. These are greenhouses without a rigid frame in which the roof is supported by air pressure from within. They differ from air-inflated greenhouses, previously discussed, which are supported by a frame and have air under pressure between two covering layers of film plastic to keep them apart for insulation purposes. The most striking of the air-supported greenhouses was a one-acre structure built in Ohio as a joint project of the Goodyear Tire and Rubber Company, the Cleveland Vegetable growers Association, and Pretzer Farms in 1969. The greenhouse measured 100 by 428 feet and was covered by a layer of vinyl film with a 3-year life expectancy. The film was anchored in the soil around the perimeter. Anchor points were established every 50 feet along the longitudinal center of the greenhouse. A plastic tube around each anchor point served as a drain for water and was connected to an underground tile system. A small portion of the total fan capacity was used for roof support so that it was possible to remove and replace a plastic film panel while maintaining inflation of the remainder of the greenhouse.

The principal advantages of such greenhouses are the low initial cost (the Goodyear greenhouse was valued at under $1 per square foot of ground covered including erection and all materials—excluding heating and cooling) and a "temporary" tax classification which exempts them from real estate taxes in most states. This greenhouse design, however, has not caught on in the industry. This is partly due to apprehension of what would happen in the event of a failure, and possibly because of the development of the low-price gutter-connected film plastic greenhouses which offer a permanent frame and low risk.

Experimental Designs

Dr. W. J. Roberts at Rutgers University developed an inexpensive cable frame design for a film plastic greenhouse (Figure 2-18). This greenhouse should not be used where snow accumulation occurs. Posts of $4'' \times 4''$ treated lumber or equivalent material are set upright in the ground on 10- to 12-foot centers. A nylon-coated steel cable anchored to the ground on both

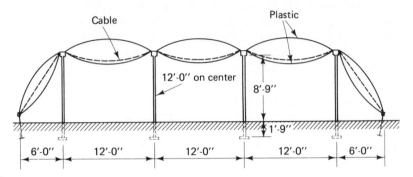

Figure 2-18. Design for a film plastic-covered cable greenhouse by W. J. Roberts, M. K. Kim, and D. R. Mears of Rutgers University that makes use of a minimal frame. Two layers of plastic are placed over the supporting cables and are separated by a positive air pressure.

ends passes over each row of posts. The layers of plastic film are applied over the cables. A small fan is then used to develop a positive pressure between the layers.

Researchers at Penn State University have studied the *thin-shell* principle of construction. They have focused attention on two variations: the multibarrel cylindrical vault and the hyperbolic paraboloid (Figure 2-19). Greenhouses of various dimensions may be constructed by repeating these units. These designs lend great strength to the structure and require only a minimal frame.

Greenhouse System for Coastal Desert Regions

A low-energy, humidity-cycle method for desalination of saline (salty) water developed by Dr. Carl Hodges of the Environmental Research Laboratory of the University of Arizona was constructed on the Gulf of California at Puerto Penasco, Sonora, Mexico by a team from the University of Arizona and the University of Sonora. The resulting desalted water was too expensive for use in conventional agriculture so the possibility of greenhouse culture was explored by the team. A model range was constructed and operated with success using the native beach sand as a root medium.

Shaikh Zayed, ruler of the prosperous Arabian principality of Abu Dhabi, recognized the potential of the greenhouse system for his soil-poor land and contracted to have such a unit developed and built on the sandy, nearly barren, and sparsely inhabited island of Sadiyat for the purpose of growing vegetables. This was completed in 1972 (Figure 2-20). Three diesel engines, which develop 580 Bhp at 750 rev/min at site conditions, are used to generate electricity for use in the greenhouse range. Waste heat is captured in

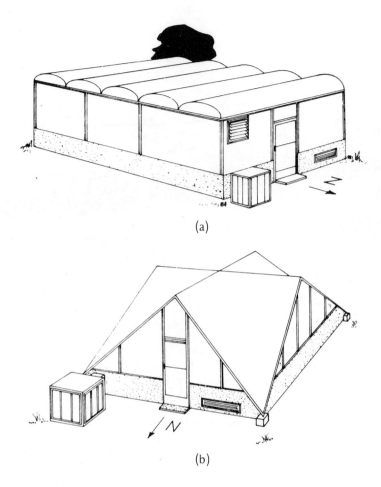

(a)

(b)

Figure 2-19. Experimental greenhouse designs studied at Penn State University by R. A. Aldrich and J. W. White. (a) Multibarrel cylindrical vault; (b) hyperbolic paraboloid.

recovery mufflers attached to each engine and used for desalting sea water. The desalinating plant has a capacity of about 70,000 gallons of water per day. The plant, in addition to providing energy and water for over four acres of greenhouses, provides electricity and about 3000 gallons of drinking water per day to the nearby fishing village.

    The greenhouse range consists of 48 air-supported polyethylene houses and four blocks of rigid frame Roper IBG houses covered with polyethylene. A variety of vegetables are grown in the range including lettuce, turnip, pepper, eggplant, radish, tomato, cucumber, bean, and cabbage. These are marketed fresh to the principality's population of 50,000, who otherwise

Figure 2-20. A greenhouse range in the Arabian principality of Abu Dhabi. Waste heat from generators producing electricity to power the range is used to desalt sea water, which in turn is used for watering vegetables grown within the greenhouses. The system was developed by a team of research scientists at the University of Arizona in the United States and the University of Sonora in Mexico. (*Photo courtesy of Environmental Research Laboratory, Tucson, AZ 85706*)

would have to import vegetables from other countries. Vegetables grown out-doors are susceptible to injury from wind-blown sand and to desiccation from the drying winds coming off the desert.

Plants are grown directly in the native sand on the floor of the green-house. Organic media are not abundant in these regions and would be pro-hibitively expensive. A very dilute nutrient solution is applied three to four times per day. Due to the climate, heating of the greenhouses is not required, but cooling is. Air is brought into the greenhouses through large evaporative pads in the walls. Salt water is passed over the pads. As it evaporates, the entering air is cooled.

The net effect of this greenhouse concept is the production of elec-tricity for powering the operation and the desalting of sea water through use of waste heat from the engines. The desalted water is used for growing high return crops which justify the cost of the water. The crops are grown in greenhouses to protect them from the adverse elements of the hot, arid, salty environment for which this system was developed. The system is economically practical.

BENCHES AND BEDS

Fresh Flowers

The first choice is whether to grow fresh flowers in a raised bench or in ground beds. If the crop is of moderate height such as chrysanthemum and snapdragon, raised benches can be used; however, these benches should be located close to the ground to keep the plants at a practical level for disbudding, spraying, and harvesting. Rose plants are grown for about five years and become exceedingly tall during this time. Most are grown in ground beds to minimize height. Carnations are grown from one to two years and also become very tall. Years ago they were commonly grown in ground beds without bottoms, but the occurrence of a bacterial wilt disease nearly destroyed this business in the northeastern U.S. and since then they have been grown in raised benches. It was not possible to pasteurize the root medium deep enough in the bottomless ground beds, and the disease continually reoccurred.

If ground beds are selected they should be constructed in a manner which isolates media contained within from external soil. In this way the root media can be thoroughly pasteurized on a routine schedule, reducing the possibility of disease. Concrete has proven best for ground beds. There are companies which will construct concrete benches on location (Figure 2-21). The bottom should be V-shaped with the longitudinal center at least 1.5 inches lower than the sides. A half tile is placed in the center over the V and the bed is sloped one inch per 100 feet to insure drainage of water. The bottom of the bed should be filled level with gravel to insure lateral movement of water to the tile. At the point where the tile contacts the lower end of the bed, a hole is located in that end to permit drainage of water. The drainage tile serves another valuable purpose since steam introduced through the tile will percolate up through the root media, pasteurizing it.

Other less expensive ground beds are constructed as well (Figure 2-22). Side walls can consist of treated wood, asbestos-cement (Transite®), or cement blocks. The wall, at least 8 inches deep, extends down to a well-drained foundation substance such as a sandy subsoil. If the base substance is not well drained, drainage tile should be installed in this substance below each bed. Walks should be filled with gravel, or if paved they should be sloped for drainage. It is important that walks be separated from beds to insure: (1) that soil in them, easily contaminated by soil carried in on shoe bottoms, does not spread into the beds, and (2) that water remains where it is applied rather than running off into the walks.

Figure 2-21. A concrete ground bed used for cut flower production. The bed is sloped one inch per 100 feet and has a V-shaped bottom. A half tile runs the length of the bed at the lowest point to conduct water to a drain hole at the end of the bed. A concrete trough running across the greenhouse collects water from all beds and carries it out of the greenhouse. Steam can be injected into the drain hole for pasteurization of the bed between crops.

Ground beds are well suited for the tall crops, roses and carnations. If raised beds are preferred for cut flowers they should be situated close to the ground. An 8-inch concrete block serves as a good post to separate the bench from the ground. The bottom should have abundant drainage holes along its length. Raised benches should be as level as possible to prevent wet and dry areas. Benches are most commonly constructed from concrete, asbestos-cement, or wood. Concrete benches can be poured in place or assembled from precast concrete boards. One board is used for each side and several boards, running lengthwise, for the bottom. The bottom boards have a ½-inch space between them for drainage. Galvanized iron brackets are used to bolt the sides to a pipe frame or concrete cross support beneath the bench floor. Asbestos-cement benches are very common because of the ease of working with this material relative to concrete and its long life expectancy. Flat asbestos-cement boards are used for bench sides and corrugated sheets for the bottom to assure strength and drainage. The corrugations run across the bench. If a single sheet is used across the bench, the corrugation valleys are set lower than the bench sides. If two sheets are used, they are sloped toward the center to insure drainage. See Figure 2-23 for some raised bench designs.

(a)

(b)

Figure 2-22. (a) Drainage tiles imbedded in gravel beneath a ground bed. (b) Ground beds with treated wood sides. The root medium is placed on the gravel base containing the drainage tile.

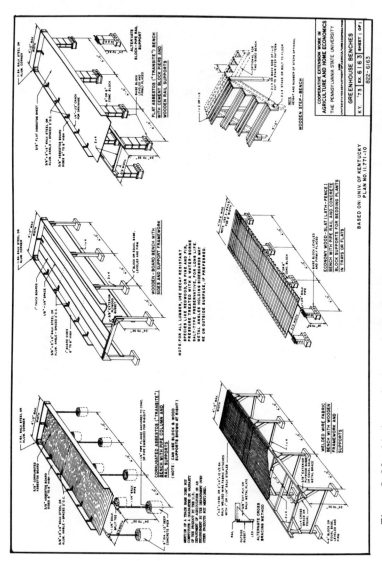

Figure 2-23. Various raised greenhouse bench designs as set forth by the Pennsylvania State University Cooperative Extension Service and based on plans developed at the University of Kentucky. The asbestos-cement benches with side walls are appropriate for fresh flower crops while the welded wire, lath and step benches are best for pot plants due to maximum

The preferred woods for bench construction are cypress, redwood, locust, and cedar because of their resistance to decay. Wooden benches should be painted with a copper naphthenate preservative. The natural preservative in redwood is corrosive to iron and steel, therefore, nails, screws, or bolts should be constructed of other types of metals such as aluminum, brass, zinc, etc.

The preferred width of cut flower benches and beds is 3.5 and 4.0 feet. Roses are conveniently grown in 4-foot wide beds because bushes are planted one foot apart in each direction. This permits four plants across the bed. The other cut flower crops may be found in either width of bed. Except in very wide greenhouses, benches are run the length of the greenhouse. The beds and benches should be 8 inches deep to accommodate 7 inches of root media. Rose beds are an exception which should be 1 foot deep. Eighteen-inch walks are used between all benches except in the center of the greenhouse where a 2-foot walk is established. This arrangement of benches allows for the use of about 67 percent of the floor area for growing.

Pot Crops

Raised benches are generally used for pot plant crops. They are 32–36 inches high for convenience of working. Benches should not exceed a 3-foot width if against a wall or 6 feet if accessible from both sides. It is difficult to handle plants in the center of wider benches and labor becomes inefficient. It is important to have air circulation around each plant to reduce the incidence of condensation on foliage and thus the possibility of disease. Pot plant benches should not have sides. The floor of the bench should be as open as possible. Redwood lath in woven wire similar to snow fencing makes excellent bench floors and is sold for this purpose. The redwood can be supported by a $2'' \times 4''$ wooden frame (Figures 2–23 and 2–24) or by a pipe frame. The frame itself is often supported by concrete blocks. One-inch square 14-gauge welded-wire fabric also makes an excellent bench floor (Figure 2–23). Both benches permit proper circulation of air.

Cut flower benches are generally laid out lengthwise in greenhouses to minimize the number of end posts needed for supporting plants and the time necessary to attach and tighten support wires. Since support is not a consideration in pot plant benches, the benches are usually run across the greenhouse to minimize handling of heavy pots. A 3- to 4-foot wide center aisle is provided along the length of the greenhouse to permit motorized equipment such as golf carts to be used for transporting plants and materials. Side walks should be 18 inches wide at most and should end three feet in from the side walls. Benches are located at the ends of the walks. Benches in this arrangement are known as peninsular benches and can result in as much as 80 percent growing area as opposed to 67 percent in the longitudinal arrangement.

Figure 2-24. A raised pot plant bench using redwood lath for the floor and 2″ × 4″ lumber frame. Cement blocks are used for legs.

A new concept in space efficiency for greenhouses equipped with pot plant benches is seen in the *Aisle Eliminator Bench System* by Simtrac, Inc. Such a system can increase production space by as much as 25 percent. By turning a crank at the end of the bench, the bench platform can be moved to either side. As a bench is moved from right to left, an aisle on the left side closes and a new aisle opens up on the right side (Figure 2-25). When several aisle-eliminator benches are used, only one aisle is needed which can be shifted to any position.

A recent concept for ridge-and-furrow ranges with a large single interior calls for paving the floor with porous asphalt or concrete and growing pot plants directly on the floor (Figure 2-26). Water percolates through the pavement to a gravel bed beneath while weeds are unable to grow up through this layer. Standard asphalt paving with a reduced quantity of binder can be used or porous concrete made from a mixture of 2800 lbs of 3/8-inch gravel, 6 bags (94 lb each) cement, and 21–22 gallons of water. This makes one cubic yard. It is generally poured in a layer 3 inches thick which will withstand a 600 pounds per square inch test. Tractors and trucks may be driven over the floor for setting up and removing crops. With this system it is possible to use 85 percent of the floor area for growing.

(a)

(b)

Figure 2-25. An aisle eliminator bench system: (a) the bench on the right is in its extreme right position; (b) the bench on the right has been moved to its left position, thus shifting the aisle to the right of this bench. (*Photos courtesy of Simtrac, Inc., Skokie, IL 60076*)

Figure 2-26. A ridge-and-furrow range in which pot plants are grown on a pavement of water-porous asphalt. Growing space is maximized in this greenhouse and tractors or trucks can be used for moving plants and materials.

SUMMARY

1. Greenhouse location is as important as the greenhouse design itself. Factors to be sought in a location are (a) reasonable tax structure at present and in the future, (b) room for expansion, (c) level, well-drained site, (d) a climate favorable to the crop intended, (e) available labor, (f) reasonable proximity to utilities and shipping routes, and (g) a plentiful supply of good quality water.

2. Glass greenhouses are permanent, lasting the owner's life expectancy or longer. The material expense and labor of periodically replacing the covering is eliminated with glass, but the overall cost of a glass structure is much higher. Light transmission through glass (90 percent) is superior to double-layer polyethylene (81 percent). There are two general styles. The high profile American greenhouses which can be free-standing or connected in a ridge-and-furrow fashion, and the low profile Dutch type greenhouses which are constructed in a ridge-and-furrow style only, due to their narrow bay width of 10.5 and 21 feet.

3. Film plastic greenhouses are the least expensive to build. They lend themselves well to temporary business ventures, businesses operated for only one season of each year, and locations where there is a tax advantage for nonpermanent structures. Film plastic greenhouses offer an inexpensive means for entering the flower growing business. On the other hand, film plastic ranges can be built on permanent, metal, ridge-and-furrow frames permitting the full degree of automation and efficiency of any glass or FRP range. Polyethylene is the most common film plastic in use and is usually applied as an air-inflated double layer. The insulating property of the double layer reduces fuel consumption by about 40 percent over a glass or a single layer polyethylene greenhouse which makes the double layer polyethylene greenhouse less expensive to purchase and operate in spite of the periodic labor and the cost of replacing the plastic.

4. A third type of greenhouse is the FRP (fiberglass reinforced plastic) panel greenhouse. FRP panels can be bent to fit most film plastic greenhouse frames. This reduces the labor of replacing film plastic since FRP, depending on grade, will last from 5 to 25 years. FRP is also used on permanent frame, metal greenhouses. In this latter case, the overall structure generally costs about the same as a glass greenhouse. The FRP covering does not last as long as glass but it is more resistant to breakage, is cheaper to heat in the winter and to cool in the summer, initially transmits more light (although this feature can be quickly lost), and has a more uniform light intensity throughout the greenhouse.

5. New greenhouse designs and concepts are under study aimed at reducing the initial purchase price and improving the heating and cooling efficiency. Considerable effort is going into growth room studies as will be discussed in Chapter 10. Some crops can be grown to maturity and many others through the seedling stage in well-insulated buildings under lights.

6. Fresh flower crops are grown in either ground beds or raised benches. Such beds are 3.5 or 4 feet wide and generally 8 inches deep—12 inches is best for rose beds. Fresh flower beds are oriented along the length of the greenhouse with 18-inch aisles between. This arrangement of beds allows for 67 percent utilization of floor space for growing.

    Pot plants can be grown on raised benches or directly on the floor. Raised benches have open bottoms constructed from wire hardware cloth ($1'' \times 2''$ mesh), redwood lath, or treated boards with at least a half-inch space between them. Sides are either not used or are low (2 inches). Benches are usually 5 to 6 feet wide and are arranged in a peninsular style. A central aisle, three feet or wider, runs the length of the greenhouse. Benches and smaller aisles radiate out from the central aisle to either side. Such an arrangement makes more efficient use of floor space—up to 80 percent can be growing area— and minimizes hand-carrying of plants. Some pot crops are grown directly on floors paved with porous asphalt or concrete. Water penetrates the floor while weed growth is inhibited. This system permits use of 85 percent or better of the floor space.

SUGGESTED READINGS

Aldrich, R. A., W. A. Bailey, J. W. Bartok Jr., W. J. Roberts, and D. S. Ross. "Hobby Greenhouses and Other Gardening Structures." Northeast Regional Agriculture Engineering Service (NRAES)-2, 1976.

Courter, J. W. "Plastic Greenhouses." University of Illinois Cooperative Extension Service Circular 905, 1965.

Gray, H. E. "Greenhouse Heating and Construction." Florists' Publishing Co., 343 S. Dearborn St., Chicago, Il, 1956.

Laurie, A., D. C. Kiplinger and K. S. Nelson. *Commercial Flower Forcing.* McGraw-Hill Book Co., New York, 1968.

Sheldrake, R. Jr. and R. M. Sayles. *Plastic Greenhouse Manual Planning, Construction and Operation.* Dept. of Vegetable Crops, N.Y. State College of Agriculture and Life Sciences., Cornell Univ., Ithaca, N.Y., 1974.

Wiebe, J. and R. E. Barrett. *Plastic Greenhouses.* Ontario Dept. of Agriculture and Food Publication, 40. 1970.

A series of leaflets from the University of Kentucky Dept. of Agricultural Engineering, Lexington, Ky. as follows:

Duncan, G. A. and J. N. Walker. *Preservative Treatment of Greenhouse Wood.* AEN-6, 1973.

____. *Greenhouse Coverings.* AEN-10, 1973.

Walker, J. N. and G. A. Duncan. *Greenhouse Structures.* AEN-12, 1973.

____. *Greenhouse Benches.* AEN-13, 1973.

____. *Painting Greenhouses and Equipment.* AEN-14, 1974.

____. *Rigid-Frame Greenhouse Construction.* AEN-15, 1973.

____. *Greenhouse Location and Orientation.* AEN-32, 1974.

Various greenhouse manufacturers offer literature concerning products and technical information.

Chapter 3

Greenhouse Heating

Heat is measured by the Btu (British thermal unit), defined as the amount of heat required to raise one pound of water 1°F. When the number of Btus becomes large, as in heating greenhouses, it is more convenient to use the larger term horsepower. One boiler horsepower is equivalent to 33,475 Btu. To convert from Btu to boiler horsepower one divides Btus by 33,475.

The requirements for heating a greenhouse reside in the task of adding heat at the rate at which it is lost. Most heat is lost by *transmission* through the covering materials of the greenhouse. Different materials, such as aluminum sash bars, glass, polyethylene, and asbestos-cement curtain walls, vary in transmission according to the rate at which each conducts heat from the warm interior to the colder exterior. For instance, aluminum sash bars conduct heat faster than wood, which results in more rapid loss of heat. (Since the upkeep of wood, however, is much greater, its use is not justified.) Glass conducts heat a little faster than FRP; thus an FRP greenhouse is cheaper to heat. Table 3-1 lists heat loss values for several greenhouse coverings. A greenhouse covered with one layer of polyethylene, for example, loses 1.2 Btu of heat through each square foot of covering every hour when the outside temperature is 1°F lower than the inside. When a second layer of polyethylene is added only 0.7 Btu is lost. This is a reduction of better than 40 percent of the heat loss.

There are limited ways for insulating the covering material without blocking light transmission. As previously mentioned, a dead air space between two coverings appears to be the best system. Forty percent of the heat requirement can be saved when a second covering is applied. The savings diminish when the air space between the two coverings increases to the point where air currents can be established in the space, generally 8 inches or greater and is completely lost when the two layers touch one another.

Although thermopane glass (panels of two layers of glass with a dead air space) significantly reduce heat loss they have been too expensive to justify. There has been some use of a double layer of polyethylene sealed together in such a way as to form numerous air cells of about 3/16-inch thickness (Figure 3-1). This material can be applied in a continuous layer by stapling to the wood sash bars inside glass greenhouses or by conventional methods of attachment inside FRP and film plastic greenhouses. An adhesive is now available for attaching it directly to FRP and glass. Thus far this material has the disadvantage of being limited to widths of four feet but does offer the great advantage of insulation. It has a heat transmission value of 0.60. A 45 percent savings in fuel is claimed when this material is applied as an inner layer in glass greenhouses and 50 percent when it is used to replace the conventional polyethylene layer on a single glazed film plastic greenhouse. This greenhouse covering looks very promising and warrants further commercial trial.

A second mode of heat loss is that of air *infiltration.* Cracks between panes of glass or FRP and around ventilators and doors permit the passage of warm air outward and cold air inward. A general assumption holds that the volume of air held in the greenhouse is lost more than twice each hour in a glass greenhouse, once per hour in an FRP house with seams between overlapping sheets of FRP, and that almost no loss occurs in film plastic greenhouses. About 10 percent of the total heat loss from a tight greenhouse occurs through infiltration loss.

A third mode of heat loss from greenhouses is that of *radiation.* Warm objects emit radiant energy which passes through air to colder objects without warming the air significantly. The colder objects become warmer. Glass, vinyl plastic, FRP, and water are relatively opaque to radiant energy (do not readily permit the passage of radiant heat), whereas polyethylene is not (Table 3-1). Polyethylene greenhouses can lose considerable heat through radiation to colder objects outside unless a film of moisture forms on the polyethylene to provide a barrier. Fortunately, a film of condensation often forms on the inside of polyethylene at night.

HEAT SOURCE

A boiler or heater must be provided to supply heat to the greenhouse at the same rate at which it is lost by transmission, infiltration, and radiation. A *central* or *localized* heat source may be utilized. In the central system, one or more boilers are located in a single position and the steam or hot water generated is piped to the various greenhouse locations. The localized system makes use of several heaters, usually hot air, each located in the area it heats. The localized system demands a lower initial investment for the greenhouse range which starts small and expands rapidly. Heaters are purchased as

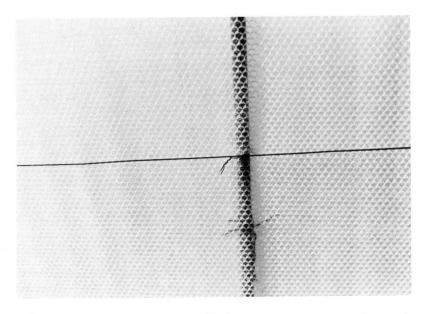

Figure 3-1. An FRP greenhouse lined with a sheet of polyethylene consisting of two layers fused in such a manner as to form air bubbles about 3/16-inch thick. This combination of coverings reduces heat loss by 50 percent or better when compared to the FRP layer alone.

needed. Much of the high initial cost of a large central boiler could not be justified until future expansions demanded the full capacity of the boiler. A central boiler system is best justified for the greenhouse range which starts out large because in the long run the large boilers of the central system are cheaper to operate and maintain than the numerous small heaters of the localized system. The large boiler can be fired on relatively inexpensive fuels such as coal and the heavier grades of oil.

Central Heat System

Years ago the central system was usually located in a boiler room separate from the greenhouse. Today it is becoming more popular to place the boilers in the greenhouse with one boiler installation handling up to three acres of floor area. When the boiler room is separate, considerable heat is lost from the pipes carrying steam or hot water to the greenhouses and from the return lines carrying condensate or cool water back to the boiler in spite of proper insulation.

American greenhouse ranges have been heated by steam as well as hot water. Hot water systems have been used in smaller ranges, i.e., less than

Table 3-1

Transmission, Infiltration, and Radiation Losses of Heat
from Various Greenhouse Coverings

| COVERING MATERIAL | HEAT LOSS | | |
	Transmission Btu/ Sq Ft	Infiltration Air Exchange/Hr	Radiation % of Total
Glass	1.13	2	4.4
PVC	0.92	1	–
Fiberglass (FRP)	0.95–1.00	1	1.0
Mylar	1.05	–	16.2
Polyethylene			
1 layer	1.20	0	70.8
2 layers	0.70	0	–
1 layer with 3/16″ air cells	0.60	–	–

Rates of transmission loss are expressed as Btu of heat passing through one square foot of covering in one hour when the outside temperature is 1°F lower than the inside temperature. Infiltration loss occurs when warm air leaks from cracks in the greenhouse and is expressed as the number of volumes of air lost from the greenhouse per hour. Radiation loss is the amount of radiant heat passing through the covering expressed as a percentage of the total radiant heat beaming upon it.

20,000 square feet of floor area. These are low pressure systems of about five pounds per square inch (psi) and the water temperature is usually set well below the temperature of steam—212°F (100°C). Large volumes of water must be used in these systems because only one Btu of heat energy can be obtained from each pound of water as it drops one degree F.

In larger ranges a steam system is used, since the volume of water needed to supply heat to a large greenhouse range would dictate the need for a prohibitively large boiler and plumbing system. One pound of water releases 970 Btu of heat energy when it changes from steam at 212°F to water at 212°F and then an additional Btu for each degree it drops below that point. For this reason much less water is needed to heat a greenhouse if it is supplied as steam. A smaller boiler and less plumbing are required.

One might wonder why hot water systems are used at all in light of the advantages listed for steam. Because small ranges may not be as well automated or supervised during the night, they are often prone to crop loss by freezing. The large volume of water in the hot water system provides a reservoir of slowly available heat which can protect the greenhouse against frost for several hours after boiler failure. The heat of steam, however, is quickly dissipated placing greater dependency on continual operation of the boiler. Clearly, hot water and steam systems both have a place in the greenhouse industry.

European systems make far greater use of hot water, even in larger ranges. These are high-pressure systems which permit a much higher water temperature and thus a greater heat capacity than low-pressure systems. This factor reduces the needed pipe and boiler sizes. Such high-pressure hot-water systems are appearing in larger American greenhouse ranges today.

Attention should be paid to the placement and height of the smoke stack in the central system. The stack should be sufficiently tall so that shifting winds cannot sweep emitted gases into the greenhouses where they can cause plant injury. It is best to place the stack in such a position that the prevailing winds carry the smoke away from the range, and also such that the stack does not cast a shadow on the crop. The north side and northeast corner, for instance, would be good locations for the boiler and stack under conditions of prevailing winds from the west.

Localized Heat System

Numerous heater designs are used in the localized heating system of greenhouses. These heaters fit into two basic categories: *unit* or forced air and *convection* heaters. The difference resides in the presence or absence of a heat exchanger within the heater. The heat exchanger transfers heat from the firebox exhaust to the air of the greenhouse.

UNIT HEATERS: Unit heaters are often referred to as forced-air heaters. They consist of three functional parts as illustrated in Figure 3-2. Fuel is combusted in a firebox to provide heat. The heat is initially contained in the exhaust which rises through a set of thin-walled metal tubes on its way to the exhaust stack. The warm exhaust transfers heat to the cooler metal of the tubes. Much of the heat is removed from the exhaust by the time it reaches the stack through which it leaves the greenhouse. A fan in the back of the unit heater draws in greenhouse air, passing it over the exterior side of the tubes, and then out the front of the heater to the greenhouse environment again. The cool air passing over the hot metal tubes is warmed. In short, the metal tubes serve as heat exchangers absorbing heat from the hot exhaust passing through the inside of them and transferring it to the cool greenhouse air passing over the outside of them.

Generally the fuel supply and fan are connected to a thermostat located in an appropriate area of the greenhouse. Heat is supplied only as needed. Automation is a distinct advantage of unit heaters. Unit heaters burn a variety of fuels including the lighter grades of oil, kerosene, LP gas, and natural gas. Fuel types, however, cannot be changed without alteration to the unit heater.

Unit heaters come in vertical as well as horizontal designs (see Figure 3-3). This refers to the direction in which the heated air is exhausted from

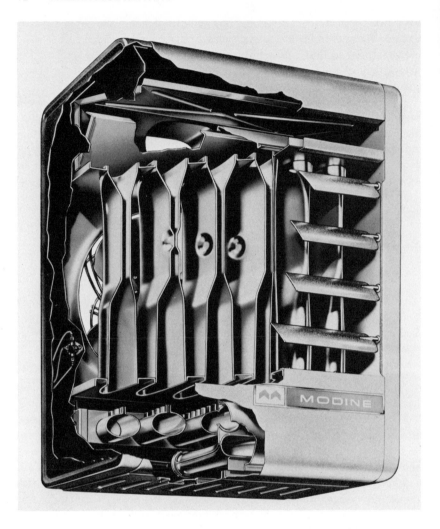

Figure 3-2. Interior view of a horizontal unit (forced air) heater. Fuel is combusted in the chamber at the bottom. Hot fumes rise inside the heat exchanger tubes, giving up heat to the walls of the tubes. Smoke exits at the top rear into a stack. A fan behind the unit forces cool greenhouse air over the outside of the tubes where it picks up heat. (*Photo courtesy of Modine Manufacturing Company, Racine, WI 53401*)

the heater. The vertical heater takes air in from the ridge area of the greenhouse and expels it downward toward the floor. These heaters are purchased in a size capable of heating an area the width of the greenhouse. They are suspended from the ridge of the greenhouse, well above head height, and are spaced along the length of the greenhouse at intervals equal to the width of

(a)   (b)

Figure 3-3. (a) A vertical unit heater typical of the early types used for greenhouse heating. (b) A horizontal unit heater commonly used today.

the greenhouse. When unit heaters first became popular in the 1940s, the vertical type were believed best for greenhouse application. Uneven temperatures and drying of the soil sometimes occurred which resulted in nonuniform growth. Horizontal units are more widely accepted today. The uneven temperature and drying problem is reduced with horizontal air distribution. It is possible to use fewer but larger heaters, thus reducing the initial cost of the heaters as well as the labor or installation. The horizontal heaters are also adaptable to the newer integrated systems of heating, cooling, and horizontal air flow.

Whenever fuel is combusted, oxygen is consumed. Older glass greenhouses may have sufficient air leaks to provide the needs of the firebox, but don't depend on it. Plastic greenhouses are tighter and there have been many cases where burners have gone out during the night after consuming the available oxygen, permitting the crop to freeze. A shortage of oxygen often leads to formation of odorless carbon monoxide gas prior to the flame going out. *An employee entering such a greenhouse could lose his life.* As a general rule one square inch of opening from the outside should be provided near the heater for every 2000 Btu capacity of the heater. A stove pipe, tile, or flexible clothes dryer tube may be placed near the burner intake, extending outside. It is frequently buried for convenience. An 8-inch diameter pipe would provide the 50 square inches required for a 100,000 Btu heater. The end of the tube should be covered with a screen to prevent the entry of animals.

Unit heaters have an exhaust stack which is generally run from the heater directly through the roof above the heater. The stack must extend above the greenhouse roof sufficiently high to permit dissipation of the smoke without reentry into the greenhouse.

CONVECTION HEATERS: Convection heaters are seen in greenhouses owing to their low purchase price. Since they are not satisfactorily automated, they are used mainly in small ranges. These heaters differ from unit heaters in that they do not have a built-in heat exchanger. Fuel of most any type including wood, coal, oil, or gas is combusted in a firebox. The resulting hot fumes pass out through an exhaust pipe which is situated along the ground either between ground beds or beneath benches (Figure 3-4).

The exhaust pipe is sufficiently long to permit cooling of the exhaust before it leaves the end of the pipe. The heater is located at one end of the greenhouse and the exhaust usually exits at the opposite end of the greenhouse. The exhaust pipe serves at a heat exchanger transferring heat from the exhaust to air in the greenhouse. The exhaust often is introduced directly into a manifold of large diameter stovepipe from which several smaller stovepipes feed out. Although stovepipe is frequently used, black polyethylene tubing can be used as well. All joints in the pipe system should be taped with fire-resistant tape to help prevent leakage of fumes into the greenhouse. To further guarantee against leakage, a low capacity fan similar to those used in an oil-fired residential burner should be installed in the outlet of the exhaust system. The fan draws out the exhaust and in so doing maintains a suction or negative pressure within the system. If leaks exist, air from the greenhouse will enter at these points rather than exhaust escaping. Polyethylene tubing does not work in this system because it collapses under negative pressure.

It is important in all greenhouse heating systems that the exhaust does not contact the crop. When the fuel source is of high purity and is thoroughly combusted only carbon dioxide and water vapor are produced, but it is rare that fuels are completely combusted. Products of incomplete combustion form, including ethylene gas, are injurious to plants (Figure 3-5). Ethylene can cause a distorted, corkscrew type of stem growth, curling of leaves, and abortion of buds. There are also impurities contained in fuels. Sulfur is commonly found in coal, oils, and gases. Upon combustion it is released as sulfur dioxide gas (SO_2). Sulfur dioxide gas dissolves into moisture films on the plant surfaces and is converted to sulfurrous acid, and after oxidation, sulfuric acid which burns the cells it contacts (Figure 3-6). Small tan spots appear or, in severe cases, the entire leaf may die.

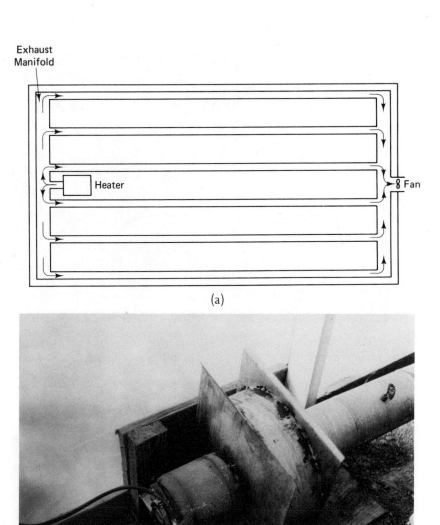

Exhaust
Manifold

Heater

Fan

(a)

(b)

Figure 3-4. (a) The physical setup of a convection heating system in a green-house. Exhaust from the convection heater enters a large-diameter stovepipe manifold in which it is distributed to several smaller diameter stovepipes running along the ground between beds or under benches to the opposite end of the greenhouse. There the exhaust is collected in a manifold and expelled to the outside. A fan located in the outlet draws out the exhaust and maintains a negative pressure in the exhaust pipe system to prevent fumes from escaping through cracks into the greenhouse. (b) A fan at the end of a stovepipe.

Figure 3-5. Ethylene gas injury to chrysanthemums caused by fumes escaping from an improperly vented unit heater inside the greenhouse. Leaves are distorted and abnormally narrow, and the terminal bud has aborted. (*From J. W. Love, Department of Horticultural Science, North Carolina State University, Raleigh, NC 27607*)

Figure 3-6. Sulfur dioxide injury on Rieger begonia foliage. Improperly vented heaters can emit the gas. Carbon dioxide generators burning fuel with an undesirably high sulfur content also produce toxic levels of this gas inside the greenhouse.

EMERGENCY HEATERS AND GENERATORS

The risk of electrical power failure is always present. If a power failure should occur during a cold period, such as a heavy snow or ice storm, crop loss due to freezing is likely. Except for manually fired convection heaters, greenhouse heaters and boilers generally depend upon electricity. Solenoid valves controlling fuel entry, safety control switches, thermostats, and fans providing air to the firebox all depend upon electrical energy.

Power failure can be damaging during the summer as well. Temperature control in newer greenhouses lacking ventilators is dependent upon electrical exhaust fans. It is likely that the temperature will rise to $120°F$ ($49°C$) in a closed greenhouse on a clear summer day if a ventilator system is not in effect. High temperatures cause delay in flowering of many crops and, if prolonged for several days, can cause flower bud abortion. Many other types of equipment used in growing crops is dependent upon electrical power. For these reasons it is important that a standby electrical generator be installed (Figure 3-7).

The generator can be wired into the greenhouse circuit in such a way that it automatically turns on in the event of a power failure. Some thought should be given to the types of equipment that will be run under this situation. It is rare that the cost can be justified for a generator capable of providing all the electrical needs. During the winter, the heating system should certainly be connected into the generator, and possibly a portion of the lighting system used for photoperiodic control of flowering time if such crops are grown. Lights used during the night for control of crop flowering draw considerable power and often cannot be handled by available generators. As will be discussed in a subsequent chapter, it is possible to use cyclic (flash) lighting in which the crop is divided into three to five zones. Only one zone is lighted at a time, thus reducing the load demand. During the summer, if the entire cooling system cannot be handled, a proportion of the fans should be maintained to insure against excessive temperatures.

A standby electrical generator is essential to any greenhouse operation. It may never be used, but if required for even one critically cold night it becomes a highly profitable investment. Generators are available from a number of used equipment sources, such as government surplus.

It is equally likely that the heating system will fail. Temperatures can drop rapidly in a greenhouse due to the poor insulating properties of the coverings. The rate of temperature decline is increased by lower outside temperatures and by increases in wind velocity. Frequently there is insufficient time to seek assistance or repair the heater before the inside temperature reaches the freezing point. In northern latitudes this period of time can be as short as three or four hours. One way or another an emergency heating system should be available. Some florists have grouped into a cooperative. When one range loses heat, the owner notifies a member of the cooperative

Figure 3-7. A standby electric generator (*left*) used in the event of power failure to maintain operation of the boiler (*right*), cooling system, and possibly a portion of the lights used for photoperiodic timing of the crop. (*From J. W. Love, Department of Horticultural Science, North Carolina State University, Raleigh, NC 27607*)

who in turn alerts other members. The members transport the emergency heaters to the stricken range and assist the owner. Other florists tackle the problem on an individual basis by purchasing their own set of emergency heaters.

The Salamander heater, seen in Figure 3–8, is a popular and inexpensive heater. A kerosene supply is maintained in the pot at the bottom. It is combusted within the bottom part of the vertical stovepipe. The fumes rise up the pipe and out the top into the greenhouse. For this reason a ventilator should be opened about a half inch to prevent concentration of the fumes. The stovepipe turns red and radiates considerable quantities of heat. One heater

Figure 3-8. A salamander heater typical of the type of heater that should be held in reserve in the event of heat failure. Kerosene contained in the lower pot burns inside the exhaust stack. Since fumes come out the top, ventilators must be opened a crack when these heaters are used.

can raise the temperature of 12,000 cubic feet of air 25°F to 30°F and is considered adequate emergency heat for up to 1500 square feet of greenhouse floor area. The heater burns between one half and one gallon of kerosene per hour. One gallon cans (#10) have been used as well for emergency heat. The top is removed and a pair of 1-inch holes are cut in opposite sides two to three inches down from the top to provide air circulation. The can is half filled with alcohol and ignited. Although risky, ranges have been saved from freezing by crumpling newspaper and tightly rolling it into a ball of about 10-inch diameter. Balls are placed in the greenhouse aisles and ignited. Due to tight packing they burn slowly. Many other systems are feasible. It is important that one be available.

FUEL

Solid, liquid, and gaseous fuels represented by coal, oil, and gas are used for greenhouse heating. Each has advantages and disadvantages which until recently entered into the decision of which fuel to use. Now the choice is heavily influenced by antipollution regulations and availability. The use of coal and high sulfur content oils has been disallowed in some areas.

Natural gas is the more desirable fuel because the initial installation is cheaper, storage tanks are not required, and it burns clean which reduces the labor of adjusting and cleaning the boiler. Propane and butane gases have many of the advantages of natural gas but are expensive.

Oil is generally the next choice. It is easily automated, but storage tanks are necessary and considerably more ash and soot result. The boiler exhaust passages, referred to as tubes, must be cleaned as often as weekly during the peak heating season and adjustments are needed at least annually in the firebox. Fuel oils are available in five grades designated No. 1, 2, 4, 5, and 6. No. 1 is slightly heavier than kerosene and is generally used to heat private homes. The oil becomes heavier, more viscous, as the number increases. Oil of grade No. 6 must be preheated before ignition, or it will not flow through the nozzle in the burner. No. 2 oil is used in small greenhouse heaters and the heavier grades in larger boilers.

Coal is available in many grades. The terms *anthracite* and *bituminous* refer to hard and soft coals respectively. Many intermediate kinds exist with no distinct lines of demarcation. Materials softer than bituminous also exist ranging all the way to peat. All are the compacted remains of plant material. Coal requires considerable above ground storage space, more labor of handling than oil, and yields large volumes of ash which must be removed and disposed of.

The quantity of fuel required for one night, or for any given period of time, can be predicted by knowing the heat value of the fuel to be used and the heat required in the greenhouse. The heat requirement can be easily calculated as will be seen later in this chapter. The heat values of the common greenhouse fuels are listed in Table 3-2.

From Table 3-2 it can be seen that the heater in a greenhouse requiring 100,000 Btu of heat per hour would burn 11.9 pounds of anthracite coal or one gallon of No. 4 oil or 133 cubic feet of natural gas. All are equivalent in heat value. Each is determined by dividing the output heat value of the selected fuel into the Btu of heat required in the greenhouse. In the case of anthracite coal, the 100,000 Btu required in the greenhouse was divided by 8392 Btu, which is the heat output of one pound of coal resulting in a need for 11.9 pounds of coal.

The cost of fuel is a strong factor in its selection. Equivalent costs of three types of fuel are listed in Table 3-3. The three figures on any line in the

Table 3-2
Typical Heat Contents for Various Types of Fuel Used for Greenhouse Heating

FUEL	HEAT VALUE	BOILER EFFICIENCY (%)	HEAT OUTPUT
Moist Coal-Mine Run	*Btu per Lb*		*Btu per Lb*
Anthracite (hard)	12,910	65	8,392
Semi-anthracite	13,770	60	8,262
Low volatile bituminous	14,340	65	9,321
Medium volatile bituminous	13,840	60	8,304
High volatile bituminous	10,750–13,090	55	5,913–7,200
Sub-bituminous	8,940–9,150	55	4,917–5,033
Fuel Oils	*Btu per Gal*		*Btu per Gal*
No. 1	132,900–137,000	70	93,030–95,900
No. 2	135,800–141,800	70	95,060–99,260
No. 4	140,600–153,300	68	95,608–104,244
No. 5	148,100–155,900	67	99,227–104,453
No. 6	149,400–157,300	65	97,110–102,245
Gases	*Btu per Cu Ft*		*Btu per Cu Ft*
Natural	1,000	75	750
Manufactured	550	70	385
Propane	2,570	75	1,928
Butane	3,225	75	2,419

The heat value is the amount of heat contained in the fuel. The boiler efficiency and heat output are the percentage of the heat value and the actual amount of heat which is obtained from the fuel when combusted in a burner.

Table 3-3
Comparative Costs of Electricity, Oil, and Gas

AN ELECTRIC RATE OF: (¢/kWh)	IS THE SAME AS IF YOU HEATED WITH	
	FUEL OIL AT: (¢/gal)	GAS AT: (¢/therm)
1.7	48.4	37.3
1.8	51.3	39.4
1.9	54.2	41.6
2.0	57.0	43.8
2.2	62.7	48.2
2.4	68.4	52.6
2.6	74.1	56.9
2.8	79.8	61.3
3.0	85.5	65.7
3.2	91.2	70.1
3.4	96.9	74.5
3.6	102.6	78.8
3.8	108.3	83.2
4.0	114.0	87.6
4.4	125.4	96.4
4.8	136.8	105.1
5.2	148.2	113.9
6.0	171.0	131.4
6.8	193.8	148.9

Adapted from a table by Clifford M. Tuck and Associates, Athens, GA 30604

Heat values: kWh = 3416 Btu, gal = 139,000 Btu, therm = 100,000 Btu

Boiler efficiency = No. 2 Fuel Oil at 70%, Gas at 75%.

table are equivalent, i.e., a Btu of heat would cost the same from each of the three fuels. Taking the eleventh line for example, 2¢ per kilowatt hour (kWh) is equivalent to paying 57¢ per gallon of No. 2 oil or 42.8¢ per therm of gas. One should check his local prices for fuel. If oil is available for 48.4¢ per gallon and electricity for 2¢ per kWh, it is much cheaper to to heat with oil. On the other hand, if gas cost 30¢ per therm each Btu of heat costs less from gas than oil.

HEAT DISTRIBUTION

Upon combustion of fuel in the firebox of the heater or boiler, the heat must be transferred to the greenhouse. It is important that only a minimum amount be lost in so doing and that once inside the greenhouse the heat be evenly distributed across the growing area. Warm air rises to the peak of the greenhouse where it is of little value and the cooler air forming at the glass surface drops to the lower area where the plants are growing. This situation raises the price of heating, but fortunately can be controlled.

Pipe Coils

Convection as well as forced-air heat distribution systems are used in the greenhouse today. Years ago convection systems were used almost exclusively. Most heat was derived from a central boiler system and delivered to the greenhouse in the form of hot water or steam through insulated pipe mains. Once inside the greenhouse, the heat mains supplied a network of smaller pipes covering the length and width of the greenhouse which served as a radiator warming the surrounding air. The warm air, due to its tendency to rise, sets up convection currents throughout the greenhouse. A detailed look at this system of heat conduction is warranted since many of today's greenhouse ranges still use it.

Hot water has been customarily supplied at a temperature of 180°F (85°C) in the greenhouse. It can be heated to higher temperatures when the heating load becomes intense. Two-inch diameter pipe is generally used. Steam systems, on the other hand, supply steam usually at a temperature of 215°F. This is three degrees above the temperature at which water turns to steam and is possible because the system is under a low pressure of five pounds or so. Since there is less resistance to the flow of steam, smaller pipes are used in the greenhouse coil, either 1½- or 1¼-inch diameter. The amount of pipe needed in a greenhouse coil can be determined by referring to the heat supply values listed in Table 3-4 for various types of pipe. A greenhouse requiring 160,000 Btu of heat per hour would need 1000 linear feet of 2-inch hot-water pipe to provide this heat. This was determined by dividing the total heat requirement for the greenhouse by the amount of heat which one linear foot of pipe can provide. In this case 160,000 Btu per hour is divided by 160 Btu per foot of 2-inch hot-water pipe yielding an answer of 1000 feet of pipe. If a 1½-inch system of steam pipes was used instead, the need would be 160,000 Btu per hour ÷ 210 Btu per hour or 762 feet of pipe.

Placement of heating pipes is very important. Since the total length of pipe will usually be several times the perimeter of the greenhouse, several layers of pipe will be necessary. If all of the pipe is stacked on the side walls

Table 3-4
Heat Available From One Linear Foot of Various Diameter Pipes
Heated by Hot Water at 180°F or Steam at 215°F

HEAT SOURCE	PIPE DIAMETER	HEAT SUPPLIED/FT. OF PIPE
Hot water 180°F (85°C)	2 in	160 Btu/hr
Steam 215°F (102°C)	1½ in.	210 Btu/hr
Steam 215°F (102°C)	1¼ in.	180 Btu/hr

The inside air temperature of the greenhouse is 60°F.

and end walls, undesirable patterns of air flow will occur as shown in the work of Dr. H. E. Gray at Cornell University. The cross-sectional view of the greenhouse in Figure 3-9 shows that the heat from the side coils of pipe rises along the side wall and part of the roof until it meets a stream of air which is being cooled by the glass and is flowing downward under the roof. The two currents mix and drop at this point, part returning to the pipe coil and part moving toward the center of the greenhouse at plant level, cooling as it moves. In the center of the greenhouse, currents meet from both sides and rise. The longitudinal section shows that heat rises from the end wall coils to the peak where it travels toward the center of the house cooling as it moves. In the center the two cool air masses meet and drop to the ground causing a cold spot in the greenhouse. The growth of plants is delayed where these cold spots occur. Cold spots can be counteracted by the placement of pipe in the regions of the downdrafts. For this reason about one third of the pipe is placed above the height of the plants running from end to end in the greenhouse as illustrated in Figure 3-9b. The remaining two-thirds of the pipe are placed in stacks along the outer walls. The overhead pipes should be six inches to one foot above the maximum plant height and can be as close as one foot from the roof. Side pipes should have a few inches of clearance on all sides to permit the establishment of air currents and should be located low enough to prevent blockage of light entering through the side walls. They are generally attached to the curtain wall.

When several pipes are stacked above one another, their effectiveness is reduced. Additional pipes must be added to compensate. Table 3-5 shows the effect. For two pipes the effect is insignificant. Five pipes in a stack, however, are only as effective as four pipes placed apart from each other. In a heating design where the heat of four pipes is needed in the side coil, five would have to be installed. Overhead pipes are spaced sufficiently far apart to avert the problem.

The expense of pipes and installation became a concern during the 1950s and alternative materials and designs were sought. Fin pipe became popular as a partial substitute for conventional pipe. Fin pipe is a conventional pipe with numerous thin metal plates radiating outward from it to increase the surface area of the pipe and thus the rate at which it transfers heat from the hot water or steam contained inside to the surrounding air.

Depending on the design, one linear foot of fin pipe can be equivalent to four or more linear feet of conventional pipe. It should be remembered that heat released from fin pipe is much more intense than from conventional, making it important to distribute the fin pipes evenly throughout the greenhouse. If a single continuous coil of fin pipe is not needed around the entire greenhouse, then the fin pipe should be alternated with conventional pipe at equidistant intervals.

Pipe coils can be arranged in two styles, either box or trombone (Figure

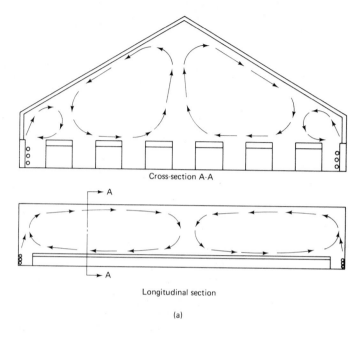

Cross-section A-A

Longitudinal section

(a)

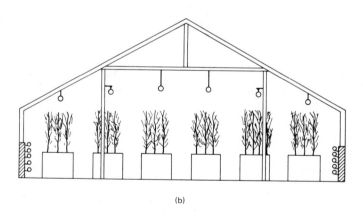

(b)

Figure 3-9. (a) Air circulation pattern in a greenhouse using only coils during the winter. (b) A desirable combination arrangement of overhead pipe and side coils for controlling downdrafts and cold spots in the greenhouse. (*From H. E. Gray, Greenhouse Heating and Construction, Florists' Publishing Co., Chicago, IL, 1956*)

Table 3-5
Heat Supply Relationship of Pipes in a Vertical Stack
Compared to Pipes Located Separately From One Another*

NUMBER OF PIPES IN VERTICAL STACK	EQUIVALENT NUMBER OF INDIVIDUAL PIPES GIVING SAME AMOUNT OF HEAT
1	1
2	2
3	2 2/3
4	3 1/3
5	4
6	4 1/3
8	5

*From H. E. Gray, *Greenhouse Heating and Construction,* Florists' Publishing Co., Chicago, 1956.

3-10). Box coils are used in hot water systems. Hot water entering the greenhouse through the pipe main is distributed in a header, also known as a branch tee, to several smaller pipes through which it passes simultaneously to the opposite end of the greenhouse. There it combines and returns to the boiler to be reheated. There is a resistance to the flow of water in the pipe. The box coil minimizes this resistance by reducing the length of pipe through which any given portion of the water must flow and by increasing the cross-sectional area of the combined pipe through which the water passes.

Trombone coils are used for steam systems. Resistance to flow is not a problem for steam, but the rapid drop in pressure and temperature along the pipe is. If a box coil were used for steam conduction, the entry end would be hot and the exit end much cooler resulting in an intolerable temperature gradient in the greenhouse. A continuous pipe is used in a trombone coil. Steam enters at the top of the coil and passes to the distant end of the greenhouse. It returns to the entry end in the second pipe down and then back to the distant end in the third pipe down. This arrangement continues until at the end of the coil water condensate and steam enter a trap which permits the return of water, but not steam, to the boiler. No temperature gradient exists along the length of the coil. The gradient exists from top to bottom of the coil and is of no consequence. The overhead pipe coil is usually a trombone coil whether hot water or steam is used. In the case of a hot-water system, two overhead trombone coils are used to reduce resistance.

When heat is distributed in the greenhouse by a pipe system, a vertical temperature gradient establishes itself. Since warm air rises, the temperature in the peak can be as much as 1°F warmer for each foot in elevation above ground level. It is only the heat at plant level that counts. Vertical air lift

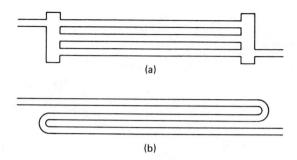

Figure 3-10. (a) Box coil used to distribute hot water through a greenhouse; (b) trombone coil used in a steam system of heating.

fans have been installed in a row beneath the ridge in greenhouses heated by pipe coils (Figure 3-11). Warm air from the peak enters the fan from the top and is distributed outward at a gentle downward angle. These fans greatly reduce the vertical temperature gradient making better use of heat and reducing fuel costs. However, these fans result in very uneven temperatures at plant height. Vertical lift fans have been used with pipe-heating systems but not with forced-air heating systems.

A more recent system for establishing uniform temperature in pipe-heated greenhouses is the horizontal air flow (HAF) system developed by J. S. Koths at the University of Connecticut and further tested by J. N. Walker at the University of Kentucky. This system uses small horizontal fans and moves the air mass with less than half the electricity required by vertical air lift fans.

Dr. Koths visualizes a 30- by 100-foot greenhouse as a large box measuring 30 × 100 × 10 feet containing 1½ tons of air. It is difficult to start the air moving, but once it is moving in a circular pattern, like water in a bathtub, it is easy to keep it moving. Turbulence creates a need for the initial startup phase. There is much more turbulence in the vertical air-lift system. The horizontal air-flow pattern of the HAF system also results in the movement of warmer air from the gable to the plant height and reduces heating costs. Temperatures at plant height are much more uniform with the HAF system.

An ideal air-flow rate has not been established for the greenhouse environment, but a minimum velocity of 40 fpm (feet per minute) has been suggested by Dr. Walker at the University of Kentucky. Below this level, air flow is erratic and uniform mixing of air cannot be assured. A velocity of 40 fpm causes slight leaf movement on plants with long leaves, such as tomato.

Specifications for the HAF system are shown in Figures 11 and 12 and are described by Dr. Koths as follows.

Figure 3-11. Vertical air lift fan installed in the peak of the greenhouse to transfer warm air down to the plant level.

FOR INDIVIDUAL HOUSES:

1. Fans of 1/12–1/10 hp are sufficient. Commercial, continuous duty motors should be used.

2. Use approximately one fan per 50 feet of wall on both sides of the house.

3. Install the first fan 15 to 20 feet from the end of the house, the last one 40 to 50 feet from the end toward which it is blowing.

4. All fans should be installed about one-quarter of the way across the house and pointed directly down the house to minimize turbulence.

FOR RIDGE-AND-FURROW HOUSES:

1. Move the air down one house, back the other. Connecting gutters must be sufficiently high to permit air movement.

2. Use large low-horsepower fans. A 1/4 hp 30-inch fan will provide more than 40 fpm (perhaps) in two 20′ × 100′ connected houses. For two 30′ × 125′ houses, place a fan in the center of each house about 30 feet from the near end of one, the far end of the other.

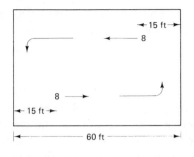

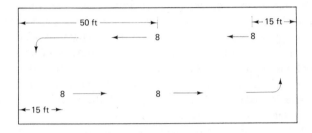

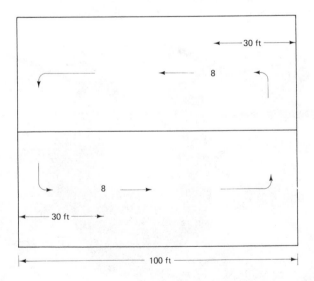

Figure 3-12. Fan arrangements for a horizontal air flow (HAF) system in various greenhouse sizes. Fans are located one-quarter of the width of the greenhouse in from the side walls in the first two single greenhouses illustrated. They are located under the ridge in the ridge-and-furrow greenhouse diagram.

3. Since a 1/4 hp fan will service perhaps 4000 square feet of green-house, it is generally not advisable to use larger fans unless the greenhouses are especially wide and long or you just happen to have one that is not being used.

Unit Heaters

Many modern American greenhouses are heated with unit heaters rather than pipe coils alone. A considerable number of greenhouses are also being imported from The Netherlands. These are sometimes heated by a high-pressure, hot-water, pipe-coil system, but otherwise unit heaters are used. Unit heaters may have a self-contained firebox or they may derive heat from steam or hot water generated in a central boiler which is then piped to the heat exchanging coil within the unit heater. Horizontal unit heaters are used.

Warm air is emitted directly into the greenhouse environment in many small greenhouses. In larger greenhouses, where circulation is a problem, a polyethylene tube is connected to the air outlet (Figure 3–13). The poly-ethylene tube is installed along the length of the greenhouse above plant height and is sealed at the distant end. Round holes of 2- to 3-inch diameter are located in pairs at opposite sides of the tube every few feet along the tube length. Warm air from the heater moves through the tube and out the side holes. The warm air comes out at a high velocity in a jet stream and

Figure 3–13. A horizontal unit heater connected to a transparent poly-ethylene tube with holes along either side for uniform distribution of heat.

quickly mixes with the surrounding air. This system insures that heat is distributed from one end of the greenhouse to the other. When neither heating nor cooling is required, many growers, rather than installing a HAF air circulation system, keep the fan in the unit heater running without heat so that air from the greenhouse is continually circulated through the tube. Air circulation gives more uniformity of temperature in the greenhouse, conserves heat, and reduces the occurrence of disease by reducing condensation on plant foliage.

Considerable heat is lost through the side walls of the greenhouse; in addition, warm plants radiate heat energy to colder objects outside the greenhouse. The result is a disproportionately high cooling effect in the outer beds of plants. In colder climates, the overhead unit heater systems are unable to completely counteract the cold spots along the walls. One or two rows of pipe are installed around the perimeter of the greenhouse. The side coil should have a heat-supplying capacity equal to the heat loss through the walls of the greenhouse. This will generally be one third or slightly more of the total heat requirement. If more than one row of pipe is required, fin pipe can be used to keep the size of the installation to a minimum. The perimeter pipe coil is generally turned on first and the overhead heaters later, as more capacity is required.

Thermostat

Except for the least expensive convection heaters, the operation of heaters and boilers is controlled by a thermostat. When the temperature drops below the desired level, an electrical switch is actuated in the thermostat which causes fuel to flow into the heater or boiler and ignite. A valve on unit heaters connected to central boiler systems is activated by the thermostat to permit entry of steam or hot water. The unit heater fan may also be activated by the thermostat unless running continuously as part of the HAF system. When the temperature in the greenhouse rises to a level a degree or two above that which caused the heating system to activate, the thermostat responds and the system shuts down.

Since temperature gradients exist in greenhouses with even the best of heating systems, placement of the thermostat is very important. It should be placed in a location which reflects the average temperature in the greenhouse. If it were placed in a location favored by the placement of the heater or a direct flow of warm air, the heater would turn on and off according to conditions in that warm spot and the remainder of the greenhouse would run colder than desired. The majority of the crop might be delayed. Thermostats are quite often placed near the center of the greenhouse. The height of the thermostat placement is also very important due to the vertical temperature gradient. The thermostat should be located at the height of the growing points of the plants. For pot plant crops, this is usually 6 to 12 inches above the pot rim. For cut flowers the height varies, and the thermostat should be attached to a post on which it can be raised or lowered. Direct or indirect rays of sunlight will raise the thermostat temperature well above the air temperature. This will prevent the operation of the heater on cold but bright winter days when heat is needed. The thermostat should therefore be shielded from the sun's rays. A very desirable system calls for placement of the thermostat in a box (Figure 3-14). The outer surface of the box is painted in a reflective color such as white or aluminum to reduce heat buildup. The ends of the box have louvers to permit air passage, but prevent entry of sun rays. A fan is installed to provide a minimum air flow through the box of 600 feet per minute. This insures that a large mass of air is continually monitored by the thermostat.

Other instruments should be located in the thermostat station. A second thermostat set at a low temperature such as 50°F (10°C) should be connected to an alarm in the manager's or owner's home. This will alert someone in the case of heat failure while there is still time to make corrections. The alarm system should be powered by a battery or a standby generator to insure that it operates during an electrical power failure. When the

Figure 3-14. An aspirated box that houses the heater thermostat, a low-temperature alarm thermostat, and a thermometer. The box has a reflective outer surface, louvered ends, and a fan to provide a minimum air flow of 600 feet per minute. It is located at the height of the growing points of the plants.

alarm is to be located a long distance from the greenhouse it is possible, working through the local telephone company, to use their existing lines.

Thermostats are not always calibrated accurately, nor certain to hold their calibration. They should be checked against an accurate thermometer periodically. A thermometer should be located in the station. It should be of high quality since much depends upon its accuracy. The thermometer can be calibrated by placing it in a bucket of ice water. Water in the presence of ice is at precisely 32°F (0°C).

HEAT REQUIREMENT CALCULATION

A-Frame Greenhouse

In order to determine the heat requirement, the surface of an A-frame greenhouse must be divided into four components as illustrated in Figure 3-15. These are: roof, gable, wall, and curtain wall. Heat lost under standard conditions through each of these areas can be found in Tables 3-6 and 3-7. All values in the tables are listed as MBtu which means thousands of Btu. A figure of 5 in the table therefore means 5000 Btu. The gable and roof losses can be found in Table 3-6. There are two wall components—the wall covered with a transparent covering and the curtain wall below it which has a nontransparent covering such as asbestos-cement or concrete block. The heat loss from each is determined separately in Table 3-7. The wall length in each

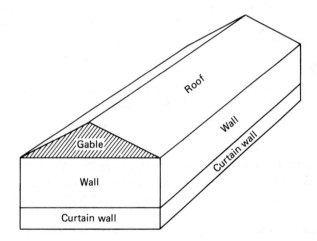

Figure 3-15. Diagram of an A-frame greenhouse showing component areas needed in the determination of the heat requirement of this greenhouse.

case refers to the total perimeter of the greenhouse since the wall extends around four sides of the greenhouse.

All heat losses thus far determined are for standard conditions which include a 70°F (20°C) temperature difference from the outside to the inside temperatures and an average wind velocity of 15 miles per hour (mph). It is likely that you will have different temperature and wind conditions for a different type of greenhouse construction. You can change the heat loss values in Tables 3-6 and 3-7 by multiplying them by two correction factors. To do this, determine the difference in temperature between your desired inside night temperature and the coldest outside temperature you expect to encounter during the winter. Local temperature probabilities can be obtained from the nearest U.S. Weather Bureau Office or by purchasing the most recent Weather Bureau Climatological Data pamphlet from the Superintendent of Documents, Government Printing Office, Washington, D.C. 20042. Next, determine the average wind velocity for your area. For most areas 15 mph will suffice; however, this can be checked out with the nearest U.S. Weather Bureau Office. Select a climate factor, K, from Table 3-8 for your particular temperature difference and wind velocity and multiply each heat loss value from Tables 3-6 and 3-7 by the factor. Select a construction factor, C, in Table 3-9 for the type of greenhouse you have, and multiply this by the heat loss values for the gable, the roof, and the wall (transparent covering only). Determine a curtain wall construction factor, CW, in Table 3-10 and multiply the curtain wall heat loss value by this factor. All greenhouse component heat losses have now been corrected. The four corrected values should be added together to determine the total heat input required to heat the greenhouse for one hour. If the heating system is located inside the greenhouse, this is the end of the calculation. Purchase a boiler with a net rating equal to the heat requirement calculated.

If a central heating system is located in a separate building, an additional quantity of heat will be necessary to compensate for heat losses from the delivery and return lines to and from the greenhouse. An engineer should be consulted to determine what this loss is and it should be added to the heat requirement calculated for the greenhouse.

EXAMPLE PROBLEM: The following steps are taken to determine the heat requirement for an all-metal, glass-covered greenhouse measuring 30 feet wide by 100 feet long. The curtain wall is 2 feet high and constructed of 4-inch concrete block. The glass wall above the curtain wall is 6 feet high. An average wind velocity of 15 mph is expected. A 60° temperature difference is expected between the outside low temperature of 0°F and the inside temperature of 60°F.

GREENHOUSE COMPONENT	STANDARD HEAT LOSS (MBtu/hr)	K (from Table 3-8)	C or CW (from Tables 3-9 or 3-10)		CORRECTED HEAT LOSS (MBtu/hr)
Gable	18 (Table 3-6)	.84	1.08	C	16.330
Roof	266 (Table 3-6)	.84	1.08	C	241.262
Wall (transparent)	123 (Table 3-7)	.84	1.08	C	111.561
Curtain Wall	41 (Table 3-7)	.84	.58	CW	19.975
			Total Heat Requirement		389.128 (MBtu/hr)

1. Sketch a chart as illustrated.

2. Find the appropriate heat loss value for both gables combined in Table 3-6 immediately below the figure for the greenhouse width. For a 30-foot width it is 18 MBtu (18,000 Btu) per hour.

3. Find the heat loss value for the combined roofs in Table 3-6 at the point where the 30-foot greenhouse width column and the 100-foot greenhouse length row intersect. It is 266 MBtu in this case.

4. Figure the length of the side wall. It is equal to the perimeter of the greenhouse which equals 100 + 30 + 100 + 30 feet or 260 feet. Find the heat loss figure for the transparent wall measuring 6 feet high and 260 feet long and for the curtain wall measuring 2 feet high and 260 feet long in Table 3-7. Since there are no figures in the table for a wall length of 260 feet, we must look up values for 200 feet and for 60 feet and add them together to arrive at our answer. For the transparent wall 95 MBtu are lost through a 200-foot wall and 28 MBtu more through an additional 60 feet of the wall. The total loss is equal to 95 + 28 or 123 MBtu/hr. The curtain wall heat loss is equal to 32 + 9 or 41 MBtu/hr.

5. Determine a K factor in Table 3-8 for a wind velocity of 15 mph and a temperature difference of 60°. The K value is 0.84 which lies at the intersection of the wind velocity column and the temperature difference row. Enter this value in the chart in the appropriate spaces after each of the four greenhouse components.

6. Determine a C factor from Table 3-9 for the type of greenhouse construction. The example greenhouse is constructed with a metal frame and a glass covering and has a C factor of 1.08. Enter this value in the appropriate boxes after the gable, roof, and transparent wall components. These are the three components constructed with the above materials.

Table 3-6

Standard Heat Loss Values for Gables and Roofs of A-frame Type Greenhouses*

GREEN-HOUSE LENGTH FEET	GREENHOUSE WIDTH—FEET														
	16'	18'	20'	22'	24'	26'	28'	30'	32'	34'	36'	38'	40'	50'	60'
GABLE LOSS (BOTH) MBTU/HR	5	6	8	10	11	13	15	18	20	23	26	29	32	50	72
ROOF LOSS (BOTH) MBTU/HR															
5	7	8	9	10	11	12	12	13	14	15	16	17	18	22	26
10	14	16	18	19	21	23	25	27	28	30	32	34	35	45	54
20	28	32	35	39	42	46	50	53	57	60	64	67	71	88	106
30	42	48	53	58	64	69	74	80	85	90	96	101	106	133	160
40	57	64	71	78	85	92	99	106	113	120	127	135	142	177	212
50	71	80	89	97	106	115	124	133	142	151	159	168	177	222	266
60	85	96	106	117	127	138	149	159	170	181	191	202	212	265	318
70	99	112	124	136	149	161	173	186	198	211	223	235	248	310	372
80	113	127	142	156	170	184	198	212	227	241	255	269	283	354	424
90	127	143	159	175	191	207	223	239	255	271	287	303	319	398	478
100	142	159	177	195	212	230	248	266	283	301	319	336	354	443	532
200	283	319	354	390	425	460	496	531	567	602	637	673	708	885	1062
300	425	478	531	584	637	690	743	797	850	903	956	1009	1062	1328	1594
400	566	637	708	779	850	920	991	1062	1133	1204	1274	1345	1416	1770	2124
500	708	797	885	974	1062	1150	1239	1328	1417	1505	1593	1682	1770	2213	2666

*Tables 3–6 through 3–11 adapted from The National Greenhouse Manufacturers' Association, P.O. Box 128, Pleasantville, N.Y. 10570 and The Greenhouse Climate Control Handbook, Acme Engineering and Manufacturing Corp., Muskogee, OK 74401.

Table 3-7
Standard Heat Loss Values for Greenhouse Walls

WALL LENGTH FEET	WALL HEIGHT–FEET				
	2′	4′	6′	8′	10′
	WALL LOSS MBTU/HR				
5	1	2	2	3	4
10	2	3	5	6	8
20	3	6	9	13	16
30	5	9	14	19	24
40	6	13	19	26	32
50	8	16	24	32	40
60	9	19	28	38	47
70	11	22	33	44	55
80	13	25	38	51	63
90	14	28	43	58	71
100	16	32	47	64	79
200	32	63	95	128	158
300	47	95	142	192	237
400	63	127	190	256	316
500	79	158	237	320	395

7. Find the CW factor for the curtain wall in Table 3-10 and enter it in the chart in the appropriate box in the curtain wall row. For a 4-inch concrete block wall it is 0.58.

8. Correct each of the standard heat loss values in the chart by multiplying it by the K factor, and then in turn by multiplying each answer by the C or CW factor in the same row. Enter these four values in the chart.

standard heat loss $\times K \times C$ = corrected heat loss

gable $18 \times 0.84 \times 1.08$ =   16.330 MBtu/hr

roof $266 \times 0.84 \times 1.08$ = 241.262

wall
(transparent) $123 \times 0.84 \times 1.08$ = 111.561

Curtain
wall $41 \times 0.84 \times 0.58$ =   19.975

9. Add the four corrected heat loss values together to arrive at the total heat loss. This value is the amount of heat which must be applied to the

Table 3–8

Climate Factors, K, for Various Average Wind Velocity and
Temperature Conditions

INSIDE TO OUTSIDE TEMPERATURE DIFFERENCE (°F)	WIND VELOCITY–MPH				
	15	20	25	30	35
30	.41	.43	.46	.48	.50
35	.48	.50	.53	.55	.57
40	.55	.57	.60	.62	.64
45	.62	.65	.67	.70	.72
50	.69	.72	.74	.77	.80
55	.77	.80	.83	.86	.89
60	.84	.88	.91	.94	.98
65	.92	.96	.99	1.03	1.07
70	1.00	1.04	1.08	1.12	1.16
75	1.08	1.12	1.17	1.21	1.25
80	1.16	1.21	1.26	1.30	1.35
85	1.25	1.30	1.35	1.40	1.45
90	1.33	1.38	1.44	1.49	1.54

Standard heat loss values from Tables 3-6, 3-7 and 3-11 are multiplied by a factor (K) to correct them for local wind and temperature conditions.

greenhouse each hour to maintain the desired temperature if the heater is located in the greenhouse. For the example greenhouse, a heater or boiler with a net rating of 389,128 Btu per hour is needed.

10. If the heater is located in a building apart from the greenhouse, the loss from the steam or hot water mains and return lines must be determined and added to the above figure.

11. In a mild climate, all heat could be provided by an overhead unit heater system; but in a cold climate, a wall coil of pipes should provide an amount of heat equal to the loss through the transparent wall plus the curtain wall. In this example the requirement would be 111.561 plus 19.975 or 131.536 MBtu/hr. The remaining heat, gable plus roof (257.592 MBtu/hr), is provided by the overhead system.

12. If desired, the fuel consumption could be calculated for an hour during the night described. Divide the total heat requirement by the heat output of the fuel used.

Table 3-9

Greenhouse Construction Factors, *C,* for the
Common Types of Greenhouses in Use Today

All metal (good tight glass house—20 or 24 in. glass spacing)	1.08
Wood & steel (good tight glass house—16 or 20 in. glass spacing)	
(Metal gutters, vents, headers, etc.)	1.05
Wood houses (glass houses with wood bars, gutters, vents, etc.—	
up to and including 20 in. glass spacing)	
Good tight houses	1.00
Fairly tight houses	1.13
Loose houses	1.25
FRP covered wood houses	.95
FRP covered metal houses	1.00
Double glazing with 1″ air space	.70
Plastic covered metal houses (single thickness)	1.00
Plastic covered metal houses (double thickness)	.70

Standard heat loss values for transparent components of greenhouses such as gables and roofs in Table 3-6, transparent side walls in Table 3-8 and ends as well as covering in Table 3-11 are multiplied by a factor (C) to correct them for the type of construction.

Table 3-10

Curtain-Wall Construction Factor, *CW,* for Various Types of
Coverings Used in the Nontransparent Curtain Wall

Glass	1.00	8″ Concrete	.60
Asbestos-cement	1.00	4″ Concrete Blk.	.58
4″ Concrete	.76	8″ Concrete Blk.	.46

The standard heat loss value for the curtain wall from Table 3-7 is multiplied by this factor to correct it for the type of covering.

anthracite coal   389,128 Btu/hr ÷   8,392 Btu/lb of coal = 46.4 lb/hr

No. 2 oil   389,128 Btu/hr ÷ 97,000 Btu/gal oil   = 4.0 gal/hr

Quonset Greenhouse

Determination of the heat requirement for a Quonset greenhouse requires a few modifications owing to the difference in shape as pictured in Figure 3-16. Quonset greenhouses are either covered with film plastic or FRP and a curtain wall is rarely used. The transparent covering usually extends to the ground. Two surface areas are considered in the heat calculation; the two ends collectively and the covering that extends for the length of the greenhouse covering the roof and walls but not the ends. Heat loss values under

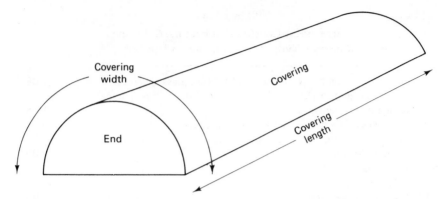

Figure 3-16. Diagram of a Quonset greenhouse showing component areas needed in the determination of the heat requirement of this greenhouse.

standard conditions through these two components are found in Table 3-11. These values must be corrected for your own conditions in the same way that the heat values for an A-frame greenhouse were corrected. The same K and C factors are located in Tables 3-8 and 3-9 respectively. The end and covering heat loss values are multiplied by each of these factors to determine the corrected heat loss value. The two corrected heat loss values are added together to arrive at the heat requirement for the greenhouse.

Listed below are steps to follow when calculating the heat requirement of a Quonset-type greenhouse. The following example is used for this purpose: A metal-frame greenhouse measuring 30 feet wide by 100 feet long and covered with two layers of polyethylene each measuring 40 feet wide. A temperature difference of 60°F and an average wind velocity of 15 mph.

1. Locate the heat loss value for the two ends combined in Table 3-11. It is the value immediately below the covering width entry of 40 feet or 40 MBtu (40,000 Btu) per hour.

2. Locate the heat loss value for the covering in Table 3-11. It is the value located at the intersection of the column below the covering width of 40 feet and the row for a house length of 100 feet. In this example, 316 MBtu are lost through the covering per hour.

3. Determine a K factor from Table 3-8 for a wind velocity of 15 mph and temperature difference of 60°F. It is equal to 0.84.

4. Find a C factor in Table 3-9 for this metal-frame greenhouse covered with a double layer of polyethylene. It is 0.70.

5. Multiply each of the standard heat loss values by the K factor and then by the C factor to determine the corrected heat loss values.

Table 3-11

Standard Heat Loss Values from Quonset-Type Greenhouses for the Combined Ends
and for the Entire Covering Along the Length of the Greenhouse

	COVERING WIDTH–FEET											
	18'	20'	22'	24'	26'	28'	30'	32'	34'	36'	38'	40'
END LOSS IN MBTU/HR	8	10	12	15	17	20	23	26	29	33	36	40
HOUSE LENGTH FEET	COVERING LOSS MBTU/HR											
5	7	8	9	9	10	11	12	13	13	14	15	16
10	14	16	17	19	21	22	24	25	27	28	30	32
20	28	32	35	38	41	44	47	51	54	57	60	63
30	43	47	52	57	62	66	71	76	81	85	90	95
40	57	63	70	76	82	89	95	101	103	114	120	127
50	71	79	87	95	103	111	119	127	134	142	150	158
60	85	95	104	114	123	133	142	152	161	171	180	190
70	100	111	122	133	144	155	166	177	188	199	211	222
80	114	127	139	152	264	177	190	202	215	228	240	253
90	128	142	157	171	185	199	214	228	242	256	271	285
100	142	158	174	190	206	221	237	253	269	285	301	316
200	285	316	348	380	411	443	475	506	538	570	601	633
300	427	475	522	569	617	664	712	759	807	854	902	949
400	570	633	696	759	822	886	949	1012	1075	1139	1202	1265
500	712	791	870	949	1028	1107	1187	1265	1345	1424	1503	1582

These values are for standard conditions including a 70°F difference from outside to inside temperature and an average wind velocity of 15 mph.

$$40 \times 0.84 \times 0.70 = 23.520 \text{ MBtu}$$

$$316 \times 0.84 \times 0.70 = 185.808 \text{ MBtu}$$

$$23.520 + 185.808 = 209.328 \text{ MBtu/hr.}$$

6. Add the two corrected heat loss values together to determine the heat requirement of the greenhouse. This is the net load of the heater when it is located within the greenhouse.

COMPONENT	STANDARD HEAT LOSS (MBTU/HR)	K (Table 3-8)	C (Table 3-9)	CORRECTED HEAT LOSS (MBTU/HR)
Combined ends	40	0.84	0.70	23.520
Covering	316	0.84	0.70	185.808
		Total Heat Requirement		209.328 MBtu/hr

Significance of K, C and CW Factors

Standard heat loss factors are multiplied by these factors to correct them for local conditions. When local conditions are the same as the standard conditions under which the heat loss values of Tables 3-6, 3-7 and 3-11 were determined, these factors are equal to 1. Obviously, multiplication by this factor does not change the heat loss values. Note in Table 3-8 that the K factor has a value of 1 for an average wind velocity of 15 mph and a temperature difference of 70°F (21°C).

If the wind velocity remained at 15 mph and the inside temperature were reduced by 10°F so that the temperature difference was now 60°F (16°C) rather than 70°F (21°C), less heat would be required in the greenhouse. This can be seen in the K factor which would become 0.84. When a factor less than 1, such as this factor of 0.84, is multiplied by the standard heat loss value, the heat loss, or in other words heat requirement, diminishes. The most highly resistant coverings to heat transmission, those which retain heat best in the greenhouse, have the lowest C factors in Table 3-9. The same is true for the curtain wall covering materials in Table 3-10.

HEAT CONSERVATION

One of the more obvious steps which can be taken to conserve heat and fuel is to apply a second covering of polyethylene. This will usually reduce fuel consumption by about 40 percent. Present day film plastic greenhouses are generally covered with two layers which are separated by air supplied by a small fan. A layer of film plastic can be, and frequently is, installed inside FRP greenhouses and glass greenhouses with wood sash bars. It can be stapled to wooden sash bars. When possible, north walls should be conventional solid, insulated construction with a reflective covering. This can reduce total heat loss up to 10 percent.

It is difficult to install a polyethylene layer on the inner side of the roof of a glass or FRP greenhouse, particularly if the frame and sashbars are metal. Recently, growers have been installing a heat barrier film from eave to eave across the greenhouse. Such a film is horizontal and just above head height.

One company, Simtrac, Inc., has developed an aluminized polyester film which can be drawn across the greenhouse at sunset and off again at sunrise. Since the film blocks most light, it must be off during the day. A polyethylene film, which has acceptable light transmission, could be used and would not need to be removed by day. However, polyethylene installed in this manner would have only about half the heat retention value of the polyester film. An eave-to-eave polyester film can retain about 60 percent of the heat normally lost from a greenhouse. A significant part of the difference is due to the relative opaqueness (blockage) of polyester to radiant heat compared to polyethylene which readily permits passage (Table 3-7).

When an eave-to-eave heat barrier is installed, a vertical barrier around the perimeter of the greenhouse should be used as well. It may be easier to attach a nonmovable film to the walls, depending upon available space and accessibility. In any event, the plant zone must be sealed off from the space above the barrier to prevent convection loss of heat to the gable.

Automatic systems are available for drawing the heat retention film across the greenhouse. One company makes use of a series of parallel tracks in which magnetic power capsules travel pulling or pushing the film. This system can be seen in Figure 10-13, where it is being used to move a light barrier covering for photoperiodic control of flowering. Such a system, including the covering, costs about 80¢ per square foot of ground covered. The automated system has a safety advantage over a permanently installed film. As illustrated in Table 3-12 the temperature in the space above the aluminized polyester film can be very cold. This reduces the speed at which snow is melted from the roof. During a heavy snow storm, the load could build up to the point of greenhouse collapse. Generally, during such a storm, the heat retention film is removed.

Some greenhouses, in which crops such as chrysanthemums that flower in response to the day–night length are grown, may already have an automated system for pulling a light barrier cover to regulate day length. This same system, and often the same cover, can be used for conserving heat.

Considerable heat can be lost through cracks between overlapping panes of glass or sheets of FRP. Aging causes these cracks to open up and may also cause the glazing compound to become brittle and fall away from the

Table 3-12
Temperatures in the Greenhouse Space Over an Eave-to-Eave
Aluminized Polyester Heat Retention Film
at Various Outside Temperatures

OUTSIDE TEMPERATURE	TEMPERATURE ABOVE FILM	TEMPERATURE BELOW FILM
20°F (−6°C)	64°F (18°C)	60°F (16°C)
10 (−12°C)	54 (12°C)	60
5 (−15°C)	49 (10°C)	60
0 (−18°C)	44 (6°C)	60
−5 (−20°C)	39 (4°C)	60
−10 (−23°C)	34 (1°C)	60

The temperature in the plant growing space below the film is 60°F (16°C).

area between the glass and the sash bar. Cracks may occur in the glass with corners falling out, or some panes of glass may slide, opening up holes. Eventually, reglazing of a glass greenhouse becomes inevitable. It should be done as soon as the need becomes evident to prevent heating bills from rising. Under the present fuel situation, it could be false economy to put off a reglazing job.

The climate factors in Table 3-8 give a good indication of the effect of wind on the heat requirement. For every 5 mph rise in average wind velocity above 15 mph there is a 4 percent increase in heat loss from the greenhouse. The velocity of wind striking a greenhouse can be reduced by providing wind rows of trees. Fast-growing evergreen trees, such as hemlock, serve well. In some cases, trees are already existent prior to construction of the greenhouse range. Care should be taken to leave these where they can perform a strategic role. While windbreaks are important, they must never cast a shadow over the growing area. This would result in loss of productivity which would be more costly than the fuel saved by the windbreak. Windbreaks on the east, west, or south side should be located away from the greenhouse a distance equal to 2.5 times the height of the windbreak to prevent winter shadows from interfering with crop growth.

Heaters will consume fuel at varying efficiencies, depending upon adjustment of the fuel-to-air ratio. For this reason, heaters should be maintained in good condition. Omission of a periodic service call can cost far more in increased fuel consumption. Soot may build up in the flue passageways of boilers providing insulation on those iron surfaces which are in actuality the heat exchanger of the boiler. Less heat is transferred to water and more goes up the smoke stack, thus increasing fuel consumption. Boilers should be cleaned on a regular basis. There are materials for coating flue tubes which reduce the tendency for soot to adhere to the surface, allowing more to pass out in the smoke effluent. On the average these tubes are more efficient heat exchangers, assuming a cleaning schedule is still maintained.

Within the range of cultivars of some crops there are cultivars which can be satisfactorily produced at lower temperatures than others. This is particularly true for poinsettias and chrysanthemums. Greenhouse crops as a whole can be produced at lower temperatures than are generally recommended, but the cropping time is increased. Arguments have been set forth for and against this procedure in reference to fuel conservation. In some cases the fuel savings are lost in forms such as overhead and fuel consumption during the period of extended growth. Before adopting this form of conservation one should test it out and keep accurate records.

SUMMARY

1. Heat must be supplied to a greenhouse at the same rate with which it is lost in order to maintain a desired temperature. Heat can be lost in three ways: by transmission, infiltration and radiation. Heat is conducted directly through the covering material in transmission loss. In infiltration loss, heat is lost as warm air escapes through cracks in the covering, and in radiation loss heat is radiated from warm objects inside the greenhouse through the covering to colder objects outside.

2. A central heating system is most efficient in large greenhouse ranges. In this system, two or more large boilers are located in a single location. Heat is transported in the form of hot water or steam through pipe mains to the growing area. Traditionally, hot water has been used in smaller ranges, up to about one-half acre, and steam in larger ranges. High-pressure hot-water systems are popular in large greenhouse ranges in parts of Europe and are making an entry into America.

3. A localized heating system is popular in small greenhouse ranges due to the low initial purchase price. In this system, small heaters with self-contained fireboxes are installed in each greenhouse unit as the range is expanded. Ultimately this system entails a higher cost of maintenance than the central system.

4. Emergency equipment is a necessity and should include a heat source such as the Salamander heater as well as an electrical generator. The generator can be installed to start automatically upon power failure. The need for heat should be signaled by a thermostat-activated alarm system in the manager's home.

5. Heat distribution within the greenhouse in the past has been through coils

of pipes supplied with hot water or steam from the central boilers. Two-thirds of the pipe were located on the side and end walls and one-third across the greenhouse above plant height running from end to end. The overhead pipe counteracted downdrafts and coldspots. Vertical air-lift fans were sometimes used and frequently today either the horizontal air flow system or the fan-tube system is used with the pipe coil system to reduce the vertical temperature gradient by moving the warm air in the peak back down to the growing area.

Today, pipe coil heat-distribution systems are used with some of the high-pressure hot-water boiler systems; but more often in America forced-air distribution is used. Unit heaters (forced air), either with self-contained fireboxes or supplied heat from a central boiler, emit warm air. The air may be emitted directly into the greenhouse in a horizontal manner. In greenhouses where distribution is a problem, the air may be emitted into a transparent polyethylene tube running the length of the greenhouse. Heat escapes from the tube through holes on either side of the tube in small jet streams which rapidly mix with the surrounding air and sets up a circulation pattern to minimize temperature gradients.

6. Thermostat placement is very crucial. The thermostat should be located at the height of the growing point of the plants and in a location typical of the average temperature of the greenhouse. It should be in a light-reflecting box which is aspirated at a minimum rate of 600 feet of air per minute. Also in the aspirated box should be other temperature-sensing controls and a thermometer which is used for testing and correcting the thermostats.

7. Relatively easy procedures have been outlined for calculating the heat requirement of greenhouses. Information necessary for determining the heat requirement of an A-frame style greenhouse is contained in Tables 3–6 through 3–10 and for Quonset-style greenhouses in Tables 3–8 through 3–11.

8. The heat requirement of greenhouses can be reduced by installing a second covering of polyethylene, by repairing broken glass and tightening existing glass, by using a wind row of trees to reduce wind velocity, by periodic adjustment and cleaning of heaters or boilers, and possibly by the use of cool temperature-tolerant varieties of plants.

SUGGESTED READINGS

Acme Engineering and Manufacturing Corp. *The Greenhouse Climate Control Handbook.* Acme Engineering and Manufacturing Corp., Muskogee, Ok., 1977. Form C7F.

Aldrich, R. A., W. A. Bailey, J. W. Bartok Jr., W. J. Roberts, and D. S. Ross. *Hobby Greenhouses and Other Gardening Structures.* Northeast Regional Agriculture Engineering Service, 1976. (NRAES)–2.

Gray, H. E. *Greenhouse Heating and Construction.* Florists' Publishing Co., 343 S. Dearborn St., Chicago, Il, 1956.

Laurie, A., D. C. Kiplinger, and K. S. Nelson. *Commercial Flower Forcing.* McGraw-Hill Book Co., New York, 1968.

National Greenhouse Manufacturers' Assoc. "How to Calculate Greenhouse Heat Loss." Natl. Greenhouse Mfg. Assoc., P. O. Box 128, Pleasantville, N.Y. 10570.

A series of leaflets from the University of Kentucky Dept. of Agricultural Engineering, Lexington, Ky. as follows:

Duncan, G. A. and J. N. Walker. *Poly-tube Heating-Ventilation Systems and Equipment.* AEN–7, 1973.

Walker, J. N. and G. A. Duncan. *Estimating Greenhouse Heating Requirements and Fuel Costs.* AEN–8, 1975.

——. *Greenhouse Heating Systems.* AEN–31, 1974.

Various manufacturers of heating equipment offer literature covering products and technical information.

Chapter 4

Greenhouse Cooling

GREENHOUSE SUMMER COOLING SYSTEM

Most localities, with the general exception of those in higher elevations, experience periods of heat which are adverse to greenhouse crops. Temperatures inside the greenhouse are frequently 10 to 20 degrees higher than those outside in spite of open ventilators. Detrimental effects of high temperatures are typified by loss of stem strength and flower size of carnations and delay of flowering or even bud abortion of chrysanthemums. Evaporative cooling systems, also known as *fan and pad cooling* (Figure 4-1) have become popular during the past two decades as a remedy for this problem.

The evaporative cooling system is based on the process of heat absorption during the evaporation of water. Along one wall of the greenhouse water is passed through a pad. Traditionally the pad has been placed in a vertical position and is composed of excelsior (wood shreds). Today other materials are used as well. Exhaust fans are placed on the opposite wall. Warm outside air is drawn in through the pads. Water in the pads, through the process of evaporation, absorbs heat from the surrounding pad and frame as well as from the air passing through the pad. The air entering the house can be as much as 10 to 25 degrees cooler than the outside temperature if the humidity is low.

Specifications

There are two main considerations in this system: (1) the rate at which warm air is to be removed, allowing cool air to be drawn in, and (2) the area of the pads. The rate of air exchange is measured in cubic feet of air per minutes (cfm). Normally the rate of removal of 8 cfm per square foot of greenhouse floor is sufficient. This applies to a greenhouse under 1000 feet in

109

(a)

(b)

Figure 4-1. An installation of (a) an evaporative pad and (b) exhaust fans used for evaporative cooling of a greenhouse during the summer.

110

elevation, with an interior light intensity of 5000 footcandles (fc) and a temperature rise of 7°F (4°C) from the pads to the fans.

The rate of air removal from the greenhouse must increase as the elevation of the greenhouse site increases. Air decreases in density, becoming lighter with increasing elevation. The ability of air to remove solar heat from the greenhouse depends upon its weight and not its volume. Thus, a larger volume of air must be drawn through the greenhouse at high elevations than at low elevations in order to have an equivalent cooling effect. Table 4-1 lists factors (F elev) used to correct the rate of air removal for elevation.

The rate of air removal is also dependent upon the light intensity in the greenhouse. As light intensity increases, the heat input from the sun increases requiring a greater rate of air removal from the greenhouse. Factors (F light) used to adjust the rate of air removal are listed in Table 4-2. An intensity of 5000 fc is accepted as a desirable level for crops in general and is achieved with a moderate coat of shading compound on the greenhouse covering.

Solar energy warms the air as it passes from the pad to the exhaust fans. Usually a 7°F (4°C) rise in temperature is tolerated across the greenhouse. If it becomes important to hold a more constant temperature across the greenhouse, i.e., to reduce the rise in temperature, it will be necessary to raise the velocity of air movement through the greenhouse. Factors (F temp) used for this adjustment are given in Table 4-3 for various permissible temperature rises.

The pad and fans should be placed on opposite walls. These walls may be the ends or the sides of the greenhouse. The distance between pads and fans is an important consideration in determining which walls to use. A distance of 100 to 200 feet is best. Any distance greater than 200 feet requires more elaborate and expensive equipment. When the distance is reduced below 100 feet, the cross-sectional velocity of air movement becomes lower and the air often develops a clammy feeling. This situation must be compensated by increasing the size of the exhaust fans or in other words the velocity of air movement. This increases the cost of the system. Factors (F vel) used to compensate for this point are listed in Table 4-4.

It is now possible to calculate the rate of air removal required for a specific greenhouse by using the factors given in Tables 4-1 through 4-4. First, determine the rate of air removal required of a greenhouse under

Table 4-1
Elevation, Feet Above Sea Level

FEET	UNDER 1000	1000	2000	3000	4000	5000	6000	7000	8000
F_{elev}	1.00	1.04	1.08	1.12	1.16	1.20	1.25	1.30	1.36

Table 4-2
Maximum Interior Light Intensity, Footcandles

FC	4000	4500	5000	5500	6000	6500	7000	7500	8000
F_{light}	.80	.90	1.00	1.10	1.20	1.30	1.40	1.50	1.60

Table 4-3
Pad-to-Fan Temperature Variation, $\Delta T^\circ F$

°F	10	9	8	7	6	5	4
F_{temp}	.70	.78	.88	1.00	1.17	1.40	1.75

Table 4-4
Pad-to-Fan Distance, Feet

FEET	20	25	30	35	40	45	50	55
F_{vel}	2.24	2.00	1.83	1.69	1.58	1.48	1.41	1.35

FEET	60	65	70	75	80	85	90	95	100
F_{vel}	1.29	1.24	1.20	1.16	1.12	1.08	1.05	1.02	1.00

Factors used for making adjustments in the standard rate of air removal in a summer evaporative cooling system when an alteration is made in the standard conditions of a greenhouse site elevation under 1000 feet, a maximum interior light intensity of 5000 footcandles, a temperature rise from pad to fan of 7°F and a pad-to-fan distance of 100 feet or more. Whenever deviations from standard conditions exist, the standard rate of air removal of 8 cfm per square foot of floor is corrected by multiplying it by the appropriate F factor. (Tables developed by National Greenhouse Manufacturers' Association, P.O. Box 128, Pleasantville, N.Y. 10570.)

standard conditions by the following equation, where L and W represent the greenhouse length and width, respectively. This equation calls for the removal of 8 cfm per square foot of floor area.

$$\text{cfm standard} = L \times W \times 8$$

Now, correct the standard rate of air removal by multiplying it by the larger of the following two factors, F house or F vel. F vel is read directly from Table 4-4. F house is calculated as follows:

$$F \text{ house} = F \text{ elev} \times F \text{ light} \times F \text{ temp}$$

Thus, the final capacity of the exhaust fans must be

$$\text{Total cfm} = \text{cfm standard} \times F \text{ house}$$

$$(\text{if } F \text{ vel is larger, use } F \text{ vel instead of } F \text{ house})$$

Next, the size and number of exhaust fans must be selected. The fans collectively should at least equal the rate of air removal required and should be rated to do such at 0.1 inch of water static pressure. The static pressure figure takes into account the resistance the fan meets in drawing air through the pad and in pushing air out against a prevailing wind. Air delivery ratings for various size fans are listed in Table 4-5. Fans should not be spaced more than 25 feet apart. If the end of the greenhouse is 60 feet wide, a minimum of three fans will be necessary. The required capacity of each fan can be determined by dividing 3 into the total cfm of air removal required. It is then a matter of finding fans in the table which are rated for this performance level. These fans should be evenly spaced along the end of the greenhouse, at plant height if possible, to guarantee a uniform flow of air through the plants.

The pad area should be determined next. Ideally, one square foot of pad should be provided for every 150 cfm of air movement. The area of excelsior pads made from aspen (the most common pads in use today) required for any given fan is presented in Table 4-5. The area listed is for one fan and should be multiplied by the number of fans required.

The pad should extend the entire length of the wall in which it is mounted and this wall should be opposite the wall where the exhaust fans are located. The necessary height of the pads is determined by dividing the total area of the pads by the length of the pads.

Water supplied to the pad is recycled. Below the pad is a reservoir. A pump is located here which delivers water to a pipe running horizontally along the top of the pad. The ends of the pipe are plugged. Small holes exist along the lower side of the pipe about every 4 inches to distribute water evenly along the pad.

To each linear foot of pad, water must be delivered at the rate of 1/3 gallon per minute regardless of the height of the pad. For a pad 75 feet long, it would be necessary to pump 25 gallons of water per minute onto the top of it. The reservoir itself should have a capacity of 1.5 gallons for each linear foot to accommodate all of the water in the system when it is turned off. Since water evaporates from the system, it is also necessary to provide fresh water. A water line with a float valve at the end works well for this purpose.

The fan and pad system can be automated or operated manually. If automated, a thermostat should be tied into two points in sequence. When the thermostat calls for cooling, the exhaust fans should turn on. If this does

Table 4-5

Air Delivery Ratings and Required Pad Areas for Various Size Fans*

FAN SIZE (IN.)	HORSEPOWER	CFM AT 0.1 IN. STATIC PRESSURE	ASPEN PAD AREA REQUIRED PER FAN (SQ FT)
24	1/4	4700	30
24	1/3	5700	36
24	1/2	6500	42
30	1/3	7400	47
30	1/2	8800	56
30	3/4	10200	65
36	1/2	10500	67
36	3/4	12600	81
36	1	14200	91
42	1/2	12500	80
42	3/4	15000	96
42	1	16800	108
48	3/4	17800	115
48	1	19600	126
54	1	22800	152
54	1½	26850	179

*Data from Acme Engineering and Manufacturing Co., Muskogee, Oklahoma.

not satisfy the cooling requirement and the temperature continues to increase, the pump providing water to the pads should be activated. When the cooling requirement is satisfied, the system turns off step by step in the reverse order.

Pad Description

The pad assembly consists of several components pictured in Figure 4-2. A pipe is suspended immediately above the pad. It is usually, but not necessarily, a plastic pipe. Holes are drilled in a line about 4 inches apart along the bottom side, and the ends of this pipe are capped. It is best to bring the water into the pipe at the midpoint if the pad is 75 feet or longer. A baffle is placed below the pipe to spread the water uniformly before it drops onto the pad. The baffle is occasionally omitted, but if it is care must be taken to space holes sufficiently close to insure thorough wetting of the pad. Fiber in the pad swells upon wetting, allowing air to flow more readily through dry spots. This reduces the overall cooling capacity. The pad is mounted below the baffle in a vertical fashion. Since the pad is flexible, it is placed inside a frame of 1-inch by 2-inch wire. A gutter is mounted under the pad to collect water and return it to a sump from which it can be recycled to

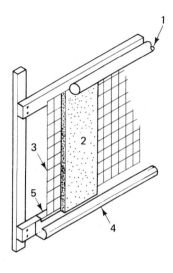

1. Water distribution pipe
2. Excelsior pad
3. Welded wire frame
4. Water return gutter
5. Galvanized flashing

6. Water distribution pipe
7. Excelsior pad
8. Water return gutter
9. Pump
10. Water inlet with float valve
11. Sump

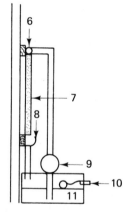

Figure 4-2. Diagram of (a) the components of a pad system for evaporative cooling and (b) the water distribution system for a cooling pad including sump, float valve, and pump.

the pads by means of a pump. A cover is placed over the exposed surface of the gutter to prevent debris from collecting in it. Water must be added to the sump from time to time, since the principle of this system depends upon water evaporation. As much as a gallon of water per minute can evaporate from 100 square feet of pad on a hot, dry day. A water line with a float valve should be plumbed into the sump.

It should be noted that there are other pad systems on the market. One pad is composed of a special corrugated cellulose paper impregnated with insoluble antirot salts, rigidifying saturants, and wetting agents. This pad has a life expectancy of ten years or greater and is available in thicknesses of 4, 6, and 12 inches. With increasing thickness the overall dimensions of the pad can be reduced. Only one square foot of 4-inch thick pad is needed for every 250 cfm of air movement, as opposed to 150 cfm for an excelsior pad. These pads, therefore, better fit the dimensions of a greenhouse than the aspen pads and also eliminate the need for annual pad replacement.

Horizontal pads are also being tried by growers. A horizontal screen is constructed outward from the greenhouse. One of a variety of materials, including gravel, vermiculite, and excelsior is placed on the screen to serve as an evaporative surface and yet permit air percolation. Mist nozzles keep the pad wet and air is drawn from outside through the pad into the greenhouse. Several pads may be installed in a stack along one greenhouse wall, offering an economy of space. Another advantage is the long life expectancy of the pads since more permanent type materials can be used.

Pads may be placed immediately inside the side or end wall (Figure 4-3). The wall adjacent to the pad should be equipped with ventilators to permit air entry during hot weather and for sealing off the outside air during cooler spring and fall nights. In this case the ventilator arms and gears are located exterior to the greenhouse. If the required pad area should exceed the area of the greenhouse wall, it is necessary to place it exterior to the greenhouse wall (Figure 4-4). The opening in the greenhouse should be at least half the area of the pad. The pad should be set back from the opening a distance of half of the height by which the pad exceeds that of the opening. Ideally, the extra height of the pad should be equally divided above and

Figure 4-3. An evaporative cooling system arrangement with the pad located inside the greenhouse and the ventilator mechanism exterior to the greenhouse. This system permits cooling on warm autumn days when the evenings are too cold for the side wall to be left open. (*Photo courtesy of J. W. Love, Department of Horticultural Science, North Carolina State University, Raleigh NC 27607*)

Figure 4-4. A cooling pad exterior to the greenhouse. This arrangement can accommodate a pad larger than the wall of the greenhouse. The pad is set back from the wall a distance at least half the excess height of the pad over the wall and is connected to the greenhouse by a transparent covering to insure that air entering the greenhouse comes through the pad.

below the opening. It is important that the pad be connected to the greenhouse on the top and ends by a transparent covering material to insure that any air drawn through the pad enters the greenhouse.

Fan Placement

Whenever possible, it is best to place the fans on the leeward side of the greenhouse and the pads on the side toward the prevailing winds so that the winds will assist rather than counteract the cooling system. If fans exhaust into the windward side, their capacity should be increased ten percent or more. When two or more houses are located adjacent to each other, more important factors dictate the placement. Fans from one greenhouse should not exhaust warm, moist air toward the pads of an adjacent greenhouse unless it is located at least 50 feet away.

When fans are located in adjacent walls of greenhouses located within 15 feet of each other, they should be alternated so that they do not blow directly against each other. Adjacent service buildings can also present a problem. There must be a clearance of one and one-half diameters of the fan between the fan and adjacent obstacles. If this is not possible, special roof-mounted fans should be installed.

A waterproof housing should enclose the fan to protect it from the elements. Air-activated louvers generally protect the outside. It is imperative that a screen or welded-wire guard be placed on the inside of the fan to protect workmen and visitors from serious injury.

The Air Stream

The pads should be located at and slightly above the plant height. This will bring the cool air in on the plants. Due to resistance of the foliage and plant supports, as well as the rising temperature, the air stream will rise at an angle of seven degrees (one foot in every eight), and will soon pass over the plants leaving a pocket of hot air below at the plant height. Transparent (polyethylene) vertical baffles should be installed in the gable of the greenhouse perpendicular to the air stream to direct the flow of air down to the plants. Baffles should be installed every 30 feet. The bottom of the baffle should be well above the plant height to permit passage of air.

If pads are located near the floor and the benches are tall, considerable air may pass beneath the benches where little benefit occurs. In this case, baffles should be placed beneath the benches near the pads.

The situation encountered in a greenhouse more than 200 feet long and less than 100 feet wide can be remedied by placing pads at each end of the greenhouse and exhaust fans in the roof halfway between the ends. In this situation the greenhouse is cooled by the equivalent of two systems each half the length of the greenhouse.

EXAMPLE PROBLEM: The following example illustrates the calculations involved in designing an evaporative cooling system. Consider a single greenhouse 50 feet wide and 100 feet long located at 3000 feet elevation. The greenhouse has a moderate coat of shading compound on it; thus the maximum light intensity inside is 5000 footcandles. A 7°F (4°C) rise in temperature can be tolerated from pad to fans. Stepwise calculations for developing a cooling system for this greenhouse are as follows:

1. Multiply the greenhouse floor width by the length and by 8 to determine the quantity of air to remove per minute under standard conditions.

$$\text{cfm std} = L \times W \times 8$$

$$\text{cfm std} = 50 \times 100 \times 8 = 40,000 \text{ cfm}$$

2. Determine a factor for the house (F house) by multiplying the three factors together: elevation, light intensity inside the greenhouse, and

the temperature rise from pad to fans. These factors are found in Tables 4-1 through 4-3 respectively.

$$F \text{ house} = F \text{ elev} \times F \text{ light} \times F \text{ temp}$$

$$F \text{ house} = 1.12 \times 1.0 \times 1.0 = 1.12$$

3. Look up the factor for velocity (F vel) in Table 4-4. Select two opposite walls for installation of the pad and fans which are 100 to 200 feet apart or as close to 100 feet as possible. The end walls which are 100 feet apart should be used in this example: F vel = 1.00.

4. Multiply the *CFM* std value from Step 1 by either F house or F vel, using whichever factor is larger—F house in this case. This is the volume of air to be expelled from the greenhouse each minute.

$$\text{Total cfm} = \text{cfm std} \times F \text{ house}$$

$$\text{Total cfm} = 40,000 \text{ cfm} \times 1.12 = 44,800 \text{ cfm}$$

5. Determine the number of fans needed. Since they should not be over 25 feet apart, divide the length of the wall housing the fans by 25.

$$50 \text{ ft} \div 25 \text{ ft} = 2 \text{ fans}$$

6. Determine the size of the fans needed by dividing the total cfm of air to be removed (from Step 4) by the number of fans needed.

$$\text{Total cfm} \div \text{no. of fans}$$

$$44,800 \text{ cfm} \div 2 = 22,400 \text{ cfm per fan}$$

7. Purchase two fans of the size determined in Step 6 and space them equidistant on one end of the greenhouse. If the fans were to be purchased from the manufacturer of equipment listed in Table 4-5 two 54-inch fans with 1 hp motors would be selected.

8. The pad area is determined next. One square foot of pad is required for each 150 cfm of fan capacity. Divide the capacity of the required fan (22,400 cfm) by 150 cfm to arrive at a required pad area of 149 square foot per fan. Since there are two fans, a total of 298 square feet of pad is required. Approximately the same value could be read directly from Table 4-5. (If a 4-inch-thick corrugated cardboard pad were used, only 90 square feet would be required since 1 square foot accommodates 250 cfm of fan capacity.)

9. The pad must cover the width of the wall in which it is to be in-stalled—50 feet in this example. The height of the pad is determined by dividing the total pad area by its width. A 6-foot tall pad should be purchased.

$$\text{pad height} = \text{pad area} \div \text{pad width}$$

$$\text{pad height} = 298 \div 50 = 5.96 \text{ feet}$$

10. The pump capacity is equal to 1/3 gallon per minute times the length of the pad and must be selected to have this flow rate for the given head under which it must operate. The head is the distance from the water surface in the sump to the top of the pads.

$$\text{Pump capacity} = 1/3 \text{ gallon per minute} \times \text{pad length}$$

$$\text{Pump capacity} = 1/3 \text{ gallon per min} \times 50 = 16.7 \text{ gallon per min}$$

11. The sump size is equal to 1.5 gallons per foot of pad length.

$$\text{Sump volume} = 1.5 \text{ gal} \times \text{pad length}$$

$$\text{Sump volume} = 1.5 \text{ gal} \times 50 = 75 \text{ gal}$$

GREENHOUSE WINTER COOLING SYSTEM

The fundamental difference between summer and winter cooling sys-tems lies in the temperature of the air that is external to the greenhouse. It is often desirable to cool the air during the summer before passing it over the plants. Large volumes of cooled air are introduced directly and uniformly over all plants. During the winter cold, external air must be introduced indirectly and mixed with the undesirably warm air within the greenhouse prior to making contact with the plants in order to prevent cold spots at the plant level. For best results, the flow of incoming air must be smooth in the summer, and turbulent in the winter so as to bring about rapid mixing.

Originally greenhouses were constructed with ventilators adjacent to the ridge. When cooling was required on winter days they were opened. Cold air, being more dense than the warm air inside, would drop to the floor beneath the ventilators. From there it would spread laterally, rising in temper-ature as it mixed with the warm air. The result was a temperature gradient across the house at plant height. This led to uneven growth rates and subse-quently to variation in maturation dates. The new *fan-tube ventilation system* used for winter cooling corrects the horizontal temperature gradient problem. It circulates the air in the greenhouse like water circulating in a bathtub.

Description of Fan-Tube Ventilation

The temperature at which winter ventilation is desired is set on a thermostat which in turn activates two events simultaneously (Figure 4-5). A louver is opened in a gable end through which cold air enters the plastic tube when an exhaust fan is simultaneously activated. The exhaust fan may be located at any location in the greenhouse since its role is merely to produce a negative pressure which will cause an influx of air into the distribution tube and provide even ventilation throughout the greenhouse.

An alternate winter cooling system makes use of the exhaust fan, inlet louver, and distribution tube but has the distribution tube separated from the inlet louver and has a pressurizing fan located in the inlet end of the distribution tube (Figure 4-6). The pressurizing fan directs incoming cold air into the tube; thus it must be at least equal to the exhaust fan. If it is smaller, incoming cold air will drop to the ground at the point of entry and cause a cold spot. When cooling is not required, the inlet louver closes and the pressurizing fan continues circulating air within the greenhouse. This step replaces the horizontal air flow (HAF) circulation system but requires more power.

Specifications

Under standard conditions, a volume of 2 cubic feet of air should be removed from the greenhouse each minute for each square foot of floor area.

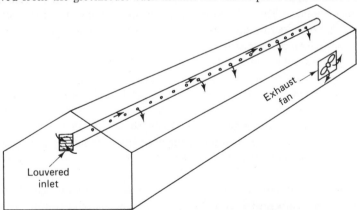

Figure 4-5. Diagram of a greenhouse showing the components of a *fan-tube* winter cooling system. When cooling is required, a thermostat activates an exhaust fan and opens the louvered inlet. Cold air enters the louver and is directed down a transparent polyethylene tube. Jets of cold air leave the tube through holes along the sides of the tube and thoroughly mix with warm greenhouse air before reaching the plants.

Figure 4-6. Air inlet components of a winter cooling system including the louvered inlet, a polyethylene distributing tube a short distance from the louvered inlet, and a pressurizing fan to direct air into the tube under pressure.

(Remember that 8 cubic feet of air per square foot of floor is required for summer cooling.) The volume obtained by multiplying the floor area by 2 would therefore define the capacity of the exhaust fan in terms of cubic feet of air movement per minute (cfm).

Various published specifications call for as little as 1.5 cfm and as much as 4 cfm of air to be exhausted per square foot of floor area. The high-capacity system costs more to set up, but can be operated earlier in the fall and later in the spring to extend the winter cooling season. This can have an advantage since frosts usually occur during these extension periods. A high-capacity fan-tube system eliminates the necessity of switching back and forth between the summer fan and pad and the winter fan-tube systems at these times.

When fan-tube ventilation is used, standard conditions specify a maximum inside temperature of 15°F above the outside temperature. The temperature inside the greenhouse can become adversely high on a winter day when the sun is shining even though the outside temperature is below the desired level. The fan-tube cooling system is designed to reduce the internal temperature to within 15°F of the outside temperature.

If a lower inside temperature is desired, cold air must be introduced

Table 4-6

Factors (F_{winter}) for Adjusting Standard Rate of Air Removal in a
Winter Greenhouse Cooling System for the Temperature Difference
Between the Inside and Outside of the Greenhouse

	GREENHOUSE TEMPERATURE ABOVE OUTDOOR TEMPERATURE ($^{\circ}$F)									
	18	17	16	15	14	13	12	11	10	9
F_{winter}	.83	.88	.94	1.00	1.07	1.15	1.25	1.37	1.50	1.67

*From National Greenhouse Manufacturers' Association, P.O. Box 128, Pleasantville, N.Y. 10570.

into the house at a greater rate. The compensating factors to be used in these cases are given in Table 4-6. As in the case of the summer cooling system, standard conditions also specify an elevation under 1000 feet and a maximum interior light intensity of 5000 footcandles. If other specifications are desired, factors must be selected from Tables 4-1 and 4-2 and used to correct the rate of air entry.

Distribution tubes are conventionally oriented from end to end in the greenhouse. Each distribution tube can be used to cool up to 30 feet of greenhouse width, although it is desirable to use two tubes for greenhouses 30 feet wide. One tube placed down the center of the house will cool houses up to 30 feet in width. Houses from 30 feet to 60 feet in width are cooled by two tubes spaced equidistant across the house. Holes along the tube exist in pairs on the opposite vertical sides. The holes vary in size according to the volume of greenhouse to be cooled. The number and diameter of tubes needed to cool a greenhouse can be determined from Table 4-7. If two or more tubes are needed, they should be of equal size and should be spaced evenly across the greenhouse. Recommendations in Table 4-7 are based on an air-flow rate of approximately 1700 cfm per square foot of cross-sectional area in the tube. When the greenhouse is large and the required number of 30-inch diameter tubes becomes cumbersome, tubes may be installed with air inlets in both ends. These inlets double the amount of cool air which can be brought in through the tube.

The winter cooling system requirements should be taken into consideration at the time when fans are ordered for the summer cooling system. In this way one or more of the summer fans could be used for the winter exhaust fan requirement. While the fans used for the summer system should all be of equal size in any one cooling area, one fan could be purchased with a two-speed motor that provides half its capacity at the lower speed.

Table 4-7

Number (N) and Diameter (D) in Inches of Air Distribution Tubes Required
for Winter Cooling of Greenhouses of Various Widths and Lengths

GREENHOUSE WIDTH	50		100		150		200		IBE		250		IBE	
	N	D	N	D	N	D	N	D	N	D	N	D	N	D
15	1	18	1	18	1	24	1	30	—		1	30	1	24
20	1	18	1	24	1	30	1	30	—		2	24	1	24
25	1	18	1	24	1	30	2	24	1	24	2	30	1	30
30	2	18	2	18	2	24	2	30	—		2	30	—	
35	2	18	2	24	2	24	2	30	—		3	30	2	24
40	2	18	2	24	2	30	2	30	—		3	30	2	24
50	2	18	2	24	2	30	3	30	2	24	3	30	2	30

GREENHOUSE LENGTH

Tubes run the length of the greenhouse and are spaced equidistant across the greenhouse. Tubes are connected to a louvered air inlet on one end only unless otherwise specified. Those open to louvered inlets on both ends are identified as *IBE*.

EXAMPLE PROBLEM: Determine the winter cooling specifications for a greenhouse measuring 50 feet wide by 100 feet long and situated at 3,000 feet elevation. The maximum interior light intensity anticipated is 5000 fc and the desired interior to exterior temperature difference is $15°F$.

1. The capacity of the exhaust fan is equal to 2 cfm times the greenhouse floor area under standard conditions.

$$cfm_{standard} = 2 \times length \times width$$
$$cfm_{standard} = 2 \times 100 \times 50 = 10,000 \, cfm$$

2. Correct the exhaust fan capacity just calculated for deviations from standard conditions. The only deviation in the sample problem is the elevation of 3000 feet which has an F elevation value of 1.12 from Table 4-1. An exhaust fan with a capacity of 11,200 cfm at a static water pressure of 0.1 inch is needed.

$$cfm_{adjusted} = cfm_{standard} \times F_{winter} \times F_{elev} \times F_{light}$$
$$cfm_{adjusted} = 10,000 \times 1.0 \times 1.12 \times 1.0 = 11,200 \, cfm$$

3. The number of air-distribution tubes can be determined from Table 4-7. Two 24-inch tubes are needed for this greenhouse having a 50-foot width and 100-foot length.

4. The diameter of individual holes along the side of distribution tubes and the distance between them must next be decided. Tables are presented in the catalogues of florist supply companies specifying the model of tube required for given tube diameters and greenhouse lengths. The model identification, unfortunately, does not indicate the size or distance between holes in these tubes.

The hole specifications can be calculated if you wish to purchase unpunched tubing or purchase tubing from a company which punches holes to your specifications. Work in England by G. A. Carpenter specifies that the total area of all holes in a single tube should be between 1.5 and 2 times the cross-sectional area of the tube. The cross-sectional area of a 24-inch tube is 3.14 square feet. Thus, the combined area of all holes in a tube should be between 4.71 and 6.28 square feet. As the required tube length increases, the distance between holes should increase to maintain a reasonable diameter hole. Distances of 2 to 4 feet are common.

5. If the winter cooling system is to be used for circulating air in the greenhouse, a pressurizing fan is needed in the inlet end of the distribution tube and the tube must be separated from the inlet louver by a distance of a few feet. The pressurizing fan should be equal to the exhaust fan in capacity.

If this is not possible, then the pressurizing fan should be larger. The two pressurizing fans needed in the example greenhouse should have a combined capacity of 11,200 cfm which is equal to the exhaust fan capacity. Each pressurizing fan thus has one half the capacity of 5600 cfm at 0.1 inch static-water pressure.

INTEGRATION OF COOLING
AND HEATING SYSTEMS

Cooling and heating are often required during the winter when days are bright and evenings are cold. In either case the same polyethylene tubes are used to distribute the cold air from the outside or the warm air from the heater. Unit heaters are placed near the open end of the tube so that the warm air emitted from them is directed into the tube. One design calls for the unit heater to be attached to the inlet end of the tube as illustrated in Figure 4-7. During the cooling phase, louver A is open and B is closed. External cold air enters as a result of an exhaust fan located elsewhere and is directed into the polyethylene tube under pressure by the fan in the unit heater. When the greenhouse is sufficiently cool, louver A closes and B opens. The unit heater fan continues to circulate air within the greenhouse. If the temperature drops, the same louver arrangement is maintained and the unit heater turns on. In this case air from inside the greenhouse is heated and distributed through the tube.

A second integrated heating-cooling design calls for a pressurizing fan in the tube inlet and placement of the unit heaters away from and perpendicular to the inlet of the tube as shown in Figure 4-8. The pressurizing fan runs continuously. A motorized louver in the greenhouse end wall opens only during cooling. An exhaust fan located elsewhere causes air to enter through the louvered inlet. This air is in turn directed into the tube for uniform distribution by the pressurizing fan. In the interim between cooling and heating, the pressurizing fan continues to circulate air within the green-house. When heat is required, the unit heaters turn on and blow warm air toward the tube inlet. When the air is in close proximity to the inlet, the pressurizing fan picks it up and directs it into the tube.

The integrated winter cooling-heating systems discussed are adequate for winter conditions but do not adequately cope with the changeable weather situation in the fall and spring. It is not unlikely during these periods to require evaporative cooling one day, winter convection tube cooling the next day, and heat the following night. All three systems can be integrated under the control of a single multistage thermostat. This system is illustrated in Figure 4-9 and can be visualized to occur in the following sequence of steps. The evaporative cooling system is operating on a hot autumn afternoon. As the afternoon wears on and outside temperatures drop, the cooling

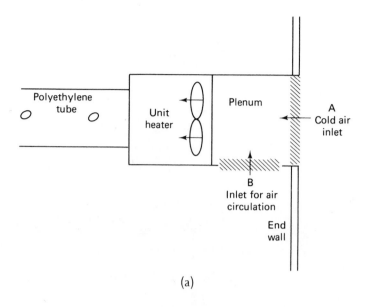

(a)

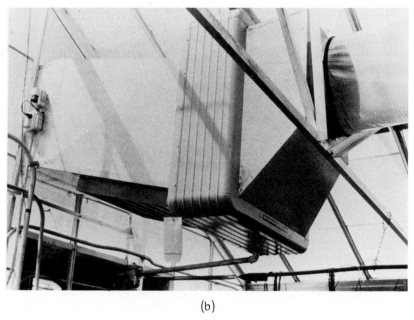

(b)

Figure 4-7. (a) An integrated winter cooling and heating system. The unit heater fan operates continuously, serving as a pressurizing fan for the tube. Only louver A is open during cooling; louver B is open and A is closed during the heating stage. When neither cooling nor heating is required, air is continually circulated within the greenhouse. (b) A commercial installation of such a system.

127

Figure 4-8. General view of an alternative winter cooling-heating system with unit heaters mounted apart from the tube inlet. Warm air is expelled from the heaters toward the tube inlet, where it is picked up by the pressurizing fan.

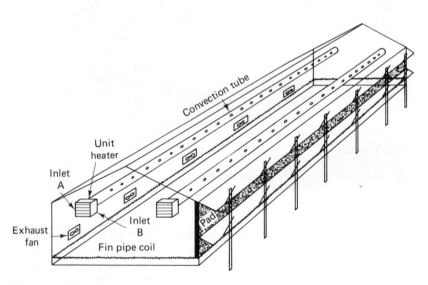

Figure 4-9. A completely integrated evaporative cooling-fan tube cooling-heating system.

requirement diminishes. A reduction in the inside temperature activates a thermostat switch that turns off the water-circulating pump in the evaporative pad. The exhaust fans continue to operate, drawing air in through the dry pads. As the need for cooling diminishes, all of the exhaust fans turn off except those needed for the winter fan-tube cooling system. The ventilators adjacent to the pads close. The winter cooling system is now in operation with the pressurizing fan in the tube running and the louvered inlet in the end wall open. As evening approaches, no cooling is necessary. The exterior louvered inlet (A) closes and the interior inlet (B) opens. Air is now circulated within the greenhouse. (A sometimes-preferred alternative to the fan-tube circulation of air at this point is the HAF system, in which case the tube-pressurizing fans would turn off and the HAF fans would turn on in their place to circulate air.) Temperatures continue to drop during the night. Heat is first supplied through the perimeter pipe coil. When this cannot hold the desired temperature, half of the overhead unit heaters are activated and later, if necessary, the remaining half. In the morning, the reverse sequence of events occurs.

COOLING HOBBY GREENHOUSES

The principles are basically the same for cooling hobby greenhouses. A fan and pad system is used during the summer. To insure proper vertical distribution of cool air, the pad should not be under two feet in height. There are cooling problems inherent with these small greenhouses that demand a higher capacity system. A minimum of 12 cfm per square foot of floor area should be exhausted from the greenhouse. If the greenhouse is attached to the east, west, or especially the south side of another building, then considerable solar heat will be collected inside the greenhouse by this wall. Half of the area of the wall should be added to the floor area when calculating the ventilator requirement.

Package evaporative coolers are practical for greenhouses with 300 square feet of floor area or less. A package cooler as pictured in Figure 4-10 consists of a cubical structure with evaporative pads on three sides. Water conduction and collection lines, as well as a pump, are built into the package. A fan is located inside the package to draw air in through the pads and expel the cool air to the greenhouse interior. A ventilator must be open at the opposite end of the greenhouse to serve as an air exit. The package coolers can be less expensive for a small greenhouse. They are easier to install and are more aesthetically pleasing than the conventional fan and pad systems.

The winter cooling system for a hobby greenhouse again follows the principles of a larger greenhouse. Fan-tube ventilation works well. Often it is not necessary to distribute heat in the winter through a distribution tube. The force with which air is expelled from these heaters is sufficient to cause

Figure 4-10. An Arctic Air® package evaporative cooler for a small or hobby type greenhouse. Water is circulated through pads on three sides of the package. A fan is located within the unit to draw air in through the pads. (*Photo courtesy of J. W. Love, North Carolina State University, Raleigh, NC 27607*)

uniform circulation throughout a hobby-size greenhouse. If this is the case, the fan-tube system can be simplified with resulting economy. For winter cooling, the polyethylene tube may be connected directly to a stovepipe elbow mounted in the wall of the greenhouse with the end outside pointing down. The elbow serves as an air inlet. When this system is off, the polyethylene tube hanging from attachments along its upper side collapses and seals itself off from the outside. The tube inflates when an exhaust fan in the greenhouse turns on. An elbow inlet should be used rather than a straight pipe to prevent wind from blowing into the system and bringing about cooling at times when it could not be tolerated. To prevent wind entry, it is best to place the inlet from this type of cooling system on the leeward side of the greenhouse.

Very small greenhouses do not require a distribution tube for winter cooling. Air entering high in the gable will mix sufficiently well with existing air along the short length of the greenhouse. When neither cooling nor heating is required, it is well to use an 8- to 12-inch fan for air circulation to prevent hot or cold spots and to keep down the incidence of disease.

SUMMARY

1. Summer cooling requires that large volumes of air be cooled and brought into the greenhouse. The cool air must pass in a smooth stream throughout the entire growing area. An evaporative cooling system is used for this purpose. It consists of pads on one wall, through which water is circulated, and exhaust fans on the opposite wall. Air entering through the pads is cooled and then drawn across the greenhouse to the exhaust fans.

2. Air is drawn through the greenhouse at the rate of 8 cfm per square foot of floor area under standard conditions of an elevation under 1000 feet, a maximum interior light intensity of 5000 fc, an air temperature rise of $7°F$ ($4°C$) between the pads and the exhaust fans, and a distance of 100 feet or more between pad and fans. If any of these factors varies, an adjustment must be made in the flow rate of 8 cfm per square foot of floor.

3. The most versatile placement of the pad is inside the greenhouse wall, allowing ventilators in that wall to open and close to adjust to weather conditions during the interim periods in spring and fall when both heating and cooling are required. If the pad area required is larger than the wall, it must be located external to the greenhouse and should be set back from the greenhouse a distance equal to half of the excess height of the pad above the opening in the wall.

4. Exhaust fan placement is important. Fans should not exhaust warm, moist air toward an intake pad unless there is 50 feet of distance separating them. When greenhouse walls are less than 15 feet apart, fans in adjacent walls should be alternated so as not to expel air toward each other. A clearance of at least one and one-half diameters of the fan should be allowed between an exhaust fan and an adjacent building. If this is not possible, roof-mounted fans should be used.

5. Winter cooling calls for the introduction of a small volume of already cold air from the outside. It must be introduced in a turbulent flow, high in the greenhouse gable so that it thoroughly mixes with the interior air before reaching the plant zone; otherwise cold spots occur. A fan-tube cooling system is used. The system consists of an exhaust fan which develops a negative pressure in the greenhouse, a louvered air inlet in the gable, and a polyethylene tube with holes along the sides for turbulent air emission that runs from the inlet along the length of the greenhouse.

6. A flow rate of 2 cfm air per square foot of floor area is satisfactory for standard conditions—of an elevation under 1000 feet, a maximum interior light intensity of 5000 fc, and a capacity to bring the inside temperature down to within $15°F$ of the colder outside temperature. Adjustment must be made in the air flow rate for any change in these factors.

7. Present day winter cooling and heating systems make use of the same polyethylene tube for distribution of the cool or the warm air. When neither cooling nor heating is required, air can be circulated through the tube if there is a pressurizing fan in the inlet end of it and that end is not attached directly to the inlet. The horizontal air flow (HAF) system is an energy efficient alternative for circulating air. Small fans are placed above plant height at 50-foot intervals down one half of the greenhouse and back the other half. The fans are designed to set up a horizontal circular air flow which will (1) conserve fuel by bringing hot air down from the gable, and (2) minimize temperature gradients at plant height.

8. Integrated systems are used today which can handle the variable requirements during the interim periods in spring and fall when both cooling and heating are needed. A multistage thermostat is used to direct the transition from summer evaporative cooling through winter fan-tube cooling to heating and visa versa.

9. The principles are the same for cooling of hobby greenhouses. Somewhat simpler systems can be utilized. When the greenhouse is attached to an existing building on any side but the north, half of the attachment wall area is added to the floor area when calculating ventilation rates. For summer cooling, a minimum air flow rate of 12 cfm per square foot of floor is necessary.

SUGGESTED READINGS

Aldrich, R. A., W. A. Bailey, J. W. Bartok Jr., W. J. Roberts, and D. S. Ross. *Hobby Greenhouses and Other Gardening Structures.* Northeast Regional Agriculture Engineering Service, 1976. (NRAES)–2.

Bartok, J. W. Jr. "Fan/Tube Greenhouse Ventilation." Connecticut Greenhouse Newsletter No. 32, 1970, pp. 9–12.

Gray, H. E. *Greenhouse Heating and Construction.* Florists' Publishing Co., 343 S. Dearborn St., Chicago, Il, 1956.

Koths, J. S. "Effectiveness of Horizontal Air Flow (HAF) in Greenhouses." Connecticut Greenhouse Newsletter No. 56, 1974, pp. 17–21.

Laurie, A., D. C. Kiplinger and K. S. Nelson. *Commercial Flower Forcing.* McGraw-Hill Book Co., New York, 1968.

National Greenhouse Manufacturers' Assoc. "Standards for Ventilating and Cooling Greenhouses–1971 Revision. Natl. Greenhouse Mfg. Assoc., P.O. Box 128, Pleasantville, N.Y. 10570, 1971.

A series of leaflets from the University of Kentucky Department of Agricultural Engineering, Lexington, Ky. as follows:

Walker, J. N. and G. A. Duncan. *Estimating Greenhouse Ventilation Requirements.* AEN-9, 1973.

——. *Air Circulation in Greenhouses.* AEN-18, 1973.

——. *Greenhouse Humidity Control.* AEN-19, 1973.

——. *Cooling Greenhouses.* AEN-28, 1974.

——. *Greenhouse Ventilation Systems.* AEN-30, 1974.

——. *An Automatic Sidewall System for Greenhouse Environmental Control.* AEN-37, 1975.

Various manufacturers of cooling and ventilation equipment offer valuable literature covering products, price, and technical information.

Chapter 5

Root Media

After greenhouses are constructed and the heating and cooling systems are set into operation, it is time for the first cultural consideration—that of selecting a root medium. Taken at surface value, this appears to be a monumental task. Some fifteen or more components including field soil, sand, perlite, polystyrene, peats of many types, barks of various origins, and sawdust are to be found in a myriad of formulations used by growers, sold as commercial preparations, or recommended by research institutions. Many are well-proven while others are ineffective. There is a magical lure about concocting one's own root medium which often leads to poor combinations of components and to the use of a greater number of components than is needed or can be justified economically. Selection of a root medium, however, should be an easy matter once some fundamentals are understood.

PROPERTIES OF GOOD GREENHOUSE ROOT MEDIA

Functions of Root Media

There are four functions that the root medium must serve in order to support good plant growth. It must serve as a reservoir for plant nutrients. It must hold water in a way that it is available to the plant, and at the same time provide for the exchange of gasses between roots and the atmosphere above the root medium. Finally, the root medium must provide an anchorage or support for the plant.

One can think of many materials which provide these four functions and still do not constitute a practical root medium. Coarse sand, for instance, has a low water holding capacity due to its low surface area per unit volume.

This necessitates frequent watering, as often as three times per day for some crops during the summer. The nutrient-holding capacity of sand is also low. The majority of nutrients held in sand are dissolved in the small quantity of water held on the surface of the sand particles.

Vermiculite (expanded mica) when used with soil is at first a good root medium, but with time and usage collapses under the weight of the soil. The average diameter of its pores diminishes, reducing the capacity for carbon dioxide (CO_2) gas produced by the roots and by microorganisms during respiration to escape from the medium. When CO_2 gas builds up in the medium, respiration, and thus growth, slows down. When CO_2 gas cannot diffuse from the medium it follows that oxygen (O_2), needed to keep the process of respiration going, cannot diffuse into the medium where the roots exist. This also adversely slows down respiration and growth.

Other materials can serve all four functions if systems are constructed to foster their use. Although rather unconventional, water alone can be used as a root medium. Water availability and nutrient retention are good, but the functions of gas exchange and support are nearly nonexistent. The process of growing plants in a substrate consisting of nutrient solution is termed _hydroponics_. To provide support, plants are anchored in trays suspended above the nutrient solution. To provide gas exchange, air is bubbled into the nutrient solution continuously. There are variations on hydroponics in which plants are grown in coarse sand, gravel, vermiculite, or other coarse solids, while the nutrient solution is periodically passed through the solids. In another variation, a similar solid is used for the root medium in watertight beds. A reservoir of nutrient solution is maintained at the bottom of the bed extending up into but not to the surface of the solid medium. The nutrient solution rises up by capillarity, coating the surface of the solid medium. A constant water content is maintained above the nutrient solution reservoir. If sufficiently large particles are used, the centers of the pores remain open for gas exchange.

The hydroponic system of plant growth has been well studied since the middle of the nineteenth century. Considerable efforts were put forth during World War II to develop it into a feasible commercial practice. It was used on board some ships and on islands in the Pacific for producing fresh vegetables during the war effort. There are greenhouse ranges today growing plants by various modifications of hydroponics (Figure 5-1). Up to the present, these systems have not offered enough of an advantage over conventional root media culture to foster their wide-scale acceptance. When water alone is used as the root medium, aeration and support are costly problems. If coarse solid particles are used in a sort of hydroponic application, such as gravel culture, the high frequency of water and nutrient application becomes a problem.

Figure 5-1. Carolina Wholesale Florist in Sanford, North Carolina, a green-house range where chrysanthemum plants are grown in a modified hydro-ponic system. Coarse African vermiculite is used in the trays as the aggregate. The concrete tanks in which the trays are suspended are filled periodically (about every two days) with nutrient solution for ten minutes and then emptied in order to replace water and nutrients in the vermiculite.

Adaptation of Field Soil to Containers

What's wrong with using field soil in greenhouse containers? Green-house crops often can be grown in the field without significant alteration of the soil, but when this soil is transferred to a container and the same crop grown, failure ensues. While all four functions are provided in the field, the function of aeration is usually not adequate in the container. Water retention and aeration go hand in hand.

As more water is held in the pores between the soil particles, less space is available for gas movement. Drainage is proportional to the depth of the soil above the water table. The bottom of any container is equivalent to a water table. Most cut flower beds contain a seven-inch depth of soil, while potted plants range from seven inches down to two inches in bedding-plant containers. The water content in a bedding-plant container shortly after watering would be similar to that in a soil situated two inches above free-standing water, in other words, a swamp situation. The soil pores would be mostly filled with water and little room would remain for gas exchange.

One dimension by which soil is classified is *texture*. Texture is the size distribution of particles in a soil. Field soil is composed of three mineral components (Figure 5-2). The finest particles, clay, extend up to a maximum diameter of 0.002 mm. Silt is composed of particles up to 0.05 mm, and the third component, is everything larger. Clay feels sticky to the touch, silt is floury, and sand is gritty. Texture terms include *sandy loam, silt loam,* and *clay loam* for soils predominating in sand, silt, and clay respectively. Loam refers to a reasonable balance of all three materials. Texture is important because it relates to the speed with which water will move down through the soil, determining how rapidly good aeration will return to the soil after watering. The texture must be coarse enough for these events to occur, but not so coarse that the soil lacks a reservoir for holding water.

It is clear that two different soils would be needed in the field and greenhouse; a relatively fine-textured soil in the deep field and a very coarse-textured soil in the shallow container.

Texture relates to water retention for a very simple reason. Water will remain in soil because it is attracted to the surface of soil particles. Water exists as a film or layer coating each soil particle. The thickness of the water layer depends upon the gravitational force attempting to pull the water out of the soil and down to the water table. The greater the distance from the soil to the water table, the stronger is the gravitational force. Within the water layer, that water which is farthest from the soil particle surface is held the

Texture

Description of particle sizes

Clay   Silt   Sand

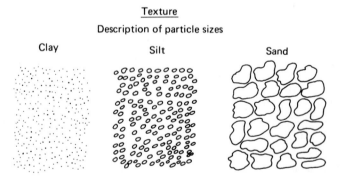

Figure 5-2. Soil is composed of three mineral components, the relative sizes of which are shown above. Clay particles are the smallest and have a maximum diameter of 0.002 mm. Silt particles have a diameter extending from 0.002 to 0.05 mm. Larger particles are termed sand. The texture classification of a soil gives an indication of the proportion of these three mineral particles contained in it.

least tightly. It is this water which will be pulled away first by the gravitational force. Thus, as the gravitational force increases, i.e., the depth of the soil increases, the thickness of the water layer on the soil particle surfaces decreases (Figure 5-3), and the air-filled center of the pore gets larger, permitting better gas exchange.

The logical solution to the shallow container problem would appear to be a change toward coarser texture, i.e., an increase in the diameter of the pores. This does solve the problem of aeration, but it creates a new problem by reducing the water-holding capacity of the soil. When the diameter of particles making up a soil is increased, the total surface area of these particles in a given volume decreases. Since water is held on the surface of these particles, the total amount of water in the soil decreases as the particle diameter increases (texture becomes coarser).

There is another dimension of soil which can be altered to increase aeration without decreasing the water-holding capacity. *Structure* is the

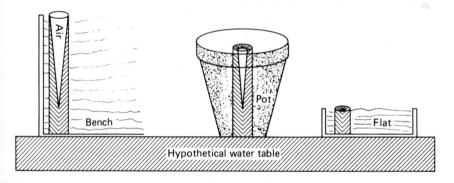

Figure 5-3. A greatly magnified soil pore is shown in various greenhouse containers filled with soil. All are shown to be perched on a water table, or reservoir of free-standing water, which is effectively the situation existing in the greenhouse shortly after watering. The pore depicts the moisture situation that exists within each container. Water is attracted to the walls of the pore and at the base the entire pore fills. Higher in the pore, the downward gravitational pull on the water becomes greater and the water farthest away from the pore wall is removed. The layer of water in the pore becomes thinner with increasing height. Spaces between soil particles in the container are interconnected and form pores running the depth of the soil. Pores in the bench are filled with water at the bottom and are mostly open at the top. Shortly after watering, roots can grow in the upper layers of soil in this bench, but not in the lower layer where there are no open pores for gas exchange. Pores in the pot do not rise as high above the water table; thus in the upper layer of soil there is more water and less aeration than in the upper layer of the bench soil. The poorest situation for growth exists in the flat where the pores are so short as to be completely filled with water.

degree of combining of particles into aggregates. A soil with good structure is said to be friable or loose. The product of organic matter degradation is humus which, along with microbial secretions and hyphae, acts as a cement to bind particles together into aggregates. This is the greatest importance of organic matter in field soils. Through the development of structure, a dimension is given to soil which cannot be achieved through alterations in texture. High-water retention of fine-textured soil can be combined with excellent drainage of coarse-textured soil. This is accomplished by extensive retention of water in the small diameter pores within each aggregate and rapid percolation of water out of and conversely good gas exchange into the large pores between the aggregates (Figure 5-4).

It should now be apparent that field soil must be prepared for use in containers by altering it to a coarser texture and by increasing its structure. A coarser texture can be achieved by mixing coarse sand into the soil while structure can be improved by incorporating large aggregate particles into the soil such as sphagnum peatmoss and bark. There are numerous materials which can be added to soil, but before a selection can be made one more set of properties should be understood. These properties pertain to greenhouse root media specifically.

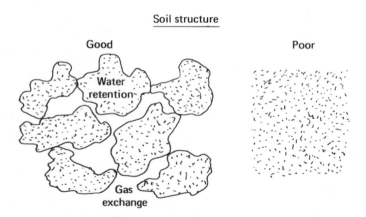

Soil structure

Good   Poor

Water retention

Gas exchange

Figure 5-4. An important property of soil is structure. The soil on the left has good structure because the particles comprising it are cemented together into larger aggregate particles. Small-diameter pores still exist within the large aggregates, and because of the large surface area of these pores a large volume of water is held in each aggregate. Between the aggregates are very large pores that do not fill with water, thus providing a channel for gas exchange. The soil on the right has very little structure. Only small pores exist. While water retention is good, aeration is poor.

Desirable Properties of a Root Medium

1. STABILITY OF ORGANIC MATTER. Organic matter added to soil in the field decomposes to form humus which acts as a cement to hold particles together in aggregates. Thus, structure is developed with time. Greenhouse root media used in pots are generally sold with the plant after a period of one to four months. Time is not afforded for all of the organic matter to decompose to humus. Good structure must exist when seed is sown or plants are potted. It is also important that decomposition of organic matter in the root medium to be used in pots be minimal. Since the volume of root medium available within the pot for root growth is small, any significant reduction in the volume during growth of the plant is detrimental. Straw and sawdust decompose rapidly and for this reason are not desirable in a root medium used for pot crops. The situation is somewhat different for fresh flower crops in benches where the root medium volume is sufficiently great to permit shrinkage. Soil is used indefinitely for fresh flower crops. With time, structure deteriorates, requiring that new aggregates be provided. This can be done either by direct addition to the root medium as an amendment, such as sphagnum peatmoss, or by development through the periodic application of organic matter which decomposes to form humus.

2. CARBON:NITROGEN RATIO. The amount of nitrogen (N) relative to carbon (C) in a root medium amendment is important. Decomposition of organic matter occurs largely through the action of living microorganisms. The largest component of organic matter (50 percent or more) is C which is utilized by the microorganisms. N in the organic matter must be available to the microorganisms in the quantity of at least one pound for every thirty pounds of C; otherwise, decomposition slows down. Anytime this ratio of 30C:1N is exceeded, i.e., more than 30 pounds of C exists for each pound of N, N already present in the root medium or N added as fertilizer will be utilized by the microorganisms rather than by the crop plants. The crop will become deficient in N. If this situation occurred slowly and continuously, a grower could easily compensate for it by increasing his N fertilizer application. The decomposition of materials such as straw and sawdust occurs rapidly, however, thereby creating a peak of N demand followed by a quickly diminishing demand for N as organic matter available to the microorganisms runs out. Only the most experienced growers can compensate for this process.

The C:N ratio for sawdust is about 1000:1. It has been reported that in addition to the small amount of N already present in the sawdust, 24 pounds of N must be added to facilitate the decomposition of one ton of sawdust by microorganisms. Bark has a C:N ratio of about 300:1 and requires an addition of 7 pounds of N to facilitate the decomposition of one ton. It is not the C:N ratio alone which determines the suitability of a root media component, but also the rate of decomposition. While bark has an undesirably wide C:N ratio of 300:1, its rate of decomposition is slow and steady, requiring as long as three years to decompose. The drain of 7 pounds of N per ton of bark carried out over three years presents a negligible N tax at each fertilization date. Bark is therefore a desirable root media component in spite of its wide C:N ratio. Sawdust, on the other hand, will decompose in a few months and has a wider C:N ratio of 1000:1. The N tax in this case is great and this material should be avoided by the inexperienced grower.

3. **BULK DENSITY**. The bulk density of root media relates to support of the plant. Nearly any solid medium will provide for anchorage of the plant roots, but it is also important that the medium be sufficiently heavy to prevent a potted plant from falling over due to the weight of the plant. A mixture of vermiculite and perlite has a density of about 32 pounds per cubic foot shortly after watering, but when dry its density is only 6.5 pounds per cubic foot. Large plants in this medium easily topple over when handled in any way. On the other hand, a high-bulk density can be uneconomical when extensive handling of root media or the potted plants is required or when the shipping distance of the marketable plant is great. An acceptable range for bulk density of potting media is 40 to 75 pounds per cubic foot after watering.

As mentioned earlier, soil must be amended with coarse particles such as sand to provide aeration. Wet clay-loam soil weighs about 90 pounds per cubic foot and builder's sand about 120 pounds per cubic foot (Table 5-1). For this reason perlite with a wet density of 25 pounds per cubic foot is often used as a substitute for sand in spite of its higher cost. The problems of bulk density are not nearly as important for media used in greenhouse benches.

4. **MOISTURE RETENTION AND AERATION**. Wet root medium is composed of three phases—the solid particles of the medium, liquid water coating the surfaces of the particles, and air occupying the center of the pores. In order to insure a suitably long interval between watering and to provide adequate aeration at all times, the balance of water and air in the root medium pores must be controlled. This is accomplished through selection of the particles comprising the medium. After watering, 10 to 20 percent of the volume of the root medium should be occupied by air and 35 to 50 percent by water. A survey of ingredients in Table 5-1 indicates that these conditions can be provided through the use of materials such as bark, sawdust, peatmoss, and vermiculite.

It should be recalled that water retention is related to the depth of the root medium. As indicated in Table 5-2 the water-holding capacity of media after watering is greater in a five-inch pot than in a seven-inch pot. The capillary force holding water in the root media is equal in each pot, but the gravitational force pulling water out of the pot becomes greater as the pot increases in depth. With decreasing water content comes an increasing air content. Fortunately the range in acceptable air and water content values is wide. Well-formulated root media with high air- and water-retention values are suitable for all greenhouse containers.

5. CATION EXCHANGE CAPACITY. Root media components such as clay, silt, organic matter, and vermiculite have negative electrical charges. These charges will attract and hold positive electrical charges (cations). Most fertilizers have electrical charges, some negative and others positive. Positively charged fertilizer components are ammonium nitrogen, potassium, calcium, magnesium, iron, manganese, zinc, and copper. Field soil and greenhouse media electrically attract and hold these nutrients so that they are not washed away during a rain or heavy watering. At the same time, these electrically held nutrients are available to the plant. Cation exchange capacity (CEC) is a measure of the magnitude of negative electrical charge and is generally expressed as milliequivalents per 100 grams (me/100g) of dry root media component. A level between 10 and 30 me/100g is considered desirable for greenhouse root media. Higher levels are not common but are also desirable. If the value becomes less than this, the medium will not act as a suitable reservoir for nutrients and it will become necessary to apply fertilizer frequently. Clay, peatmoss, vermiculite, and most composted organic matter have a high CEC, while sand, perlite, polystyrene, and noncomposted materials such as rice hulls and peanut hulls have an insignificant CEC. When preparing a root medium, it is important to include a component with a high CEC.

6. pH. The importance of root media pH level will be brought out in Chapter 8 on fertilization. It is sufficient to say here that the pH level controls the availability of nutrients to the plant. Greenhouse crops fall into two categories. Most grow best in a slightly acid pH range of 6.2 to 6.8. A small number of crops are termed "acid-loving" since they grow best in a strongly acid pH range of 4.5 to 5.8. Sphagnum peatmoss, pine bark, and many composts are acid. Peatmoss can have a pH level below 4.0 Sand and perlite are neutral (pH 7.0). Vermiculite and some hardwood barks are alkaline (pH above 7.0). Field soil can range from acid (pH 3.5) to alkaline (pH 8.5). It is important to check the pH level of the medium one has formulated and adjust it to the proper level prior to planting. Instructions are given in Chapter 8. Commercial root media are usually adjusted to the proper pH level by the manufacturer.

7. FERTILIZER CONTENT. It is customary for manufacturers of root media to incorporate complete fertilizer (nitrogen, phosphorus, and potassium) in it sufficient to carry the needs of the plant for two to four weeks

Table 5-1
Physical Properties of Amendments, Soils, and Mixtures

MATERIAL	BULK DENSITY (DRY)	(LB/CU FT) (WET)	WATER RETENTION (% OF VOL)	AIR CONTENT AFTER DRAINAGE (% OF VOL)
Bark, fir, 0-1/8″	14.3	38.0	38.0	31.5
Bark, fir, 1/8-5/8″	11.5	20.8	15.0	54.7
Loam, clay	58.8	93.3	54.9	4.7
Loam, sandy	98.0	122.0	35.7	1.8
Peat, sedge AP	13.1	46.0	52.3	17.0
Peatmoss, hypnum	11.6	19.4	59.3	12.4
Peatmoss, sphagnum	6.5	43.3	58.8	25.4
Perlite, 1/16-3/16″	6.0	24.6	47.3	29.8
Rice hulls	6.4	14.3	12.3	68.7
Sand, builders	104.0	120.0	26.6	9.4
Sand, fine	93.5	115.0	33.7	2.5
Sawdust, redwood	10.9	41.8	49.3	27.9
Vermiculite, 0-3/16″	6.8	40.0	53.0	27.5

Manure, dairy	21.5	63.0	66.7	7.6
50:50 (v/v) mixture clay-loam with:				
Peatmoss, sphagnum	33.8	72.7	61.0	10.0
Sand, builders	79.0	104.6	40.8	6.2
Sawdust, redwood	34.3	70.6	57.6	14.4
Sandy-loam with:				
Peatmoss, sphagnum	53.7	88.7	52.8	6.3
Sawdust, redwood	49.3	82.5	52.7	10.1
Fine sand with:				
Bark, fir, 0–1/8"	52.8	76.5	37.4	15.2
Peat, sedge	57.5	88.2	49.0	4.5
Peatmoss, hypnum	53.8	84.3	49.0	6.5
Peatmoss, sphagnum	46.2	75.8	47.3	9.4
Perlite, 1/16–3/16"	53.2	80.0	42.6	7.6
Sawdust, redwood	57.5	81.2	40.5	12.1
Peatmoss with:				
Perlite 3/16–1/4"	6.9	37.5	51.3	23.6

Adapted from *Horticultural and Agricultural Uses of Sawdust and Soil Amendments*. Technical bulletin published by Paul Johnson, 3106 Simbar Road, Bonita, CA 92002, 1968.

Table 5-2
Effects of Container Size on the Average Moisture-Holding
Capacity of Various Root Media

MEDIA	CONTAINER WATER CAPACITY (% OF VOL)	
	5" POT	7" POT
Sand, builder's	27.7	24.3
Perlite	39.6	27.0
Peatmoss, sphagnum	91.0	67.8
1 sand:2 peatmoss	64.2	42.4

(about one pound each of calcium nitrate and potassium nitrate). This is an advantage for the grower who is using the medium for germinating seeds, since it will not be necessary for him to fertilize the seedlings prior to transplanting them. The grower using media for growing established plants will generally purchase a different medium. In this case, the presence of complete fertilizer can be a disadvantage if the grower is: (1) growing fertilizer-sensitive plants typified by a number of green plants, or (2) storing the medium under moist conditions for several months which permits too much of the fertilizer to change over to an available form and reach a toxic level. It would be better in these cases not to incorporate nitrogen and potassium into the root medium. Phosphorus, however, should be included because it does not build up to toxic levels and is cheaper and less complicated to add into the medium prior to planting than it is to apply it through the fertilization program during crop culture. Relatively inexpensive single (20 percent) super-phosphate at the rate of 2.5 pounds per cubic yard of root medium will supply the phosphorus needs for a year or more.

Soilless media containing peatmoss and bark tend to result in micro-nutrient deficiencies particularly iron and boron deficiencies; thus it is customary to incorporate a commercial preparation of fritted micronutrients into them at the rate of 2 ounces per cubic yard. Soilless media also tend to be excessively acid; therefore limestone must be added to bring the pH level up to that desired. It is best to use dolomitic limestone in this case since it contains two essential nutrients—calcium and magnesium. Calcitic limestone supplies only one essential nutrient, calcium. The amount to use will depend upon the pH adjustment to be made and will be dictated by the soil-testing laboratory which tests your root medium sample.

In summary, only two nutritive ingredients need to be added to a soil-based root medium: single superphosphate and a material to adjust the pH level, dolomitic limestone, if the level must be adjusted upward. A third ingredient is needed for soilless media, a mixture of micronutrients. A low-balanced level of nitrogen and potassium is desirable in media to be used for seed germination.

COMPONENTS OF ROOT MEDIA

Numerous materials exist from which the components of a root medium can be selected. Listed in Table 5-3 are the more common components, the roles that each perform, and the cost of these. Alternative components exist for each of the four needed functions of a root medium. Selection of components is based on cost and availability.

Field Soil

Prior to the practice of soil pasteurization, which took hold in the early 1950s, it was customary to replace greenhouse media annually, usually during the summer. Much attention was paid to the type of field soil used. Soil with a high degree of structure and a loam texture proved to be the most desirable.

Texture was insured by locating the greenhouse range in a region of proper soil type. There was a degree of latitude here because a sandy loam field soil could be altered in the greenhouse media by using a larger amount of field soil to provide sufficient silt and clay and a lesser amount of sand to

Table 5-3
Root Media Components in Use, Their Functions,
and Cost of Those Commercially Available

	WATER RETENTION	NUTRIENT RETENTION	AERATION	LIGHT WEIGHT	COST PER CU. FT. ($)
Field soil	X	X			.15–.30
Sphagnum peatmoss*	X	X			.65–.80
Bark (0–3/8″)*	X	X			.18–.30
Sawdust (rotted)	X	X			.10–.30
Manure	X	X			.15–.50
Compost	X	X			—
Vermiculite*	X	X		X	1.05
Calcined clay*	X	X	X		1.75
Bark (3/8″–3/4″)*	X	X	X		.18–.30
Floramull®	X			X	—
Sand (concrete grade)			X		.15–.30
Perlite*			X	X	.95
Polystyrene (ground scrap)			X	X	.30–.50

*The cost of delivery is not included. In all other entries it is included.

avoid excess sand particles. Clay loam soil was amended with larger than usual amounts of sand since it was lacking in this component. Structure was developed in the field soil by growing a mixed crop of grasses and clover on the soil for one to three years. These crops continually renew their root systems leaving behind vast quantities of roots which decompose into humus and lead to good structure development.

Crops commonly used were Kentucky bluegrass, timothy, red-top, red clover, alsike clover, and ladino clover. The seed bed was prepared by proper liming and the application of 300 pounds of complete fertilizer such as 5-10-10 per acre. Spring and fall applications of manure plus 500 to 600 pounds of complete fertilizer, high in phosphorus content, per acre were made. The crop was mowed twice per year and allowed to lie on the ground. The fall previous to the summer when the soil was to be moved into the greenhouse, the crop was disked and the soil was placed in piles where decomposition of the crop took place.

Since fresh flower growers no longer replace their media, it is important only at the time of establishing the greenhouse range that a proper field soil be developed. Pot plant growers, however, must have a continuous supply of proper field soil if they utilize soil-based media. Many established greenhouse areas have been inundated by residential and commercial development, and newer ranges have located in regions of poor soil to take advantage of other factors such as transportation, labor supply, and utilities availability. Such businesses, lacking suitable field soil, have purchased soil with sporadic success, due to cost or variation from one lot to another. These growers have found it expedient to use soilless media.

Peatmoss and Peats

There are different types of peat. Peatmoss that is light tan to brown is the least decomposed and is formed from sphagnum or hypnum moss, mostly the former. It has a nitrogen content between 0.6 and 1.4 percent and decomposes slowly; thus nitrogen tie-up is not a problem. It has the highest water-holding capacity of all the peats, holding up to 60 percent of its volume in water. Sphagnum peatmoss is the most acid of the peats with a pH level between 3.0 and 4.0 and requires between 14 and 35 pounds of finely ground limestone per cubic yard to bring the pH level up to the 6.2 to 6.8 level which is best for most crops. In areas with hard water containing calcium, the lower rate may be suitable. One to 1.5 pounds per cubic foot may be necessary in areas low in calcium.

The fine structure of the moss can still be seen in peatmoss. Large quantities of water are held on the extensive surface area of the moss while good gas exchange occurs in the large pores between the aggregates (chunks) of peatmoss. For this latter reason peatmoss should not be finely ground down to the level of fibers prior to use.

Reed-sedge peat is brown to reddish brown in color and is formed from swamp plants including reeds, sedges, marsh grasses, and cattails. It occurs in varying degrees of decomposition, but is generally more highly decomposed than peatmoss. As a result, more fine particles are present giving a poorer structure than peatmoss. The water-holding capacity of reed-sedge peat also is lower than peatmoss. Depending on the source, reed-sedge peat can vary from a pH level of 4.0 to 7.5. Although sphagnum peatmoss is preferred for the general range of greenhouse applications, reed-sedge peat can be used in root media for pot and bench crops if the pH is properly adjusted.

Peat humus is dark brown to black in color and is the most highly decomposed of the peats. It is usually derived from hypnum peatmoss or reed-sedge peat. Original plant remains are not distinguishable and water-holding capacity is less than other peats. The pH level can range from 5.0 to 7.5. Peat humus has a moderately high nitrogen content which makes it undesirable in seed flat media or media used for salt-sensitive plants. Ammonium nitrogen is released from the peat humus which can build up to levels that are toxic to the more sensitive plants such as young seedlings, African violets, snapdragon, and azalea. Ammonium nitrogen is released during microbial decomposition of peat humus because there is more than one pound of nitrogen available per 30 pounds of carbon. Peat humus is rarely used in the greenhouse.

Bark

Redwood and fir bark have been used on the west coast for many years as a component of nursery and greenhouse root media. Pine bark (Figure 5-5) is extensively used along the eastern seaboard and the gulf states into Texas. Hardwood barks are used in many of the interior states. All are highly satisfactory.

Bark is very inexpensive compared to the materials it replaces in root media, mainly sphagnum peatmoss and soil. Small quantities of bark are used for industrial purposes, but by and large most bark constitutes a waste-disposal problem and can be obtained for a nominal price or just the cost of transportation. Until recent years much bark was disposed of by burning, but antipollution laws now prevent this in many areas. Due to the need to compost bark prior to use in root media, several companies are now processing bark for this purpose. This, of course, adds to the price; however, the price advantage over materials replaced by bark is still great.

Fresh bark contains a variety of chemical materials, some of which decompose very rapidly. Because the C:N ratio is wide, 300:1, and initial decomposition is fast, there can be a troublesome tie-up of nitrogen during this time. Microorganisms breaking down the bark use the carbon in it for their own cells and along with it need nitrogen. If there is not enough nitrogen in the bark for them, they will take it from the soil. When bark is removed from logs, varying quantities of cambium and young wood are

Figure 5-5. Barks of various origins are widely accepted throughout the United States today as a substitute for peatmoss. Pine bark is pictured here. Typical processing calls for composting in a pile for three months or longer and then screening into different sizes for various markets. Particles passing through a 3/8-inch mesh screen are used in pot plant media (*left*); those between 3/8 and 3/4 inch are used for fresh flower media amendment (*right*); and larger particles are used for landscape mulches (*center*).

included. These materials decompose even faster than bark and further accentuate the nitrogen tie-up problem. The wood content tends to be highest in the spring when growth is most active. A period of composting rids bark of these components and brings it to a stage where the rate of decomposition is slow and steady; thus nitrogen tie-up is not a problem.

Some hardwood and softwood barks contain various types and quantities of phenolic compounds which are injurious to plants. During composting these compounds are destroyed. A period of at least thirty days is required for this to occur. Composting has an additional beneficial effect for bark and sawdust as well. Fresh bark and sawdust do not hold fertilizer nutrients very well because of a low cation exchange capacity of about 8 me/100 g. After composting, the CEC rises to a level of 60 me/100 g or higher, which imparts a very strong nutrient retention capacity to the bark and sawdust.

Composting is accomplished in two ways. Nitrogen is mixed in at the rate of three pounds of actual nitrogen per cubic yard and the bark is set in piles in the field. Ammonium nitrate is a good source of nitrogen and is used at the rate of nine pounds per cubic yard since it contains 33 percent nitrogen. A period of four to six weeks is sufficient to complete the rapid phase of decomposition. In the second system, no nitrogen is used and three months to a year are required. The first system better guarantees a satisfactory endproduct. Composting in either case results in destruction of phenolic compounds, degradation of wood, and the fragmentation of larger particles into smaller ones. The piles must not be too deep, i.e. over 12 feet, because during the process of composting heat is given off that, if permitted to become too intense, can set the pile on fire. The surface layer should be turned into the pile after one to two weeks of composting to insure that all of the bark has been processed. The heat given off by fermentation is sufficient to pasteurize the bark. Harmful disease organisms, insects, nematodes, and weed seeds are thus eliminated. It is important that subsequent handling be carried out in a way to maintain this cleanliness. The bark should not be piled where crops have been grown or the run-off from crop lands has accumulated. Equipment used for moving bark should be sterilized first if it has been used on crops. If the bark is bagged, clean handling is almost insured. Larger growers find economy in purchasing bark in bulk (unpackaged). Prior to sale, bark is screened for various purposes. Particles 1/8 inch and under are used as soil conditioners in applications such as golf course greens. Particles 3/8 inch and under are preferred for greenhouse pot media, and 3/8 to 3/4 inch for organic matter amendment of greenhouse fresh flower media. Larger pieces are used for landscape mulching.

Since the large part of the cost of bark often lies in the shipping expense—costing one dollar or more per mile for a 60 cubic yard truckload—it is important to obtain bark from local sources. For this reason, numerous types of bark are used throughout America. In general, processed bark will cost from one-fourth to two-thirds the price of imported sphagnum peatmoss.

Sawdust

Sawdust in many respects is similar to bark. It should be partially composted because in the fresh state its rate of decomposition and nitrogen tie-up is excessive and it may contain toxic substances such as resins, tannins, or turpentine. Even after composting, sawdust decomposes at a faster rate than bark and, due to its wider C:N ratio (1000:1), a greater amount of nitrogen is tied up in the root media. Whereas the problem is insignificant with bark, it must be taken into account when fertilizing a medium containing composed sawdust.

Abandoned piles of sawdust are often available for the cost of transportation in forested areas. If the pile has existed for a year or more, the sawdust below the surface layer should be well composted. Care should be taken to avoid unleached areas deep in the pile which are strongly acid and injurious to plants. These areas could not receive sufficient oxygen during fermentation and, as a result, volatile organic acids were formed and trapped here. These problem areas can be identified by the exceptionally dark color of the sawdust and its pungent, acrid odor. This sawdust can be reclaimed by exposing it to the air and to leaching rains for a season, but it still will be more acid than the properly composed sawdust.

Sawdust composted with additional nitrogen for one month to the stage appropriate for use in root media is itself acid and requires limestone to neutralize it. In this stage it is granular and a medium dark brown color. It continues to decompose during use in the pot or greenhouse bench. Various types of pine and some types of hardwood sawdust require further additions of limestone as time passes. Sawdust, like other plant materials, ends up close to neutral in pH when thoroughly composted; however, this is well beyond the stage at which it is initially used in greenhouse root media.

Manure

Annual addition of manure was a standard practice in fresh flower beds and quite frequently was used in bedding and potted plant media until the middle of this century. When soil pasteurization became popular, problems arose as a result which discouraged the further use of manure. There are ways around this problem which will be discussed in Chapter 6 on media pasteurization. A few growers use manure today and realize good benefits from it.

Manure has a high cation exchange capacity which serves as a reservoir for nutrients. In addition it is a good source of nutrients and micronutrient deficiencies rarely occur when manure is used. As a matter of fact, micronutrient deficiencies were rare in the days when manure was routinely used. Today such deficiencies present a serious problem. Manure also contains small levels of nitrogen, phosphorus, and potassium (Table 5-4). Because large quantities of manure are used in media, a significant part of the total requirement of these three nutrients is met. Manure also has a high water-holding capacity, a basic requirement of greenhouse media.

Peatmoss perhaps comes the closest to manure in the functions that it serves in root media and, indeed, has been the component substituted for manure in recent years.

Rotted cow manure is the best type to use in the greenhouse. Other types are stronger and must be used cautiously and in smaller quantities. Often, as in the case of poultry manure, the ammonia content is too high and causes root and foliage injury to the plant. Cow manure is incorporated into media at the volume rate of 10 to 15 percent. The media is then pasteurized with steam or chemicals. This is necessary in order to rid the medium of harmful disease organisms, insects, nematodes, and weed seed. Manure contains a sizeable quantity of weed seed which would otherwise become troublesome. Following pasteurization, it is very important that each time water is

Table 5-4
Primary Fertilizer Nutrient Content of Some Types of Animal Manure

TYPE OF MANURE	NUTRIENT CONTENT (% OF DRY WEIGHT)		
	Nitrogen (N)	Phosphorus (P_2O_5)	Potassium (K_2O)
Cattle (cow)	0.5	0.3	0.5
Chicken	1.0	0.5	0.8
Horse	0.6	0.3	0.6
Sheep	0.9	0.5	0.8
Swine	0.6	0.5	1.0

required, a sufficient quantity be applied to insure leaching so that a buildup of ammonium nitrogen originating from the manure does not occur. Even if a crop is not planted in the medium, it must be leached periodically. A buildup of ammonium nitrogen contributes to the total soluble salt content of the root medium and can be detected readily by a soluble salt test. This is an easy test which can be performed by the grower; it will be discussed in Chapter 8.

Manure has been used in a moist state which renders it a difficult material to introduce into a mechanized system of media preparation. Its after-pasteurization problems preclude its use in media to be stockpiled for later use. Its messy physical condition and heavy weight prevent its being shipped more than a few miles from the farm. Until a process is devised for drying, grinding, and getting around the ammonium nitrogen buildup problem of manure, its use will be limited to a few growers who have a local supply and the technical knowledge to handle it.

Crop By-Products

Straw is occasionally used, but must be chopped into pieces three inches or less in length to permit uniform incorporation into the soil and the labor input is expensive. Since straw decomposes rapidly it must be added two or three times per year, again an expensive proposition. A variety of other organic amendments are occasionally used including peanut hulls, bagasse (sugar cane fiber), and rice hulls. All of these can be used successfully but require knowledge and careful handling. Materials such as straw, peanut hulls, bagasse, and rice hulls have a wide C:N ratio that causes the tie-up of nitrogen. If this is gauged, and extra nitrogen is added, no problem arises.

Flower crop stubble, the foliage, stems, and roots left in the bench after harvesting cut flower crops, has logically been looked upon as a source of organic matter. Growers have chopped the stubble into small pieces and rototilled it into the root medium. Because this organic material is the very crop being grown, it is an excellent host for carrying diseases over from one crop to another. It should be pasteurized with the root medium. Since many growers do not pasteurize after each crop, crop remains are generally removed from the greenhouse. Crop remains thoroughly composted outside the greenhouse can be used successfully as a root media amendment.

Composted Plant Materials

There are numerous plant by-products available, including sawdust and bark. Although materials such as rice hulls, peanut hulls, and seaweed can be used in root media, in their original state their CEC and water-holding capacities are low. Straw, as previously mentioned, is in the wrong physical shape to be uniformly incorporated into media and also results in extensive tie-up of nitrogen as it decomposes. Many of the undesirable traits of these materials are corrected during composting. Conversion during composting to smaller but more numerous particles results in greater surface area and water-holding capacity. Reduction of some of the organic matter to high CEC humus yields a great increase in nutrient-holding capacity. Plant materials low in nitrogen, but high in carbon, pass through their period of extensive nitrogen tie-up during composting. Composting, therefore, can improve the desirability of many materials for use in root media.

Composted plant materials are not free of problems. Small resultant particle sizes can increase the need for coarse texture particles to insure aeration. Materials of moderately high nitrogen content such as leafy plant wastes, manure, and sewage sludge can end up high in ammonium nitrogen which is injurious to sensitive crops. In this case the amount of compost used must be limited and ample water applied in the early stages of growth to insure leaching. In spite of such difficulties composting is a valuable process for obtaining root media components which can constitute excellent substitutes for peatmoss, bringing nutrient and water retention to the medium. The list of materials which can be composted is extensive. The end-products, however, should be tested in the greenhouse on a small scale before incorporation into any commercial program.

Composting requires a special technology and for this reason is generally not practiced by greenhouse growers today. When a large, continuous supply of organic matter is available for little more than the cost of handling, composting can be a profitable endeavor. An excellent explanation and description of composting methods is given by R. P. Poincelot in Connecticut Agricultural Experiment Station Bulletin 754, *The Biochemistry and Methodology of Composting.*

Quantities of compost required by small greenhouse ranges can be provided by the pile method. Organic matter to be composted is arranged in piles measuring seven feet wide by seven feet or greater in length at the base and five feet high. The sides are tapered so that the top is two feet narrower than the base. Materials to be composted are classified as (1) *carbonaceous*—low in nitrogen and comparatively high in carbon such as leaves, straw, hay, wood chips, or shavings, sawdust, and rice hulls, or (2) *nitrogenous*—high in nitrogen content relative to carbon such as grass clippings, green plants, manure, garbage, digested sewage sludge, and soil. Materials to be composted should be mixed in the proportion of 75 percent carbonaceous to 25 percent nitrogenous (Figure 5-6). Often the pile is built on a six-inch layer of brush to insure aeration necessary for proper composting. A one-foot layer of mixed carbonaceous-nitrogenous organic material is added. Often a two-inch layer of nitrogenous material such as manure is added next, followed by a one-inch layer of soil. Subsequently, brush is omitted and the mixed carbonaceous-nitrogenous layer is reduced to six inches as the pattern is repeated until the pile is five feet deep.

The top is concave so as to collect water. Water is important to the process of composting and the water content of the pile should remain between 50 and 60 percent of its weight. When dry materials are added to the pile they should be moistened. Copious quantities of oxygen are needed by microorganisms involved in the breakdown of organic matter. If the pile is excessively wet, to the point where it feels soggy or becomes compacted during decomposition, oxygen will be used faster than it can penetrate into the pile. Different types of microorganisms will then take over, resulting in a foul odor and a pale green color in the center of the pile—an entirely undesirable situation. A pile deeper than six feet tends to compost excessively, whereas a shallow pile of two feet is not suitably insulated to maintain the high temperature needed for composting.

The pile should be thoroughly mixed from time to time to reestablish pores permitting aeration and to move to the interior of the pile the surface materials which have not undergone composting. The frequency of mixing determines the speed with which composting occurs. If turned every six weeks, a spring pile can be composted by fall or a fall pile by spring. It is possible to complete the process in as short a period as two weeks if the pile is kept moist and turned after four, seven, and ten days.

Microorganisms needed for decomposition are provided in the manure and soil added to the pile. The nitrogen needed by the microorganisms is obtained from the nitrogenous materials added to the pile. If insufficient nitrogenous materials are available, fertilizer must be added to the carbonaceous materials to satisfy the needs of the microorganisms. If this is not done, the reaction time is greatly lengthened.

Large growers must resort to higher capacity composting and will generally use a wind-row technique. Rows of considerable length, eight to twelve feet wide at the base and four to six feet in height, are constructed as previously described. These rows are periodically turned by means of a

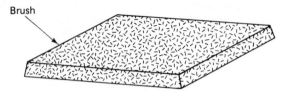

Brush

1. The base usually consists of a 6-inch layer of brush.

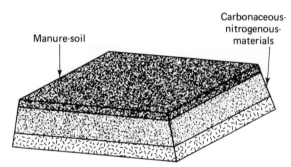

Manure-soil

Carbonaceous-
nitrogenous-
materials

2. This is followed by a 1-foot thickness of mixed wastes,
2 inches of manure or a substitute, and 1 inch of soil.

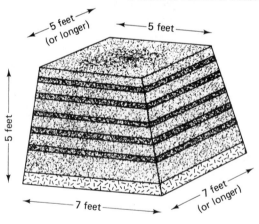

5 feet
(or longer)

5 feet

5 feet

7 feet

7 feet
(or longer)

3. Remaining layers are a repeated pattern of 6 inches of mixed carbonaceous-
nitrogenous wastes, 2 inches of manure or a substitute, and 1 inch of soil.
The final pile is tapered, 5 feet high, and completely moist. A depression is
commonly formed on top to catch rain and the pile is often covered with bur-
lap, hay, or soil to conserve heat. Microbiological activity is aided by keeping the pile moist and the decomposition is speeded by thoroughly mixing the
pile at 6 and 12 weeks.

Figure 5-6. Diagrammatic illustration of an Indore compost pile. (*From R.
P. Poincelot, "The Biochemistry and Methodology of Composting," Connecticut Agricultural Experiment Station Bulletin 727, 1972*)

156

bucket mounted on a tractor. In some operations, a perforated plastic pipe is placed under the center of the pile. Air pumped through it aerates the pile and eliminates the need for mixing.

Limestone is not currently recommended for use in composting since it may raise the pH level to a point where ammonium nitrogen formed can be converted to ammonia gas and lost. The nutrient content of the compost is not sufficiently high to qualify it as a fertilizer. Dry compost generally has an analysis of 1.5 to 3.5 percent nitrogen, 0.5 to 1.0 percent phosphorus and 1.0 to 2.0 percent potassium. When considering the quantity of compost used in root media, this can have a significant impact. The final pH level is usually neutral to slightly alkaline.

The process of composting occurs in several stages. Each stage involves different microorganisms. The pile, initially in the mesophilic stage, rises in temperature from that of the surrounding air to 104°F (40°C) at which point it enters the thermophilic stage. Finally it reaches a level of 158°F (70°C) where it stabilizes for a short time. This can occur in as short a time as two to three days. Thereafter the temperature gradually cools to that of the surrounding air. The pH level also undergoes shifts. Initially, organic matter derived from fresh plant material will be slightly acid, around pH 6.0. As it decomposes, organic acids will be formed which will result in a drop to 4.5 to 5.0. As the temperature rises, further chemical conversions take place and the pH rises to an alkaline level of 7.5 to 8.5. Finally the pH levels off at a neutral to slightly alkaline level of 7.0 to 7.5.

Composted Garbage

Many municipalities combine the collection and disposal of kitchen wastes and solid household trash. When producing a compost from this waste most metals, rags, and large items are first reclaimed; then the remaining refuse is ground and set out in heaps to compost. Heat generated in these heaps from the action of microorganisms breaking down the organic matter destroys harmful organisms and results in a dark brown, somewhat granular product. Glass is ground fine enough to prevent its becoming a safety hazard. The pH level is about 8.5 and the salt content moderately high but subject to removal by leaching.

Processed garbage has worked well as a mulch in landscaping, but has not been as satisfactory as a root medium component. The problem stems from the variation in refuse ingredients. When a high proportion of kitchen waste is present, a product rich in humus is produced which makes a good peatmoss substitute in the traditional soil-based media. When high proportions of wood, paper, plastic, or other such materials are present, a product is produced which can tie up nitrogen in root media or simply act as an inert component which would be a better sand replacement. This variability within single batches of product has led to variable results within trials ranging from excellent to poor. More work is needed before this product can be fully accepted as a component of greenhouse root media.

Floramull®

Floramull®, earlier known as Hygromull® in America, is a white, water-absorbing synthetic resin produced by BASF Corporation of West Germany (Figure 5-7). Because of its moisture-holding capacity, it can serve as a partial substitute for soil and peatmoss in root media. It does not replace the cation exchange capacities of these two components, and thus does not substitute for their nutrient-holding capacities. Floramull® will hold water equal to approximately 50 percent of its volume. Although Floramull® has a pH value of 3.0 it does not appreciably affect the root medium pH level.

Floramull® is a urea formaldehyde type resin that is formulated into blocks which are in turn ground into flakes of 0.1 to 0.5 inches in diameter for greenhouse use. The resin contains 30 percent total nitrogen but only 0.25 percent of soluble nitrogen; thus it is not toxic to plants. It breaks down at the rate of 3 percent per year providing some nitrogen for use by the crop. The resin is very light in its dry state, weighing 18 ounces per cubic foot or

Figure 5-7. Floramull® being mixed into root medium. Floramull is a lightweight (18 oz/cu ft) resin that will hold approximately 50 percent of its volume in water. It is an effective component in pot media for increasing water-holding capacity. (*Photo courtesy BASF-Wyandotte Corporation, Wyandotte, MI 48192*)

less. It can easily be crushed between the fingers. When used with soil and sand, tilling of the media, as is done in fresh flower beds, can result in collapse of the resin. Floramull$_®$ has worked out well in soil-base potting media and in lightweight soilless media in general. It has been used successfully in America, but is most extensively utilized in Europe. It can be considerably cheaper than field soil or the peatmoss which it partially replaces.

An interesting application of Floramull$_®$ is found in landscaping where it is used to establish grass on bare sites. A slurry of Floramull$_®$, grass seed, and fertilizer is pumped through nozzles out over the landscape. The slurry is pumped 1,200 feet or more so that vast areas such as roadways, industrial landscapes, or slag heaps can be conveniently seeded. The Floramull$_®$ provides a source of moisture for the germinating seed and also serves as a mulch to reduce evaporation of water from the soil beneath. Although light in weight, Floramull$_®$ bonds to the soil so that it will not blow away.

Vermiculite

Vermiculite ore is mined principally in the United States and in Africa as a micalike, silicate mineral. The ore itself has a bulk density of 55 to 65 pounds per cubic foot, but when expanded to the state used in root media, the density drops to 7 to 10 pounds per cubic foot (Figure 5-8). This lightweight property makes it very desirable in pot media. Each particle of vermiculite ore contains numerous thin plates lying parallel to each other. Between the plates is moisture that expands when heated to high temperatures, causing the plates to move apart into an open accordianlike structure. The expanded volume can be as much as sixteen times the volume of the original ore. The water-holding capacity of expanded vermiculite is high because of the extensive surface area within each particle. Aeration and drainage properties are also good due to the larger pores between particles. The common particle size is 6-10 mesh (USS).

There are numerous negative electrical charges on the surface of each vermiculite platelet giving rise to its high cation exchange capacity of 19 to 22.5 me/100 g. The predominant fertilizer nutrients in vermiculite are potassium, magnesium, and calcium. The potassium content of American vermiculite will provide a small part, but certainly not the total needs, of a crop. The magnesium content of African vermiculite is high and has been known to provide the total needs of a greenhouse crop. Vermiculite varies in pH level. American vermiculite is essentially neutral while African vermiculite tends to be alkaline with pH levels approaching 9 in some cases. The alkaline African vermiculites constitute no problem when combined with an acidic media component such as peatmoss or bark. If used alone, in a propagation bed or in a hydroponic operation, the pH level of African vermiculite should be adjusted down. American vermiculite can be used without alteration.

Figure 5-8. Expanded vermiculite as it is used in greenhouse media. The exceptional water- and nutrient-holding capacities of vermiculite make it an excellent component of soilless media. (*Photo courtesy W. R. Grace & Co., 62 Whittemore Avenue, Cambridge, MA 02140*)

Vermiculite is a very desirable component of soilless root media because of its high nutrient and water retention, good aeration, and low bulk density. It is commonly included in commercially prepared soilless media; but because it is expensive compared to components such as bark and sand, it is not always included in media prepared by growers. Expanded vermiculite can be compressed easily between the fingers. Under the weight of soil-base media expanded vermiculite tends to compress, which greatly reduces aeration. Vermiculite is generally not used with soil.

Calcined Clay

Aggregates of clay particles are heated to high temperatures (*calcined*) to form hardened particles which resist breakdown in root media. These aggregates are large, mostly 8–45 mesh, and irregularly shaped. As a result they fit together loosely in the root medium creating large pores for drainage and aeration. Within each calcined clay aggregate are numerous clay particles forming a myriad of small water-holding pores. One pound of calcined clay can contain over thirteen acres of surface area within its structure. Calcined clay, therefore, brings the property of structure to root media in the form of a hardened, buff-colored aggregate weighing about 30 to 40 pounds per cubic foot. The pH levels of different calcined clay products range from acid to alkaline (4.5-9.0), but they have only a small influence on the pH level of root media. Calcined clays have a sizable CEC, from 6 to 21 me/100 g, which gives them the good property of nutrient retention. The variation in properties of calcined clays stems back to the type of clay used, e.g., *montmorillonite* clay from the Mississippi Valley and *attapulgite* clay from Florida and Georgia. Lusoil₍ᵣ₎, made from attapulgite clay has a pH of 7.5 to 9.0 and a CEC of 21 me/100 g. Terragreen₍ᵣ₎ and Turface₍ᵣ₎ are derived from montmorillonite clay.

Calcined clays should be used in a quantity equal to 10-15 percent of the volume of fresh flower media. For pot plant media they should constitute 25 to 33 percent of the total volume; the remainder being composed of either soil, peatmoss, or a combination of the two.

Sand

Sand is used in root media for adding the coarser texture needed to insure proper drainage and aeration. For this reason concrete grade sand (a sharp, coarse sand) is used. Concrete grade sand has the specifications listed in Table 5-5. Washed sand should be purchased since it is nearly free of clay, silt, and organic matter. In regions where there are snowfalls, caution should be exercised during the winter to avoid purchasing sand containing road salt (sodium chloride). Road salt is added to batches of sand to be sold to highway departments because it melts road ice. The level used in sand is injurious to greenhouse crops. It raises the total soluble salt level in the medium to the point where roots are killed.

Table 5-5
ASTM (American Society for Testing and Materials)
Specifications for Concrete Grade Sand

% OF TOTAL PASSING THE SCREEN	SCREEN SIZE
100	3/8 inch
95-100	No. 4*
80-100	No. 8
50-85	No. 16
25-60	No. 30
10-30	No. 50
2-10	No. 100

*These figures refer to the number of holes per inch. A No. 4 screen has holes slightly smaller than one-quarter inch due to the width of the wire between each hole.

Perlite

Perlite is a good substitute for sand for providing aeration in root media. Its main advantage over sand is its light weight of about six pounds per cubic foot as compared to 100-120 pounds per cubic foot for sand. Perlite is a siliceous volcanic rock which is crushed and when heated to 1800°F (982°C) expands to form white particles with numerous closed, air-filled cells. Water will adhere to the surface of perlite, but it is not absorbed into the perlite aggregates. Perlite is sterile, chemically inert, does not have a cation exchange capacity, and is nearly neutral with a pH value of 7.5. It does not appreciably affect the pH level of root media. Perlite costs considerably more than sand. As a result, it is used when root media density constitutes an economic advantage.

Polystyrene Foam

This material is known more commonly as Styrofoam®, Styropor®, and Styromull®. Like perlite, it constitutes a good substitute for sand, bringing improved aeration and light weight to root media. It is a white synthetic product containing numerous closed cells which are filled with air. It is extremely light, weighing less than 1.5 pounds per cubic foot. Like sand, it does not absorb water and has no appreciable cation exchange capacity. It is neutral and thus does not affect root media pH levels.

Polystyrene can be obtained in beads or in flakes. Beads of 1/8-to 3/16-inch diameter and flakes of 1/8- to 1/2-inch diameter are satisfactory for pot plant media. Larger particles may be used in bench media and for epiphytic plants such as orchid (Figure 5-9). Depending upon the source, price can vary considerably. The edges cut from large blocks prior to cutting into sheets, or the leftover pieces when desired shapes are stamped from sheets can be ground to form an excellent media component. Polystyrene should be given more consideration by greenhouse growers.

Other Coarse-Textured Components

Numerous substitutes will appear in the future for sand derived from minerals, or perhaps by-products of industry. Their usefulness will be determined by their bulk density, size, shape, and cost. A few interesting and effective products appeared on the market in the past few years. One product consists of short lengths of plastic wirecoating stripped from the ends of electrical wire during the process of making electrical components. The pieces

Figure 5-9. Equal parts of polystyrene foam (Styromull®) and sphagnum moss makes a good root medium for the orchid plant shown above. Polystyrene is an excellent lightweight substitute for sand in root media. *(Photo courtesy of BASF-Wyandotte Corporation, Wyandotte, MI 48192)*

are inert, relatively lightweight, and range in size from about 1/16 to 3/16 of an inch in diameter. A second product, Polytrol®, consists of pellets and flakes 1/8 to 1/4 inch in size made from plastics. Reject plastic materials which cannot be used in prime products are combined with recycled municipal solid waste plastics to make this product. Many other substitutes can be found for sand if one bears in mind the function of sand.

SOIL-BASED MEDIA

The largest division in root media types falls between those containing soil and the soilless types. One type is not necessarily superior to the other. Equal quality plants can be grown in each if adjustments are made. Selection of a root medium type is made on the basis of economics and the physical situation which it must serve. Ten years ago a discussion of soilless media would have been included in this book more as a curiosity or a prediction of things to come. Today, when one looks around the pot plant industry it seems conceivable that a discussion of soil-based media will be obsolete in a few years. This should not be the case where a grower has an abundant source of good, uniform soil and has developed an efficient mixing procedure.

Formulation

Perhaps half of the pot plants in the United States are grown in soil-based media. By contrast, virtually all of the cut flower crops are grown in this type media. Traditionally, the soil-based medium has been composed of equal parts by volume of loam field soil, concrete grade sand, and sphagnum peatmoss amended with phosphorus and adjusted to the proper pH level. Sandy field soil is compensated by an increase in the proportion of peatmoss and field soil and a decrease in sand, while clay soil calls for more sand.

Sand is used in soil-based media to develop large diameter pores for good aeration. Two materials, perlite and polystyrene, have proven to be good substitutes. Like sand, both materials resist compaction and absorption of water. Unlike sand they are very light in weight, six pounds or less per cubic foot as opposed to 100 pounds or more per cubic foot for sand. A moist mixture of equal parts of soil, sand, and peatmoss weighs about 90 pounds per cubic foot which is suitable for use in a greenhouse bench, but not for pot plants which must be handled frequently or moved great distances. Substitution of perlite or polystyrene for sand reduces the wet weight of this medium to less than 60 pounds per cubic foot which is acceptable. There is a price for doing this—perlite can cost as much as ten times the price of sand. Polystyrene, however, is more reasonably priced.

Field soil provides reasonable nutrient (CEC) and water-holding capacities. When one-third of the soil is replaced by sand these two properties are significantly reduced. To restore them, sphagnum peatmoss, an amendment with a high CEC and water-holding capacity, has been traditionally added into the medium at the expense of an additional one-third of the field soil. Coarse peatmoss should be obtained when possible. Some peatmoss is hydrolically mined and the particles are so small much of the effect of structure is lost. The large pieces of sphagnum peatmoss fit together loosely to form wide pores for aeration. The intimately fine leaf structure of the sphagnum moss comprising the peatmoss forms copious narrow pores for holding water. Sphagnum peatmoss has one of the greatest water-holding capacities of any medium amendment, holding upwards of 60 percent water by volume when moist. Thus, sphagnum peatmoss provides good water-holding capacity and a fair amount of aeration. Sand provides the balance of aeration.

Sphagnum peatmoss is compressed into bales for shipment and sales purposes. If large pieces appear when opened, they should be broken with a hoe or passed through a soil-shredding machine. If passed through the machine more than once, however, the pieces are nearly broken down to individual moss filaments and much of the desirable aeration property is lost.

Maintenance

The structure of root media is sufficiently stable to persist until the time when the final purchaser of potted plants would ordinarily repot these plants. At that time, one to two years, some of the old root media can be removed and a new media prepared to fill the larger pot, thus restoring the original level of structure. In any event, loss of structure is not a problem for the grower of potted plants. It is a problem for the cut flower grower since he maintains soil permanently in his ground beds and benches.

The action of decomposition results in loss of organic matter and the periodic need to add more. This is customarily done once each year at the time when the root media is pasteurized. The standard additive has been coarse sphagnum peatmoss rototilled into the bench in a quantity equal to about 10 percent of the volume of the root media in the bench. Coarse bark (3/8 to 3/4-inch screening) has also proven to be a very good annual amendment in bench media. The decomposition rate is slow, requiring up to three years for complete breakdown. These materials provide excellent drainage properties. The first year a quantity equal to ten percent of the bench volume should be incorporated into satisfactorily drained media and 15 percent into poorly drained media. As a rule of thumb, each year thereafter a quantity equal to 5 percent of the bench volume is added.

Sometimes the organic matter level is adequate but the clay content is too high. Poor drainage and excessive cracking of the root media upon drying (Figure 5-10) are symptoms of this condition. This is particularly prevalent when clay soil is used. The problem is remedied by a single addition of concrete grade sand to these media. Perlite is generally not used since weight is not a problem in benches. Calcined clay is sometimes used because in addition to providing macropores for drainage and aeration, it contains numerous micropores within each particle to improve water-holding capacity and a high CEC that improves nutrient retention. A quantity equal to 10 to 15 percent of the bench volume is incorporated into the medium. It is expensive but need only be applied once since it is resistant to breakdown.

SOILLESS MEDIA

Soilless media is growing rapidly in popularity. Growers who do not have field soil of their own have found it difficult to purchase soil of proper structure and texture. They also have found the soil to vary from load to load. This requires alternatives in their media formulations and thus considerable attention on the part of managers. Occasionally changes in the field soil are overlooked and the resulting root medium leads to a poor crop and loss of profits. Soilless media are attractive to these growers.

Figure 5-10. A fresh flower medium containing too much clay. Note the cracks that occur upon drying. This medium has inadequate gas exchange, as witnessed by symptoms of oxygen deficiency in the chrysanthemum plants. Growth is stunted, leaves are light green in color with veins lighter than the rest of the leaf blade, and the plants wilt on bright days.

Other growers are involved in shipment of potted plants long distances by truck and must have a finished plant as light as possible. Soilless media can be formulated in lighter densities than soil-based media.

Still other growers look on soilless media as a form of automation since it can be purchased ready for use, thus eliminating the need for any labor input or mixing facilities. Such growers may be in a labor market of high wages or in a situation of limited labor availability.

Components of Soilless Media

So many materials are available for soilless media that growers make the mistake of mixing too many or the wrong types together. The four functions of root media—plant support, aeration, nutrient retention, and moisture retention—should be considered when developing a formulation. Organic matter or clay is needed to provide cation exchange capacity for nutrient retention. Unless the organic matter or clay is in coarse aggregates to facilitate aeration, coarse-textured particles such as sand, perlite, or polystyrene will be required. If the organic matter or clay selected has a high water-holding capacity, as does peatmoss, no further components are necessary.

On the other hand, if organic matter or clay of insufficient water-holding capacity is used, such as coarse bark, it will be necessary to include a second organic material or clay component (such as peatmoss or calcined clay) to increase the water-holding capacity. The desired density of the medium can be attained by avoiding heavy coarse particles or clay components.

As will be seen in the next section, good root media need not contain more than one to three components. The selection of components will generally depend upon their availability and cost. A grower who markets peatmoss, and thus can obtain it at wholesale cost, or who is located close to the point where it is dug, so that transportation costs are minimal, should use peatmoss for its superior water-holding capacity and CEC. If weight is not a problem, he (or she) should mix it with the cheapest coarse-textured component which is sand. If light weight is required, the considerably more expensive components perlite or vermiculite may have to be used. If light weight is required and the grower is fortunate enough to be located near a source of polystyrene flakes or beads, the lighter density can be achieved with less cost than perlite.

A grower located in a timber area will probably find bark to be economical. If he (or she) is large enough to process it, or if there is a processing firm in the area so that a fine-textured, decomposed product free of wood is available, bark alone may be used as the root medium. If the bark is excessively fine-textured or contains wood which will decompose rapidly to form very fine-textured particles which reduce aeration, sand should be incorporated for aeration and possibly sphagnum peatmoss added to restore the needed water-holding capacity.

Formulations

PEATMOSS-BASED FORMULATIONS. One of the earliest commercially prepared soilless media developed was Einheitserde (standardized soil), a mixture of half peatmoss and half well-aggregated subsoil clay amended with nitrogen, phosphorus, and potassium and limed to a pH level between 5 and 6. It was introduced by Dr. A. Fruhstorfer in Hamburg, Germany in 1948. Einheitserde is marketed by several companies in Europe and is used for a wide range of crops and applications from seed germination to plant finishing.

The UC (University of California) mixes were some of the earliest soilless media adopted in America during the 1950s. These are a series of five media ranging from 100 percent sphagnum or hypnum peatmoss to 100 percent fine sand with intermediate combinations of the two. These media are formulated by individual growers. The more popular greenhouse pot media of this series is the half peatmoss, half fine sand mixture. Several fertilizer amendments are recommended, but one that works well when the medium is to be stored for some time prior to planting is presented in Table 5-6. The designation of fine sand indicates sand between 0.5 and 0.05 mm in diameter, which is equivalent to 1/50 to 1/500 of an inch, or to sand that passes a 30-mesh screen but is retained on a 270-mesh screen.

The Peat-Lite mixes were introduced by Drs. J. W. Boodley and R. Sheldrake at Cornell University in the early 1960s. Mix A is composed of half sphagnum peatmoss and half horticultural grade vermiculite. Mix B contains horticultural perlite in the place of vermiculite. Various fertilizer amendments are recommended for these media depending upon the fertilizer requirement of the crop to be grown. Typical amendments for general pot plant culture are presented in Table 5-6.

While some growers formulate Peat-Lite mixes, there are a number of commercial preparations of soilless media on the market similar to Peat-Lite Mix A. Some of these are Redi-Earth®, Jiffy Mix®, and Pro-Mix® A, the latter with 60 percent peatmoss and 40 percent vermiculite. These media should, and usually do, contain ground limestone sufficient to raise the pH to a satisfactory level of about 6.0. They also generally contain a full complement of micronutrients, phosphorus to meet the needs of a crop, and sufficient nitrogen and potassium to provide the needs for two to four weeks of a lightly fertilized crop.

It is significant that the media thus far discussed have been composed of only two components. This is possible because one is peatmoss which has the highest water-holding capacity of any of the components discussed, a significant CEC, and a modest degree of aeration if not too finely shredded.

Table 5-6
Formulations for the UC Mix C and Peat-Lite Mixes A and B

| | QUANTITY PER CU YD | | |
INGREDIENT	UC Mix C	Peat-Lite A	Peat-Lite B
Sphagnum peatmoss	13.5 cu ft	13.5 cu ft	13.5 cu ft
Vermiculite		13.5 cu ft	
Perlite			13.5 cu ft
Fine sand	13.5 cu ft		
Potassium nitrate	4.0 oz		1.5 lb
Calcium nitrate		1.5 lb	
Potassium sulfate	4.0 oz		
Fritted trace elements		2.0 oz	2.0 oz
Single superphosphate			
(0-20-0)	2.5 lb	2.5 lb	2.0 lb
Dolomitic limestone	7.5 lb	10.0 lb	5.0 lb
Calcitic limestone	2.5 lb		
Wetting agent		3.0 oz	3.0 oz

In the cases where sand, perlite, or clay aggregates were used, increased aeration was provided. Clay and vermiculite additions increased the CEC along with aeration. Peatmoss comes very close to an ideal medium by itself if it contains coarse aggregates. European growers have learned to grow top quality crops in it. This concept is just beginning to come into the American industry for pot plant culture. If this system is used, it is important to guard against overwatering. This comes about from watering too frequently. Because peatmoss effectively retains nutrients, it is important that overdoses of fertilizer not be applied and that the medium is thoroughly watered each time water is needed to insure that excess nutrient salts are leached from the medium.

Formulators of soilless media must remain competitive. A significant part of the expense of these media to the grower is the shipping cost. For this reason media are in a rather dry state when shipped. Dry peatmoss, particularly when finely ground, can be exceedingly difficult to wet because it repels water. This is the reason that wetting agents are used in these media. See Table 5-7 for a partial list of wetting agents suitable for this purpose.

The wetting agent, however, does not completely correct the problem. The peatmoss-vermiculite media pose no problem when used for seed germination because the newly seeded flat is usually placed under a mist irrigation system which gently and thoroughly moistens the media without permitting drying of the surface during the process. When some of these media are used for pot plant or cut flower culture in beds they require a prohibitively long initial wetting period. Upon flooding the surface of the medium, a period of time must be allotted for the water to penetrate. Then the surface is flooded again and the procedure repeated several times until water finally penetrates to the bottom.

This tedious procedure can be partially avoided by adding coarse-textured particles to the media such as sand or perlite. These components provide large pores which allow quicker penetration of water throughout the media. Lateral as well as vertical movement of water occurs in the initial soaking of smaller peatmoss pores, resulting in a saving of time. Some commercially available media which contain sand and/or perlite in addition to peatmoss and vermiculite are Pro Mixes $BX_{\circledR}$ and $C_{\circledR}$, Metro $Mix_{\circledR}$, and Grower's Choice$_{\circledR}$. Some growers with a source of well-drained field soil add 10 to 20 percent by volume to these media to improve wettability, reduce cost, and increase post-sale consumer satisfaction.

BARK-BASED FORMULATIONS. As previously discussed, the use of bark is economically expedient in many areas. Water- and nutrient-holding capacities of bark are generally not as good as peatmoss. As a result, vermiculite or peatmoss are commonly used in commercial preparations of bark media. Commercial media containing composted pine bark and vermiculite

Table 5-7

Some Wetting Agents, Sources, and Rates That Can be Used for the
Initial Wetting of Dry Peatmoss-Based Soilless Media

CHEMICAL[1]	SOURCE	PERCENT ACTIVE	RATE/YARD[2] (oz)
Aqua Gro	Aquatrols Corp. of America Box 385 Delair, New Jersey 08110	100%	3
Ethomid 0/15	Armak Company 8401 West 41st Street McCook, Illinois 60525	100	3
Hydro-Wet (L 237)	Colloidal Products P.O. Box 621 Petaluma, California 94952	87.5	3
Surf Side	Monto Products Corp. P.O. Box 404 Ambler, Pennsylvania 19002	100	3
Tetronic 908	Wyandotte Chemical Co. Wyandotte, Michigan 48192	100	3
Triton B-1956	Rohm & Haas Company Independence Mall W. Philadelphia, Pennsylvania 19106	77	3

From J. W. Boodley and R. Sheldrake, Jr. *Cornell Peat-Lite Mixes for Commercial Plant Growing*, New York College of Agriculture and Life Sciences Extension Information Bulletin 43, 1977.

[1]No endorsement of products is intended, nor is criticism of unnamed products implied.

[2]The simplest way to add wetting agents is in the granular formulation. If used as a liquid, dilute the 3 ounces in 5 to 10 gallons of water and add to the mix. To wet dry mixes after preparation, use a drench of 1 pint per 100 gallons. This is equivalent to about 1 teaspoonful per gallon for small amounts.

include Choice Greenhouse Mix$_®$ and Choice Nursery Mix$_®$. In addition to these two ingredients, Ball Growing Mix$_®$ contains perlite. Metro Mix 300$_®$ contains composted pine bark, vermiculite, and peatmoss, as well as sand and perlite for drainage. Metro Mix 350$_®$, in addition to sphagnum peatmoss, vermiculite, and sand, contains specially processed pine bark.

Pine bark is sometimes used alone, requiring only an upward adjustment of the pH level with ground limestone plus the addition of micronutrients and phosphorus. Pine bark containing particles up to 3/8-inch diameter generally has sufficient aeration for such an application. Finer pine bark, hardwood bark, as well as redwood bark and sawdust are commonly mixed with sand to provide aeration. Commonly about 30 percent sand is used in these mixtures. Occasionally in the summertime, when the drying action is so much greater, peatmoss may be added to these mixtures to increase water-holding capacity. A ratio of 3 bark:1 sand:1 peatmoss is favored.

The most acid of the barks is pine bark. To raise the pH level of pine bark media to 6.5, which is best for crops in general, ten pounds of dolomitic limestone and two pounds of hydrated lime should be mixed into each cubic yard. Dolomitic limestone alone will suffice for hardwood barks and lesser amounts can be used depending upon the initial pH. Some hardwood barks are alkaline (pH level above 7) and may require no limestone at all; they may even require sulfur to lower the pH level to 6.5.

FUTURE FORMULATIONS. Media discussed thus far include the more common components. Numerous other components exist and many new ones will be developed as the trend away from soil-based media continues. You should now be able to determine with only a minimum of testing whether these components are useful to you and how they should be used. First select a component which provides adequate moisture and nutrient retention. If one component does not provide both functions adequately, two components may be required. Seek components which have aggregate structure so that optimum aeration is provided. If this is not possible, a coarse-textured component will be needed to provide aeration. The fewer components the better because of the cost of mixing. Be sure that none of the components provides an excessive quantity of nutrients or salt such as excessive ammonium released by rapidly decomposing peats or from chicken manure.

Chemical Amendments

The grower who prepares his or her own soilless media should make the following chemical amendments. Adjust the pH level to 6.2 to 6.8 for crops in general or to 5.0 to 5.8 for acid-loving crops. Use limestone to raise the pH level and either sulfur or aluminum sulfate to lower it. Instructions for the use of these materials are given in Chapter 8. The phosphorus needs for one year should be provided through the addition of 2.5 pounds of single super-phosphate (0-20-0) per cubic yard of medium. A complete trace element mixture is imperative since peatmoss and bark media commonly tend toward iron and boron deficiencies, and to a lesser extent other trace element deficiencies. A fritted trace element mix is best because it is a slowly available form providing all of the trace elements required by the plant for a period of ten months or more. Fritted trace elements are incorporated into media at the rate of two ounces per cubic yard. Commercial preparations of soilless media usually contain nitrogen and potassium sufficient to last two to four weeks. This is good for seed flat media since it eliminates the need for applying nutrient solutions to the young seedlings, a procedure which can easily be overdone. It is best if high levels of nitrogen and potassium are left out of media to be used for established plants. Crops may be categorized according to fertilizer-level tolerance. Many of the newer house plants and flowering pot plants are lightly fertilized and are sensitive to moderate fertilizer levels. Unless slow-release forms of nitrogen and potassium are used in media it is going to be necessary to establish a fertilizer program after planting; thus there is only a minimal advantage to applying a two- to four-week supply of these two nutrients prior to planting. Slow-release forms of nitrogen and potassium which will provide safe levels of these nutrients for three months or longer may be mixed into media during formulation. The media should be used as soon as prepared because the slow-release fertilizers begin to release nutrients immediately and, in storage, may soon lead to toxic levels.

Economics of Soilless Media

The greenhouse grower who elects to use soilless media must decide whether to purchase it ready-for-use or to formulate it. This decision must be made individually and is based on economics. The grower should calculate the cost of media he or she formulates and compare it with the price of commercial media including shipment. When calculating the formulation cost be sure to include the depreciation cost of the mixer, any conveyor belts and front-end loaders used to fill the mixer, buildings used for holding components of the media, the cost of pasteurization if this is necessary, and all labor costs. Whether you formulate a soil-based or a soilless medium, you may be startled by the true cost. Commercial media, while expensive at face value, are not very different in cost from media individually formulated and can actually be cheaper if a steady source of relatively inexpensive components are not available.

Several of the widely available brands of commercial media cost about $1.90 per cubic foot when purchased in two- to six-cubic foot packages. Some brands are available in bulk at lower prices. There are numerous local formulators who sell at even lower prices, some as low as $0.50 per cubic foot. The figure of $1.90 per cubic foot appears to be high, but isn't necessarily intolerable. Eighteen six-inch azalea-type pots used for pot mum culture can be filled from one cubic foot of medium (Table 5-8) at a cost of $0.11 per pot. If each finished pot wholesales for $3.50, the medium cost will be less than 3 percent of the total costs of production.

MEDIA PREPARATION AND HANDLING

You have now made several important decisions. First you have decided whether to use a soil-based medium or a soilless one. Then you have decided whether to purchase or prepare your own medium. If you have decided to formulate your own medium, you have determined the minimum number of components necessary to insure reasonable nutrient and moisture retention without sacrificing aeration. You have further studied all possible component substitutes for the expedience of economy, investigating materials ranging from bark, sawdust, and sewage to polystyrene and reprocessed plastic beads. Now you have worked out a formulation which is tailored to

Table 5-8
Number of Pots That Can Be Filled
from One Cubic Foot of Root Medium

POT SIZE (INCH)	NUMBER PER CU FT
Standard Type	
2¼	296
2½	176
3	120
4	44
5	24
6	14
7	9
8	5.6
12	1.6
Azalea Type	
4	64
5	32
6	18
Low Pan	
5	40
6	31
7	14

your conditions and needs. It meets the required functions of a root media, has the proper weight for your format of handling and shipping, and incorporates the most economical combination of various components available in your locality. You must complement this plan with an efficient system for mixing and handling.

Small Batch Handling

Very small batches (up to five or six cubic feet may be mixed by hand shovel on a potting bench or on any hard surface (Figure 5-11). Components are piled on one another and the nutrient amendments, including limestone, superphosphate, and micronutrient mix, are broadcast over the pile. The pile is thoroughly mixed in three or four shifts. The pile is methodically removed by shovel from its base in the front. As material is removed, other material higher up tumbles downward mixing as it falls. The new pile is built in front of the original pile by continually dropping material on the top point of this conically shaped pile. As material is added it tumbles down all sides of the pile mixing as it goes. This procedure is repeated two or three times more by moving the pile to the side and then to the back.

Intermediate Volume Handling

Preparation of larger batches requires motorized equipment. Cement mixers ranging from the hobby size (two cubic feet) to those mounted on concrete trucks (six, seven, eight, or 10 cubic yards) are used (Figure 5-11). Growers often purchase old concrete trucks. The mixer is removed, reconditioned, and set up for greenhouse operation. The mixer is located near piles of medium components which are fed into the mixer either by a conveyor belt or a tractor-mounted front-end loader. Upon mixing, the medium is automatically discharged from the mixer into a potting trailer.

The bed of one commercial design trailer has a perforated plate with a chamber below it. For homemade trailers, a series of 1¼-inch pipes one foot apart are fixed to the bottom of the trailer. The pipes are connected to a manifold pipe which has a single steam inlet. The other ends of all pipes are capped. Holes 1/8 to 1/4 inch in diameter are drilled in pairs every six inches along the opposite sides of the pipe system to permit the escape of steam. When the trailer is filled with medium, a tarp is fastened over it and steam is injected into the chamber below the false bottom or into the pipe distribution system. Steam rises through the perforations and percolates up through the root medium, thereby destroying harmful disease organisms, insects, and weed seeds. This pasteurization process requires about two hours. The tarp is then removed and the soil permitted to cool. At that point the trailer is moved to a convenient location for potting plants and the sides are lowered to a horizontal position to serve as a potting bench (Figure 5-12).

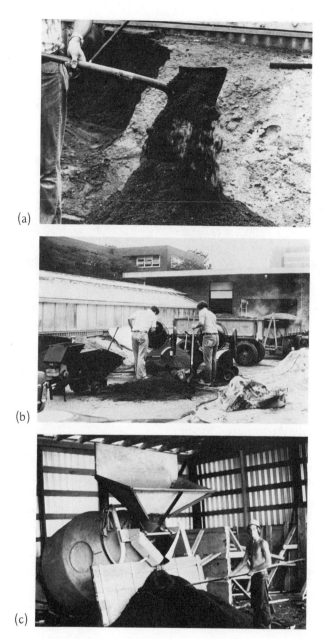

(a)

(b)

(c)

Figure 5-11. (a) A hand shovel procedure for mixing small batches of root media. (b) A small scale root media mixing operation. The soil shredder on the left is used to break up clods in field soil and sphagnum peatmoss. Components of media including fertilizer amendments are mixed in the two cubic foot cement mixers. The freshly prepared medium is placed in the pasteurizing wagons in the background and is pasteurized. (c) An intermediate size root media mixing operation making use of the mixer from a concrete truck.

175

Figure 5-12. A potting trailer with sides lowered to the horizontal position to serve as a potting bench.

Large, Fully Automated Systems

Large growers are in the best position to automate. A soil-handling system can be purchased ready-built (Figure 5-13) or can be designed and assembled by the grower. Where an automated system is justified, it is generally in daily use and for this reason is placed under a roof to permit its use regardless of weather. The system begins with storage bins for media components which can be filled directly by trucks. Components are then moved by tractor to a hopper mounted over a conveyor belt, which feeds them into a mixer. Chemical amendments are added directly to the mixer. Upon mixing, steam is injected into the mixer to pasteurize the root medium. The medium is then expelled into a storage bin by reversing the mixer. Later it can be moved from the storage bin to an automatic pot or flat-filling machine.

SUMMARY

1. Root media must serve four functions: provide water, supply nutrients, permit gas exchange to and from the roots, and provide support for the plant.

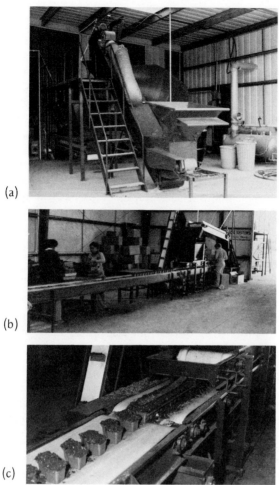

(a)

(b)

(c)

Figure 5-13. A root medium mixing system for large operations. (a) Media components are placed in the hopper, through which they drop into a grinder and then pass up an elevator into a mixer. Perlite and chemical amendments are added directly into the mixer from above. Root medium is steam pasteurized in the mixer with steam produced in the portable steam generator at the right. After pasteurization, the rotation of the mixer is reversed to expel the medium into the six-cubic-yard storage hopper on the left. The duct over the elevator is used to blow cool air into the mixer when it is emptying in order to reduce the time before the root medium can be handled. (b) Further along the system, root medium is automatically brought by conveyor belt to a pot-filling machine as needed. In the scene above, 157 three-inch pots are being filled per minute. Pots leave the filling machine on a belt and can be planted directly or can be removed and planted elsewhere. (c) A close view of the pot-filling machine. Excess soil is recycled back to the hopper on the filling machine. This machine can fill flats or pots of any size, including three-gallon cans. (*Photos courtesy of Soil Systems, Inc., Apopka, FL 32703*)

2. Desirable properties of greenhouse root media include:
   a. For pot plant media, a stable organic matter content which will not diminish significantly in volume during growth of a crop
   b. Organic matter with a reasonable carbon:nitrogen ratio and rate of decomposition so that nitrogen tie-up is not troublesome
   c. For pot plant media, a bulk density light enough to enhance handling and shipping but sufficiently heavy to prevent toppling of plants (40 to 75 pounds/cubic foot when wet)
   d. High moisture retention coupled with good aeration (35 to 50 percent water and 10 to 20 percent air by volume after watering)
   e. A high cation exchange capacity for nutrient reserve (10 to 30 me/100 g of dry medium)
   f. A pH level between 6.2 and 6.8 for crops in general, lower for acid requiring plants
   g. Sufficient level of all nutrients other than nitrogen and potassium to prevent a deficiency for the duration of at least one crop

3. A long list of potential components exists for use in greenhouse media. One should select components for his or her root medium on the basis of meeting the four functions of root media, economics, steady availability, and use of a minimal number of components.

4. Soil-based media has traditionally been used in greenhouses. Soil provides water and nutrient retention. Concrete grade sand is added to increase aeration and peatmoss is used to restore moisture and nutrient retention lost by the addition of sand. A standard formulation of 1 loam soil: 1 sand:1 peatmoss can be altered to accommodate various soil textures.

5. Soilless media are an asset where soil procurement is a problem. Peatmoss alone or combined in equal volume amounts with fine sand, perlite, or vermiculite constitutes an effective root medium. Composted bark of species ranging from pine to hardwoods also provides a good base for soilless media. Successful formulations include: (a) bark in combination with 25 percent coarse sand, and (b) bark in combination with 20 percent coarse sand and 20 percent sphagnum peatmoss by volume.

6. It is important to adjust the pH level of root media at the time of mixing. Generally an upward adjustment is required and dolomitic limestone is the favored material to use. Common rates range from 5 to 10 pounds/cubic yard for soil-based media and 10 to 15 pounds/cubic yard for soilless media. Single superphosphate (0-20-0) is applied at mixing time at a rate between 2½ and 3 pounds/cubic yard to meet phosphorous and sulfur needs for one year. Since peatmoss and bark-based media tend toward micronutrient deficiencies, a micronutrient mixture is also added to these media during their formulation.

7. Root media preparation and handling poses an important economic consideration for growers. It may be purchased already mixed, chemically amended and pasteurized, thus circumventing considerable labor, or it may be formulated by the grower. Various degrees of automation are available for formulating and handling media and should be considered.

SUGGESTED READINGS

Baker, K. F. ed. "The U. C. System for Producing Healthy Container-Grown Plants." University of California, Division of Agriculture Science, Experiment Station-Extension Services Manual 23, 1957.

Boodley, J. W. and R. Sheldrake, Jr. "Cornell Peat-Lite Mixes for Commercial Plant Growing." New York College Agriculture and Life Sciences Extension Information Bulletin 43, 1973.

Coker, E. G. *Horticultural Science and Soils.* Vol. 2: *Soils and Fertilisers.* Macdonald and Co., Ltd. London, 1971.

Johnson, P. *Horticultural and Agricultural Uses of Sawdust and Soil Amendments.* Paul Johnson. 1904 Cleveland Ave., National City, CA 92050, 1968.

Poincelot, R. P. "The Biochemistry and Methodology of Composting." Connecticut Agricultural Experiment Station Bulletin 754, 1975.

Potter, C. H. "Bedding Plants 6: Choosing a Soil: The Real Thing or a Mix?" *Florists' Review* 147(3819):32–33, 71–74. 1971.

White, J. W. "Criteria for Selection of Growing Media for Greenhouse Crops." *Florists' Review* 155(4009):28–30, 73–74. 1974.

White, J. W. *Growing media.* In *Bedding Plants,* 2nd ed. J. W. Mastalerz ed. PA Flower Growers, 103 Tyson Bldg., University Park, PA 16802, 1976.

Chapter 6

Root Media
Pasteurization

Subtropical conditions exist in the greenhouse which are conducive to the development of plant disease organisms. The environment never freezes, the atmosphere is continually moist, and temperatures are always warm. The continuous culture of one, or at best a few crops, accentuates the disease problem by providing a continuous host on which disease organisms can build.

Before 1950, in order to combat the soil-borne disease problem, root media were removed from greenhouses annually and replaced with media which had been carefully prepared by a proper succession of crops in the field and by composting, as described in the previous chapter. During the 1950s, this cumbersome labor-consuming system became less prevalent as root medium pasteurization was adopted.

Root medium pasteurization is a standard practice for virtually all greenhouse ranges today. It generally is done on an annual basis; although a number of growers are pasteurizing their media between every crop. The need for such an increase in frequency is occasionally dictated by the build-up of disease in the greenhouse. For a relatively short crop such as chrysanthemums this could be every twelve to sixteen weeks. The summer has been a preferred time for pasteurization because crop production is usually at a low point, student labor is more available, root media are warmer, and, in the case of steam pasteurization, all or much of the boiler capacity is available at that time.

Root medium pasteurization, in addition to eliminating disease organisms, is used to control nematodes, insects, and weeds. Field operators have been known to pasteurize soil for the single benefit of weed control.

Pasteurization may be accomplished by means of injecting steam into the soil or by the injection of one of several chemicals such as methyl bromide and chloropicrin. These two methods will now be discussed separately.

181

STEAM PASTEURIZATION

Temperature Requirements

There are a number of organisms which are injurious to plants and each has its own condition under which it is destroyed as set forth in Figure 6-1. It has been customary to apply steam for 30 minutes beyond the time when the coldest spot in the batch of root medium being pasteurized reaches

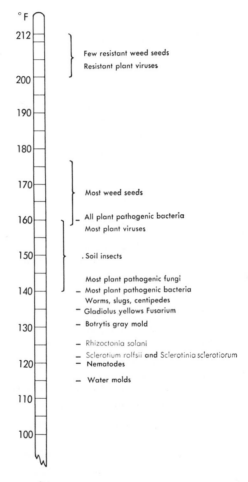

Figure 6-1. Temperature necessary to kill pathogens and other organisms harmful to plants. Most of the temperatures indicated here are for thirty-minute exposures under moist conditions. (*From Baker, K. F., ed., "The U. C. System for Producing Healthy Container-Grown Plants," California Agriculture Experiment Station and Extension Service Manual 23, 1957*)

180°F (82°C). While this guarantees 30 minutes at a minimum temperature of 180°F, the medium temperature usually rises to 212°F (100°C), the temperature of steam.

This chapter refers to pasteurization rather than sterilization because sterilization would imply destruction of all organisms in root media whereas pasteurization indicates that only selected organisms are killed. Root media contains, in addition to the harmful disease organisms, many beneficial organisms. A root medium heavily occupied by beneficial organisms is not readily infected by disease organisms. By virtue of their strong foothold, the beneficial organisms compete successfully for oxygen, space, and nutrients and present resistance to the establishment of the disease. Pasteurization at a temperature of 212°F results in considerable destruction of beneficial organisms. This situation is not bad if beneficial organisms are the first to re-innoculate the medium. However, if a disease organism is first, it will develop rapidly without resistance or competition.

Equipment is available today which will mix air with steam (Figure 6-2). The temperature of the mixture can be adjusted to a desired level below

Figure 6-2. A steam aerator that permits pasteurization of root media at a temperature (140–160°F) below that of steam (212°F). Steam from a boiler enters the aerator at the right while a blower introduces air. The two gases mix in the tank at the top and are then conducted through the hose on the left to a covered potting wagon containing root medium to be pasteurized. A hand valve is used to regulate the amount of air introduced, which in turn controls the temperature of the mixture. The temperature is indicated on the temperature gauge shown.

212°F and injected into the medium. The medium will rise to that temperature and no higher. This system is known as *aerated steam pasteurization*. Several recommendations call for a temperature of 140°F (60°C) for 30 minutes although many growers pasteurize at a temperature of 160°F (71°C) for 30 minutes. Most harmful organisms are destroyed while only a minimum of beneficial organisms are killed.

Root Media Preparation

The root medium should be loosened before pasteurizing. If it is in a bench it should be rototilled. Heat moves most rapidly within the medium by convection, i.e., by movement of the steam through the pores. There are large pores in loose media which facilitate the movement of steam and thereby cut down the length of time required to pasteurize a bench or container of root medium.

The root medium should not be dry. Dry soil acts very much as an insulator resisting the conduction of heat and causing the medium to warm up slowly. The addition of water speeds up the rate of pasteurization but there is an optimum level of water beyond which further additions again slow down the speed of pasteurization. Water requires five times as much heat to raise its temperature as does an equal weight of soil. Since all of the excess water in the root medium must also be raised to the desired temperature of pasteurization (160°F) the process becomes very slow and consequently expensive. As a general rule the root medium should be at the moisture level one would desire at the time of planting a crop. For soil-based media this is about fifteen percent moisture by volume.

There are a few types of weed seed which can survive temperatures approaching 212°F. Some of these are morning glory, buttonweed, bur clover, shepard's purse, and Klamath weed. This problem can be circumvented by moistening the root medium a week or two prior to pasteurization. As soon as seed begins the germination process of taking up moisture, it is easily killed at lower temperatures typically used for pasteurization.

Since root media must be mixed prior to pasteurization, it is desirable to add the various chemical and physical amendments at that time. Superphosphate, limestone, fritted micronutrients, inorganic complete fertilizers, and the slow-release fertilizer MagAmp can undergo the process of pasteurization without adverse effect. The slow-release fertilizer Osmocote requires further consideration. It can withstand temperatures up to 200°F (94°C) without damage to the coating; however, the rate of release may increase. If pasteurized with the medium, it should be used within 20 days to avoid an injurious buildup of salts. Pasteurization of Osmocote containing medium at 160°F is considerably safer.

Bench media require periodic additions of organic matter such as peatmoss or bark. This is most easily incorporated at the time the medium is rototilled prior to pasteurization. It is also a good practice to carry these amendments through the pasteurization process to destroy any harmful organisms which might be in them.

Steam Sources

The temperature of one cubic foot of greenhouse root media on the average can be raised one degree Fahrenheit by the addition of 24 Btu of heat. The lower the initial temperature of the medium, the greater the heat which must be applied to pasteurize it. Table 6-1 lists the heat required to raise a cubic foot of soil-based media to 180°F from various starting temperatures.

Steam pasteurization efficiency may be as low as 50 percent. Half of the heat generated in the boiler may be lost from the boiler itself, the lines leading to the root medium, the walls of the bench, and the cover over it. It is therefore necessary to double the figures in Table 6-1 when determining the size boiler needed. Since one boiler horsepower (hp) is equal to 33,475 Btu per hour, a total of about six cubic feet of medium at 65°F (18°C) can be pasteurized with one boiler hp of heat. This would be equivalent to about twelve square feet of bench area.

Boilers can also be rated in terms of pounds of steam generated. In this case they are referring to one pound of water heated to the state of steam. When one pound of steam at 212°F changes state to one pound of water at 212°F it releases 970 Btu of heat. One more Btu is released for each degree the water drops below this point. If the root medium is pasteurized at 180°F, the water will drop 32° releasing an additional 32 Btu beyond the 970 Btu released when it changed states. Thus, one pound of steam contributes 1,002 Btu to the job of pasteurization. About six pounds of steam are required to pasteurize one cubic foot of root medium.

Table 6-1
Heat Required to Raise 1 Cubic Foot of Greenhouse Root Media
Containing 15% Moisture from Various Starting Temperatures to 180°F

| STARTING TEMPERATURE | | HEAT REQUIRED (BTU) |
°F	°C	
70	21	2,650
60	15	2,880
50	10	3,120
40	4	3,340
30	−1	3,600

From Gray, H. E. "Steam Sterilization." *Florists' Review* 127, pp 13–14, 77–79, 1960.

A steam boiler used for heating a greenhouse can be used for pasteurization. A tee and valve should be installed in the main steam line at a convenient point in each greenhouse from which steam can be obtained.

Hot water boilers may also be used for pasteurization if they can be converted to produce steam. The hot water boiler pictured in Figure 6-3a has sufficient space above the flue to lower the water level so that there is a space for steam to form and collect as pictured in Figure 6-3b. For this conversion a glass water gauge is installed so that the water level can be seen. An automatic water feed with safety alarm is installed to maintain a safe water level in the boiler since water is lost through steam. The hot water boiler type pictured in Figures 6-3c and 6-3d should not be converted to steam because the smoke flues are too high to remain covered with water

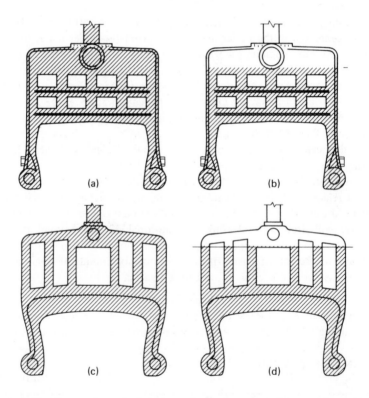

Figure 6-3. Conversion of a hot water boiler to steam: (a) a section of boiler filled with water for hot water heat; (b) the same section with the water line lowered to leave a steam dome for steam pasteurization of soil; (c) section of a boiler designed only for hot water; (d) cannot be used for steam sterilization because when the water line is lowered the tops of the flueways are exposed to the direct heat of the fire without water protection. (*From Ball, V., ed., 1975. Ball Red Book, 13th ed., George J. Ball, Inc., West Chicago, IL*)

during steam formation and would probably crack open as a result. Before converting a hot water boiler to steam one should check with the boiler manufacturer.

A greenhouse range without a boiler capable of producing steam may also use steam for pasteurizing. Portable steam generators (Figure 6-4) are available. A generator capable of generating 425,000 Btu per hour can be purchased for $2,300 to $2,500 and will pasteurize up to 300 square feet of raised bench area in two hours.

Steam does not have to be generated under high pressure for pasteurization purposes. Once it is released in the root medium, it is under very low pressure, considerably less than one pound per square inch (psi). Pressure at the boiler serves the purpose of driving the steam through the lines to the root medium. For this purpose, a pressure at the boiler of 10 to 15 psi is practical. It is true that the heat content of steam rises as it is put under pressure. However, the increase in heat content is small and a high pressure system must be justified on other grounds, such as heat distribution in a large greenhouse range. When steam pressure is increased to 50 psi, the temperature rises to about 297°F (146°C) and the additional heat content increases by only 29 Btu over steam at zero pressure.

Figure 6-4. A portable steam generator used for producing steam for root media pasteurization in situations where steam cannot be generated by the heating system of the greenhouse range. (*Photo courtesy of J. W. Love, Department of Horticultural Science, North Carolina State University, Raleigh, NC 27607*)

Steam Distribution

Steam should be conducted from the portable steam generator or main steam line in the greenhouse through a low pressure steam hose with a two-inch inside diameter. Couplings on the hose should be full flow, i.e., with a full 2-inch inside diameter. The hose costs about $3.60 per linear foot and couplings are $6.00 each. If steam is provided from a central boiler, there should be a valve in each greenhouse section from which steam can be obtained (Figure 6-5).

Steam is distributed in fresh flower ground beds through buried perforated pipes. For beds three feet wide, one row is buried; for four-foot beds, two rows are used. Used rain gutters, used boiler flue tubes, irrigation pipe, and other materials can be used for this purpose. A pair of holes 1/8 to 1/4 inch in diameter should be drilled on opposite sides every six inches to distribute steam. The end of each pipe is plugged with a cap. A simple pipe manifold can be assembled to distribute steam from the inlet hose to each pipe (Figure 6-6).

Many older ground beds, particularly in rose ranges, were constructed with a concrete V-shaped bottom. At the lowest point in the V a drainage tile

Figure 6-5. When steam is provided by a central boiler for root media pasteurization, it is best to have a permanent steam line in each greenhouse from which steam can be obtained for this purpose. A subsurface steam line with periodic risers is used in the above situation to minimize the length of steam hose and the amount of labor required.

Figure 6-6. An easily constructed steam line manifold. The four-foot-wide bench pictured above is best pasteurized with two perforated steam conduction pipes buried in the root medium.

was installed along the length of the bed. Steam can be very effectively applied through this tile, minimizing the equipment and labor of set-up needed. Ground beds without bottoms can present another problem. Disease organisms and nematodes can exist below the point that the soil has been loosened. Steam does not penetrate rapidly into this hard area. Harmful organisms below this point can return to the upper levels where roots grow after pasteurization. It is best to bury the steam conduction pipes at the bottom of the rototilled root medium. This results in deeper penetration of steam and also prevents nematodes and symphillids from escaping by burrowing deeper ahead of the steam.

Raised benches filled with root medium may be pasteurized with or without buried steam conduction pipes. If used, they are buried at half the depth of the soil. Other growers inject steam between the cover and the root medium through five-inch diameter canvas hoses. Once the cover is inflated, steam readily penetrates the loosened root medium. Time required to reach the minimum temperature for pasteurization can be shorter when the conduction pipes are used, particularly in heavy media.

Empty raised benches also can be pasteurized with steam distributed through a five-inch diameter canvas hose costing about 40 cents per linear foot. The hose is slipped over the end of the steam hose and tied in place. It is then placed on the root medium and the distant end is tied closed with a piece of wire. The hose should be wet before pasteurizing to speed up the initial release of steam. Although an easier system to set up than the buried steam pipes, it can require a longer time for steam to penetrate the root medium.

Potting media is best pasteurized in a wagon equipped with perforated steam pipes at the bottom or a perforated false bottom with steam chamber below. Such wagons have already been described in Chapter 5. Ideally the sides of such wagons can be lowered to a horizontal position to serve as potting benches.

Fields of soil also can be steam pasteurized and are commonly done so in chrysanthemum production areas such as Florida and California. It would be quicker to inject methyl bromide into the soil by tractor, but this would not completely kill verticillium wilt—a very devastating and prevalent disease of chrysanthemums in the production fields. Steam is effective against this disease. The boiler may be in a fixed central location or may be mounted on a truck so that it may be moved from field to field. Steam is conducted from the boiler by a steam hose across the field to a steam rake (Figure 6-7). The rake consists of a four-inch pipe header 12 feet long which is drawn perpendicular to a cable which pulls it across the field. Projecting down into the soil from the header are 16- to 18-inch blades spaced nine inches apart. Behind each blade is a ½-inch pipe carrying steam from the header to the soil at the lower rear side of each blade. A winch is often used to draw the rake across the field at a rate of 10 to 20 inches per minute. One acre of soil can be pasteurized by a single rake in 40 to 70 hours of operating time. A sterilizing cover is attached to the back side of the header and is thus dragged across the field. The cover should be sufficiently long to require 30 minutes to pass over any given point in the field. The cover should be 600 inches (50 feet) long for a rake moving at 20 inches per minute. The cover serves to hold the steam in the soil so that the soil temperature will be maintained at or above 160°F for 30 minutes.

The coldest spot during pasteurization is at the end of the bench or trailer where the steam enters and usually near the outer wall at this end. A thermometer should be placed in the coldest spot. Pasteurization should not be stopped until the coldest spot reaches the temperature and time conditions desired. If the thermometer were placed in a warm spot, pasteurization would stop before harmful organisms were killed in the colder areas. These areas would become a source of innoculation for the remainder of the soil. Because of the lack of competition, the harmful organisms would spread rapidly. It would be better not to pasteurize the soil than to do an incomplete job such as this.

The cold spot in a greenhouse bench can be corrected by applying an extra quantity of steam at that point. Figure 6-8 shows a system for doing this. A short piece of pipe is connected to and run parallel to the steam conduction pipe at the point where it enters the root media being pasteurized.

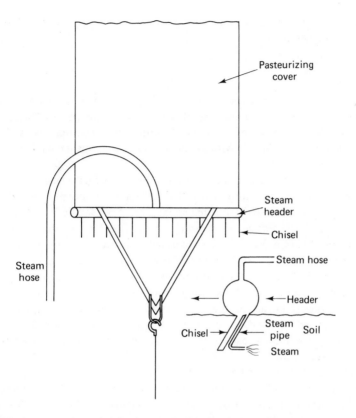

Figure 6-7. A steam rake used for pasteurizing soil in the field. Steam is conducted via hose to a a 12-foot-long header. Chisels about 9 inches apart project into the soil at a distance of 16 to 18 inches. Small pipes behind each chisel carry steam into the soil to the depth of the chisels. A pasteurizing cover is drawn behind the rake to maintain a high soil temperature for 30 minutes. The rake itself often is drawn across the field by a cable and winch.

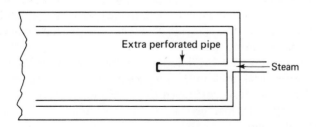

Figure 6-8. An extra perforated steam conduction pipe (center of bed) used to deliver additional steam to the cold end of a bed to prevent excessive pasteurization time.

The extra piece of pipe has numerous perforations on opposite sides spaced about two inches apart.

Covers

Without a cover, steam will quickly rise through the root medium and be lost, further reducing the efficiency of an already inefficient use of steam. Covers are placed over media during pasteurization to catch and hold steam in close contact with media so it can be of further value in raising the temperature.

Basically there are three types of covers—polyethylene, vinyl, and neoprene-coated nylon fabric. Polyethylene film has the shortest life expectancy but is the cheapest, costing about 2 cents per square foot. It may be used several times during one season of pasteurization but does not store from season to season. Vinyl covers are usually purchased in 8 mil thicknesses. They are advertised to last for up to 25 uses. Actually these covers last much longer if handled properly and stored away from sunlight. Ultraviolet light breaks down vinyl plastic. These vinvyl covers cost about 8 cents per square foot. The longest lasting of the covers is the neoprene-coated nylon fabric which is claimed to stand use up to 100 times, but will actually last well beyond 200 times if dried each time it is stored. These covers cost about 24 cents per square foot.

Covers used on benches with smooth outer side walls do not have to be fastened to benches. They should overhang each side by one foot or more. As steam contacts the inner side of the cover it condenses and moistens that side. The film of water which forms between the outer side of the bench and the inner side of the cover causes the two to stick together preventing the cover from blowing off as steam builds up under it. Covers used on benches with outside posts or rough side boards must be fastened to the bench. The simplest method is to lay a chain or other heavy object over the cover against the inner side wall of the bench (Figure 6-9). Some growers squeeze the cover between the top of the bench side and a lath strip with a clamp. Other growers with wooden benches place a lath strip over the cover at the top, outer sides of the bench and nail the lath to the bench. This puts holes in the cover which is undesirable, particularly in the case of the higher quality cover which must be used many times.

Thirty minutes after 160°F has been achieved the steam should be shut off. The cover will fall back to the root media and then it can be cautiously removed. When the media has cooled to a comfortable working temperature, seeds and young plants may be planted. This can require from four to eight hours depending upon depth and moisture content. Media pasteurized with aerated steam can be cooled much faster by using the aerator to pass cool air through the soil for 30 minutes after the cover has been removed.

Figure 6-9. When the outer side of a bed or bench wall is uneven, rough, or short, the pasteurizing cover must be fastened to prevent lifting by steam beneath. The simplest method is to weight it down with heavy objects such as chain or pipe.

After-Steaming Problems

There are two toxicity problems that can occur as a result of steam pasteurization. One is manganese toxicity and the other is ammonium toxicity. Large quantities of manganese exist in many soils. Fortunately, a small but adequate amount is available for plant use while the majority is in an unavailable form. Steam pasteurization results in further conversion of unavailable to available manganese. The longer the soil is steamed, the greater is the buildup of available manganese and, hence, the greater the risk of manganese toxicity. It is important that media containing field soil be pasteurized at the recommended temperature for only the length of time necessary, 30 minutes. Soilless media usually constitute no problem since the components contain little or no manganese.

A high level of manganese in the plant is toxic in itself causing tip burn of leaves. High levels of manganese in the root medium also interfere with the root uptake of iron; in fact, iron deficiency is commonly caused by high available manganese levels.

Root media which contain organic matter rich in nitrogen can release ammonium nitrogen during pasteurization and may continue to release it for a few weeks. Manure, highly decomposed peats, leaf mold, and composts are examples of such materials. Microorganisms feed upon the organic matter for the carbon, nitrogen, etc. contained in it. When there is an overabundance of nitrogen contained in it, much will be released for plant use. As illustrated in Figure 6-10, ammonifying bacteria convert nitrogen in organic matter to ammonium nitrogen and then nitrifying bacteria convert the ammonium nitrogen to nitrate nitrogen.

Most plants grow best on a mixture of ammonium and nitrate forms of nitrogen. Many may be injured by ammonium nitrogen alone, e.g., poinsettia and rose, or will grow less vigorously. Normally, ammonium nitrogen is continuously converted to nitrate nitrogen by soil bacteria so there is always a mixture. During pasteurization ammonifying and nitrifying bacteria are nearly eliminated. In a few weeks the ammonifying bacteria population builds back to an effective level and sizeable quantities of ammonium nitrogen are released from organic matter. It is not until three to six weeks after pasteurization that nitrifying bacteria generally build back to a population size where they can cope with the ammonium nitrogen being released. In the meantime, two to six weeks after pasteurization, toxic quantities of ammonium nitro-

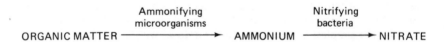

Figure 6-10. Ammonium toxicity can be a problem when organic materials rich in nitrogen are pasteurized with either steam or chemicals. Nitrogen contained in organic matter is released as ammonium when ammonifying microorganisms, including bacteria, fungi, and actinomycetes, break down the organic matter in order to utilize its carbon content. Nitrifying bacteria, in turn, convert ammonium to nitrate nitrogen. During pasteurization, both populations of microorganisms are reduced to low levels. The ammonifying organisms build back to an effective level before the nitrifying organisms. During the interim period, plants are prone to ammonium injury.

gen may develop. This may burn the roots of plants and cause stunting of the entire plant as well as wilting of the tops. Most any type of nutrient deficiency can ensue as a result of the root injury. Once the nitrifying population becomes large, the high levels of ammonium nitrogen are converted to nitrate nitrogen which is less toxic to plants and is more readily leached from the root medium during watering. Because of these lower levels and the fact that many plants can tolerate higher levels of nitrate than ammonium nitrogen, the problem usually ends at this time.

It is mainly for this reason that the use of manure gave way to peatmoss during the 1950s when pasteurization became popular. Peatmoss, because of its low nitrogen content and slow rate of decomposition, does not support a toxic buildup of ammonium nitrogen.

There is a third event which can occur from oversteaming of media that attracts considerable attention but is not harmful. The fungus *Pezziza ostrachoderma* will build into a large conspicuous population when competition from other microorganisms is reduced by overpasteurization (too high a temperature or excessive time). The fungus forms spores at the medium surface which are at first white, then yellow, and finally brown. Another fungus, *Pyronema* sp., forms pink spores. These fungi do not attack plants, but their common occurrence serves to illustrate the ease with which a disease organism can get a foothold in overpasteurized media where competition has been suppressed.

CHEMICAL PASTEURIZATION

Chemicals offer an alternative to steam for the grower who does not heat with a steam boiler and is too small to afford a portable steam generator. It is also appealing to the grower who grows only one crop a year, such as bedding plants, and as a result does not want to invest much in initial equipment. The field grower of crops other than chrysanthemum would also see a value in chemical pasteurization because it can be applied much more rapidly than steam.

Counterbalancing these three advantages of chemicals are three disadvantages. Chemically treated media cannot be used for young plants for ten days after treatment. For fresh flower crops, costly overhead continues during this time. Chemicals are injurious to humans and stringent safety precautions must be taken. While steam amd methyl bromide may be used in a greenhouse containing plants, chloropicrin may not.

Methyl Bromide

Methyl bromide is available under various trade names and in different combinations with chloropicrin. Methyl bromide is extremely hazardous to humans and for this reason a small quantity, usually 2 percent, of tear gas (chloropicrin) is added as an irritant to warn against exposure. It is available in 1- and 1-1/2-pound cans or larger cylinders for tractor mounting. It is a liquid under pressure which turns to gas when released. Methyl bromide is effective against disease organisms, insects, nematodes, and weed seeds.

Root media should be worked up to a loose state for rapid penetration of the gas and should be at a moisture content desired for planting. Media at 40°F (4°C) or lower should not be treated. It is best if the media is 50°F (10°C) or higher. A potting medium is placed in a container or on a hard, flat surface preferably not over one foot deep. Cans of methyl bromide are placed adjacent to the pile or to the bench and are used at the rate of one pound per cubic yard of medium. The can is placed in an applicator as pictured in Figure 6-11. A tube extends from the applicator to the top of the root medium where it is placed in an open saucer or can to collect any liquid that might come out with the gas. From here it can quickly evaporate. If it were to enter the medium as a liquid it might take several days longer to evaporate than anticipated and in the meantime would be injurious to plants. A polyethylene cover is placed over the bench or pile. In the bench it can be weighted down by chain along the edges and for the pile application it can be weighted down along the edges with sand. Clay pots or wooden blocks should be placed on the root medium to hold the cover up so that the gas can contact all of the surface.

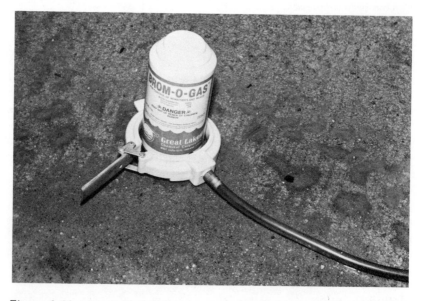

Figure 6-11. An applicator for small cans of methyl bromide. The can is placed in a ring. As the ring is clamped tight, a hollow spike punctures the can. Methyl bromide liquid under pressure expands to gas as it exits from the spike into a plastic tube that conducts it to the root medium pile. It is used at the rate of 1 pound per cubic yard of medium.

When the medium is ready for pasteurization, the handle on the applicator is closed. As this is done a hollow spike is driven into the can allowing methyl bromide to escape through the tube to the space between the medium and the cover. The medium should be exposed to the gas with the cover on for at least 24 hours at temperatures of 60°F (15°C) and higher. At the cooler temperature of 50°F the exposure time should be 48 hours. The cover is then removed and the medium is left undisturbed to aerate for 24 hours (48 hours at 50°F). After this time it may be handled. Seeds can be safely planted after three days of aeration but plants including cuttings and seedlings should not be planted for seven to ten days.

Methyl bromide should not be used in a greenhouse where there are other plants unless full ventilation can be provided during the process. Carnations are susceptible to even slight concentrations of methyl bromide so it is best not to use this chemical for this crop. Cauliflower, salvia, and snapdragon may sustain a moderate degree of distorted growth from media not thoroughly aerated.

Methyl bromide can be applied by tractor in the field. A cylinder of methyl bromide is pressurized and the gas conducted through plastic tubes to a row of chisels mounted behind the tractor six to eight inches apart (Figure 6-12). The gas is released at the bottom of the chisels four to six inches deep. Also mounted to the back of the tractor is a roll of polyethylene film. The end is buried at the beginning of the row to anchor it. As the tractor moves across the field the plastic sheet is unrolled. The leading edge of the first sheet is buried with soil by a disc mounted to the tractor. Subsequent sheets are glued to the preceding sheet to form one continuous covering over the field.

A rig such as the one described sells for about $1,200 and can be depreciated over ten years. Three men with one tractor rig can treat up to five acres in one day. Other materials include two rolls of 1 mil polyethylene 7.5 feet by 4,000 feet ($170) and 240 pounds actual methyl bromide ($210) per acre. Custom applicators can be hired at a rate of about $700 per acre by those who are not set up to apply the chemical themselves.

Methyl bromide, like steam, greatly reduces the populations of ammonifying and nitrifying bacteria. The same toxic build-up of ammoniacal nitrogen can occur if organic matter rich in nitrogen and capable of rapid breakdown is used.

Chloropicrin

This fumigant, also known as tear gas, is a popular choice for carnation crops because of their sensitivity to methyl bromide. Chloropicrin, however, cannot be used in a greenhouse where there are plants. Another disadvantage of chloropicrin is its poor penetration into plant tissue in root media.

Chloropicrin is used at the rate of three cc (cubic centimeters) per square foot of bench or field surface and for bulk media at the rate of three

(a)

(b)

(c)

Figure 6-12. Tractor-mounted rig for injecting gaseous chemicals into field soil for pasteurization. (a) Chisels extend into the soil. Behind each is a tube that delivers the gas into the soil. A rake follows to seal the holes made by the chisels. (b) A roll of polyethylene film is located behind the rake. At the beginning of the row the end of the polyethylene is anchored by burying it in the soil. As the tractor moves across the field, the film unrolls. (c) One side of the film is buried by a disc while the other side is glued to the previous sheet of plastic. Up to five acres of field can be treated by three people in one day with a single tractor. (*Photo courtesy of W. A. Skroch, Department of Horticultural Science, North Carolina State University, Raleigh, NC 27607*)

to five cc per cubic foot. Chloropicrin is injected into media in the greenhouse by a hand injector. A spike at the base of the injector is pushed by foot into the medium. As this occurs three cc of liquid chloropicrin is released from the end of the spike. The injector is inserted on twelve-inch centers. After application, the bench or pile of medium is covered with a polyethylene cover. Chloropicrin may be injected through tractor-drawn chisels in the field. The usual practice outdoors is to thoroughly moisten the top inch of soil with water to seal in the chloropicrin.

Chloropicrin should not be used at media temperatures below $60°F$ ($15°C$); $70°F$ ($21°C$) is best. An exposure time of one to three days is needed, the longer time being needed at $60°F$. Media should be aerated for seven to 10 days before planting in it.

Residue Test

Wet, heavy, or cold media are slow to release chemical fumigants upon aeration. A grower must be certain that the residue is below an injurious level before planting his crop. A simple lettuce test can determine this.

Fill a few jars 3/4 full with treated medium. The medium should be at a moisture content for planting. Wet it if necessary. Place wet, one-inch squares of absorbent cotton on the medium and on each square of cotton place ten to fifteen lettuce seeds which were presoaked in water for 30 minutes. Seal the jars tightly as soon as possible and place at room temperature in an area where they receive daylight. (Lettuce seed will not germinate in the dark.) Prepare some other jars in the same manner, using untreated medium as a control. After two days the seed in the control should have germinated as well as those in the treated medium jars if the residue is down to a safe level. If the seeds fail to germinate in the treated media jars, aerate the medium longer. It will help to mix or rototill the medium.

RE-INOCULATION

Root media pasteurization serves the purpose of eradicating biological pests. It does not provide a resistance to these pests. The grower must think through all his operations in which he might introduce contaminated media to clean media.

Pots and flats are of first concern. If they have been used before, they contain media and possibly plant tissue which could be contaminated. These should be cleaned. Clay and wooden containers can be steamed along with root media. Plastic pots, however, will distort at that high temperature. Plastic pots as well as clay and wooden containers can be treated with the chemical fumigants.

Tools are another source of disease inoculum. They should be periodically disinfected to prevent the spread of any disease which might be present in the range and certainly before using a recently pasteurized medium. A solution of a disinfectant such as LF-10$_{®}$ (sold by florist supply houses) should be maintained in a bucket conveniently located in the head house and in the greenhouses so that tools can be easily dipped in it. Household bleach diluted 1:9 with water serve well also but it will break down in the sunlight in a few days.

Another common source of contamination is the soil on the soles and heels of shoes. It is a great temptation to place one foot on the side of a bench when conversing with someone else in a greenhouse. This is an efficient way to transfer inoculum. Most visitors have an interest in plants and have probably been in another greenhouse range or a garden recently. The probability of them carrying contaminated soil is great. It should be a standard rule around the greenhouse that feet are to be kept off the benches. Some growers place a fiber mat in a shallow tray of a disinfectant solution at the entry to their range so that everyone steps through it, disinfecting his shoes before entering. This is particularly wise for a propagation greenhouse where disease prevention is an even more serious matter.

Plastic watering systems become distorted when left under the cover during steam pasteurization. They are customarily removed or raised above the bench during pasteurization. They should be syringed with household bleach diluted 1:9 with water or with a disinfectant such as LF-10$_{®}$ before placing them back on the root medium. In a small operation these pipes may be wiped with a rag saturated with disinfectant. The thin tubes and weights used in automatic pot watering systems should be dipped in a container of disinfectant. Wire and string supports for fresh flowers should likewise be sterilized before being reused on a recently pasteurized bench.

For pasteurization to be effective, the grower must think through all operations to identify and correct those which can cause re-inoculation of the growing media. Means exist to insure a clean range. Where failure occurs it is due to a lack of foresight.

ECONOMICS

Steam pasteurization is the cheapest system when the steam can be obtained from an already existent heating system. An average of 5600 Btu of boiler capacity are required to supply the 2,800 Btu needed to pasteurize one cubic foot of root medium. One gallon of oil with an approximate heat content of 135,000 Btu and a burning efficiency of 75 percent provides sufficient heat to pasteurize 18 cubic feet of soil. The fuel cost per cubic foot is therefore $0.022 per cubic foot based on a price of $0.40 per gallon.

Methyl bromide in one pound cans can be purchased for $1.25 and is sufficient to treat 27 cubic feet of soil. The unit price here is $0.045 per cubic foot, about twice the cost of steam.

There are other considerations. A large operator could easily depreciate the cost of a portable steam generator and still end up pasteurizing his root media for less than $0.045 per cubic foot. A small grower, or one who operates only during one season per year, often finds that he cannot stay under the cost of chemical pasteurization if he must purchase a portable steam generator.

For the purpose of illustration, a one-acre greenhouse range could be expected to have 29,000 square feet of bench area containing 16,900 cubic feet of root media. A $2400 steam generator depreciated over ten years would add $0.014 to each cubic foot of media for a total oil plus equipment cost of $0.036, which is cheaper than chemical pasteurization.

One last factor must be considered and that is the cost of labor required to carry out each method of pasteurization. Preparation of media is the same in each alternative, calling for a loose, moderately moist condition. Covers are needed for each alternative also. The difference lies principally in the steam conduction hose or pipes to the bench and in the bench. This is a very small consideration and would not be likely to influence the decision as to which system to use.

SUMMARY

1. Greenhouse root media should be pasteurized at least once per year, and more often as required, to rid them of harmful disease organisms, nematodes, insects, and weed seed.

2. Numerous microorganisms develop in root medium which are not harmful. These can be beneficial by providing competition for harmful microorganisms which might otherwise proliferate. For this reason root media are pasteurized and not sterilized, i.e., only some organisms are killed.

3. Root media may be pasteurized with steam by raising it to a temperature of 140–160°F for 30 minutes.

4. Volatile chemicals also are used for pasteurizing root media. Methyl bromide is most popular although chloropicrin is used as well, mostly for carnation crops since this crop is injured by methyl bromide residues for a few months after application. Chemical pasteurization precludes the need for a steam boiler, an advantage for small growers.

5. Both steam and chemical pasteurization require that the root medium be loose and of a moisture content suitable for planting. Amendments such as peatmoss, manure, and bark should be incorporated prior to pasteurization to prevent introduction of diseases or pests.

6. Pasteurization can result in ammonium and manganese toxicities in certain situations. If the root medium contains organic matter rich in nitrogen, such as manure, steam and chemical pasteurization can result in an excessive release of ammonium, particularly in the period of two to six weeks after pasteurization. Either these materials should be avoided or an adjustment be made in the watering practice to insure adequate leaching of ammonium.

Many soils contain large levels of manganese, most of which is unavailable. Steam pasteurization causes a conversion of unavailable manganese to an available form. A toxic level is sometimes reached. This is another case for pasteurizing root media at a low temperature (160°F) and for only the necessary length of time (30 minutes).

7. Pasteurization of root media is designed to eliminate harmful organisms. It does not protect against future infestation. Good sanitation practices must be employed to maintain clean conditions. Some considerations include disease-free seeds and plants, sterilization of containers and tools, a pesticide program, foot baths, a clean working area, sanitation outside the greenhouse, and proper control of temperature and humidity.

SUGGESTED READINGS

Baker, K. F. ed. "The UC System for Producing Healthy Container-Grown Plants." University of California, Agricultural Experimental Station-Extension Service Manual 23. 1957.

Ball, V. ed. *The Ball Red Book.* Geo. J. Ball, Inc. West Chicago, IL, 1975. pp. 91–117.

Bunt, A. C. *Modern Potting Composts.* The Pennsylvania State University Press, University Park, PA 1976. pp. 229–251.

Gray, H. E. 1960 "Steam Sterilization." *Florists' Review* 127(3292):13–14, 77–79.

Griffin, R., R. Maire, and W. Humphrey. "Sterilizing Nursery Soils with Steam—a New Method." University of California, Agricultural Extension Service Publication AXT-177. 1965.

Chapter 7

Watering

Watering is the greenhouse operation that most frequently accounts for loss in crop quality. Taken at face value it would appear to be the simplest operation. When performed correctly it is simple and perhaps a bit boring. For this reason the task is often assigned to one of the less experienced employees. If this inexperienced employee waters at the wrong time or uses an incorrect amount of water the crop is injured. The original quality cannot be regained.

The decision of when to water should be made by the greenhouse manager. He should inspect every bench of plants daily and he should supervise the watering operation when it is carried out by another employee. Actually with the wide variety of inexpensive automatic watering systems available today, the range should be equipped with a system simple enough to permit the manager to do the actual watering as he inspects the range. The few minutes it takes for each section to be watered affords him a chance to further inspect plants in that section for insects, disease, nutritional disorders, and any other problems. Success or failure is not due so much to the quantity of labor expended but rather to the correct timing of the various labor operations. It is of utmost importance that the greenhouse range be inspected daily by the most knowledgeable person and that work plans be altered by his findings.

EFFECTS OF WATERING ON PLANTS

Underwatering

When water is not applied frequently enough the plant wilts, retarding photosynthesis and slowing growth. The elongation of young developing cells is reduced, resulting in smaller leaves, shorter stem internodes (the length of stem between leaves), and in general a hardened appearance to the plant. In more extreme cases a burn may begin on the margin of leaves and spread inward, affecting the whole leaf. On some types of plants the leaves drop off.

Overwatering

When water is applied a little too frequently, new growth may become large but soft as a result of high water content and, as a whole, plants tend to be taller. This is an undesirable situation because some of these plants wilt easily under bright light or dry conditions and do not ship or last well. If water is applied even more frequently, the oxygen content of the root medium is reduced by the higher average content of water in the pores, resulting in damage to the roots. A damaged root system cannot readily take up water or nutrients. This causes wilting, hardened growth, an overall stunting of the plant, and several nutrient deficiency symptoms.

RULES OF WATERING

Rule 1. Use a Well-Drained Medium

The importance of texture and structure was brought out in Chapter 5. If your medium is not well-drained and aerated then it is not possible to water properly. Either you will underwater to achieve aeration or you will provide the required water at the expense of aeration. In either case poor plant quality will result. A well-drained medium of high water-holding capacity is required for use in containers. This calls for coarse texture and a high degree of stable structure—in short, a formulated medium and not field soil alone.

Rule 2. Water Thoroughly Each Time

Because media cannot be partially wetted, it is important to water all of the medium in a container each time water is applied (Figure 7-1). Water applied to the medium surface enters the pores at the top and adheres to the particle surfaces making up the pore walls. Additional water causes the layer on the particle surfaces to become thicker. Eventually the layer of water becomes thick enough that any additional water is too far away from the particle surface to be held and gravity pulls it down to the next particle below. There it is attracted to the particle surface, and as more water enters, the water layer on this particle grows thicker. This process keeps repeating itself until water finally reaches the particles at the bottom of the container. Additional water then flows through the medium and out the bottom of the container.

Figure 7-1. Only half of the amount of water the soil in the beaker is capable of holding was applied. Instead of all the particles being partially wetted, those at the top are thoroughly   wetted, while those at the bottom remain completely dry. This points out the fallacy of trying to partially water a root medium.

If six ounces of water are required to water the root medium in one pot and only three ounces of water are applied, the medium in the top half of the pot will be thoroughly wetted while medium in the lower half will remain dry. Late in the afternoon or on Saturdays there is always a temptation to water a crop partially to carry it over until more time is available for watering. From the discussion above one can readily see the fallacy of doing this. Medium in the lower part of the pot or bench would not receive water and as it continued to dry, roots would die.

It is important to apply, in addition to the amount of water needed for wetting all medium, an additional amount. Ten percent of the water applied to a pot or bench should run out of the bottom of the container. This is done to leach excessive fertilizers and nonfertilizer elements which might otherwise build up to toxic levels. Some of the fertilizers used contain elements which are not used in large quantity by the plant. As fertilizer is repeatedly applied to provide the elements needed in large quantity, these other elements accumulate.

As a general rule of thumb for soil-based media, 1/15 gallon of water should be applied to each square foot of bench for each inch of root medium depth. A typical eight-inch-deep bench containing seven inches of medium should receive 7/15 gallon of water, or in practical terms, 1/2 gallon of water per square foot. A six-inch azalea pot requires about six ounces of water. This rule applies to the application of nutrient solution as well as straight water. These quantities of water should be checked out for your situation since media vary in water-holding capacity. Larger or smaller quantities may be justified for various soilless media.

Rule 3. Water When Moisture Stress Occurs

It is apparent from Rule 2 that overwatering does not refer to the amount of water applied during a single application. Overwatering indicates that water is applied too frequently. When this is done too much of the lifetime of the root is spent under conditions of minimum aeration and as a result root development is suppressed.

Water should be applied just before or, for some crops, when the plant enters into the early symptoms of water stress. For each plant these signs are different. Some plants such as chrysanthemum take on a darker leaf color, others such as begonia turn toward a grey-green leaf color. By observing a crop one can quickly learn the early warning signs of moisture stress. It is important that the color and feel of the root medium associated with early moisture stress also be learned. Some crops, such as azalea, do not show signs of moisture stress until permanent damage occurs to the roots. Judgment of when to water rests entirely on media appearance, feel, and weight.

WATER QUALITY

It is very important that the chemical content of water be known before using it in the greenhouse. A common problem is that of a high salt content. This occurs frequently along coastal areas where seawater may infiltrate the ground water. Quantities of sodium bicarbonate or sodium chloride can become high enough to be injurious. Ground water in the southwestern United States can contain excessive quantities of sodium and boron. A total soluble salt reading gives a good assessment of this problem.

Table 7-1 lists several classes of water quality based on total salt content, relative sodium content, and boron content. If your water source is rated permissible, precautionary measures must be taken. The specific elements making up the salts in your water should be avoided or at least reduced in the fertilizer program. The influence of these salts on media pH should be assessed and compensated. The most common problem is with alkaline (high pH) water which can cause a rise in root media pH. Adjustment of the pH level of the water is expensive. It is easier to adjust the pH of the media downward periodically with an application of sulfur or aluminum sulfate. When high salt levels exist in the water supply the medium should never be allowed to dry excessively since this tends to concentrate the salts and

Table 7-1
Permissible Limits for Electrical Conductivity, Total Dissolved Salts, Percent Sodium,
and Concentration of Boron for Several Classes of Irrigation Water

CLASS OF WATER	ELECTRICAL CONDUCTIVITY (mho/cm × 10⁻⁵ at 77°F–25°C)	TOTAL DISSOLVED SALTS (ppm)	SODIUM (% of Total Salts)	BORON (ppm)
Excellent	< 25	< 175	< 20	< 0.33
Good	25–75	175–525	20–40	0.33–0.67
Permissible	75–200	525–1,400	40–60	0.67–1.00
Doubtful	200–300	1,400–2,100	60–80	1.00–1.25
Unsuitable	> 300	$> 2,100$	> 80	> 1.25

Source: Wilcox, L. V. 1948. "The Quality of Water for Irrigation Use." USDA Technical
Bulletin 962, pp. 15, 27.

aggravate the problem. If your water falls into the doubtful or unsuitable
categories you should seek a different water source, or if need be, locate in a
different area.

City water is not free of problems. Chlorination of water normally does
not affect greenhouse crops. Fluoridation does cause injury to some crops.
The 1 ppm concentration of fluoride which is added to many water supplies
to reduce the incidence of tooth decay is injurious to some green plants;
notable among them is *Cordyline terminalis* Kunth, Baby Doll. Here it is
best to avoid fluoridated water. The pH level of the root media can also be
raised to tie up fluoride.

WATERING SYSTEMS

Hand Watering

Hand watering today is uneconomical. A grower can only afford hand
watering where a crop is still concentrated, such as in seed flats or when he is
"spot watering," i.e., watering a few select pots or areas which have dried
sooner than other areas. We will consider first the price of hand watering a
bench 4 feet wide by 100 feet long and then compare this to automatic systems in a bench of equal size. The price of materials in each system is based
on minimum order rates which maximizes the cost. The water main to the
base of each bench is not calculated into the cost of each system. The labor
of installation is not included either, but is quite minimal. In all cases the
labor saved will pay for the system in less than one year.

A 400-square foot bench with a fresh flower crop requires 200 gallons of water at each watering. The frequency of watering can range from once a week in the darker part of the winter to more than three times a week during the summer. Taking a conservative average of two times per week, this bench is watered 104 times in a year. At a water flow rate of 8 gallons per minute which is not uncommon for a 3/4-inch hose, 25 minutes is required to apply 200 gallons. For the whole year 43.3 hours are spent watering one 4 by 100 foot bench. At an hourly rate of $3.00 per hour, this costs $130.00

It soon will be apparent that this cost is too high. In addition to this deterrent, there is a great risk of applying too little water or of waiting too long between waterings. Hand watering requires considerable time and is very boring. It is usually performed by the lower paid employees. Often the temptation to speed up the job or put it off to another time wins out. Automatic watering is rapid and easy and is performed by a manager. The temptation to submit to error is greatly lessened.

Where hand watering is practiced, a water breaker should be used on the end of the hose as pictured in Figure 7-2. Such a device breaks the force of the water, permitting a higher flow rate without washing root media out of the bench or pot. It also lessens the risk of disrupting the structure of the medium surface.

Figure 7-2. The device on the end of the hose is a water breaker. It reduces the force of water striking the root medium by increasing the cross-sectional area through which it flows. Reduced water pressure results in minimized breakdown of root medium structure and loss of medium from containers.

Perimeter Watering for Fresh Flowers

Perimeter watering consists of a plastic pipe around the perimeter of the bench with nozzles which spray water over the root medium surface below the foliage (Figure 7-3). Either polyethylene or PVC pipe can be used. While PVC pipe is more expensive it does have the advantage of being very stationary. The polyethylene pipe tends to roll if not anchored firmly to the side of the bench. This causes nozzles to rise or fall from proper orientation with the root medium surface.

Nozzles are made of nylon or a hard plastic and are available to put out a spray arc of 180° or 45°. For benches of fresh flowers other than roses up to 42 inches wide and rose benches up to 48 inches wide the 180° nozzles are used and are spaced 30 inches apart. For fresh flowers other than roses in benches 48 inches wide, 180° and 45° nozzles are alternated 20 inches apart. The 45° nozzles project water further than the 180° nozzles. Regardless of the types of nozzles used, they are staggered across the bench so that each projects out between two nozzles on the opposite side. A hole is punched in the polyethylene pipe or drilled in the PVC pipe and the treaded nozzle is then turned in with a wrench.

Figure 7-3. A perimeter watering system for fresh flower production in benches or beds. A polyethylene or PVC pipe carries water around the perimeter of the bed. Plastic or nylon nozzles screwed into the perimeter pipe spray water into the bed below the foliage.

Perimeter watering systems with 180° nozzles require one water valve for benches up to 100 feet in length. For benches over 100 feet and up to 200 feet, a water main should be brought to the middle of the bench and 3/4-inch water valves should be installed on either side, one to service each half of the bench. This system applies 1/10 gallon of water per minute per foot of pipe. Where 180° and 45° nozzles are alternated, the length of the bench serviced by one water valve should not exceed 75 feet.

The cost of this system for a 4- by 100-foot bench with alternate 180° and 45° nozzles is $36.01. This includes PVC pipe and two water valves.

2	3/4″ valves	$ 9.90
12	3/4″ PVC pipe fittings	3.09
210-ft	3/4″ PVC pipe	16.24
120	nozzles	6.78
		$36.01

Dew-Hose® for Fresh Flowers

The Dew-Hose® system utilizes 1-¼-inch wide (when flat) polyethylene tubes which run the length of the bench 8 inches apart. The Dew-Hose® is connected to a 3/4-inch polyethylene pipe which runs across the end of benches up to 60 feet long or crosses the bench at the midpoint of benches up to 120 feet long (Figure 7–4a). Individual Dew-Hose® lengths must not exceed 60 feet. A single 3/4-inch water supply can handle up to 1,200 square feet of level bench.

The Dew-Hose® is manufactured from a flat piece of black, 8 mil polyethylene which is sewn into a tube with plastic thread. Water oozes from the stitching when under pressure (Figure 7–4b). A water pressure of 4 to 9 psi within the Dew-Hose® is applied. To prevent plugging, a 200 mesh strainer should be installed in the water supply.

The cost for this system for a 4- by 100-foot bench is $32.64. It includes a 3/4-inch valve and a header at the midpoint of the bench.

600 ft	Dew-Hose®	$25.08
	Header kit	1.34
5	3/4″ plastic pipe fittings	1.27
1	3/4″ valve	4.95
		$32.64

Ooze-Headers® for Fresh Flowers

This system is similar to the Dew-Hose® except that the tube is run across the bench every 8 inches from a ½-inch polyethylene header pipe along the length of one side of the bench (Figure 7-5). The ooze tubes are

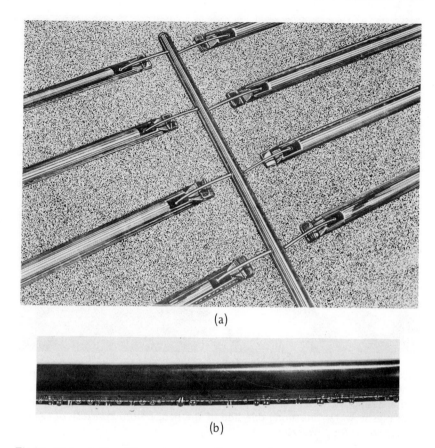

(a)

(b)

Figure 7-4. A Dew-Hose® system of automatic watering for fresh flower production. (a) A supply tube connection for a Dew Hose® or a Twin Wall® watering system. Hoses run the length of the bench and are spaced eight inches apart. (b) Water seeps out of the stitching along one side of each hose. The same method of release occurs in the Ooze Header® and Jumbo Header® systems. (*Photo courtesy of Chapin Watermatics Inc., Watertown, NY 13601.*)

of the same construction as Dew-Hose® but they are 5/8 of an inch wide. They are used in lengths 2 inches shorter than the width of the bench to accommodate the header pipe. Each ooze tube is sealed at both ends, but extending from one end is a thin polyethylene supply tube which is inserted into a hole in the ½-inch polyethylene header pipe. Brass inserts may be installed in the header pipe and holes can be made in the header pipe with a hand punch fashioned after an ice pick or with a Quik-Punch® tool available commercially. The handle of this tool is squeezed and in so doing a punch is driven through one wall of the pipe. The supply tube is immediately pushed into the hole. The flexible wall of the header pipe expands toward the center of the hole, thus squeezing the supply tube to make a watertight seal.

Figure 7-5. An Ooze-Header® system of automatic watering for fresh flower production. Ooze-Headers® run across the bed at eight-inch intervals and are supplied water through a thin polyethylene tube connected to a half-inch plastic water line along one side of the bed. (*Photo courtesy of Chapin Watermatics, Inc., Watertown, NY 13601*)

A water pressure of 4 to 9 psi is used in this system. As much as 1,200 to 1,600 square feet of bench can be handled by a 3/4-inch water supply system.

The Ooze-Header® system drips water slowly onto the root medium surface and depends upon lateral movement of water a distance of 4 inches from either side of each tube. Some media which are unusually porous may undergo channeling of the water downward without sufficient lateral movement to wet all areas of the medium, particularly at the upper surface. If this is the case, puddling from a more rapid application is needed. Jumbo-Oozers® are used for this purpose. These are the same as Ooze-Headers® except that they are 1-¼ inches wide and are attached to a 3/4-inch polyethylene pipe along the length of the bench. One 3/4-inch water supply system will handle 600 to 800 square feet of bench.

The Ooze-Header® system for a 4- by 100-foot bench costs $38.48. This includes a 3/4-inch valve and a ½-inch polyethylene header pipe with 5/8-inch Ooze-Header® tubes every eight inches across the bench. Components of the system are as follows:

100 ft	½" polyethylene pipe	$ 3.78
150	46" Ooze-Headers®	27.89
7	plastic pipe fittings	1.86
1	3/4" valve	4.95
		$38.48

Twin-Wall Hose® for Fresh Flowers

The Twin-Wall® system is becoming more popular than the Dew-Hose® or Ooze-Header® systems because longer lengths of bench can be handled from a single header (up to 250 feet) and because this hose better equalizes water pressure along the length of sloping benches (slopes up to 2 percent). It is one of the best systems for a bench built on a slope.

The Twin-Wall Hose® is made from either 4 mil or 8 mil black polyethylene and is actually a hose inside a hose. Longer benches can be handled with the 8 mil thickness. The inner hose has one hole in its wall for every six holes in the wall of the outer hose (Figure 7-6). For greenhouse purposes an 8-inch spacing between holes in the outer hose is most common. For very porous media a hose with holes 4 inches apart is used. There are several other

Figure 7-6. A Twin-Wall® system for automatic watering of fresh flower crops. The water delivery line consists of a tube within a tube. Water enters through the inner tube, passes through holes in its wall to the space between the two tubes, and finally through holes in the outer tube to the root medium. Holes in the outer tube are spaced four inches apart for coarse-textured media and eight inches apart for finer-textured media. *(Photo courtesy of Chapin Watermatics, Inc., Watertown, NY 13601)*

wider spacings used for field application. Listed in Table 7–2 are the maximum lengths of bench which can be handled by a single 3/4-inch header for level benches and benches with a 1 percent slope (12 in. per 100 feet). For sloping benches the water header should be at the high end.

The Twin-Wall Hose® is purchased in rolls 3000 feet long for 4 mil and 1,500 feet long for 8 mil thicknesses. It is placed on the surface of the medium from end to end in the bench. Individual hoses are spaced 8 inches across the bench. Each end of each hose is folded over double and pinned to the ground with "end holders" supplied by the manufacturer. A small hole is made through the walls of the Twin-Wall Hose® near the inlet end with a piercing tool and a supply tube is inserted through the hole into the inner Twin-Wall Hose®. The other end of the supply tube is connected to a 3/4-inch polyethylene header running across the end of the bench (Figure 7–4a). The recommended working pressure on the inner hose is 3 psi.

A Twin-Wall Hose® system for a 4- by 100-foot bench making use of six lengths of 8 mil hose with outlets every 8 inches and a 3/4-inch polyethylene header with a valve costs $30.70 for components. The cost breakdown is as follows:

600 ft	8 mil Twin-Wall Hose®	$21.60
6	supply tubes	0.48
12	end holders	2.28
1	3/4″ valve	4.95
6	3/4″ plastic fittings	1.39
		$30.70

Table 7–2

Water Flow Rate per 100 feet and Maximum Lengths
of Twin-Wall® Hose from the Inlet for 4 and 8 mil Hoses with
Holes in the Outer Hose Spaced 4 Inches or 8 Inches Apart

OUTLET SPACING (in.)	FLOW PER 100 FT (GPM)	MAXIMUM LENGTH (FT)	
		level	1% slope
	4 mil hose		
4	1.54	140	160
8	0.77	220	270
	8 mil hose		
4	1.54	160	180
8	0.77	250	300

Viaflo® Tubing for Fresh Flowers

Viaflo® porous plastic tubing is made from a patented sheet structure based on linear polyethylene. It is purchased in rolls up to 4,000 feet long as a flattened tube approximately one inch wide. Water is supplied at a pressure of 2 to 5 psi. The tube then becomes round with a 5/8-inch diameter and water passes out through the wall. This tube may be used on the root medium surface or it may be buried. Often in the field it is buried in the ground. Viaflo® tubing is run lengthwise in a bench application. Tubes are spaced 8 inches apart across the bench and are connected to a 3/4-inch polyethylene header running across the bench.

One end of the tubing is tied off and at the water inlet end a feeder tube is inserted and secured with a connector cone and o-rings. The other end of the feeder tube is pressed into a hole punched in the side of a 3/4-inch polyethylene header pipe running across the bench.

Care should be taken not to apply too much pressure since the walls of the tube can rupture. Algae should be cleaned from the tube when it builds up since this will clog the porous wall.

The cost of materials for a Viaflo® system in a 4- by 100-ft bench is $24.94. This includes a valve, 3/4-inch polyethylene header across the end of the bench and six lengths of Viaflo® tubing. Feeder tubes and o-rings are included with each roll of Viaflo® tubing.

600 ft	Viaflo® tubing	$18.60
1	3/4″ valve	4.95
6	3/4″ plastic pipe fittings	1.39
		$24.94

Tube Watering for Potted Plants

This has been the standard for automatic pot watering. Water is carried to each pot by a thin polyethylene tube (Figure 7-7). The tube is available in various inside diameters from different sources including 0.036, 0.045, 0.060, 0.075, and 0.076 inches. The number of pots which can be watered from a single 3/4-inch water main depends upon this inside diameter. The 0.036-, 0.060-, and 0.076-inch tubes can handle 1600, 700, and 400 pots respectively. The narrower diameter tubes are used for small pots where the density is high in the bench and the water requirement per pot is low. This minimizes the expense of laying water lines. The 0.060-inch size is popular for six-inch pots and the 0.075- or 0.076-inch sizes for two to five gallon containers for such items as poinsettia stock plants.

The tube must have a weight at the end in the pot to prevent it from

Figure 7-7. The "tube system" is used for automatic watering of potted plants. Water is carried the length of the bench in a plastic pipe generally located down the center. Each pot is connected to the central pipe by a separate small polyethylene tube. A weight is attached to the end of the tube in each pot to anchor the tube and to break the force of the water before it reaches the root medium.

being thrown from the pot when the water is turned on. The weight further serves the purpose of breaking the force of water so that it does not dig a hole in the root medium. Usually there is a baffle in the weight opposite the end of the tube which breaks the flow of water and permits it to trickle out either side. The weight also prevents light media components from being drawn into the tube and plugging it. When the water is turned off, a suction often occurs which can draw particles into the tube. There are various types of weights sold. One weight consists of a plastic cylinder with the tube entering through the side (Figure 7-7). Drop-in® weights are conical in shape and are made of noncorrosive metal. On-off® tubes are available in the 0.076-inch size and are made from noncorrosive metal. When a pot is removed, the tube can be sealed by pushing the On-off® weight. A quick pull on it turns it on again.

Generally water is provided along the bench by a 3/4-inch polyethylene or PVC pipe. The latter has a longer life expectancy and lies straighter. Tubes to each pot may be connected directly into holes punched or drilled into the water pipe which is usually run down the center of the bench from end to end. The tube can be pushed into the hole directly or a brass insert can be pressed into the hole first and the tube inserted into it. The brass insert facilitates subsequent removal and replacement of tubes. Plugs are available to fill holes left by removed tubes. Each tube must be the same length because the flow rate depends upon the length of the tube. To cut down on the quantity of tubing, particularly in benches with numerous small pots, Long-Header$_{\circledR}$ and Add-A-Header$_{\circledR}$ systems are used. In each case, a number of tubes run from a plastic header, the header in turn being connected to the water main by a single larger tube.

Tube watering can be used for hanging baskets as well (Figure 7-8). A plastic water line is run along the length of the row of baskets. A separate thin polyethylene tube connects each pot to the water line. Some growers install a galvanized water pipe and hang pots directly from it.

Some growers prefer to install a manual valve on the water main and exercise all judgment as to time and duration of water application. Others decide when to water and at that time turn on a Watermatic Scale$_{\circledR}$. The scale is preset to the number of ounces of water desired in each pot. When this quantity is reached the scale tips and turns off the water. A similar scale, EV-2$_{\circledR}$, turns off the water by means of a solenoid switch. Some growers leave the decision of when and how much to water entirely up to automation in the form of a Moist-Scale$_{\circledR}$ (Figure 7-9). The scale is placed on the bench in a position of average dry conditions and a potted plant is set on it. When the pot dries to a preset amount, the scale turns the water system

Figure 7-8. An automatic tube watering system for hanging baskets. Each pot is connected to the plastic water line above by a thin polyethylene tube.

Figure 7-9. A Moist Scale® device for turning water on and off automatically. A representative plant is placed on the scale. It becomes lighter as water is lost and the scale platform rises. A switch beneath the platform activates a solenoid valve which turns the tube watering system on. When a sufficient weight of water has been delivered to the pot and the scale platform settles down, the switch beneath it closes the solenoid water valve.

on by means of a solenoid. Water is delivered to the pot on the scale by a tube the same as all other pots on the bench. As water is applied, the pot becomes heavier and finally reaches a weight which lowers the platform of the scale to a point where a switch under it turns off the water by a solenoid switch. The Moist-Scale® must be periodically adjusted for the increase in plant weight. This system has been very satisfactory where careful attention to the adjustments of the scale have been made.

A tube system of pot plant watering for a 4- by 100-foot bench costs $51.18. This system has a manual valve, a 3/4-inch PVC water main the length of the bed in the center and 400 24-inch tubes with plastic weights and brass inserts where each is connected directly to the water main. The cost of individual components is listed below.

100 ft	3/4″ PVC pipe	$ 9.38
400	24″ 0.060 ID tubes with plastic weights	32.80
400	brass inserts	2.76
1	3/4″ valve	4.95
6	3/4″ PVC pipe fittings	1.29
		$51.18

The manual valve could be replaced in the above system by a Water-matic Valve℞ for $41.00 which can handle up to 1,600 pots with 0.036-inch diameter tubes or by a Moist-Scale℞ package including solenoid and transformer for $94.45. With a 3/4-inch solenoid 1600 pots can be handled by the Moist-Scale℞ and with a 1-¼-inch solenoid 4,400 pots can be handled on 0.036-inch diameter tubes. It is not a fair comparison to enter the price of these automatic controls into the above calculations because undoubtedly a much larger area than 400 square feet would be controlled by these valves.

Mat Watering for Potted Plants

Mat (capillary) watering offers a very good alternative for the pot plant grower who has different pot sizes in his benches during the year (Figure 7-10). The tube system would require a constant removal and addition of tubes to suit the changing pot density. Mat watering is also beneficial to the grower of small potted plants where it is best not to wet the foliage. The number of tubes in such a system would be cumbersome. The mat watering system uses a mat 3/16 to 1/2 inch thick which is kept constantly moist. Pots are set on the mat and take up water by capillarity through holes in the

Figure 7-10. A mat (capillary) watering system for pot plant crops. Water is applied to the mat several times a day through tubes such as Twin-Wall℞, Viaflo℞, or Dew-Hose℞ that are spaced two feet apart. Water moves by capillarity from the mat into the root medium in the pot and maintains a constant moisture content in the pot at all times. Various types of mats are available.

bottom of the pot. Pots of any size can be placed on the mat at one time. No adjustment is needed for shifting pot sizes.

Mat watering is an old system based on subirrigation. Years ago sand was placed in a watertight bench and kept moist. Pots were set in the sand and water continuously rose by capillarity into the root medium in the pots. This system maintains a constant moisture content in the pot and greatly reduces the labor of watering. Several mats developed in Europe are used extensively there. The system has only recently caught on in America.

A number of mats are available, but to use them the bench should be level. A polyethylene sheet is placed on the level bottom of the bench. It is preferable, but not necessary, that it be black to reduce algal growth. A thin sheet of 2 mil is sufficient since its role is to serve as a water barrier. The mat is placed on the polyethylene sheet. Care should be taken to keep the edges of the mat level with the plane of the mat. If they are lower they act as a wick drawing water from the mat and dripping it to the ground. Mats can be cut with a scissors and more than one piece can be used to line a bench by butting the edges together.

Various types of mats are used. One brand makes use of reprocessed cloth while others are composed of virgin synthetic fiber. Three or four layers of newspaper spread over the polyethylene film can serve as a mat. This practice is used commercially in Europe and has been tested successfully in this country.

Watering tubes including Viaflo®, Twin-Wall Hose®, and Dew-Hose® are used to deliver water to the mat. These tubes run the length of the bench and are placed two feet apart. The mat should be kept moist at all times. This will often require water application several times per day. A time clock can be set to activate a solenoid water valve. Overwatering is not a problem because excess water simply drips from the edge of the mat.

Algae is a problem in that it is very unsightly on the mat and on pots, harbors insects, and emits a foul odor upon dying. Some mats will withstand steaming which kills algae. Much of the algae can be washed off periodically under a strong stream of water from the hose. Caution should be exercised here since some mats may not stand up to the pressure. Disinfectants may also be used but should be washed from the mat after use.

Thus far, most fertilization of pots or mat watering in America has been by means of slow-release fertilizer in the root medium. Clear water has been applied to the mat. Nutrient solutions can be applied to the mat but excessively heavy populations of algae build up.

The cost of materials in a mat watering system can range from $53 to $69. The variation is due to the type of mat used. The example system includes a 3/4-inch manual valve, 3/4-inch header system, two lengths of Twin-Wall Hose® for water distribution, and a 2 mil black polyethylene underliner.

400 sq ft	*Mat*		$36.80-$52.17
	Vattex P$_{®}$	$52.17	
	Cap-Mat$_{®}$	52.00	
	Water-Mat$_{®}$	36.80	
200 ft	Twin-Wall Hose$_{®}$		
	plus connectors		5.60
400 sq ft	black, 2 mil polyethylene		4.85
1	3/4″ valve		4.95
5	3/4″ plastic header		
	fittings		1.39

$53.59-$68.96

Overhead Spray for Potted Plants

While the foliage on the majority of crops should be kept dry for disease control purposes there are a few crops which tolerate wet foliage. These crops can most easily and cheaply be irrigated from overhead. Bedding plants, field grown fresh flowers, and azalea liners are crops commonly watered from overhead.

A pipe is installed along the middle of a bed. Riser pipes are installed periodically to a height well above the final height of the crop. Usually 2 feet above bedding flats and 6 feet in fields is sufficient. A nozzle is installed at the top of each riser. Nozzles vary from those which throw a 360° pattern continuously to types which rotate around a 360° circle. Nozzles with a 180° arc can be obtained for the ends of beds. The spray diameter of various nozzles can range up to 36 feet or more.

FURTHER CONSIDERATIONS FOR AUTOMATIC WATERING SYSTEMS

Life Expectancy

It is difficult to assess a life expectancy for each watering system and yet this must be done in order to give proper economic consideration to this form of automation. In general, it can be assumed that the more delicate parts of these systems such as 8 mil polyethylene tubes and plastic nozzles will last five to six years if properly maintained. The mains, valves, and overhead metal nozzles can last considerably longer, particularly if PVC is used.

Problems arise when particles are not strained from well or pond water. These accumulate in the smaller tubes and nozzles. A 100 to 200 mesh strainer should be used in most of these systems. Algae will tend to grow on tubes such as Viaflo$_{®}$, Dew-Hose$_{®}$ and Ooze-Header$_{®}$. Root media particles may build up on them. In order to prevent clogging, such components should be removed and soaked in a disinfectant solution as dictated by the buildup of these materials.

Sterilization

The plastic components of automatic watering systems should not be steam sterilized. This tends to reduce the life expectancy of the polyethylene components and to distort the PVC pipe and plastic nozzles. Prior to steaming, the flexible tubes should be rolled up and the plastic pipe mains should be lifted above the bench and secured to the superstructure above.

Once removed, the watering system must also be sterilized; otherwise there is the risk of recontaminating the bench medium with particles adhering to the watering system. A sponge or rag can be dipped in a pail of disinfectant such as bleach or LF-10® and the pipe and nozzles wiped with this. These materials could also be proportioned into the water line and applied by hose. The flexible water tubes can be removed and soaked in a barrel of disinfectant.

The problem is not so great for pot plant benches because here there isn't any media to be pasteurized. These benches including the watering system may be hosed with a disinfectant.

Automation

It is perhaps best for smaller growers to use manual valves on the watering system. In this way the owner or manager can check each bench daily and the expense of further automation is avoided. Larger ranges tend to have a heavier investment in management which better guarantees careful daily monitoring of all growing areas. Because of the extensive area to be watered, these ranges sometimes install automatic valves.

The simplest control is a time clock. A 30 minute recycle timer in connection with a 7 or 14 day time clock (cost about $65) can control a solenoid valve to apply between 15 seconds and 30 minutes of water at a number of intervals such as hourly for mat watering, daily for pots, and every other day or less frequently for fresh flower beds.

While some growers use a very well drained medium and water every day, most, due to the type of crop or medium, water as needed. Bright and warm conditions increase this frequency and cold or overcast conditions reduce it. The time clock does not always give appropriate control. A solar control switch is better. This instrument has a remote light sensing mechanism which measures solar energy at the point in the greenhouse where the sensor is installed. A given level can be set on the instrument and when it is reached any electrical system plugged into it, such as a solenoid switch on the watering system, can be turned on. Such solar instruments begin at $70.

Invariably, a range investing in automatic water valves will have numerous water zones, each with a solenoid valve. To cut down on the size of the water main and pump, one area is watered at a time. A sequential control instrument is used to coordinate the watering of a number of areas. The sequential control instrument may be turned on manually or it may be activated by a solar control instrument. Once activated, it will open and close any number of solenoid valves, one at a time, for any preset time from 15 seconds to 30 minutes. Manual sequential controllers begin at $200 for eleven-station systems and increase in price according to features included and number of stations activated.

Economics

As one manufacturer states, "Automatic watering doesn't cost, it pays." This is more true of automatic watering than most other systems of automation in the greenhouse. The systems discussed ranged in materials cost from $25 to $69 as compared to a labor cost of $130 for hand watering an equivalent 4- by 100-foot bench for one year. Of course the cost of labor to install the automatic system must be taken into account. Fortunately these systems are constructed of plastic, which is simply slipped together and clamped in the case of polyethylene, or glued together in the case of PVC. Two people could install the system on one bench starting from the water main already existent under or over the bench in about one hour. Even at a wage of $5 per hour this would add only $10 to each system. The labor of operation throughout the year is very negligible since it simply entails opening and closing valves. It can be done by the manager during the rounds he or she would ordinarily make. In a large range a sequential timer could insure that this time is minimized. Taking all materials and labor into consideration, the automatic systems cost less the first year than does hand watering.

Other factors make automatic watering a necessity for greenhouse operators: (1) as already mentioned the ease of watering better insures that water will be applied when needed and in the quantity required; (2) automatic watering provides a means of applying water without wetting the foliage which is very important for the control of disease in African violet, gloxinia, Rieger begonia, primula, cyclamen, and the lower foliage of fresh flower crops; and (3) automatic water systems provide the means through which liquid fertilizer can be automatically applied.

SUMMARY

1. Watering would appear at face value to be a boring, unimportant operation but is probably the most common cause of poor greenhouse crops. Underwatering can have as deleterious an effect on crops as overwatering.

2. Proper watering depends upon three rules:

   a. Use a well-drained medium having good structure. This will allow for ample moisture retention along with good aeration, even immediately after application of water.

   b. Water thoroughly each time. Soil cannot be partially wetted. Water should be applied until it flows from the bottom of the container. As a rule a 10 to 15 percent excess of water is applied. In general, for soil-based media, water is applied at the rate of two quarts per square foot of bench, or six ounces per 6.5-inch azalea type pot.

   c. Water when initial moisture stress occurs. This can be determined in most crops by the occurrence of subtle foliar symptoms such as texture, color, and turgidity changes. Some crops, such as azalea, do not show symptoms until root damage has occurred. Color, feel, and weight of the root medium are the cues in these cases.

3. Water quality is very important and is often overlooked. Levels of the total salt content, of individual ions such as sodium and boron, and of pH can all have a serious bearing on crop success. There are corrections for some quality problems and not for others. The water source should be tested before a greenhouse is established. Generally, the upper permissible level of total soluble salts is 200 mhos/cm $\times$ 10^{-5}. Sodium should not exceed 60 percent of the total dissolved solids and boron should not exceed a concentration of 1 ppm.

4. Hand watering is too expensive in today's labor market. Numerous automatic watering systems exist for both fresh flower and pot plant production. These can pay for themselves inside of one year. In addition to having an economic advantage over hand watering, automatic watering systems better guarantee that sufficient water will be applied on time because of the ease of application they offer. Automatic watering systems help to foster disease control by keeping foliage dryer. The automated water system is further used for the automated application of fertilizer.

SUGGESTED READINGS

Anon. Florist Supply Company Catalogs. These catalogs are available annually to greenhouse growers and are a primary source of information. The manufacturers themselves are another good source of literature.

Ball, V. *The Ball Red Book*. 13 ed. Geo. J. Ball, Inc. W. Chicago, IL, 1975.

Waters, W. E., J. NeSmith, C. M. Geraldson, and S. S. Woltz. "The Interpretation of Soluble Salt Tests and Soil Analysis by Different Procedures." *Florida Flower Grower* 9(4):1–10, 1972.

Chapter 8

Fertilization

Greenhouse fertilization has no equal in agriculture. Heavy plant growth is forced year-round under subtropical conditions. Root media volume is minimal by field standards. As a result, nitrogen applications of 4,000 pounds are commonly applied to an acre of chrysanthemums in a year. Excessive levels and imbalances of fertilizer nutrients frequently account for the difficulties encountered. Micronutrient deficiencies are on the increase as soils are continually held in intensive production under conditions of heavy leaching.

A typical plant is composed of about 90 percent water. The solid materials in the plant, commonly referred to as dry weight, are comprised of seventeen essential nutrient elements (Table 8-1) plus any of a number of nonessential elements which happen to be available in the root environment. Nearly 90 percent of the dry weight can be attributed to carbon, hydrogen, and oxygen, three essential elements which are not provided in a fertilization program but are obtained pursuant to other cultural procedures.

Carbon and oxygen are derived from carbon dioxide (CO_2) in the air while oxygen and hydrogen are derived from water. Carbon deficiency is common in the greenhouse and is covered in Chapter 9. Oxygen and hydrogen deficiencies are essentially nonexistent. Since only a small quantity of water is needed to provide these requirements, water stress injuries are usually related to other factors such as reduction in photosynthesis due to closing of stomates or to desiccation of cells.

The remaining 10 percent of the dry weight includes fourteen essential elements which must be provided through a fertilization program. These fall into two categories: the macronutrients which are present in the plant in large (macro) quantities and the micronutrients which are present in small (micro) quantities.

Table 8-1
Essential Plant Nutrients, Related Chemical Symbols, Classification,
and Typical Foliage Composition for Greenhouse Crops
Expressed as a Percentage of the Leaf Dry Weight

NUTRIENT ELEMENT	CHEMICAL SYMBOL	CLASSIFICATION	TYPICAL PLANT CONTENT (% of dry wt)
Carbon	C	Nonfertilizer	
Hydrogen	H	Nonfertilizer	89.0
Oxygen	O	Nonfertilizer	
Nitrogen	N	Macronutrient– primary	4.0
Phosphorus	P	Macronutrient– primary	0.5
Potassium	K	Macronutrient– primary	4.0
Calcium	Ca	Macronutrient– secondary	1.0
Magnesium	Mg	Macronutrient– secondary	0.5
Sulfur	S	Macronutrient– secondary	0.5
Iron	Fe	Micronutrient	0.02
Manganese	Mn	Micronutrient	0.02
Zinc	Zn	Micronutrient	0.003
Copper	Cu	Micronutrient	0.001
Boron	B	Micronutrient	0.006
Molybdenum	Mo	Micronutrient	0.0002
Sodium	Na	Micronutrient	0.03
Chloride	Cl	Micronutrient	0.1

FERTILIZATION PROGRAM

A new chapter in greenhouse fertilization began about the middle of this century when the practice of soil pasteurization eliminated the need for periodic replacement of soil. Prior to that time, nutrients were available from the humus in the rich soils used to replace the greenhouse soils every year or two. Annual applications of manure provided additional nutrients including most, and often all, of the required micronutrients. Further nutritional needs were satisfied as dictated by soil testing, usually once a month. Dry fertilizer carriers were used including such organic sources as dried blood, cotton seed meal, and tankage, while inorganic sources included nitrate of soda, muriate of potash, superphosphate, ammonium sulfate, etc.

The earlier system worked quite well, but in time it had to shift in order to come into line with changes in other cultural procedures. The perpetual use of soil made possible by soil pasteurization and dictated by economics, as well as the virtual elimination of manure necessitated by after-pasteurization problems, greatly increased dependency on a continuous system of fertilization. Heavy watering practices further aggravated the problem through leaching of nutrients, particularly micronutrients. The advent of automated watering provided an easy and economical means of applying nutrients periodically, but has necessitated the use of highly soluble fertilizers.

Today the standard practice is to dissolve high analysis fertilizer carriers into concentrated solutions. The concentrate is then proportioned by means of an injector into the water line of the greenhouse at the final concentration desired for crop application. Automatic watering systems connected to this line deliver the fertilizer solution to individual pots or to the soil surface in cut flower beds. Fertilizer is most commonly applied either with each watering or on a seven-to-ten day basis.

Pre-Plant Fertilization

It would be a very difficult task to provide all of the fourteen essential fertilizer elements on a continuous basis. Fortunately, several may be applied prior to planting without further application. The results of a soil test provide the basis for pre-plant nutrient additions.

The root media pH level should be between 6.2 and 6.8 for most greenhouse crops. Some crops may be successfully grown in the range of 4.5 to 7.5 but these are exceptions. Nutrient availability is controlled to a sizable degree by the soil pH level as illustrated in Figure 8-1. Lowering the pH level escessively results in a disproportionately high release of iron, manganese, and aluminum, all of which react with phosphorus to render it insoluble and thus unavailable. The available levels of calcium, magnesium, sulfur, and molybdenum decrease at low pH levels. High pH levels, on the other hand, result in the tie-up of phosphorus, iron, manganese, zinc, copper, and boron. It is readily apparent in Figure 8-1 that the best compromise of nutrient availability lies in the pH range of 6.2 to 6.8.

Most greenhouse media are of an acid (low) pH due to the use of acidic amendments such as peatmoss and pine bark. Finely ground limestone (all through a 10 mesh screen and 40 percent through a 100 mesh screen) is used to raise the pH level. Unless the soil report indicates a high magnesium level, which is rare, dolomitic limestone should be used. This material contains magnesium, an essential nutrient, in addition to calcium, whereas regular limestone contains primarily one essential nutrient, calcium. Rates of addition vary for each type of root medium and the magnitude of the pH correction needed, but in general they range from five to twenty-five pounds per

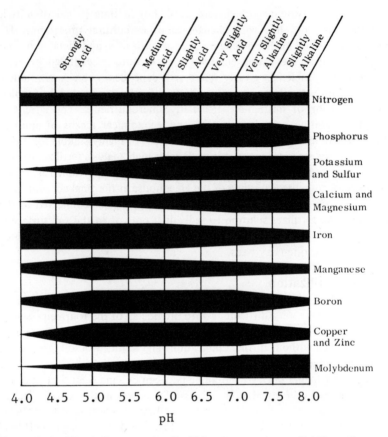

Figure 8-1. The influence of soil pH level upon the availability of essential nutrients. (*From Koths, J. S., 1973. Effects of pH on Availability of Plant Nutrients in Greenhouse Soils. Connecticut Greenhouse Newsletter No. 54, p. 11*)

cubic yard. This is sufficient to provide the required calcium and magnesium for up to one year. Where media are of neutral pH and do not require limestone additions, five pounds gypsum (calcium sulfate) should be incorporated into each cubic yard. This will provide sufficient calcium for one year; however, it will now be important to check the magnesium status of the crop (perhaps through foliar analyses) to determine when an occasional application of this nutrient is required. A good application, when called for, consists of 0.5 pounds of epsom salt (magnesium sulfate) dissolved in sufficient water to treat one cubic yard of medium. A second very important reading in the soil test is that of phosphorus. Unless it is high, make an application of three pounds of superphosphate (0-20-0) per cubic yard. If it is very low, five pounds is appropriate. One application will provide the necessary phosphorus for a year. It also provides the necessary sulfur and a sizable amount of calcium, since 20 percent superphosphate is approximately half gypsum (calcium sulfate). It is because of the gypsum content that 20 percent superphosphate (0-20-0) is more desirable than the high analysis treble superphosphate as a pre-plant amendment. If 0-20-0 superphosphate is not available, use equal parts of 0-45-0 superphosphate and gypsum and apply a combined weight of the two equal to the weight recommended for 0-20-0 superphosphate.

These two amendments provide four of the fourteen essential fertilizer nutrients. Six more, the micronutrients iron, manganese, zinc, copper, boron, and molybdenum, can also be applied in a single application. Fritted micronutrient mixes may be incorporated into the root medium during preparation and will last for ten to twelve months, or a liquid application of commercial mixes can be made the first week after planting which will last three to four months. The two remaining micronutrients, chloride and sodium, are of questionable value for many crops. Since they occur as contaminants in other fertilizers, they are disregarded, except in the case of carnation fertilization, where a small quantity of sodium is used.

Continual Fertilization

All the nutrients but nitrogen and potassium have been applied at this point. These two nutrients are not retained long enough in the root media to warrant pre-plant application exclusively. They are applied periodically as needed except where slow-release fertilizer is used. Two programs of application are most common. In the first, nitrogen and potassium are applied at a concentration of 200 parts per million (ppm) of each in the irrigation water every time the crop is watered. Surprisingly, this one rate works for many crops. The second program calls for an application of liquid fertilizer at weekly intervals. The concentration must be higher since the frequency of application is less. Concentrations range from 240 ppm nitrogen and potassium for sensitive crops such as bedding plants and elatior begonias, to 720 ppm of each for crops such as chrysanthemum and poinsettia (1.0 to 3 pounds of a 20 percent nitrogen fertilizer per 100 gallons).

A small number of growers apply liquid fertilizer on a bimonthly basis at higher concentrations. There are also a few growers who adhere to the older system of applying dry fertilizer to the soil surface as needed, usually monthly. All of these systems may result in a successful crop. There is an advantage of safety built into the high-frequency application systems. Lower concentrations of fertilizer are applied, thus reducing the risk of a burn (Figure 8-2). The greater frequency of application also reduces the chances of falling into a deficient nutrient range.

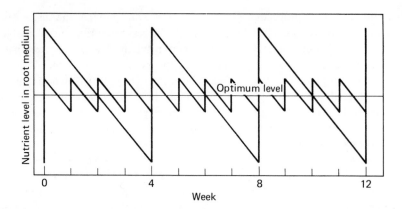

Figure 8-2. Relative root media levels of available fertilizer nutrients during weekly and monthly programs of application.

CONCENTRATION EXPRESSION AND CONVERSIONS. Fertilizer recommendations are either expressed in terms of ppm or in pounds and ounces per 100 gallons of water. One must be able to convert from one expression to the other in order to utilize the available literature. If we could purchase nitrogen or potassium by itself, these conversions would be straightforward, but this is not the case. Fertilizers always contain two or more elements. Some of the elements are essential plant nutrients while others may not be. Complete fertilizers always contain the three primary macronutrients, nitrogen, phosphorus, and potassium, and are labeled with a numerical grade such as 10-5-10. The first number indicates the percentage of elemental nitrogen (N), the second indicates the percentage of phosphorus in the oxide form (P_2O_5), and the third the percentage of potassium also in the oxide form (K_2O). The most common fertilizer grade used in the greenhouse is 20-20-20. Although this is a very high analysis fertilizer, there is still a sizable proportion of it unaccounted for. This is due to the content of other elements such as sulfate, chloride, hydrogen, etc.

Fertilizer recommendations expressed in terms of pounds or ounces per 100 gallons pose no problem since they generally refer to the fertilizer carrier rather than to the specific essential nutrient, e.g., two pounds of 20-20-20 grade fertilizer dissolved in 100 gallons of water, one pound of potassium nitrate per 100 gallons. Recommendations expressed as ppm generally refer to the essential nutrient. For example, a recommendation for a concentration of 200 ppm of nitrogen does not give any indication of the amount of 20-20-20 or potassium nitrate to use in 100 gallons of water.

To determine the amount of fertilizer carrier needed use Equation 8-1. In this case we must divide the desired ppm of nitrogen by 75 and then divide the resulting answer by the decimal fraction of nitrogen contained in the 20-20-20 grade fertilizer to be used.

Equation 8-1

$$\frac{\text{desired ppm} \div 75}{\substack{\text{decimal fraction of desired} \\ \text{nutrient in fertilizer}}} = \substack{\text{oz of fertilizer} \\ \text{carrier per 100 gal}}$$

Let us assume that a recommendation calls for 200 ppm of nitrogen and we have a 20-20-20 grade fertilizer available. Using Equation 8-1, we divide 200 ppm by 75, resulting in a value of 2.67, and then divide this number by 0.20, which is the decimal fraction of nitrogen in the 20-20-20 fertilizer, to obtain a final answer of 13.35 oz of 20-20-20 fertilizer per 100 gallons of water.

$$\frac{200 \div 75}{0.20} = 13.35 \text{ oz}/100 \text{ gal}$$

Since this fertilizer also contains 20 percent each of phosphorus and potassium we end up with a final solution containing 200 ppm N + 200 ppm P_2O_5 + 200 ppm K_2O.

Assume now that we have potassium nitrate available and want 200 ppm of potassium. This fertilizer carrier contains 13 percent nitrogen and 44 percent potassium (K_2O). Applying Equation 8-1 we find that 6.1 ounces must be dissolved into each 100 gallons of water to yield a final concentration of 200 ppm of potassium (K_2O). We also obtain nitrogen from this fertilizer carrier and it is important to know what quantity.

$$\frac{200 \div 75}{0.44} = 6.1$$

Equation 8-2 is used to generate this information. Applying the equation to our problem, we find that the concentration of nitrogen in the final solution is 69.5 ppm.

Equation 8-2

oz fertilizer carrier per 100 gal $\times$ 75 $\times$ decimal fraction
of desired nutrient in the carrier = ppm of desired nutrient

6.1 $\times$ 75 $\times$ 0.13 = 59.5 ppm

These equations can be cumbersome to use in the field. A simplified alternative is to use Table 8-2. Take again the situation where we desire to

Table 8-2
Conversion Table for ppm of Desired Nutrient to Ounces of Fertilizer Carrier per 100 Gallons of Water and Vice Versa*

OUNCES OF FERTILIZER CARRIER IN 100 GAL	PERCENTAGE OF DESIRED NUTRIENT IN FERTILIZER CARRIER										
	13	14	16	20	20.5	21	33	44	45	53	60
	ppm										
1	9.7	10.5	12.0	15.0	15.3	15.7	24.7	32.9	33.7	39.7	44.9
2	19.5	21.0	24.0	29.9	30.7	31.4	49.4	65.9	67.4	79.3	89.8
3	29.3	31.4	35.9	44.9	46.0	47.2	74.1	98.8	101.0	117.0	134.7
4	38.9	41.9	47.9	59.9	61.4	62.9	98.8	131.7	134.7	158.7	179.6
6	58.4	62.9	71.9	89.8	92.1	94.3	148.2	197.6	202.1	238.0	269.4
8	77.8	83.8	95.8	119.7	122.7	125.7	197.6	263.4	269.4	317.3	359.2
16	155.7	167.7	191.7	239.5	245.5	251.5	395.2	526.9	538.9	634.6	718.5
24	233.5	251.5	287.5	359.2	368.2	377.2	592.7	790.3	808.3	952.0	1077.7
32	311.4	335.4	383.4	479.0	490.9	502.9	790.3	1053.7	1077.7	1269.3	1436.9
40	389.2	419.2	479.2	598.7	613.7	628.6	987.9	1317.2	1347.1	1586.6	1796.2
48	467.0	503.0	575.0	718.5	736.4	754.4	1185.5	1580.6	1616.5	1903.9	2155.4
56	544.9	586.9	670.9	838.0	859.2	880.1	1383.0	1844.0	1886.0	2221.2	2514.6
64	622.7	670.7	766.7	958.0	981.9	1005.8	1580.6	2107.5	2155.4	2538.6	2873.9

*From Dr. J. W. Love. North Carolina State University, Raleigh, N.C. 27607

know how much potassium nitrate carrier to use in 100 gallons of water to supply a concentration of 200 ppm of potassium (K_2O). In stepwise fashion

1. Locate the percentage of the desired nutrient (K_2O) in the fertilizer carrier (potassium nitrate) in the upper row of Table 8-2; in this case the value is 44.

2. Read down the column under 44 until you arrive at the desired ppm, 200 in our case; however, 197.6 is close enough.

3. Read to the left across the row in which 197.6 is located to locate the figure in the extreme left column which is the number of ounces of fertilizer carrier to dissolve in 100 gallons of water, six ounces of potassium nitrate in this case. This answer corresponds to that which could be obtained by using Equation 8-1.

Realizing that potassium nitrate also supplies nitrogen, it becomes desirable to know the concentration of nitrogen. Using Table 8-2 the following steps are taken.

1. Locate the ounces of potassium nitrate needed per 100 gallons in the extreme left column, 6 in this problem.

2. Read across that row to the right until you locate a value (58.4) in the column headed by 13, the percentage of nitrogen in potassium nitrate. The value 58.4 is the concentration of nitrogen in ppm provided by six ounces of potassium nitrate in 100 gallons of water and is equivalent to the answer that could be obtained using Equation 8-2. Occasionally values will be sought in the table which are not printed. In these cases it becomes necessary to estimate their position.

SPECIFIC CROP RECOMMENDATIONS. The most common fertilizer used in the greenhouse is 20-20-20. Several companies formulate this grade and include in it the essential micronutrients as well as a dye which is used for tracing the fertilizer in the water lines. If the pre-plant recommendations are followed, the phosphorus content of this fertilizer is superfluous and thus it would be better to use a 20-0-20 grade. In some parts of this country (the northeast for example) potassium is readily fixed in soils; thus a 20-0-30 fertilizer serves better. Crops in new root media may be fertilized with a 1-0-1 or 2-0-3 ratio fertilizer until such time as the crop is established and soil tests and foliar analyses might dictate otherwise. The concentration of fertilizer varies widely from crop to crop. Table 8-3 lists several crops and concentrations of a 20 percent nitrogen fertilizer to be used for weekly and constant (with every watering) fertilization programs.

Table 8-3
Standard Concentration Requirements of Fertilizers
Containing 20% Nitrogen for Several Greenhouse Crops

CROP	CONCENTRATION CATEGORY	CONCENTRATION (oz/100 gal)	
		WEEKLY	CONSTANT
Tulip	None	–	–
Daffodil	None	–	–
Iris	None	–	–
Hyacinth	None	–	–
Snapdragon	Very light	16	6
Bedding plants	Very light	16	13.5
Elatior begonia	Very light	17	8.5
Azalea	Light	20	–
Rose	Moderate	32	10
Carnation	Moderate	32	13.5
Geranium	Moderate	32	13.5
Chrysanthemum	Heavy	40	13.5
Poinsettia	Heavy	48	17

It is not necessary to use a fertilizer containing 20 percent nitrogen. Fertilizer ratios of 1-0-1 and 1-1-1 are available in grades such as 15-0-15, 15-15-15, 25-0-25, etc. If the fertilizer contains 15 percent nitrogen use one third more or if it contains 25 percent nitrogen use one fifth less quantity in each 100 gallons of water than you would if it were a 20 percent nitrogen containing fertilizer.

A few crops do not develop well on a fertilizer equally balanced in nitrogen and potassium. The elatior begonia grows faster and develops more side shoots if fertilized with a ratio of 2 parts nitrogen to 1 part potassium. The azalea requirement is similar in that a 3-to-1 ratio is best. The carnation requirement is quite different since a 2 nitrogen:3 potassium ratio is favored.

As time passes the concentration and balance of nitrogen and potassium in the root medium usually changes, necessitating adjustments in the concentration and ratio of fertilizer applied. A large range of fertilizer ratios and grades are commercially available to serve these needs.

FORMULATING FERTILIZERS. Complete fertilizers, i.e., containing nitrogen, phosphorus, and potassium, are commercially available in a number of grades. Many florists formulate their own fertilizers, thus saving a significant part of their fertilizer bill and making possible a wider range of grades. Most fertilizers are formulated from combinations of two or more of eight fertilizer carriers. For example, one pound of potassium nitrate added to one pound of ammonium nitrate yields two pounds of 23-0-22 grade fertilizer.

wrong

A 20-20-19 grade fertilizer can be formulated by blending three pounds of ammonium nitrate plus three pounds of di-ammonium phosphate plus one pound of urea together. A number of formulations which the grower can easily make himself are presented in Table 8-4. While these fertilizers do not contain micronutrients or dye, there is a commercial preparation (Compound 111®produced by Robert Peters Co., Inc., Allentown, PA 18104) which when added to the macronutrient formulation will provide them.

None of the formulations listed in Table 8-4 contains sulfate or phosphate in combination with calcium. This would be permissible if fertilizers were formulated at the strength desired for direct application to the crop. This is not the usual case. To take advantage of automated application, fertilizer solutions are first made in concentrated form and are then diluted as they are metered into the greenhouse water system through mechanical proportioners. Calcium will precipitate (settle out as a solid) with sulfate or phosphate when formulated into a concentrated fertilizer solution; therefore, these combinations are avoided unless appropriate two-stage injection systems are used.

Care should be taken when selecting fertilizer carriers to bring about the proper soil reaction or pH. Ammonium nitrate, ammonium sulfate, and di-ammonium phosphate are acidic—lower the soil pH—while calcium nitrate, sodium nitrate, and potassium nitrate are basic—raise the soil pH. Potassium chloride is neutral. Moderate changes in root media pH can be brought about by proper selection of the fertilizer formulation. In general, ammonium nitrate is used as the nitrogen source when a lower pH is desired and calcium nitrate when a higher pH is desired.

There are two forms of nitrogen generally used for fertilization, nitrate (NO_3^-) and ammonium (or ammoniacal) nitrogen (NH_4^+). Plants vary in response to these forms. Plants, such as azalea and rhododendron, that grow well in highly acid root media develop best on a high proportion of ammonium nitrogen. Poinsettia, however, may be injured when more than 25 percent of the total nitrogen is provided as ammonium. It will develop well on nitrate exclusively. The chrysanthemum is perhaps typical of most of the greenhouse crops. When grown on all ammonium or all nitrate nitrogen, growth is inferior to that obtained from a combination of nitrogen sources. The best combinations contain from 25 to 75 percent ammonium nitrogen.

Different fertilizers are recommended for blue and pink hydrangea crops in Table 8-4. Aluminum serves to regulate flower color in hydrangea. Copious quantities of aluminum exist in most soils. When the pH is low, much of the aluminum is available to the plant and flowers are blue. When the pH is high, aluminum is rendered unavailable and flowers are pink. High levels of phosphorus also render aluminum unavailable. You will note that fertilizer formulations for blue flowers are devoid of phosphorus and are very acid, while those used for pink flowers contain large quantities of phosphorus and are not very acid.

Table 8-4
Formulating Soluble Fertilizers

FORMULA NAME		33-0-0	13-0-44	15.5-0-0	16-0-0	21-0-0	45-0-0	0-0-60	12-62-0	21-53-0	% of N as NO_3	COST PER LB. (¢) (b)	REACTION IN SOIL (c)
Ammonium nitrate	33-0-0	x									50	12	A
Potassium nitrate	13-0-44		x								100	26	N
Calcium nitrate	15.5-0-0			x							94	10	B
Sodium nitrate	16-0-0				x						100	10	B
Ammonium sulfate	21-0-0					x					0	5	
Urea	45-0-0						x				0	14	SA
Potassium chloride	0-0-60							x			—	8	N
Monoammonium phosphate	12-62-0								x		0	34	A
Diammonium phosphate(a)	21-53-0									x	0	16	SA
C'mum green	18-0-22	1	2			1					53	17	A
General summer	20-10-24	1						1	2	1	17	12	A
General low phosphate	21-4-20	7						4	1		45	12	A
General summer	21-17-20	1						2	3	3	10	12	A
General	17-6-27							4	1		43	11	A
UConn Mix	19-5-24	6	2					2	1		51	22	N
Editor's favorite	20-5-30	13						4		2	43	22	SA
20-20-20 substitute	20-20-22	4						1		3	33	21	SA
Starter and Pink Hydrangea	12-41-15	1							2		35	31	SA
Starter and Pink Hydrangea	17-35-16							1	4	10	0	14	SA
N-K only	16-0-24	2			1			2			60	10	SA
N-K only	20-0-30	1	2					2			72	21	SA
Blue Hydrangea	13-0-22					2		1			0	6	VA
Blue Hydrangea	15-0-15					3		1			0	6	VA
Acid	21-9-9	3	1			7		1		2	21	10	VA
Spring carnation	11-0-17				5			2			100	10	B
Winter nitrate	15-0-15		1	2							95	15	B
Winter potash	15-0-22		1	1							96	18	B
Lily substitute	16-4-12	1	4	6					1		78	16	N
High K	15-10-30		7	1					2		72	22	N

(a) Diammonium phosphate may be pelletized and coated. To dissolve, use very hot water and stir vigorously. Don't worry about sediment. Use crystalline potassium chloride if possible.

(b) Based on lowest available prices published by greenhouse supply firms.

(c) B = basic, N = neutral, SA = slightly acid, A = acid, VA = very acid.

From: Koths, J. S. et al. Nutrition of greenhouse crops. U. of Ct. Coop. Ext. Ser. Bull. 76-14, 1976.

AUTOMATED FERTILIZER APPLICATION. The most expedient method for applying fertilizer is the automatic watering system present in most greenhouses. The fertilizer must be dissolved into a concentrated solution in order to conserve space in the mixing and holding tanks. This necessitates the use of an injector, otherwise known as a proportioner. This device mixes precise volumes of concentrated fertilizer solution and water together. By plumbing the proportioner into the main water line serving a greenhouse range, all lines will carry a single strength fertilizer solution. The proportioner is located on a bypass line so that either water or fertilizer solution can be obtained from the lines (Figure 8-3).

It is advisable, and in most states mandatory, that in a potable water system a backflow preventive be installed on any water supply fixture that has an outlet which may be submerged (Figure 8-4). Such fixtures include fertilizer proportioners and hoses used to fill spray tanks or equipment wash-tubs. The backflow preventive stops backsiphoning of contaminated water into the water system in the event that a negative pressure (suction) develops. Nitrate, commonly supplied in fertilizers, is potentially lethal to humans. Babies are particularly susceptible to low levels of nitrate. Backflow preventives are not required when there is a gap equal to twice the diameter of

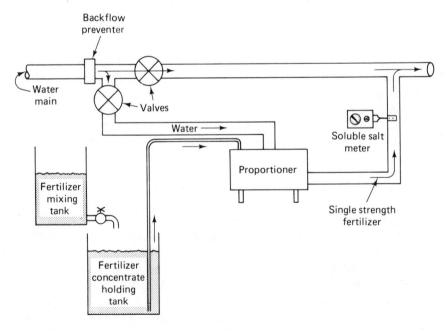

Figure 8-3. A typical arrangement of fertilizer-mixing tank, holding tank, proportioner, and soluble salt meter along the main water line in a greenhouse range.

Figure 8-4. A backflow preventive first in the open position permitting normal flow of water. When water pressure drops to a predetermined level, the check valve closes and shuts off the flow of water. At this point air can enter the device, thus eliminating the negative pressure and any backflow of water. (*From J. W. Bartok, Jr., 1973. "Preventing Backflow From Your Fertilizer Injector," Connecticut Greenhouse Newsletter No. 52, pp. 1–3*)

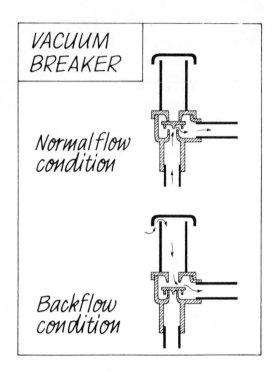

the supply line between the water supply line and the highest possible level of water in a mixing tank receiving the water. In such a setup, it is not possible for contaminated water to enter the water supply line.

Most greenhouse fertilizer is purchased in solid form. It is dissolved in a settling tank (Figure 8-3) where it is allowed to stand for the better part of a day to permit settling of solids which occasionally occur, especially when using less expensive fertilizers. A tap is located an inch or two from the bottom of the settling tank for transferring the clear liquid to a holding tank. The proportioner draws fertilizer concentrate from the holding tank. This sequence of tanks prevents unwanted solids from getting into and plugging the porportioner and automatic watering system.

Several types of proportioners are used, depending upon the application (Figure 8-5 and Table 8-5). Some proportioners, such as the Hozon®, operate on the venturi principle whereby water passing at a high velocity through an orifice sets up a suction in a line entering from the side. Fertilizer concentrate is drawn in through the side line. This is an inexpensive proportioner which serves well in a small greenhouse but is limited in application due to its fixed, narrow proportioning ratio of approximately 1:16. Where large volumes of fertilizer solution are needed, the concentrate tank would become prohibitively large. The 3/4-inch thread size and 3-gallon-per-minute flow rate limits the area which can be fertilized at one time.

Figure 8-5. Five fertilizer proportioners typical of the many types in use. (a) Hozon®, (b) Commander®, (c) Smith®, (d) Fert-O-Ject®, and (e) Gewa®.

Table 8-5
Fertilizer Proportioners and Their Specifications

BRAND	MODE OF ACTION	MAX. FLOW RATE (gpm)	RATIO	THREAD SIZE (in.)	CONCENTRATE CAPACITY (gal)
Hozon®	Venturi	3	1:16	3/4	Any
Hydrocare®	Pump	7.5	1:24	3/4	Any
M-P®	Pressure or Venturi	–	1:50 to 1:200	3/4-3	.5, 2, 5, 15
Commander®	Pump	6.6	1:128	3/4	Any
Fert-O-Ject®	Pump	560	1:100 or 1:200	3/4-6	Any
Smith Measuremix®	Pump	700	1:100 or 1:200	3/4-6	Any
Gewa®	Pressure		1:15 to 1:350	3/4-2	4, 6, 15, 26
HPA®	Solenoid-Pump	400	1:25, 1:50, 1:100, 1:200, 1:400, 1:800, 1:1600	1-4	Any

The Hydrocare® proportioner has a fixed ratio of 1:24 permitting its use in larger operations, but is still limited to a 3/4-inch water line. This proportioner draws in fertilizer concentrate by means of a pump driven by water passing through it. The Commander® proportioner satisfies the problem of concentrate volume with a fixed ratio of 1:128, but still has a 3/4-inch thread. Fert-O-Ject® and Smith® proportioners also have wide, fixed ratios— 1:100 or 1:200—but can be purchased to fit pipe sizes up to six inches. Their flow rates, which go up to 700 gallons per minute, permit simultaneous fertilization of many benches.

The Gewa® proportioner adds versatility since its ratio is adjustable from 1:15 to 1:350. This proportioner includes a concentrate tank available in 4-, 6-, 15-, and 26-gallon sizes and fits up to a 2-inch water line. The concentrate is contained in a rubber bag positioned inside an iron tank. Entering water builds up pressure between the rubber bag and the iron tank wall, thereby pressing concentrate out into the line.

All of these proportioners are satisfactory in the operations for which they are intended. For any given situation a proportioner should meet the following needs: (1) be matched to the water main size, (2) have a flow rate great enough to handle simultaneous watering of the desired number of benches or beds, and (3) have a proportioning ratio that will permit a concentrate tank of reasonable size.

A soluble salt meter should be installed in the plumbing downstream from the proportioner. The same meter used for testing root media can be used but the probe containing the electrodes is different in that it is inserted, permanently, into the water line. Each time the proportioner is turned on the soluble salt level of the solution coming from the proportioner should be checked. It should always be the same for a given fertilizer at a given concentration.

SLOW-RELEASE FERTILIZERS

Many of the nutrient sources used in the early days of greenhouse culture were in effect slow-release fertilizers. They were mainly organic materials of plant and animal origin which upon degradation slowly gave up their nutrient content to the soil. Today slow-release fertilizers are synthetically produced which have slow, sustained release patterns ranging from three months to several years. For greenhouse culture the three month release period is most popular. There are five common categories of these fertilizers. Some, when incorporated into the soil prior to planting, will provide all the necessary nitrogen, phosphorus, and potassium for the entire crop period thus eliminating the need for a continual fertilization program. Others provide micronutrients in an equally effective manner.

Slow-release fertilizers are in one sense a form of automation since they eliminate the need for a continual input of labor into fertilization. These fertilizers are more efficient than water soluble fertilizers in that a greater percentage of applied nutrients are utilized by the plant. Conversely, less nutrients leach from the root zone into the water table. This will become a more important factor as abatement of ground water pollution is further necessitated by government agencies. Traditionally, little emphasis has been placed on researching the keeping quality of potted plants after purchase by the final consumer. Proper use of slow-release fertilizers by the grower can insure adequate nutrition during the post-market period. Although crops can be fertilized exclusively with slow-release fertilizers, currently many growers use these fertilizers in conjunction with a continual fertilization program merely as an insurance program against nutrient shortage.

Plastic-Encapsulated Fertilizers

A notable example of the plastic-encapsulated slow-release fertilizers are the products under the tradename Osmocote®. They consist of plastic coated spheres of dry, water soluble fertilizers formulated from such carriers as potassium nitrate and ammonium sulfate. Particle diameters are about 1/8 inch or less.

These fertilizers are mixed into the root media prior to planting. Water vapor in the soil atmosphere enters the capsule through pores in the plastic coating. Once inside, the water vapor condenses on the fertilizer surface because the fertilizer lowers the vapor pressure. This reduces the moisture content of the atmosphere inside the capsule to a level lower than that in the moist soil atmosphere outside. As a result, water vapor continues to diffuse into the capsule in an attempt to equalize the moisture content of the atmosphere on both sides of the plastic film. Soon sufficient water has condensed inside to dissolve the fertilizer. As water continues to enter and pressure builds up inside, the walls of the capsule enlarge and fertilizer solution leaks through the expanded pores to the soil solution where it can be taken up by plant roots. The longevity of this process is controlled by the composition and thickness of the plastic coating.

Osmocote® is available for greenhouse fertilization in 14-14-14, 19-6-12, 12-0-41, and 26-0-0 grades which have a release period of three to four months, in an 18-6-12 grade which has a nine-month release period, and in an 18-5-11 grade which has a 12- to 14-month release period. The former fertilizers are well suited to most greenhouse crops which have a 12- to 14-week cultural requirement. The latter fertilizers are better suited to long term crops such as azalea, carnation, and rose. Table 8-6 lists recommended rates of application for the Osmocote® fertilizers.

Table 8-6
Rates of Application for Osmocote® Slow-Release Fertilizers for Standard Greenhouse Crops

	14-14-14		19-6-12		18-5-11 Range of Rates		
	Light, Coarse-Textured Media	Heavy, Medium-Textured Media	Light, Coarse-Textured Media	Heavy, Medium-Textured Media	Low	Medium	High
Incorporated in Root Medium							
1 cu ft	7 oz	6 oz	6 oz	5 oz	6½ oz	8¼ oz	10 oz
1 bushel	9 oz	8 oz	7 oz	6 oz	8¼ oz	10¼ oz	12 1/3 oz
1 cu yd	13 lb	11 lb	10 lb	8 lb	11 lb 2 oz	13 lb 14 oz	16 lb 11 oz
100 sq ft, 6 in. deep	—	—	—	—	20 lb 10 oz	25 lb 11 oz	30 lb 14 oz
Top Dressed on Established Plantings	Maximum Rate		Maximum Rate				
4-in. standard pot	½ teaspoon (heaping)		½ teaspoon (level)		1/10 oz	1/8 oz	1/6 oz
5-in. standard pot	1 teaspoon (heaping)		1 teaspoon (level)		1/4 oz	1/3 oz	2/5 oz
6-in. standard pot	1 tablespoon (level)		1 teaspoon (heaping)		2/5 oz	1/2 oz	3/5 oz
100 sq ft, 6 in. deep	—		—		20 lb 10 oz	25 lb 11 oz	30 lb 14 oz

The 14-14-14 and 19-6-12 grades supply nutrients for 3 to 4 months and the 18-5-11 grade for 12 to 14 months. The 18-5-11 grade is particularly useful on long-term crops such as rose and carnation. The rate of application of 14-14-14 and 18-9-13 grades should be reduced to half when used on fertilizer-sensitive crops such as azalea, African violet, orchid, heather, and certain varieties of ferns.

Slowly Soluble Fertilizers

Gypsum and superphosphate are two examples of fertilizers which are mostly insoluble. When applied to the soil, a small percentage will dissolve. As the dissolved component is depleted through plant utilization or leaching, more dissolves to replace it.

A good example of a complete fertilizer in this category is MagAmp®. It is a coprecipitate of magnesium ammonium phosphate and magnesium potassium phosphate. MagAmp® has the grade 7-40-6 and is available in coarse and medium granule size. The coarse size, having less surface area per unit of weight, requires a longer period of time for dissolution. It is an effective source of nitrogen, phosphorus and potassium for eight months or more; the medium size lasts only three to five months. It is designed to be mixed into the root medium. Recommended crops and rates of application appear in Table 8-7.

The unusually high level of phosphorus in MagAmp® can result in the reduced availability of iron, manganese, copper, and zinc in the root media. Careful attention should be paid to the micronutrient fertilizer program as a result. This fertilizer also contains 12 percent magnesium (Mg) which is high enough to antagonize the uptake of calcium in some plants and result in serious nutritional problems. Special care should be exercised to maintain calcium at a moderately high level in the root media to avert a deficiency. This problem is particularly important in areas where the water supply has a low calcium content. Osmocote® at one-third the normally recommended rate supplemented with periodic liquid fertilizer is suggested in New England.

Urea Formaldehyde

This slow-release nitrogen containing fertilizer is sold under several tradenames including Borden's 38®, Ureaform®, and Uramite®. It contains 38 percent nitrogen and is slowly available, about two-thirds being released

Table 8-7
Recommended Uses and Rates of Application for MagAmp®
Slow-Release Fertilizer

CROP	RATE	MAGAMP® GRADE
Bedding plants	8–10 lb/cu yd	Medium
Cut flowers	15 lb/100 sq ft	Medium
Foliage plants	10 lb/cu yd	Coarse
Geranium	10–12 lb/cu yd	Medium
Pot mums, Easter lily, poinsettia	15–20 lb/cu yd	Medium

the first year and successively smaller amounts in succeeding years. This fertilizer has gained considerable prominence as a source of nitrogen for home lawns and golf courses. Much of the urea formaldehyde exists in long chemical chains which cannot be taken up by plant roots. Once in the soil, microorganisms feed upon these chains, breaking them down into smaller pieces, some of which are urea. Urea is a form of nitrogen readily utilized by the plant. This breakdown process occurs slowly over a long period of time.

Urea formaldehyde has not been used extensively in greenhouse culture, except in mixed formulations, because (1) it provides only the nutrient nitrogen leaving the need for a potassium source, and (2) it provides nitrogen in the form of urea which is ultimately converted to ammonium either in the soil or in the plant. Most plants do not respond well to ammonium nitrogen exclusively. Urea formaldehyde is used by some azalea growers as a top dressing to guarantee against nitrogen deficiency because of the high requirement of this crop for nitrogen relative to potassium. It is used at the rate of one rounded teaspoon per 6-inch pot at two month intervals during periods of heavy growth.

Fritted Nutrients

Discussion of urea formaldehyde logically leads to the topic of fritted potassium since both are slow-release fertilizers. When used together they can eliminate the need for a continual fertilization program in the greenhouse. Frits are glasslike materials. They can range from insoluble to readily soluble in water. For the purposes of slow-release fertilizer, a slowly soluble frit is heated to its liquid form, the desired nutrients are added to the liquid and then it is solidified by pouring it into a cold water bath. Immediately upon solidification, the frit fractures. The fractured particles are collected, dried, and ground to the consistency of powder (200 mesh or smaller). When applied to the soil the frits slowly dissolve, giving up their nutrient content to the soil solution. Sufficient quantities can be applied to the soil to sustain this process of release for up to ten months. The release characteristics of fritted potassium make it a natural partner for use with urea formaldehyde and, indeed, the two have been combined with superphosphate and pressed into tablets for use as a slow-release source of N-P-K in nursery applications. Little attention has been paid to the use of fritted potassium in the greenhouse. Fritted micronutrient mixes are much more popular and, as indicated earlier, constitute an excellent preplant source of fertilizer lasting upward of a year.

Chelated Micronutrients

The word *chelate* is derived from a Greek word meaning claw. It is appropriate because chelates are large organic chemical structures which encircle and tightly hold micronutrients including iron, manganese, zinc and copper. Plant roots can absorb the micronutrient-chelate combination. The micronutrient is then released inside the plant. When the soil pH is higher than that desired for a specific crop, iron, manganese, zinc, and copper are precipitated, i.e., rendered unavailable, if not chelated.

Roses were traditionally grown in a moderately acid media of pH 5.5 to 6.0 With time it was learned that the benefit of the low pH level was the heavy release of available iron, a feature necessary for this poor accumulator of iron. Actually the rose grows better at a higher pH level, providing sufficient iron is available. Today iron is routinely applied in the chelated form at the rate of one pound per 1,000 square feet of bed at a frequency of about every three months. Although the alternative source of iron, iron sulfate, is much cheaper pound for pound, under adverse soil conditions it can be more expensive due to the need to apply it at a greater frequency than chelated iron.

The chelated forms of iron, manganese, zinc, and copper are the most common forms used in the premium greenhouse fertilizers. Their high solubility compared to alternative forms make them very desirable to fertilizer formulators. When correcting individual micronutrient deficiencies, there is usually an advantage to using chelated iron. Chelated manganese, zinc, and copper, however, do not share this advantage. Unless the soil pH is adversely high, the extra expense of the chelated forms of manganese, zinc, and copper is not usually warranted. The sulfate form works well for reasons of economics and effectiveness.

NUTRITIONAL MONITORING

Nutritional problems will develop even in the best of fertilization programs. The careful grower makes use of three systems for monitoring nutrient status and is thus able to forecast problems as well as develop remedies. These are: visual diagnosis, soil testing, and foliar (leaf) analysis. Each test provides some information which is not provided by the others.

Visual Diagnosis

Visual diagnosis can be employed only after damage has occurred. Often the damage is only partially reversible. For this reason one should not rely on visual diagnosis as a routine measure of nutrient status. It is very helpful after an error has been made. For each nutrient deficiency there are visual symptoms common to many crops. These are presented in the following key and in Figures 8-6 through 8-17. It should be noted that there are a few crops which will not develop some of these symptoms and there are many more crops which, in addition to these symptoms, will develop others. Only the more typical symptoms are presented.

(a)

(b)

Figure 8-6. Nitrogen deficiency and toxicity. Nitrogen deficiency appears first on the lower foliage and then progresses up the plant. Leaves turn light green, then yellow and finally necrotic. If the plant is one that forms an abscission layer, those leaves will drop off. The overall plant is stunted. (a) A series of Rieger begonia plants fertilized with increasing levels of nitrogen from deficient on the left to toxic on the right. Deficient plants are stunted, have poor secondary shoot development, and have chlorotic foliage. Toxic plants are stunted, have poor secondary shoot development, and are deep green in color. In addition to these symptoms of nitrogen toxicity, there are typical symptoms of soluble salt injury such as wilting during the bright part of the day, necrosis of foliage, and root death. Nitrogen and potassium toxicities are often complicated by high soluble salt injuries because of the high levels of these nutrients required in the root medium to get a toxicity. (b) Nitrogen deficiency of carnation exhibits itself in a very distinctive symptom known as "curly tip." The tips of leaf pairs tend to hook together so that subsequent leaves do not have adequate growing room and as a result become folded as they develop. Nitrogen deficiency also results in narrow, stiff leaf formation in carnation, often referred to as "grassiness," as seen in the plant on the left.

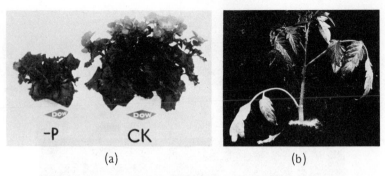

(a)   (b)

Figure 8-7. Phosphorus deficiency. (a) Foliage appears very healthy as it becomes darker green than normal. The deficient plant is well proportioned but is generally smaller than normal as seen in the contrast with a normal Rieger begonia plant above. (b) Foliage eventually turns chlorotic, as seen in the tomato plant above, and later, leaves become necrotic. Some plants develop purple pigmentation as in the case of this tomato plant. (*Photograph (b) by Woolley and Broyer and courtesy of The Fertilizer Institute, Washington, D.C. 20036*)

(a)   (b)

Figure 8-8. Potassium deficiency occurs first on older foliage as chlorosis which quickly progresses to necrosis. Symptoms may start at the leaf margin in some plant species such as begonia or may be scattered across the leaf in other species such as carnation (a). The necrotic spots spread and eventually destroy the entire leaf as seen in the tomato leaves above (b). The overall plant shows a progression of injury from the base of the plant upward. (*Photograph (b) by Woolley and Broyer and courtesy of The Fertilizer Institute, Washington, D.C. 20036*)

(a)

(b)

(c)

Figure 8-9. Calcium deficiency is generally expressed at the top of the plant as a rather irregular chlorosis of foliage and incomplete formation of tissue. Leaves of the chrysanthemum plant above (a) are incompletely formed giving the appearance of long, narrow "strap" leaves. Often the growing point (*meristem*) stops developing and takes on a blunt appearance as seen in the above chrysanthemum and rose plants (b). Note the incompletely formed leaves on the lower left side of the rose shoot. Flower tissue may also be incompletely formed, as in the case of petunia above (c). Collapse of tissue in the petal lobes and corolla tube is evident.

Figure 8-10. Magnesium deficiency. Symptoms of magnesium deficiency, like nitrogen and potassium deficiencies, begin at the base of the plant and progress upward. Interveinal chlorosis of foliage is the predominant symptom, as seen in the petunia plant above.

Figure 8-11. Sulfur deficiency. The plant as a whole is affected. Foliage becomes uniformly lighter green in color. Chrysanthemum leaves above show symptoms increasing in intensity from left to right. Some plants develop a beige cast in addition to chlorosis. (*Photograph courtesy of A. M. Kofranek, University of California, Davis, CA*)

250

(a)   (b)

Figure 8-12. Iron deficiency. Symptoms of iron deficiency are similar to those of magnesium deficiency in that interveinal chlorosis is the principal symptom, but they differ in that iron deficiency appears at the top of the plant first. (a) A close-up of interveinal chlorosis on a young Rieger begonia leaf. (b) An iron-deficient petunia plant.

Figure 8-13. Manganese deficiency. Symptoms of manganese deficiency start out the same as iron deficiency with interveinal chlorosis of young foliage. In the later stages of manganese deficiency, however, tan to grey spots develop in the chlorotic areas as seen in the above chrysanthemum leaves. (*Photograph courtesy of A. M. Kofranek, University of California, Davis, CA*)

251

(a)

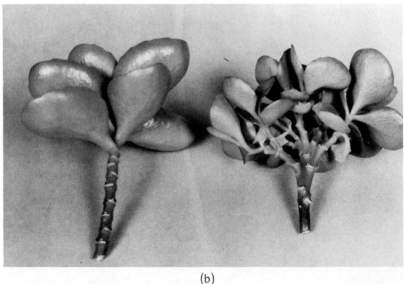

(b)

Figure 8-14. Zinc deficiency. Reduced leaf size is very typical of zinc deficiency; in fact, zinc deficiency is frequently called "little leaf disease" in field crops. Shortened internodes and irregular chlorosis of young foliage is also typical. (a) Zinc-deficient carnation shoots on either side of a normal shoot. Symptoms include small leaves and very short internodes. (b) Kalanchoe are more prone to zinc deficiency than most other greenhouse crops. Prolific branching from a broad, flattened stem is indicative of this deficiency in kalanchoe. The stem on the left is normal, while that on the right is deficient in zinc.

252

(a)

(b)

(c)

(d)

Figure 8-15. Copper deficiency. The early symptom is interveinal chlorosis of young foliage. It is different from that caused by iron deficiency because lobes and points at the leaf margin tend to be deeper green than the inner portion of the leaf blade, as seen in the above chrysanthemum leaves (a). When copper deficiency progresses in chrysanthemum, the first fully expanded leaves suddenly turn necrotic (b) as the upper leaves partially regain a green color. With time, the chlorosis of the plant tip intensifies and necrosis occurs again. Some crops exhibit veinal chlorosis as a late stage of copper deficiency as seen in the chrysanthemum plant above (c). Copper deficiency in rose (d) is seen as irregular interveinal chlorosis of young leaves. When leaves are forming, necrosis occurs on the leaf blade, resulting in the development of very small leaves. The pattern of small leaves may be cyclic, giving an hourglass effect.

(a) (b)

(c) (d)

Figure 8-16. Boron deficiency. Leaves become thickened and leathery in some plant species and irregular chlorosis develops as in the case of the petunia above (a). Other plant species develop crinkled leaves with irregular chlorosis of young leaves, as seen in the Rieger begonia plant (b). Rust colored cracks are common on stems, petioles, flower stalks, and sometimes on the leaf blades of many plants. Cork develops over the cracks (b). A cross-section of tissues of many boron-deficient plants would show rust coloration and a breakdown of vascular tissue. The boron requirement of reproductive (floral) growth is greater than that for vegetative growth; thus, abortion of the meristem often occurs when the flower bud begins to form. Side shoots develop and in turn abort only to give rise to more and more side shoots. Eventually a "witch's broom" forms, as seen in the above carnation shoots (c). If flowers should form, they are usually incomplete. Carnation flowers frequently have split calyx and a low petal count. The gladiolus flower on the left above (d) shows incompletely formed petals as a result of boron deficiency.

Figure 8-17. Molybdenum deficiency. This deficiency is rare in greenhouse crops except for poinsettia, where it is common. As pictured above, median poinsettia leaves develop a chlorotic margin which turns yellow and later necrotic. These symptoms spread inward, eventually killing the entire leaf.

A few definitions will be a help in reading the key. *Chlorosis* refers to a process whereby green chlorophyll is lost. The leaf tissue turns progressively lighter green and finally yellow. *Necrosis* refers to the death of cells and is identified as various shades of brown. *Interveinal chlorosis* is chlorosis occurring between the veins (vascular tissue) of the leaf. The veins remain green in color.

A *witch's broom* is a typical boron deficiency symptom because more boron is required for flower bud formation than for vegetative shoot development. When the plant reaches the stage of flower bud formation, it aborts, giving rise to lateral vegetative shoots. These develop but in turn abort as flower buds are initiated. This process continues until a proliferation of developing shoots gives the appearance of a broom. *Strap-leaves* are typical of calcium deficiency and are long thin leaves which have the appearance of a strap.

Soil Testing

Analyses of greenhouse soils will generally include a measurement of the pH and soluble salt levels in the soil. Neither of these levels are determined by visual diagnosis or foliar analysis procedures. Only a portion of most nutrients in the soil are immediately available to the plant. Soil test

Key to the Classical Symptoms of Various Nutrient Deficiencies

	THIS SYMPTOM MAY BE
a. The dominant symptom is chlorotic foliage.	
b. Entire leaf blades are chlorotic	
c. Only the lower leaves are chlorotic followed by necrosis and leaf drop	Nitrogen
cc. Leaves on all parts of plant are affected and sometimes have a beige case.	Sulfur
bb. Yellowing of leaves takes form of interveinal chlorosis.	
c. Only recently mature or older leaves exhibit interveinal chlorosis	Magnesium
cc. Only younger leaves exhibit interveinal chlorosis. This is the only symptom.	Iron
d. In addition to interveinal chlorosis on young leaves, grey or tan necrotic spots develop in chlorotic areas.	Manganese
dd. While younger leaves have interveinal chlorosis, the tips and lobes of leaves remain green followed by veinal chlorosis and rapid, extensive necrosis of leaf blade.	Copper
ddd. Young leaves are very small, sometimes missing leaf blades altogether and internodes are short giving a rosette appearance.	Zinc
aa. Leaf chlorosis is not the dominant symptom.	
b. Symptoms appear at base of plant.	
c. At first, all leaves are dark green and then growth is stunted. Purple pigment often develops in leaves, particularly older leaves.	Phosphorus
cc. Margins of older leaves become chlorotic and then burn or small chlorotic spots progressing to necrosis appear scattered on old leaf blades.	Potassium
bb. Symptoms appear at top of plant.	
c. Terminal buds die giving rise to a witch's broom. Young leaves become very thick, leathery, and chlorotic. Rust color cracks and corking occur on young stems, petioles, and flower stalks. Young leaves crinkled.	Boron
cc. Margins of young leaves fail to form sometimes yielding strap-leaves. Growing point ceases to develop leaving a blunt end. Light green color or uneven chlorosis of young tissue. Root growth is poor in that roots are short and thickened.	Calcium

procedures must give an estimate of the proportion of each nutrient which is available. Soil testing is commonly practiced during crop growth, but is equally valuable prior to planting. The pH level of greenhouse media is best adjusted prior to planting due to the need to thoroughly mix limestone or sulfur into it. A soil test prior to planting will also support the decision of which nutrients can be provided in a single application at that time.

Most soil testing is performed by institutional and commercial laboratories. Growers can purchase equipment to test their own root media. Inexpensive test kits generally purchased for nutrient tests are only moderately accurate giving just an approximate indication of nutrient level. Very accurate equipment, however, can be purchased by growers for testing pH and soluble salt levels. Every greenhouse business should own a pH meter (beginning at $100 and up) and a soluble salt meter (about $200). These two tests can be run in 30 minutes time and are extremely valuable in root media preparation, monitoring of general nutrient status, and for diagnosing nutritional problems.

An important decision in soil testing is that of the number of samples to be drawn. No set area can be assigned to a sample. To determine the boundaries of the area included in one sample, one should consider the origin of the media and its fertilization history. The wide variety of components in greenhouse media react differently with plant nutrients. Clays tend to tie up potassium, some more than others, while pine bark and peatmoss-based soil-less media are often associated with micronutrient deficiencies, particularly iron. Although two media might be handled under the same fertilization program, in time the available levels of nutrients will vary so much that separate soil tests will be needed.

On the other hand, a single medium might have been subjected to two fertilization programs perhaps dictated by two different crops. Even though only one crop might be growing in these areas at present, it is necessary to take two soil samples. Residual nutrients such as phosphorus may have been applied in greater quantity to one area than the other. There are other more subtle factors to consider which one will come to recognize as he or she becomes familiar with the greenhouse range. A chrysanthemum grower a few years ago experienced root injury, necrosis of leaf margins, and overall stunting of plants in specific sections of ground beds during rainy seasons. The problem was due to poor drainage in the low spots of the beds. Under this condition of low soil oxygen content, an excessive proportion of the large manganese reserve of the soil was converted to an available form and in turn resulted in manganese toxicity. The higher areas of the beds were sufficiently drained and aerated to prevent an excessive conversion of unavailable to available manganese. To identify this problem it was necessary to recognize and sample the problem section only.

There are state soil-testing laboratories in most states which offer services for no fee to a nominal cost. There also are a number of commercial laboratories which offer soil testing, foliar analysis, and consulting services. The customary volume of soil submitted is one pint. It is important that this sample be collected properly so that it is truly representative of the several thousand square feet of greenhouse benches it may represent. A soil-sampling tool should be used such as the one shown in Figure 8-18. The top half-inch of soil is scraped aside and the soil sampling tube is then pressed into the soil until it makes contact with the bottom of the pot or bench. In this way the entire root zone is sampled. The top half-inch is avoided because abnormal levels of fertilizer salts build up there as a result of water evaporation and also because roots rarely grow there due to rapid drying. At least ten soil cores should be taken for one sample. Some should be taken from the edge of the bench and others from the center since drying conditions, which affect salt accumulation, differ in these locations. The ten cores should be collected from all sectors of the sample area.

The soil sample should be mailed to the testing laboratory without delay. If the soil is wet enough to cause a breakdown of the package during shipment, it should be partially dried in the sun or on a warm surface, such as a boiler, prior to shipping. It is very important that information sheets supplied by the testing laboratory be completed and sent with the sample. This information aids in identifying problems and developing recommendations.

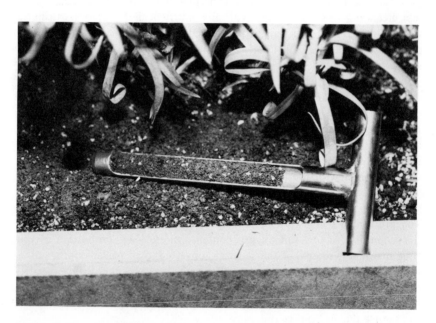

Figure 8-18. A sampling tool used for obtaining cores of soil from pots or beds in greenhouses for soil-testing purposes. The side of the tube is cut away to permit removal of the soil core.

pH: The soil-testing laboratories will interpret most of the results and make recommendations; however, it is still important for the grower to be able to interpret the test results. The soil pH level has far-reaching effects. The soil is neutral at pH 7.0, alkaline if above, and acid if below (Figure 8-19). The soil pH level controls the availability of all essential plant nutrients to one degree or another, as illustrated in Figure 8-1. Iron, manganese, zinc and copper increase in availability as the pH level decreases. Increased availability of Fe is held to be the reason acid-loving crops grow better at low pH levels. Apparently these crops are inefficient accumulators of iron. Availability of phosphorus, calcium, magnesium, and molybdenum lessens with decreasing pH. Problems of equal magnitude can occur at alkaline pH levels, i.e., above 7.0. Availability of iron, manganese, zinc, copper, and boron can diminish to the point of deficiency. The greatest average level of availability for all essential plant nutrients exists in the pH range of 6.2 to 6.8. It is possible to grow successful crops at much higher and lower levels, but the further one strays from the recommended range the greater are the odds against success.

Most greenhouse media require an upward adjustment of pH. This can

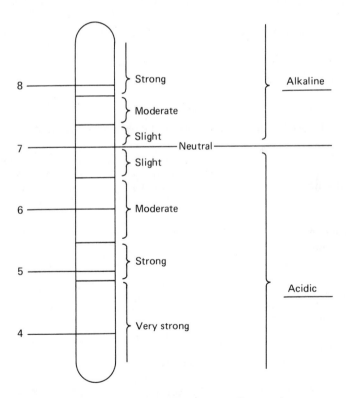

Figure 8-19.   Classification of soil pH levels according to plant response.

be accomplished at the time of mixing by incorporating finely ground dolomitic limestone into the media. Rates vary for each media type with clay, peatmoss, and pine bark requiring the heaviest rates. In general, three pounds of limestone per cubic yard of soil based medium will raise the pH about 0.3 to 0.5 units. Soil-test reports will indicate more precise amounts.

Ground limestone dissolves very slowly; thus it is important that it be mixed into the root medium to speed up the process of release into the medium solution. This process cannot occur once the crop is planted, but two procedures can be used for raising the pH level after planting. When a small upward adjustment is needed, i.e., 0.5 pH unit or less, one can switch to alkaline fertilizers in the continuous liquid program. Table 8-8 indicates the acidity and alkalinity of several common fertilizers. To adjust the pH level up, sodium, potassium, or calcium nitrates can be used. A good fertilizer program for poinsettia calls for two pounds of calcium nitrate in combination with one pound of potassium nitrate in 100 gallons of water applied weekly. If one carries out the appropriate mathematics, he finds that this program is equivalent to applying 3.4 ounces of ground limestone per cubic yard of root media each week. This is a small addition, but in time it has an effect. Fertilizer adjustment of soil pH works for the grower who through periodic testing of the soil sees pH change before it becomes injurious. The grower who permits a severe drop in pH level to occur during culture of the crop must use more drastic measures which can entail an element of risk. It may be necessary to apply hydrated lime (calcium hydroxide), referred to as *builder's*

Table 8-8

Effect of Various Fertilizers on the pH Level of Root Media

FERTILIZER	ALKALINE (LB OF LIMESTONE EQUAL TO 10 LB OF FERTILIZER)	ACIDIC (LB OF LIMESTONE NEEDED TO NEUTRALIZE 10 LB OF FERTILIZER)
Sodium nitrate	2.9	—
Potassium nitrate	2.6	—
Calcium nitrate	2.0	—
Ammonium sulfate	—	11.0
Urea	—	8.4
Diammonium phosphate	—	7.4
Ammonium phosphate	—	6.5
Ammonium nitrate	—	5.9
Superphosphate	Neutral	
Potassium chloride	Neutral	
Potassium sulfate	Neutral	

From Anon. *Dictionary of Plant Foods.* Farm Chemicals, Meister Publishing Co., 37841 Euclid Avenue, Willoughby, OH 44094, 1968.

lime. This material is injurious to young foliage and in large quantities can damage roots. A rate of 1.5 pounds per 100 square feet is recommended. The hydrated lime can be applied dry to the soil surface and then immediately syringed with water to remove any from the plant surfaces as well as to begin dissolving and moving the lime into the soil. Hydrated lime can also be applied by mixing 1 pound of it into 5 gallons of water and applying the dissolved portion to 20 square feet of medium. Hydrated lime is more soluble than ground limestone, but not completely water soluble. It reacts much faster than ground limestone, yet has a shorter residual effect in the root media. If one application does not solve the problem, a second one can be made after three weeks.

The high pH level of hydrated lime can cause a conversion of ammonium nitrogen to ammonia gas. This gas is injurious to roots and foliage. This can be a problem when a large proportion of the nitrogen fertilizer requirement is being met by the use of urea or ammonium nitrogen during the time of the pH adjustment with hydrated lime.

It may be necessary to lower the pH level of the root media. This can be accomplished by the use of sulfur, aluminum sulfate, or iron sulfate with a crop absent or present. All of these sources react in the soil to ultimately form sulfuric acid. Rates of application are listed in Table 8-9. These recommendations are designed to lower the pH level to 5.0, a level required for producing a crop of blue-flowered hydrangeas. The table is useful for determining other changes. To lower the pH level from 6.5 to 6.0 one would use 0.5 pounds of sulfur per cubic yard—the differences between 2.0 and 1.5 pounds listed in column 2—or 1.5 pounds of aluminum sulfate—the difference between 5.25 and 3.75 pounds listed in column 3.

Iron sulfate is used at the same rates as those listed for aluminum sulfate. All three materials can be mixed into the soil dry. They also may be

Table 8-9

Quantities (lb per cu yd) of Sulfur or Aluminum Sulfate Necessary to Lower the pH Level of Greenhouse Root Media from Various Levels to 5.0*

pH CHANGE	SULFUR	ALUMINUM SULFATE
8.0 to 5.0	3.5	8.75
7.5 to 5.0	3.25	7.75
7.0 to 5.0	2.5	6.5
6.5 to 5.0	2.0	5.25
6.0 to 5.0	1.5	3.75
5.5 to 5.0	0.75	2.0

*From H. K. Tayama, Ohio Florists' Association Bulletin 442, 1966.

added to water and applied to the soil during mixing or to the surface of the soil of an existing crop. Aluminum and iron sulfates are water soluble whereas sulfur is not and, therefore, must be held in suspension. The sulfates react very rapidly while sulfur must be oxidized by soil microbes, a process requiring several weeks or more if the medium has been pasteurized.

Another valuable test provided only through soil testing is the measure of the soluble salt level. Salt concentrations in the soil solution and in the root cells determine to a large extent the flow of water between the two. Water flows in the direction of the higher salt concentration which generally exists in the root cells. For various reasons salt levels in the soil solution can build up so that water no longer moves into the root. Following transpirational loss of water from the foliage, cells begin to desiccate (lose adverse amounts of water).

An excessive level of soluble salts in the root medium is first seen as wilting of plants during bright times of the day even though the root medium is moist. Overall growth slows down. Roots die from the tips back, particularly in the dryer zones of the root media. Leaves become necrotic, in some cases along the margin and in others as circular spots scattered across the leaf blade. Ultimately, deficiency symptoms of many nutrients will occur as a result of acutely impaired nutrient uptake by the injured root system.

Soluble salts come from various sources. Soluble fertilizers are soluble salts. Initially insoluble slow-release fertilizers dissolve with time releasing nutrients into the root medium which are themselves soluble salts. Thus, some soluble salt must be present to insure a proper level of fertilizer, but the level must not be too high. Other sources may not be desirable. Occasionally a well is drilled which yields water of low quality; i.e., it contains quantities of impurities. The impurities may be sulfate in areas of old coal mine shafts, sodium chloride (table salt) or sodium bicarbonate (baking soda) along coastal areas, calcium bicarbonate in areas of limestone deposits, and sodium in the alkali areas found in arid parts of the world.

Organic matter of high N content that undergoes rapid decomposition constitutes another source of soluble salts. Manure and highly decomposed peats may have sizeable N contents which are rapidly released through degradation in the root medium as ammonium-N. Ammonium-N can quickly build up to a toxic level because it is not as readily utilized in many plants as nitrate N and because its positive electrical charge causes it to be strongly held in the root medium.

Fertilizers vary in the manner in which they affect the soluble salt level. Table 8-10 lists the relative salt effect of several fertilizers. Sodium nitrate was arbitrarily set at 100. Potassium chloride is shown to have a fifteen percent greater effect on raising the soluble salt level of root media than sodium nitrate while urea has only three-fourths of the effect of sodium nitrate. The nutritive value of these fertilizers should be taken into account

Table 8-10
Relative Salt Index for Several Fertilizers

FERTILIZER	SALT INDEX
Sodium nitrate (nitrate of soda)*	100
Potassium chloride (muriate of potash–60%K_2O)	116
Ammonium nitrate	105
Urea	75
Potassium nitrate	74
Ammonium sulfate	69
Calcium nitrate	53
Potassium sulfate	46
Magnesium sulfate	44
Diammonium phosphate	34
Concentrated superphosphate	10
20% superphosphate	8
Gypsum	8
Limestone	5

From: Rader, L. F. Jr., L. M. White and C. W. Whittaker. The Salt Index–A Measure of the Effect of Fertilizers on the Concentration of the Soil Solution. *Soil Sci.* 55:201–208, 1943.

*Sodium nitrate was arbitrarily set at 100. The lower the index value the smaller the contribution which the fertilizer makes to the soluble salt level of the root medium.

along with their salt index. As the fertilizer is utilized by the plants the influence upon the soluble salt level is reduced. Ammonium nitrate has a high salt index of 105 but is comprised of ammonium N and nitrate N only. These nutrients in combination are readily utilized by the plant; thus the salt effect of this fertilizer is quickly reduced to an insignificant level. Although sodium nitrate has a lower salt index of 100, it is comprised of sodium and nitrate N. The nitrate N is readily utilized but the sodium is not. Repeated applications of this fertilizer will lead to a buildup of sodium and ultimately a high soluble salt level. Chloride has an effect similar to sodium. For this reason, sodium and chloride containing fertilizers are generally avoided in the greenhouse. Excessive levels of soluble salts are a rare problem for field crops, but in the greenhouse where unusually high levels of fertilizer are applied, it is a very common problem.

Soil testing laboratories vary in the manner in which they conduct their testing. The amount of water used to remove the salts from the root medium is the variable in the soluble salt test. Basically there are three tests: (1) the saturated paste extract test in which only enough water is applied to the root medium sample to saturate it, (2) a 1 to 2 dilution test in which 2 volumes of water are added to 1 volume of dry medium, and (3) a 1-to-5 dilution test in which 5 volumes of water are added to 1 volume of dry medium. The root medium is left in contact with the water for at least 30 minutes to permit movement of the salt into the water. The electrical conductivity of the water is then measured by placing two electrodes in the water and measuring the flow of current between them. The higher the salt content, the greater the flow of electrical current through the water. The electrical conductivity (EC) is measured in terms of mho/cm (the opposite to ohms of electrical resistance). The conductivity is very low so it is recorded in fractions of a mho, thousandths of a mho in the case of the saturated paste extract (mho/cm $\times$ 10^{-3} also called millimho) and hundred-thousandths of a mho for the other tests (mho/cm $\times$ 10^{-5}). These terms will be of little concern to the grower. Each laboratory will use one test only and will make available an interpretation chart. Interpretation charts are presented in Table 8-11 for the three test procedures.

Seedlings are more sensitive to high soluble salt levels than established plants. Established plants vary in their resistance to high soluble salt levels. African violets and azalea are particularly sensitive and should not be grown in media with a level exceeding 80 on the 1:2 dilution test. Snapdragon is moderately sensitive and should be grown at levels below 125 on the 1:2 dilution test. Several of the house plant crops which have recently become popular are sensitive as well. Little research has been conducted on each of these many crops, and soluble salt interpretations are missing for most. The exact level at which injury occurs depends to a large degree on watering practices. If the root media is not permitted to dry, then a high salt content may be tolerated. When the media dries, the salts become more concentrated than indicated by the test and injuries may ensue. Ordinarily it is not wise to

Table 8-11
Interpretation of Soluble Salt Levels

DILUTION		SATURATED PASTE EXTRACT (millimho/cm)	INTERPRETATION
1:2	1:5		
(mho/cm $\times$ 10^{-5})			
0–25	0–10	0–1	Insufficient nutrition
26–50	11–25	1–2	Low fertility unless applied with every watering
100	50	3–5	Maximum for planting seedlings or rooted cuttings
51–125	26–60	2–4	Good for most crops
126–175	61–80	4–8	Good for established plants
176–200	81–100	8–16	Danger area
over 200	over 100	over 16	Usually injurious

maintain root media at a high moisture content, but between the time that a high salt level is identified and the cure is administered it is expedient to do so.

Fortunately soluble salts, as the name implies, are water soluble and can be leached from the root media. The standard corrective recommendation calls for application of one gallon of water per square foot of root medium for bench crops or per half cubic foot of root medium for pot crops, a waiting period of a few hours and then a second application of water at the rate of two quarts per square foot of root medium surface. The waiting period gives the more slowly soluble salts time to dissolve.

Oftentimes a root medium with a soil base is adversely affected by the second application of water. The soil structure breaks down. This is particularly harmful in carnation and rose root media where the crop is maintained for one, two, or five years without an opportunity to amend the medium. Researchers at the University of Connecticut have developed a more desirable procedure for leaching in these cases. Up to five gallons of water are applied to each square foot of root medium in one application, preferably with a trickle-type irrigation system. This procedure utilizes more water but eliminates the destructive second application of water when the soil is excessively wet and subject to breakdown of structure.

Soil testing is quite well justified by the benefits derived from the pH and soluble salt tests alone, yet a major portion of the analysis is given over to determination of the available levels of essential nutrients including nitrate-N, phosphorus, potassium, calcium, magnesium, manganese and sometimes ammonium-N, iron, and zinc. It is important to remember that soil tests are designed to estimate the available fraction of each nutrient tested rather than the total quantity of that nutrient present in the root medium.

This point is exemplified in the situation of iron. The crust of the earth contains about 4 percent iron which amounts to 80,000 pounds in the upper six inches of a one-acre field. Fe deficiency often develops in such a field and when it does it can be corrected with an application of as little as five pounds of iron. It would appear that the addition is insignificant, but in relation to the pool of plant-available iron in the field, the five pound addition is large. Somewhat less than 0.1 percent of the total iron is available.

An extracting solution must be used in a soil test which will draw out the available but not the unavailable iron in the same fashion that the root does. Since the nutrient holding power of soils and the extracting power of roots vary, it is difficult, if not impossible, to develop a perfect extracting solution. Several extracting solutions have been developed over the years which are in use today. None is perfect and each yields different numerical values. Within each testing system the numerical levels of individual nutrients are related to crop response. A phosphorus level of 50 in one test is indicative of an adequate level for growth while a level of 6 may be adequate

Table 8-12
Interpretative Table for the Spurway Test*

	LOW	MEDIUM	HIGH	VERY HIGH	TOXIC
Ammonium N	Below 2	2	5	10	Over 15
Calcium	Below 40	60–120	150	Over 200	—
Nitrate N	Below 5	10–20	25–50	50	Over 60
Phosphorus	Below 2	5	5–10	10–15	Over 15
Potassium	Below 10	20	30–50	50	Over 60

*From: University of Connecticut, Plant Science Dept. Greenhouse Soil Report Form.

Values are listed in parts per million (ppm). Medium levels are suggested for establishing seedlings and rooted cuttings while high levels are generally appropriate for established plants.

in another. In either case the grower uses the standards provided by the testing laboratory.

There are about five tests in use for greenhouse soils in America, but the most widely used is the Spurway test. Interpretative tables have been well developed for this test. Table 8-12 lists recommended levels of various nutrients included in the test for greenhouse crops in general. There are other tests, e.g., the double acid test, for which interpretative tables have not been developed in the floriculture field. Growers who use tests for which there are no standards should record and relate over the years their crop responses to fertilizer applications and soil test results. This procedure ultimately indicates to the grower the levels of each nutrient which should be maintained for best growth. Whether interpretative tables exist or not one should take monthly soil samples and should keep a log book in which are recorded crop responses, soil test and foliar analysis results, dates of water, fertilizer, pesticides, and any other factors affecting growth. Quite often it is necessary to adapt values in the interpretative table to individual situations. This can be accomplished through the logging procedure.

After an individualized interpretative table is developed, monthly soil sampling should be continued. This permits identification of faulty samples which might infrequently occur as a result of poor sampling procedure or an error in testing. Note in Figure 8-20 the March value for sample A which is abnormally high. This is an indication of a faulty sample. It also indicates the direction in which nutrient levels are changing in the root medium. Note again in Figure 8-20 that the potassium levels in root media represented by samples A and B in May are equal. If this were a desirable level no action would be taken, yet in one medium the level of potassium application should be diminished at this time while in the other it should be increased so that

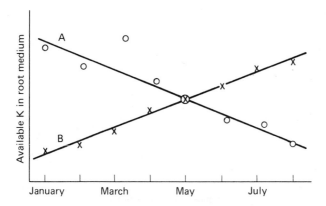

Figure 8-20. An illustration of the value of monthly soil sampling as opposed to a single sample date. Samples A and B drawn in May would indicate similar nutrient situations. This is erroneous since the root medium represented by sample A is decreasing in K level while that represented by sample B is increasing. These facts are borne out only by sequential sampling.

imbalances do not occur the following month. Only sequential sampling could bear out these points.

Foliar Analysis

Foliar analysis constitutes a third system for determining the nutrient status of crops. Like soil testing it is valuable because it can be used to assess a problem before damage occurs. Foliar analysis is an analysis of representative leaves from a crop to determine the quantities of essential and potentially hazardous nonessential elements which the crop has taken up. The laboratory conducting the analysis compares the results to standards developed at many research institutions around the world and draws the necessary conclusions for the grower.

Foliar analysis works well because of the strong relationship between leaf composition and plant response which is illustrated in Figure 8-21. Except in the zone of *luxury consumption,* where changes in leaf composition have no effect upon growth, the nutrient content of the leaf can be used to predict the growth of the plant. It is fortunate that the zone of luxury consumption exists because it lessens the chance of injury from overapplication of fertilizer.

Foliar analysis is not a substitute for soil testing. Although it and soil testing are intended for the same purpose of assessing nutrient status, each provides some information which the other does not. Where both do yield an

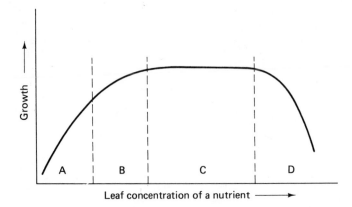

Figure 8-21. When all other factors are adequate, the leaf content of an essential nutrient strongly affects growth. Little growth occurs at low concentrations of the nutrient, but with small additions of the deficient nutrient large increases in growth occur (zone A). When the rate of growth comes closer to the optimum level, increases in the leaf content of the deficient nutrient bring about continually diminishing growth responses (zone B) until a point is reached beyond which no growth response is effected by increases in leaf concentration of the nutrient (zone C). This is the zone of *luxury consumption*. Eventually nutrient increases in the leaf reach a toxic level, resulting in decreases in growth and eventually in death (zone D).

assessment of the same factor, it is derived in a different manner which strengthens the conclusions. Foliar analysis does not give a measure of root medium pH or soluble salt levels but, unlike soil tests, it does give an analysis of all essential nutrients. Soil tests give information about the present and future by indicating levels of nutrients available for uptake. Foliar analysis gives information about the levels of nutrients already accumulated by the plant; thus it is directed from the past to the present. Just as one would not enter a serious medical operation without two independent assessments of the situation, one should not base the nutritional future of crops on one system of assessment.

The strength of soil testing in combination with foliar analysis is seen in a situation which occurred in a carnation range some years ago in New York. The crop was growing slowly and showing symptoms of potassium deficiency. Contrary to this observation, a soil test indicated that levels of nitrogen and potassium were high. Foliar analysis indicated that potassium was very deficient while nitrogen was only moderate to high. This combination of information led to the conclusion that potassium uptake was blocked by a high soil level of nitrogen. This is an antagonism which frequently occurs. The conclusion was verified when four weeks after reducing the rate of 20-20-20 fertilizer application to half of the previous level the grower observed a twofold increase in the foliar level of potassium and the disappearance of potassium deficiency symptoms.

Foliar analysis samples should be taken every four to six weeks and the results logged. The optimum level of nutrients in the foliage of each crop is different, necessitating the taking of a different sample for each crop. If one crop is growing in two dissimilar media or has been fertilized in two different manners two samples must be taken for that crop. It is important that the correct leaves be sampled since the nutrient level in each is different from the rest. The age of the crop is also important because the nutrient levels in each leaf change with time. The laboratory conducting the foliar analysis tests will provide a mailing envelope for the leaves and a set of instructions for collecting the proper leaves.

Rose plants are sampled by picking the two uppermost five-leaflet leaves on a stem whose flower calyx is cracking and whose color is just beginning to show. Thirty leaves with petioles attached should be collected.

Carnation plants that have not yet been pinched are sampled by collecting the fourth and fifth leaf pairs up from the base of the stem (area A in Figure 8-22). Sampling continues in area A after pinching and until the resulting lateral shoots develop seven pairs of leaves. Then the fifth or sixth leaf pairs are sampled on the new shoots (area B), counting the first pair of leaves to be separated for one-half the length of the leaves as the first leaf pair. Sampling continues in area B until a flower bud appears on that shoot. At that time, sampling should be shifted to secondary lateral shoots, again using the fifth and sixth leaf pairs from the terminal end of the shoot (area C). When secondary lateral shoots develop flower buds, sampling is shifted to tertiary lateral shoots, and so on.

Chrysanthemums are typical of plants in general in that the youngest fully expanded leaves are sampled. These leaves are usually found on chrysanthemum plants about one-third of the distance down the stem from the top. Chrysanthemums are generally sampled five to six weeks after planting for a single stem crop, or after pinching for a pinched crop.

Foliar analysis kits contain an information form as pictured in Figure 8-23. This form permits laboratory personnel to gather the information necessary to enable them to draw conclusions and make nutritional recommendations.

Ordinarily the leaves are placed in the mailing envelope as collected and mailed immediately to the testing laboratory. If it is apparent that nutrient residues are on the leaf surfaces from foliar fertilization, nutrient containing pesticides, etc., the leaves should be soaked in water for one minute, blotted dry, and then mailed. Deionized water is preferred, but if unavailable, clear tap water will do. The charge for foliar analysis is considerably more than for soil testing, ranging from $3 to $10 or more per sample. This charge is nominal considering the total investment in a crop and is well justified.

Considerable research has been conducted to determine the optimum

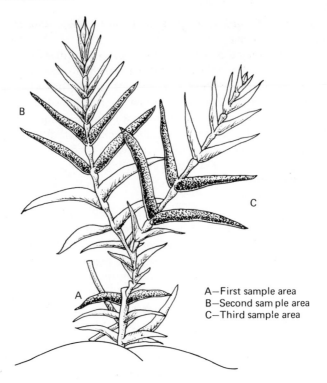

A—First sample area
B—Second sam ple area
C—Third sample area

Figure 8-22. Leaf sampling instructions for foliar analysis of florists' crops as used at North Carolina State University.

levels of nutrients in foliage. Carefully developed standards exist for many florists' crops and for other crops good estimates have developed from years of observation. Table 8-13 lists the minimum critical levels for several nutrients for some of the major crops. Concentrations below these levels are associated with deficiency. Macronutrient standards vary sharply with each crop; whereas micronutrient standards remain rather constant for most crops. There are few crop variations for the general micronutrient standards listed in Table 8-13. Listed in Table 8-14 are acceptable ranges of macronutrients for 27 tropical foliage plants. Macronutrients are expressed as a percentage of the dry weight of the leaf tissue analyzed. This would not be convenient for micronutrients since they constitute only a small fraction of one percent. A smaller term, parts per million (ppm), is used. The conversion from percent to ppm is simple, with 1 percent being equal to 10,000 ppm. The testing laboratories report their results on a form more or less similar to that reproduced in Figure 8-24. Generally the numerical level of each nutrient is reported along with an indication of which of five categories each of the nutrient levels fits:

MAILING ADDRESS: PLANT ANALYSIS LABORATORY — DEPARTMENT OF HORTICULTURAL SCIENCE
N. C. STATE UNIVERSITY, RALEIGH, N. C. 27607

SAMPLE INFORMATION FOR FLORICULTURE CROPS		LAB USE ONLY
Name of Grower:	County:	Date Sample Received:
Street, Route:	Date Sampled:	Condition of Sample:
City, State, Zip Code:	Grower Sample No:	Grower #
Telephone No:	Name of Crop:	County #
Identification of Field Sampled:	Description of Sample Site (which field):	Sample #
		Date Analysis Received:

SAMPLE INFORMATION

1. Name of crop _____ 2. Variety _____ 3. Date planted _____ .

4. Date pinched (if applicable) _____ .

5. This sample represents (a) an average condition _____ (b) a problem area _____

   (c) a spotty or sporadic situation _____ .

6. Appearance or condition of plant and/or leaves _____

_____

7. Location of sample on plant_____

_____

8. Previous crop _____ _____ 9. What is your fertilization program for the crop represented by this sample?

   (List fertilizers used, rates, and frequency of application).

_____

10. What ammendments did you use during preparation of the soil mix in which this crop is growing (List such

    materials as dolomitic limestone, superphosphate, fritted trace elements and the rates used).

_____

_____

North Carolina State University Agricultural Experiment Station
and North Carolina Agricultural Extension Service, Cooperating

FARMER OR GROWER COPY

Figure 8-23. A typical information form to be completed by the grower and submitted to the foliar analysis laboratory as an aid in the interpretation of results.

Table 8-13

Minimum Critical Foliar Levels of Nutrients for Florist Crops in General and for a Few Specific Crops

NUTRIENT	GENERAL CROPS	ROSE	CARNATION	CHRYSANTHEMUM	POINSETTIA	GERANIUM	RIEGER BEGONIA
N %	–	3.0	3.0	4.5	3.5	2.4	4.7
P %	0.3	0.2	0.45	0.3	0.2	0.3	0.2
K %	–	1.8	3.0	3.5	1.0	0.6	0.95
Ca %	–	1.0	1.0	1.0	0.5	0.8	0.5
Mg %	0.3	0.25	0.3	0.3	0.2	0.14	0.25
Fe ppm	50–60	–	–	–	–	–	–
Mn ppm	30	–	–	–	–	–	–
Zn ppm	20	–	–	–	–	–	–
Cu ppm	5	–	–	7	–	–	–
B ppm	25	–	–	–	–	–	–

Concentrations above these are sufficient while those below are associated with deficiency. Macronutrient standards are specific to each crop. Few micronutrient standards have been developed for specific crops. Fortunately, micronutrient standards do not vary much among crops.

Name of Grower:	Paul Nelson		County:	Wake		Date Sample Received:	3-19-76
Street, Route:	29 Main St.		Date Sampled:	3-17-76		Condition of Sample:	Good
City, State, Zip:	Raleigh, N. C. 27607		Grower Sample #:	2		Grower #:	27
Telephone No.:	737-3132		Name of Crop: Cut Chrysanthemum			County #:	13
Identification of Field Sampled:	III		Description of Sample Site (Within The Field):			Lab Sample #: 1971 Date Analysis Received: 3-26-76	

COUNTY SAMPLE NUMBER	FARMER OR GROWER SAMPLE NUMBER	N %	P %	K %	Na %	Ca %	Mg %	Mn ppm	Fe ppm	B ppm	Cu ppm	Mo ppm	Zn ppm	Al ppm
	2	4.50	0.85	2.10	0.02	1.2	0.38	125	150	23	9	1	44	
RANGE														
DEFICIENT				X										
LOW										X				
SUFFICIENT		X			X	X	X	X	X		X	X	X	
HIGH			X											
EXCESS														

COMMENTS AND RECOMMENDATIONS.

1. Potassium is low. Apply potassium nitrate (13-0-44) for the next two weekly applications at the rate of 2 lbs. per 100 gal.

2. Phosphorus is too high. After correcting the potassium problem use a 1-0-1 ratio fertilizer rather than the 1-1-1 you have been using.

3. Boron is approaching the deficiency level. Apply one ounce of borax per 100 sq. ft. of bench space once.

Mailing Address: Plant Analysis Laboratory, Department of Horticultural Science, N. C. State University, Raleigh, N. C. 27607 **FARMER OR GROWER COPY**
North Carolina State University Agricultural Experiment Station and North Carolina Agricultural Extension Service, Cooperating.

Figure 8-24. A typical foliar analysis report as it is received by the grower.

273

Table 8-14

Acceptable Ranges of Nitrogen, Phosphorus, Potassium, Calcium, and Magnesium in 27 Tropical Foliage Plants*

PLANT FAMILY PLANT NAME	CONCENTRATION (PERCENTAGE)				
	N	P	K	Ca	Mg
Acanthaceae					
Aphelandra squarrosa	2.0 – 3.0	.20 – .40	1.0 – 2.0	0.2 – 0.4	0.5 – 1.0
Agavaceae					
Dracaena deremensis 'Janet Craig'	2.0 – 3.0	.20 – .30	3.0 – 4.0	1.5 – 2.0	0.3 – 0.6
Dracaena deremensis 'Warneckii'	2.5 – 3.5	.15 – .30	3.0 – 4.5	1.0 – 2.0	0.5 – 1.0
Dracaena fragrans 'Massangeana'	2.0 – 3.0	.15 – .25	1.0 – 2.0	1.0 – 2.0	0.5 – 1.0
Dracaena Sanderana	2.5 – 3.5	.20 – .30	2.0 – 3.0	1.5 – 2.5	0.3 – 0.6
Dracaena surculosa	1.5 – 2.5	.20 – .30	1.0 – 2.0	1.0 – 1.5	0.3 – 0.5
Sansevieria trifasciata 'Laurentii'	1.7 – 3.0	.15 – .30	2.0 – 3.0	1.0 – 1.5	0.3 – 0.6
Araceae					
Aglaonema commutatum 'Fransher'	2.5 – 3.5	.20 – .35	2.5 – 3.5	1.0 – 1.5	0.3 – 0.6
Anthurium Andraeanum	1.6 – 2.1	.20 – .40	1.0 – 2.3	1.2 – 1.7	0.7 – 1.0
Dieffenbachia exotica	2.5 – 3.5	.20 – .35	3.0 – 4.5	1.0 – 1.5	0.3 – 0.8
Epipremnum aureum	2.5 – 3.5	.20 – .35	3.0 – 4.5	1.0 – 1.5	0.3 – 0.6
Monstera deliciosa	2.5 – 3.5	.20 – .35	3.0 – 4.5	0.4 – 1.0	0.3 – 0.6
Philodendron scandens oxycardium	2.0 – 3.0	.15 – .25	3.0 – 4.5	0.5 – 1.5	0.3 – 0.6
Syngonium podophyllum	2.5 – 3.5	.20 – .30	3.0 – 4.5	0.4 – 1.0	0.3 – 0.6

Araliaceae					
Brassaia actinophylla	2.5 – 3.5	.20 – .35	2.5 – 3.5	1.0 – 1.5	0.3 – 0.6
Dizygotheca elegantissima	2.0 – 2.5	.40 – .60	1.5 – 2.5	0.5 – 1.0	0.2 – 0.3
Bromeliaceae					
Aechmea fasciata	1.5 – 2.0	.40 – .70	1.5 – 2.5	0.5 – 1.0	0.4 – 0.8
Liliaceae					
Asparagus retrofractus	1.5 – 2.5	.30 – .50	2.0 – 3.0	0.1 – 0.3	0.1 – 0.3
Chlorophytum comosum	1.5 – 2.5	.10 – .20	3.5 – 5.0	1.0 – 2.0	0.5 – 1.5
Marantaceae					
Maranta leuconeura Kerchoviana	2.0 – 3.0	.20 – .30	3.0 – 4.5	0.5 – 1.5	0.5 – 1.0
Stromanthe amabilis	2.5 – 3.0	.20 – .50	3.0 – 4.0	0.1 – 0.2	0.3 – 0.5
Moraceae					
Ficus benjamina	1.8 – 2.5	.10 – .20	1.0 – 1.5	2.0 – 3.0	0.4 – 0.8
Ficus elastica	1.3 – 1.6	.10 – .20	0.6 – 1.0	0.3 – 0.5	0.2 – 0.4
Palmae					
Chamaedorea elegans	2.5 – 3.0	.20 – .30	1.0 – 2.0	0.4 – 1.0	0.3 – 0.4
Chrysalidocarpus lutescens	1.5 – 2.5	.10 – .20	1.0 – 2.0	1.0 – 1.5	0.3 – 0.6
Polypodiaceae					
Adiantum caudatum	1.5 – 2.5	.40 – .80	2.0 – 3.0	0.2 – 0.3	0.2 – 0.4
Rubiaceae					
Coffea arabica	2.5 – 3.5	.15 – .25	2.0 – 3.0	0.5 – 1.0	0.3 – 0.5

*From Poole, R. T., C. A. Connover and J. N. Joiner. "Chemical Composition of Quality Tropical Foliage Plants." Proc. Fla. State Hort. Soc. 89:307-308, 1976.

1. Deficient—showing deficiency symptoms

2. Low—hidden hunger

3. Sufficient

4. High—hidden toxicity

5. Very high—showing toxicity symptoms

Also included are recommended fertilization changes to correct any existent nutrient problems.

CORRECTIVE PROCEDURES

Recommendations

Fertilization systems were recommended in the earlier part of this chapter. Under ideal conditions these will work well but conditions are not always ideal. The optimum rate of fertilizer application relates to the rate of plant growth which in turn can be adversely affected by inclement weather, a poor root medium which does not drain well, over- or underwatering, a dirty greenhouse covering, nutrient tie-up by constituents of the root medium, antagonisms by other nutrients, and many other factors. Some nutrients are affected more than others; thus it is not only important to adjust the rate of fertilization but also to change the ratio of nutrients in the fertilizer. Occasionally a single nutrient will go far enough out of balance that it alone must be applied. Nitrogen and potassium adjustments can be accomplished through alterations in the continual fertilization program as indicated earlier (refer to Table 8–4). Corrective procedures for ten other nutrient deficiencies are listed in Table 8–15.

Phosphorus deficiency is uncommon but not altogether nonexistent. Its occurrence would indicate failure to incorporate phosphorus into the root medium prior to planting and could easily be corrected by switching to a complete, phosphorus-containing, fertilizer such as 20–20–20 in the continual program. Calcium and magnesium deficiencies do not often occur where the root medium pH level has been properly adjusted with dolomitic limestone. Poinsettia was traditionally, and in many cases still is, grown in an acid medium to minimize the development of root rot organisms. Calcium and magnesium deficiencies often occur under these conditions. The new varieties of poinsettia are prone to magnesium deficiency even when the medium pH level is adjusted to the range of 6.2 to 6.8. Easter lilies are very susceptible to calcium deficiency. A combination of 2 pounds of calcium nitrate and 1 pound of potassium nitrate per 100 gallons of water applied weekly works

Fertilizer Sources and Rates for Correction of Various Nutrient Deficiencies*

DEFICIENT NUTRIENT	FERTILIZER SOURCE	RATE OF APPLICATION
P	Switch to a complete fertilizer containing N–P–K for the continual program	
	OR diammonium phosphate	1 lb per 100 sq ft
	OR monopotassium phosphate	1 lb per 100 sq ft
Ca	Switch the N source to calcium nitrate for a few weeks	1 lb per 100 sq ft OR 2 lb per 100 gal
Mg	Magnesium sulfate (Epsom salts)	1 lb per 100 sq ft
S	Magnesium sulfate	1 lb per 100 sq ft
	OR switch N or K source to ammonium or potassium sulfate for a few weeks	
Fe	Iron chelate (Sequestrene 330)	1 lb per 1000 sq ft (1 oz/30 gal)
Mn	Manganese sulfate	1 lb per 1000 sq ft
	OR foliar spray manganese chelate	8 oz per 100 gal
Zn	Zinc sulfate	8 oz per 1000 sq ft
	OR zinc chelate	4 oz per 1000 sq ft
	OR switch to the fungicide Zineb and spray at the recommended rate monthly	
Cu	Copper sulfate	8 oz per 1000 sq ft
	OR copper chelate	4 oz per 1000 sq ft
	OR foliar spray tri-basic copper sulfate	4 oz per 100 gal
B	Borax	0.25 oz per 100 sq ft
	OR Solubor	0.12 oz per 100 sq ft
Mo	Foliar spray sodium or ammonium molybdate with a spreader-sticker	2 oz per 100 gal

*These corrective procedures are to be applied once. Subsequent applications should be made only after soil and foliar analysis tests indicate the need. All fertilizers are to be applied to the root medium unless a foliar spray is specified. A rate of root medium application of 1 lb per 100 sq ft equates to 2 lb per 100 gal for a soil-based medium, since 100 gal of water will saturate 200 sq ft of root medium.

well as a source of nitrogen, potassium, and calcium for both of these crops. Sulfur deficiencies tend to relate to the soil type used in root media. For this reason it is prevalent in specific geographical regions. It is a rare problem in soilless media or any medium where superphosphate (0-20-0) is used at 3 pounds per cubic yard or gypsum at 1.5 pounds per cubic yard.

It is generally safe to apply a micronutrient mixture when symptoms of a single micronutrient deficiency occur if such a mixture has not been applied within three months (nine months in the case of fritted micronutrients). If the mixture has been applied within this period, the deficient nutrient should be identified by a foliar analysis test or by treating small test plots with the suspected deficient nutrient. The deficient nutrient alone should be applied. Micronutrient excesses can be far more troublesome than deficiencies because they are difficult and sometimes impossible to remove from the root media.

Iron deficiency is common in rose hydrangea, and azalea. It also readily occurs in crops grown in soilless media if iron has not been incorporated into the media. Most rose crops are on a continuous program of iron fertilization. The frequency of application ranges from every six to twelve weeks. The symptoms of manganese deficiency are similar to those of iron deficiency and on occasion the two will occur together. Manganese deficiency is much less prevalent than iron deficiency. Zinc deficiency is rare in greenhouse crops except in the case of the *kalanchoe* (Figure 8-14). The young stems become flattened and highly branched, a condition termed *fasciation.* The stem, being very broad, gives the appearance of several stems fused together in one plane. Leaves are small and often chlorotic.

Copper deficiency occurs in specific soil types and, thus, follows geographical patterns. Soils of the southeastern United States are very prone to copper deficiency. The rose crop is an exception in that the deficiency occurs almost universally. Certain varieties are most sensitive. These are Golden Wave, White Butterfly, and Mary DeVor. The variety Forever Yours is moderately sensitive.

Boron deficiency is a problem with carnation and snapdragon crops. The requirement for boron is similar in these and other crops, but the ability of these crops to take up boron is lower. Boron is readily taken up by chrysanthemum. When carnation or snapdragon crops follow a chrysanthemum crop, boron deficiency often occurs. The pink varieties of carnation are most prone.

Molybdenum deficiency often occurs on poinsettia but is practically nonexistent in other greenhouse crops. The symptoms for poinsettia are chlorosis along the margin of leaves of intermediate age which spreads inward between the main veins and eventually causes the entire leaf to be chlorotic. Patches of necrosis develop along the leaf margin finally causing these leaves to fall off.

Interactions

Before attempting to correct a nutrient deficiency one should always be certain which nutrient is the cause of the problem. The carnation problem previously cited in which potassium deficiency was induced by an excessive soil level of nitrogen is a good example. A first indication would have been to apply potassium fertilizer, but this would not have solved the problem; it might have led to an excessive soluble salt level. The potassium deficiency was caused by an excessive level of nitrogen and only a reduction of nitrogen in the soil would correct the deficiency. Such relationships are known as *antagonisms*. Once the basic antagonisms are known, it is a simple matter to identify them in soil and foliar analysis reports. The more common antagonisms are listed in Table 8-16. When a deficiency of one of the nutrients in the right column of Table 8-16 is identified, it should be determined if an abnormally high level of the nutrient in the left column exists. If so, corrective action should involve reduction of the concentration of the nutrient in the left column. Note that some, but not all, of the nutrient antagonisms are reciprocal. A high level of iron will reduce manganese uptake and reciprocally a high level of manganese will reduce iron uptake.

Table 8-16
Common Antagonisms Occurring in Crops in General

NUTRIENT IN EXCESS	INDUCED DEFICIENCY
N	K
K	N, Ca, Mg
Na	K, Ca, Mg
Ca	Mg
Mg	Ca
Ca	B
Fe	Mn
Mn	Fe

High root media levels of nutrients in the left column bring about deficiencies of the nutrients listed in the right column.

SUMMARY

1. It is expedient to supply all essential nutrients, except possibly nitrogen and potassium, in sufficient quantity to last the full term of the crop at the time of preparing the root medium. A pH adjustment with dolomitic

limestone provides calcium and magnesium. An application of three pounds of 20 percent superphosphate per cubic yard of root medium supplies phosphorus, sulfur, and more calcium. Micronutrients can be incorporated into the medium in the form of a dry fritted mixture or immediately after planting as a single application of a liquid mixture.

2. Nitrogen and potassium are commonly applied as a liquid formulation with every watering or once per week. The rate and ratio of these two nutrients varies according to the crop.

3. The nitrogen and potassium formulation is prepared as a concentrate to conserve space and reduce the labor of mixing, and then is diluted and metered into the greenhouse water line by equipment known as fertilizer proportioners. It is delivered to the bench or pots through the automatic watering system.

4. Nitrogen and potassium can be alternatively applied in a single application of a dry slow-release fertilizer that, depending on formulation, can provide N-P-K for three to fourteen months. Different formulations and types of slow-release fertilizers are available, eliminating the need for any regular fertilization during the crop schedule.

5. Identification of nutritional disorders is as important as the fertilization program itself. Visual diagnosis of disorders can be effective, but unfortunately depends upon the presence of an injury which may not be completely reversible.

6. Soil testing is a valuable diagnostic tool in that it gives a measure of the root medium pH and soluble salt levels as well as a determination of the available levels of many, but not all, nutrients. It is inexpensive.

7. Foliar analysis is an excellent diagnostic tool to be used with soil testing. It provides a different view of the status of all the essential nutrients, some not included in soil testing.

8. The pH level of the root medium is important because it regulates the availability of all essential nutrients to one degree or another.

9. The problem of excessive soluble salts is prevalent in greenhouse culture due to heavy fertilization procedures. High soluble salt concentrations result in reduced water availability to the plant which leads to desiccation and death of roots.

SUGGESTED READINGS

Bunt, A. C. *Modern Potting Composts.* The Pennsylvania State University Press, University Park, PA, 1976.

Criley, R. A. and W. H. Carlson. "Tissue Analysis Standards for Various Floricultural Crops." *Florists' Review* 146:19–20, 70–73, 1970.

Jones, J. B., Jr. *Plant Analysis Handbook for Georgia.* Georgia Cooperative Extension Bulletin 735, 1974.

Koths, J. S.; R. W. Judd, Jr.; J. J. Maisano, Jr.; G. F. Griffin; J. W. Bartok; and R. A. Ashley, "Nutrition of Greenhouse Crops." University of Connecticut Cooperative Extension Service Bulletin 76-14, 1976.

Pinkerton, T. C., H. C. Moore, and A. L. Mehring. *Dictionary of Plant Foods.* Farm Chemicals, Meister Publishing Co., Willoughby, OH, 1968.

Poole, R. T., C. A. Connover and J. N. Joiner. "Chemical Composition of Quality Tropical Foliage Plants." Proc. Fla. State Hort. Soc. 89:307–308, 1976.

Sprague, H. B. *Hunger Signs in Crops*, third ed. David McKay Co., New York, 1964.

Walsh, L. M. and J. D. Beaton. *Soil Testing and Plant Analysis*, revised ed. Soil Science Society of America, Inc., Madison, WI, 1973.

White, J. W. "Fertilization," in Mastalerz, J. W., ed., *Bedding Plants.* Pennsylvania Flower Growers, 103 Tyson Building, University Park, PA, 1976.

Chapter 9

Carbon Dioxide Fertilization

ROLE OF CARBON

Carbon is an essential plant nutrient and is present in the plant in greater quantity than any other nutrient. About 40 percent of the dry matter of plants is composed of carbon. Plants obtain carbon from carbon dioxide gas (CO_2) in the air. For the most part, CO_2 gas diffuses through the stomatal openings in leaves when they are open. Once inside the leaf CO_2 gas moves into the cells where, in the presence of energy from the sun, it is used to make carbohydrates (sugars). The carbohydrates are translocated to various parts of the plant and transformed into other compounds needed for growth or maintenance of the plant. The process whereby CO_2 is utilized by the plant is known as *photosynthesis* and occurs in the green chloroplasts within cells. The process is summarized in the following equation:

$$CO_2 + \text{water} + \text{energy from sunlight} \rightarrow \text{carbohydrate} + \text{oxygen}$$

Air, on the average, contains about 0.03 percent CO_2. This is equivalent to 300 parts per million (ppm)—in each one million pounds of air there are 300 pounds of CO_2. The level of CO_2 in air outdoors can vary from 200 to 400 ppm. Levels of 400 ppm are common in industrial areas where fuels are combusted. The carbon in fuels is converted to CO_2 during the process of combustion. The CO_2 level also will be higher in areas such as swamps and river bottoms where large quantities of plant material are decomposing. Microorganisms feeding upon plant or animal remains respire CO_2 gas much as we humans do when we utilize·plant- and animal-derived foods. This CO_2 gas is evolved through a process called *respiration* which is summarized as follows for carbohydrates:

$$\text{carbohydrate} + \text{oxygen} \rightarrow CO_2 + \text{energy} + \text{water}$$

Respiration is the opposite of photosynthesis. It is a process which releases energy originally captured from sunlight in the process of photosynthesis. The energy released is used by the plant for various functions of growth, such as nutrient uptake.

A CO_2 level of 300 ppm is sufficient to support plant growth as we know it in the world today. Most plants, however, have the capacity to utilize greater concentrations of CO_2 and, in turn, attain more rapid growth. This genetic capability apparently stems back to primordial times when plants adapted to CO_2 levels 10 to 100 times the level that currently exists on earth.

CARBON DEFICIENCY

There are times in the winter when greenhouses are closed during the day to conserve heat. This may occur for several consecutive days during periods of inclement weather in the northern production areas of America. During the daylight hours CO_2 is removed from the air by plants through the process of photosynthesis. The level continually drops in a closed greenhouse and the rate of photosynthesis decreases until a point is reached at which growth stops.

It has been reported that an active sunflower leaf can consume the CO_2 in a column of air eight feet above it in an hour. Not all crops utilize CO_2 at that rate; however, in a matter of a few hours the CO_2 level in a closed greenhouse can drop to the compensation point where growth stops. The actual level where this happens varies for different crops, but for greenhouse crops in general it occurs near a level of 125 ppm CO_2. Carbon deficiency can occur for several days at a time, prolonging the culture time of the crop by the same number of days or reducing the quality of the crop.

CARBON DIOXIDE INJECTION

Effects on Plants

Researchers were surprised to find that plant responses continued to increase as CO_2 levels were raised above the 300 ppm level present in the atmosphere. Levels of 2,000 ppm continued to evoke growth responses in some crops. Apparently, as previously stated, this stems back to the earlier adaptation of plants to higher CO_2 levels in primordial times.

Very high levels of CO_2 have adverse effects on humans. The maximum level tolerated in submarines is 5,000 ppm. Levels of 1,000 to 1,500 ppm are common for greenhouse injection and are not harmful to people.

Crop responses vary according to the extent to which elevated levels of CO_2 can be maintained. Our studies in North Carolina (latitude 35°N) have indicated that the mild, fair weather conditions of winter are such that CO_2

can be injected for only an hour or so each day in the morning. After that, the ventilators are opened or the cooling fans are turned on. When ventilators are opened two inches or more it is not possible to hold CO_2 levels above that of the incoming air. CO_2 injection will pay for itself in North Carolina during winter seasons with a great deal of inclement weather, but not during bright winters. Raleigh is situated along the border below which CO_2 injection is not effective. Colder regions of America experience sizeable benefits from CO_2 injection on nearly all crops tested.

CO$_2$ injection on rose crops has resulted in increases in productivity up to 53 percent. Specific effects include a decrease in the number of blind shoots, increased stem length and weight, greater number of petals, and a shorter cropping time in the winter. A test at Pierce Brothers Greenhouses in Massachusetts showed a 53 percent increase in weight of roses cut when 1,000 ppm CO_2 was injected.

Chrysanthemum yields increase in the form of thicker stems and greater height when CO_2 is injected (Figure 9-1). Excess stem lengths reduce the value of pot mums and in the case of cut mums are left behind in the bench when the flowers are cut. The increased height, however, can be translated into a reduction in the length of time required to flower the crop. Because the flower date is controlled by manipulating the length of day, it is possible to program chrysanthemums to flower up to two weeks earlier with-

Figure 9-1. Dramatic increases in growth can be achieved by enriching the CO_2 level of the greenhouse atmosphere as seen in the pot mums above. *(Photo courtesy of Dr. Roy Larson, Department of Horticultural Science, North Carolina State University, Raleigh, NC 27607.)*

out a reduction in height when CO_2 is injected. This is a considerable savings in the production cost, considering a normal crop time of 12 to 16 weeks.

Carnation yields have been increased up to 38 percent by CO_2 injection. The weight of flowers and strength of stems have been increased and the time required for shoots to reach flowering has been reduced by as much as two weeks. Equally beneficial effects have been obtained for carnation stock plants. Cuttings of greater quality and number have been produced and the useful life of the stock plant has been increased as well.

CO_2 injection has caused a variety of beneficial effects on a number of other crops. Fall crops of snapdragons were of better quality while spring crops were reported to have flowered 13 days early in Connecticut. Rooting of geranium cuttings was improved and the height, as well as number of branches on subsequent plants, was increased. Blindness was decreased in Dutch iris. The number, quality, and size of blooms on orchid plants were increased, as were poinsettia bract diameters. Greenhouse vegetables have benefitted as well. Lettuce crops have been produced in 20 percent less time while tomato yields have been increased by better than 50 percent.

Increased growth stimulated by CO_2 injection has necessitated other changes in the cultural programs of some crops. Growers often fertilize lightly in the winter because slow growth is expected. Enrichment of the atmosphere with CO_2 leads to heavier rates of growth and ultimately a nutrient shortage. If a heavier rate of fertilizer is applied, the growth rate continues to increase in response to applied CO_2.

Light is often another limiting factor. When light intensity is low, the rate of photosynthesis is slowed down. Once sufficient CO_2 is added to achieve the maximum rate of photosynthesis at the low light intensity, further additions of CO_2 have no effect. If light intensity is increased by cleaning the glass on the greenhouse or by using supplemental lights during the daytime, higher levels of CO_2 will stimulate further increases in growth.

Heat is another limiting factor. Temperatures established before the era of CO_2 injection are not always adequate now that the limiting factor of CO_2 has been eliminated. Raising daytime temperatures for crops fertilized with CO_2 has been generally beneficial, while raising nighttime temperatures has not. An increase of as much as $10°F$ ($6°C$) has been recommended for roses. Geranium, snapdragon, chrysanthemum, and carnation have also been shown to respond to increased day temperature when CO_2 is injected. Temperature increases of five to ten degrees F appear to be in line, although the maximum beneficial daytime temperature for carnation was found by Holly, Goldsberry, and Juengling to be $69°F$ ($20°C$).

When injecting CO_2, the grower should be certain that the greenhouse covering is clean enough to insure the maximum light intensity possible that can be tolerated by the crop. He or she should experiment with raising the daytime temperature five to ten degrees, as well as increasing the fertilization rate, and in general insuring that all cultural procedures are practiced in a manner that promotes optimal growth.

Method of Carbon Dioxide Injection

Since CO_2 injection is only effective during the daylight hours when photosynthesis occurs, it should be injected from sunrise until one hour before sunset. It should be injected only when the ventilation fans are off or, in the case of geeenhouses cooled by ventilators, when the roof ventilators are open less than two inches. CO_2 cannot be injected during the warm seasons because cooling generally coincides with the daylight hours. Depending on the latitude of the greenhouse range's location, the season for CO_2 injection will begin between late September and early November and extend to April or early May.

The Johnson CO_2 generator is popular today (Figure 9-2). This equipment sells for close to $170 with automatic controls and will provide 1,500 ppm CO_2 in an average 24- by 200-foot greenhouse (4,800 sq ft of floor area). It burns LP or natural gas. This generator has a burner range up to 60,000 Btu per hour; thus it can consume 60 cubic feet of natural gas per hour.

Carbon dioxide generators are hung above head height along the center of the greenhouse. Within each is a precisely calibrated burner with an open flame. Under conditions of complete combustion, gas is converted to CO_2 which rises out of the burner into the greenhouse atmosphere. Convection currents move the gas about the greenhouse.

Gas consumed in the CO_2 generator must be of a high purity level as sulfur contained in it is converted to sulfur dioxide gas. When sulfur comes in contact with moisture on plant surfaces it is converted to sulfurous and eventually to sulfuric acid. This burns the plant (Figure 3-6). The sulfur content of natural gas should not exceed 1 grain per 100 cubic feet and only an H.D. 5 grade of propane should be used (7,000 grains = 1 pound; 1 grain = 64.86 mg).

Incomplete combustion will cause the formation of ethylene and carbon monoxide gases which are injurious (Figure 3-5). Internodes on the plant become shortened, branching increases, and flowers become distorted and injured. It is important that only a burner designed for CO_2 production be used in the greenhouse and that this be periodically calibrated. The burner should be kept clean and adjusted to a clear blue flame. The plumbing should be checked for gas leaks since the unburned fuel may be injurious to plants. It is also important to provide sufficient oxygen to support complete combustion of the fuel. An air inlet must be provided in a film plastic greenhouse or a glass greenhouse located in an area where it is prone to ice formation on the surface. The rule for heating systems applies here where one square inch of opening is provided per 2,000 Btu of burner capacity per hour.

Figure 9-2. A Johnson CO_2 generator. This equipment enriches the greenhouse atmosphere with CO_2 for the purpose of increasing photosynthesis and growth. *(Courtesy of Johnson Gas Appliance Co., Cedar Rapids, IA 52405)*

Various automatic control devices are used. The CO_2 generator can be turned on in the morning and off in the evening by either a time clock or a light sensor. If one of these is used alone, the generator would be turned on and off manually throughout the day when ventilation occurs. It is also possible to wire a switch into the ventilating fan circuit which turns off the CO_2 generator whenever the fan is running. Mechanical switches can be installed on the roof ventilators which will activate the CO_2 generator only when the vents are open less than two inches.

Considerable progress has been made in the 20 years since injection of CO_2 was commercialized. The concept actually dates back to the earlier part of this century, but it was not until commercial methods of application were available that extensive efforts were put forth to develop a system. Early research by Professor Holley at Colorado State University in the late 1950s, as well as work in Holland and England, led to commercial systems using liquid CO_2 or dry ice which is solid (frozen) CO_2.

CO_2 gas under pressure becomes liquid. At a low temperature it can be solidified into dry ice. In the early 1960s liquid CO_2 tanks were installed at the greenhouse range and were serviced by CO_2 distributors. CO_2 gas formed above the liquid in these tanks and was carried by a metal tubing to the greenhouses. A set of pressure-regulating valves reduced the pressure to a low level. Once in the greenhouse, the gas was distributed the length of the greenhouse in a plastic tube 1/8 to 1/4 inch in diameter with needle holes each foot along the length.

Liquid and solid CO_2 proved a more expensive source of CO_2 than the combustion of fuels. Burners were developed. Some early equipment was large and had to be located outside the greenhouse. The exhaust, essentially pure CO_2, was brought into the greenhouse through a duct and distributed along the length of the greenhouse through the conventional winter tube ventilation system described in Chapter 4. Such a generator was priced at $800 in 1965 and could maintain 1,500 ppm CO_2 in a greenhouse of 13,300 square foot floor area.

Smaller generators were developed which were installed overhead in the greenhouse. These produced CO_2 in open flame burners using kerosene, propane, or natural gas. Being simpler systems, they cost less to purchase. Depending upon the equipment purchased they could handle greenhouse areas from about 5,000 to 15,000 square feet. The cost of equipment for 5,000 square feet is about $170. This is the generation of CO_2 generators that are in use today.

CO_2 Level Measurement

Co_2 generators will not have the same net effect in all greenhouses. The CO_2 level will be lower in glass greenhouses, where air leaks exist, than in film plastic greenhouses. In order to adjust the fuel pressure on some generators, it is important to know what level is being maintained in the greenhouse atmosphere.

A CO_2 tester can be purchased for under $100. It consists of a small hand pump which passes air through a glass tube. The tube contains a CO_2-sensitive chemical which changes color as CO_2 is absorbed. The pump is stroked a given number of times. The length of the tube which changed color is measured on a scale which directly indicates the level of CO_2 in the air passed through the tube. The tubes are disposable.

Economics of CO_2 Injection

Professor Jay Koths at the University of Connecticut sums up the topic very well. The following discussion is taken directly from his article "Save Heat with CO_2," which appeared in the *Connecticut Greenhouse Newsletter* 77:18-19, January 1977:

Does carbon dioxide (CO_2) enrichment of greenhouse atmospheres save fuel? In most every circumstance, the answer is yes! Where CO_2 is being used, day temperatures are generally allowed to increase an extra 5°F or so when the sun is shining before the vents are opened.

With chrysanthemums, a decrease in growing time of two weeks with equal or better quality may be achieved. This in itself saves fuel. But in addition, the vents may remain closed until interior temperatures are 5°F higher than without CO_2. The greenhouse acts as a solar collector. Structural members, plants, soil and walks warm up, storing heat. When the sun sets, this stored heat reduces the demand on the heating system.

With snapdragons the quality is improved in late fall and early winter crops. The growing time is decreased for spring crops. But, in addition, the heat stored by virtue of higher day temperatures reduces the demand at night.

Carnations do not exhibit much of an increase in productivity until late spring. Most of the benefit is in better quality. But again, the higher day temperatures permitted allow the storage of solar heat.

For practically all crops, better quality and decreased production time are effects in addition to reducing heating costs with solar heat storage.

One might conjecture that for each hour of 5°F elevation in temperature during the day, a commensurate saving in heat will be attained. Or, for each hour of elevated temperature, a 5°F decrease in heating load would be achieved.

For example, assuming three hours of elevated temperature and an outside temperature 30°F lower than inside at night, one sixth of the heat would be saved for the equivalent of three hours. Assuming a 50 Btu/sq ft/hour load in a 10,000 sq ft greenhouse, this would be 500,000 Btu X 3 ÷ 6 = 250,000 Btu, or roughly 2½ gallons of oil, or $1.00 per day. Peanuts? Every little bit helps.

Another thought. Providing 1000-1500 ppm CO_2 for 10,000 sq ft will cost roughly $300 per year. About half of this ($150) is recovered as heat from the CO_2 generator if using propane or natural gas. If solar radiation storage is utilized, another $100-$150 may be saved. The CO_2 costs next to nothing. And the benefits in reduced cropping time and increased quality may be considered to be free.

SUMMARY

1. Carbon is an essential plant nutrient and is supplied as CO_2 gas in the atmosphere. A concentration of about 0.03 percent (300 ppm) is present in the atmosphere.

2. CO_2 is used during daylight hours in the process of photosynthesis. When the greenhouse is closed on cold winter days, the CO_2 concentration in the air inside the greenhouse can be lowered in a few hours to a level where the rate of carbohydrate manufactured in photosynthesis equals the rate of carbohydrate breakdown through respiration. Net growth ceases at this point, delaying the crop or reducing quality.

3. CO_2 is often added to the greenhouse atmosphere during daylight hours of months when greenhouses are not ventilated. The common method of addition is through the burning of kerosene, LP gas, or natural gas in special burners inside the greenhouse.

4. Re-establishment of a normal level of CO_2 (about 300 ppm) results in dramatic growth responses. Interestingly, further increases in CO_2 concentration up to 2,000 ppm or above induce even greater growth responses. Concentrations of 1,000 to 1,500 ppm are the levels generally established in the greenhouse.

SUGGESTED READINGS

Gaastra, P. "Some Physiological Aspects of CO_2 Application in Glasshouse Culture." *Acta Horticulturae* 4:111-116, 1966.

Holley, W. D. "The CO_2 Story." *In* Ball, V. ed. *The Ball Red Book, 13th ed.* George J. Ball, Inc., W. Chicago, IL 60185, 1975, pp. 156-59.

Mastalerz, J. W., Chapter 15, "Environmental Factors Light, Temperature, Carbon Dioxide." *In* Mastalerz, J. W., and R. W. Langhans, eds. *Roses: A Manual on the Culture, Management, Diseases, Insects, Economics and Breeding of Greenhouse Roses.* Pennsylvania Flower Growers, N.Y. State Flower Growers Assoc., Inc. and Roses, Inc., 1969, pp. 95-108.

Nelson P. V. and R. A. Larson. "The Effects of Increased CO_2 Concentrations on Chrysanthemum and Snapdragon." *North Carolina Agricultural Experiment Station Technical Bulletin.* No. 194, 1969.

Shaw, R. J. and M. N. Rogers. "Interaction Between Elevated Carbon Dioxide Levels and Greenhouse Temperatures on the Growth of Roses, Chrysanthemums, Carnations, Geraniums, Snapdragons, and African Violets." *Florists' Review* 135(3486):23-24, 88-89; (3487):21-22, 82; (3488): 73-74, 95-96; (3499):21, 59-60; (3491):19, 37-39, 1964.

Wittwer, S. H. "Carbon Dioxide and Its Role in Plant Growth." *Proceedings 17th International Horticultural Congress* 3:311-322, 1966.

Chapter 10

Light and Temperature

LIGHT INTENSITY FOR PHOTOSYNTHESIS

Photosynthesis

Visible light constitutes a source of energy for plants. Light energy, CO_2, and water all enter into the process of photosynthesis through which carbohydrates are formed.

$$CO_2 + \text{water} + \text{light energy} \rightarrow \text{carbohydrate} + \text{oxygen}$$

Considerable energy is required to reduce carbon that is combined with oxygen in carbon dioxide gas to the state in which it exists in carbohydrate. The light energy thus utilized is trapped in the carbohydrate. Later the carbohydrate can be translocated (moved) from the green stem and leaf cells where photosynthesis occurs to all other parts of the plant. The carbohydrate can be converted into all other compounds needed in the plant. Amino acids may be formed and then combined into chains called protein. Fats may be formed from carbohydrates. From all of these compounds yet other compounds arise such as cellulose for cell walls, pectin to cement the walls together, hormones to regulate growth, and DNA to constitute chromosomes. Energy of the sun is passed along in all of these compounds. These processes result in growth of the plant which can be detected as an increase in dry matter.

Energy must be liberated at times to power other processes in the plant. The uptake of nutrients, formation of proteins, division of cells, maintenance of membranes, and several other processes require an input of energy. This energy is obtained when compounds formed as a direct or indirect result of photosynthesis are broken down in very much the reverse process of photosynthesis, a process called *respiration*.

$$\text{carbohydrate} + \text{oxygen} \rightarrow CO_2 + \text{water} + \text{energy}$$

Respiration occurs in all living organisms at all times. It is temperature dependent, increasing with increases in temperature. When animals eat plants they obtain energy from the compounds they ingest. This energy was originally derived from light through photosynthesis. It can be released from these compounds by the animals through respiration. The same holds true for humans when we eat animal or plant tissue. Thus we see that most living organisms are ultimately dependent upon light energy.

When all factors such as CO_2 level, temperature, and water are optimized for photosynthesis, an optimum light intensity can be determined. If the light intensity is diminished, photosynthesis (and growth) slows down. If higher than optimal light intensities are provided growth again slows down because the chloroplasts are injured. Chloroplasts are the organelles within green cells in which photosynthesis occurs.

Greenhouse crops are subjected to light intensities as high as 12,000 footcandles (fc) on clear summer days to below 300 fc on cloudy winter days. For most crops neither is ideal. Many crops become light-saturated (photosynthesis does not increase at higher light intensities) at about 3,000 fc. Of course, this is assuming that all leaves are exposed to an intensity of 3,000 fc, which is rarely the case. Upper leaves cast shadows on lower leaves, thus reducing the light intensity at the lower leaves. As illustrated in Figure 10-1, an individual leaf at the top of the plant may saturate at 3,000 fc while the plant as a whole may not reach light saturation until 10,000 fc.

Rose and carnation plants will grow well under full summer light intensities. Poinsettia foliage is deeper green if the greenhouse is shaded to the extent of about 40 percent from midspring to midfall. This is typical of most crops. In addition to shading crops to prevent chloroplast suppression, crops such as chrysanthemum and geranium are shaded to prevent petal burn. The high light intensity is believed to raise the temperature of the petal tissue to an injurious level. Other crops require even more shading. Foliage plants are burned at light intensities over 2,000 to 3,000 fc and African violets lose chlorophyll at intensities of 1,500 fc and higher. The optimum light intensity for African violet is near 1,000 fc. As will be seen later in this chapter many foliage plants, gloxinia, African violet, and annual seedlings can be grown quite satisfactorily in growth rooms at a light intensity of 600 fc. Thus, it is apparent that light intensity requirements of photosynthesis vary considerably from crop to crop.

Light Quality

Not all light is useful in photosynthesis. Light is classified according to wavelength (nm). This classification is referred to as *quality*. Ultraviolet (uv) light has short wavelengths, below 400 nm (Figure 10-2). For the most part

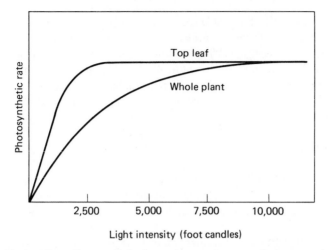

Figure 10-1. The effect oт light intensity on the rate of photosynthesis of a single leaf at the top of a plant and of the whole plant. While the single leaf reaches its maximum rate of photosynthesis at 3,000 fc, an intensity of 10,000 fc might be required for the whole plant in order to raise the light intensity within the leaf canopy to 3,000 fc.

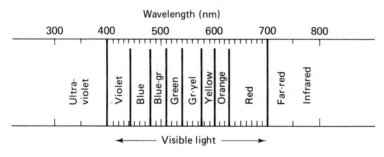

Figure 10-2. Types of radiant energy having wavelengths of 300 to 800 nm. Visible light is in the range of 400 to 700 nm.

uv light cannot be seen by the human eye and in larger quantities it is harmful to plants. Glass screens out most uv light and all below a wavelength of 325 nm. Visible or *white* light occurs between the wavelengths of 400 and 700 nm. At the shortest wavelength visible light appears violet. Blue, green, yellow, orange, and red light occur around wavelengths of 460, 510, 570, 610, and 650 nm respectively. Far-red light (700–750 nm) occurs at the limit of our visual perception and has an influence on plants other than through photosynthesis. Infrared energy occurs at longer wavelengths and is not involved in plant processes.

In is primarily the visible spectrum of light that is used in photosynthesis (Figure 10-3). There are peaks in the blue and red bands where photosynthetic activity is higher. When blue light alone is supplied to plants, growth is shortened, hard, and dark in color. When grown in red light, growth is soft and internodes are long resulting in tall plants. From Figure 10-3 it is apparent that all visible light qualities (wavelengths) are readily utilized in photosynthesis.

Maximizing Light Intensity

It is important to insure the highest light intensity possible during the darker portion of the year from midfall through early spring for all crops except the low-light group already mentioned. In this way growth is maximized.

RANGE DESIGN. Maximization of light begins in the planning stage of the greenhouse range. The simpler the frame and the further apart the sash bars, the greater the light intensity inside. A very significant stride forward was made when all metal greenhouses were popularized in the 1950s. Because of the strength of the metal members of these greenhouses, fewer sash bars were necessary to support the heavy weight of the glass. Glass widths increased

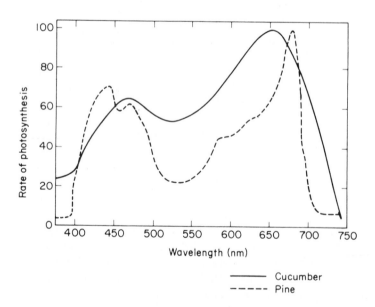

Figure 10-3. Rates of photosynthetic activity occurring under different qualities of light between the ultraviolet wavelength of 350 nm and the far-red wavelength of 750 nm. *(From The Electric Council, Growelectric Handbook No. 1, London, England)*

from 16 to 24 inches, reducing the number of sash bars by one-third. Fewer shadows in the greenhouse meant more light.

Frame simplicity is particularly important in film plastic greenhouses. The wooden frame plastic greenhouses, which have almost entirely passed by the wayside now, required very massive frames which greatly reduced interior light intensity. If you are operating such structures, it is very important to keep the wood painted white so that it reflects light into the greenhouse rather than absorbing it. The same is true of wooden sash bars on glass greenhouses. These should be painted every other year on the outside and about every five years (or as needed) on the inside. The pipe-frame quonset and all metal gutter-connected plastic greenhouses are very good in terms of their minimal frames.

The importance of the greenhouse design can be seen in light transmission figures presented by Professor W. D. Holley of Colorado State University. The frame blocks 10 percent of the sunlight, the sash bars another 5 percent and the glass another 7 percent.

frame	90% light transmission
frame + sash bars	85% light transmission
frame + sash bars + glass	78% light transmission

The covering material is another consideration. Glass transmits about 90 percent of light impinging on it. Fiberglass has a very similar transmission value under high light intensities but a vastly superior value under low light intensities. If light transmission remained constant over the years for fiberglass, it would be an undisputably superior covering. With time, however, the surface erodes, light transmission diminishes, and resurfacing becomes necessary. The guaranteed life expectancy of fiberglass (up to 25 years) is much shorter than the life expectancy of glass. Resurfacing and replacement costs must be weighed against the value of increased light during the early life of the fiberglass. It is difficult to quantitize these factors; but it can be said that fiberglass is definitely not replacing glass in this industry, except in areas where light is plentiful and where hail damage occurs very frequently.

Polyethylene transmits less light than glass, a single layer about 88 percent and a double layer about 81 percent. The lower light intensity is partially, but not completely, compensated by the absence of sash bars in the film plastic greenhouse. Light must be considered as a source of energy for crop production much the same as heat energy is. The uncompensated light energy reduction of polyethylene is more than balanced by the 30 to 40 percent savings in heating fuel afforded by a double layer of polyethylene. In the case of crops requiring high light, such as carnation, this is not a fair conclusion, but for the vast majority of crops it is safe.

In general, design and maintenance of the greenhouse frame will be based on maximizing light intensity while the choice of the covering itself will generally be based on other factors such as cost of construction, heating costs, use to which the greenhouse is to be put, available labor pool, etc.

The orientation of the greenhouse is another very important consideration in the planning of a greenhouse, particularly at northern latitudes where the angle of the sun is low in winter. L. G. Morris made the calculations presented in Table 10-1 in England at a latitude of about 50°N. They leave little doubt that the ridge of a single greenhouse should run from east to west. The difference in light intensity due to orientation is not great during the summer when the angle of the sun is large. A difference shows up in the winter when light is an important issue. The further toward the equator one goes the less importance orientation has. Certainly in the northern two-thirds of the United States it is important. J. N. Walker at the University of Kentucky reports that ridge-and-furrow greenhouses present a different situation and that a north-south orientation of the ridges is best at all latitudes. If oriented east-west, the roof of one greenhouse shades the south roof of the next greenhouse.

CLEAN GLASS. Most greenhouses are shaded during the summer to reduce light intensity. A residue of shade may still remain at wintertime. In addition, dust will usually accumulate on the glass. These deposits reduce light intensity. Twenty percent reductions in light due to such residues commonly occur. Dirty glass should be washed as the dark season approaches, usually in November. Commercial glass cleaning products are available through greenhouse supply companies. Professor J. W. Boodley of Cornell University outlined for cleaning glass the following formulation which you may make yourself.

To 1 gallon of very hot water add 4-1/2 pounds of sal soda (washing soda, $Na_2CO_3 \cdot 10 H_2O$) and 1 pound of tri-soda (sodium ortho-phosphate, $Na_3PO_4 \cdot 12 H_2O$).

Stir thoroughly until the powders are dissolved, then add 1 gallon of commercial hydrofluoric acid (52 percent) and pour this compound into 23 gallons of *cold water*. The solution is ready for immediate use.

Table 10-1
Effect of Greenhouse Orientation on Light Transmission
in the Midsummer and Midwinter at a Latitude of Approximately 50°N

ORIENTATION	% TRANSMISSION	
	Midsummer	Midwinter
N–S	64	48
E–W	66	71

Paint on with large brush or spray on with a sprayer; rinse off with hose within a few minutes. No scrubbing required.

Harmless to everything except silk. May be stored in any container.

FRP greenhouses need cleaning as well. A household detergent can be applied with a sponge or rag at the end of a pole. Sometimes the inside of glass becomes dirty as well. Professor Boodley's formulation can be sprayed inside the glass greenhouse and hosed off, providing it does not contact plants. Benches containing plants should be covered with polyethylene during cleaning.

PLANT SPACING. Plants tend to proliferate within a bench until the available light energy is fully utilized. In other words, an equal amount of dry matter will be produced in a bench whether plants such as chrysanthemum are spaced on five- or seven-inch centers. In the former case, smaller stems and blooms are produced. The size and quality of product desired will dictate the proper plant spacing.

Generally a greater amount of space per plant is provided in the winter than in the summer because of less available light. Catalogues provided by suppliers of plant material will indicate the proper spacing for various seasons of the year. It is best to follow their recommendations.

Some growers of fresh flowers have found it best to leave an open space along the center of the bench from end to end as pictured in Figure 10-4. This permits light to enter the center of the bench where it would normally be darkest. There is a resultant increase in overall quality. The same number of plants are used in a bench in this system. They are simply spaced closer to compensate for the open space in the center.

Reducing Light Intensity

The need for reducing light intensity during the midspring to early fall period has already been pointed out. This may be accomplished in two ways— by spraying a shading compound on the greenhouse or by installing a screen fabric over the greenhouse or in the greenhouse above head height.

When the entire greenhouse range needs shading, the spray method is generally used because it is less expensive. Commercial shading compounds can be purchased from florist supply companies or can be made on the premises by mixing white latex paint with water. One part paint in 10 parts water provides a very heavy shade while one part paint in 15 to 20 parts water provides a standard shade. The shading compound can be sprayed on from the ground by means of a pesticide sprayer. In some large operations, it is sprayed on from the air by a helicopter. Most of the shading compound will wear off by early fall. If it does not, it needs to be washed off.

Figure 10-4. A winter planting arrangement for chrysanthemums that allows for a space along the center of the bench to increase light intensity at that point with the resultant effect of improved quality.

When shade is desired for a single stage of growth, sheets of screening are often used where needed. Chrysanthemums and geraniums may be grown at full light intensity in northern areas but the flowers must be protected from sunburn. Cheesecloth was commonly used years ago and is still used when it affords a price advantage. Longer lasting synthetic fabrics are more popular today including such materials as polypropylene, polyester, and saran. They can be purchased in different densities of weave providing many shade values from 20 to 90 percent.

Supplemental Lighting

During the darker seasons of the year light intensity is below optimum for many crops. While the previous list of methods for maximizing light intensity help, they do not completely solve the problem. Growth of crops affected is slow and final quality is reduced. There is an increase in blindness (failure of shoots to develop) on crops such as rose and orchid. This situation can be rectified for some crops by using supplemental lighting. Such lights are installed in the greenhouse and are used to increase the light intensity during the daylight hours as well as during part of the dark period. A sufficient intensity is applied to support a desirable rate of photosynthesis.

LAMP TYPES. There are many lamps that can be used in the greenhouse. Basically they fall into three groups: incandescent, fluorescent, and high intensity discharge (high-pressure mercury, metal-halide, low-pressure sodium, and high-pressure sodium). Light emissions typical of each can be seen in Figure 10-5.

Incandescent (tungsten-filament) lamps (Figure 10-5a) are generally not used for supplemental lighting because of excessive heat. Light quality is acceptable for some plants but insufficient at the low intensities needed to avoid excess heat. For other plants the high proportion of red and far-red light emitted causes tall, soft growth and other changes in plant form. These lamps are also very inefficient, converting only 7 percent of the electrical energy consumed into light energy. Much of the energy is converted into heat, which at times is of value and at other times a detriment.

Fluorescent lamps are more commonly used in growing rooms and over small germination areas rather than in full-size greenhouses. Some supplemental lighting of crops has been done using eight foot tubes often without external reflectors. The results have been encouraging but the economics are questionable. In Europe these lamps have been used for cucumber and tomato crops, providing an additional 1,000 and 2,000 lux (95 and 185 fc) respectively. In separate trials E. D. Bickford and J. W. Mastalerz increased the yield of roses using Gro-Lux$_®$ (plant growth A) fluorescent lamps. Best results were obtained by placing the lamps between the plants.

Among the more efficient of the fluorescent lamps are the cool white and warm white tube types. These convert 23 percent of electrical energy consumed to visible light energy and have similar spectral light emissions. Cool white (Figure 10-5b) is perhaps the most commonly used fluorescent lamp for plant growth. Light emitted tends to predominate in the blue region. There are a number of other fluorescent lamps with special phosphors for emitting a spectrum of wavelengths more in line with the requirements of photosynthesis. These are categorized into two groups. Plant growth A (Figure 10-5c) are the earlier lamps with enhanced radiation in the red range while plant growth B (Figure 10-5d) is the later generation of lamps with extended spectral emission beyond 700 nm.

A limiting factor to the use of fluorescent lamps for supplemental lighting is the low power (wattage) of the tubes available. This increases the number of tubes and the total cost of fixtures and wiring needed to do the job. The larger number of fixtures increases the area of shadows cast on the crop.

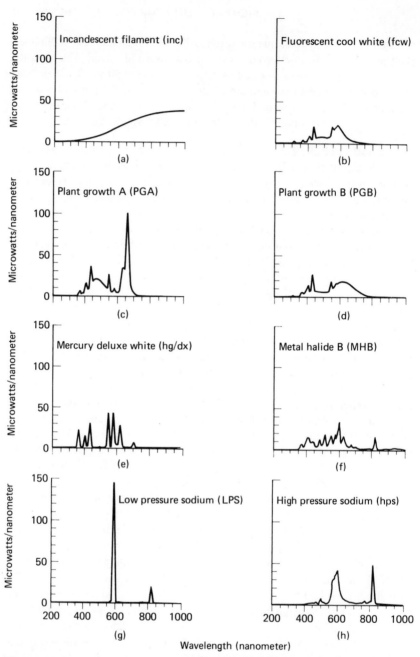

Figure 10-5. The spectrum of light emissions measured as radiant power per lumen from 8 types of lamps considered for use in greenhouses. *(From L. E. Campbell, R. W. Thimijan, and H. M. Cathey. Spectral Radiant Power of Lamps Used in Horticulture. Transactions of the American Society of Agricultural Engineers 18(5):952-56, 1975)*

High intensity discharge (HID) lamps are the subject of research today (Figure 10-6) and some types are in commercial greenhouse use. The high-pressure mercury discharge type HID lamps are more commonly used for supplemental lighting in Europe than in the United States. Light emissions from these lamps are somewhat similar to fluorescent tubes. Model MBFR/U (popular in Europe) has fluorescent powder on the inner surface of the glass bulb which converts much uv light to visible wavelengths, particularly red. This makes the lamp more desirable for plant growth and increases its efficiency to 14.9 percent. Similar American lamps are the Mercury Clear and Mercury Deluxe White (Figure 10-5e) which are often seen along roadways. These lamps are available in sizes up to 1,000 watts. They have been used for up to 10,000 hours and at that point still had 70 percent of their original output.

High pressure metal halide type HID lamps (Figure 10-5f) have been developed more recently. These lamps are available in sizes up to 2,000 watts and can convert 22.4 percent of electrical energy into light in the 400-700 nm waveband. Further study of these lamps is needed since they cost considerably more than the high pressure mercury lamps, have a shorter life, and lose their output level faster.

Low-pressure sodium type HID lamps (Figure 10-5g) come in sizes up to 180 watts and convert 35 percent of electrical energy to light energy. The high efficiency means that there is about as much usable light energy from this lamp as from a 400-watt high-pressure mercury lamp. These lamps are rather large, thus throwing a significant shadow, and the light emitted is primarily at the wavelength of 589 nm in the yellow range. This light quality

Figure 10-6. High pressure mercury and high pressure sodium type HID lamps under test to supplement the natural winter daylight for the purpose of increased photosynthesis.

has caused strap leaves on lettuce in northern Europe but not in the United States where winter light intensity is higher and days are longer. The problem is believed to be due to low levels of blue light. These lamps are used to a limited degree because they are only available in an exceptionally large street-light fixture. With a smaller fixture they could be promising as a supplemental light source.

High pressure sodium-type HID lamps (Figure 10-5h) also offer a potential for supplementary lighting of crops. These lamps produce a whiter light, that is, a broader range of wavelengths are emitted than from the low-pressure sodium lamps. This helps to alleviate the problem experienced in northern Europe with lettuce under low-pressure sodium lamps. The efficiency is lower at 27 percent but is still higher than the high-pressure mercury lamps. These lamps can be purchased in sizes up to 1,000 watt and when used in large sizes cost less per square foot of ground illuminated than the high-pressure mercury lamps.

High-pressure sodium and low-pressure sodium lamps are approximately equal in greenhouse performance. Low-pressure sodium lamps can be used closer to plants with better light distribution, thereby increasing overall efficiency. This is possible because less radiant heat is emitted into the plant zone.

COMMERCIAL APPLICATION. There are relatively few greenhouse ranges in America using supplemental lighting. The heaviest commercial use is in northern Europe. Considerable development has occurred in England and The Netherlands. Those countries lie at $50°N$ latitude and above, where winter light intensities are very unfavorable to growth.

Tests in America have shown phenomenal growth responses to supplemental lighting. The main question hinges on economics. Some growers feel they can profit from its use while many others are skeptical. Although great strides have been made in developing lamps of greater efficiency, much room still exists for improvement.

Supplemental lighting in Europe may be applied to the whole crop or more commonly to just an initial stage of the crop when the seedlings are concentrated in a minimal area. Tomato seedlings are illuminated starting at the time of germination for a period of two to three weeks at an intensity of 5,000 lux (465 fc). Plants are in seedling flats and soil blocks. In some cases light is applied for 12 hours per day, enabling the lighting arrangement to be transferred to a second batch of seedlings each day. The switching of lights occurs at midnight and at noon. In this way each batch of seedlings can be exposed to a 16-hour day-length since an additional four hours of daylight will be obtained when they are not under the lights. Day-lengths of more than 16 hours duration are avoided since they retard growth and flowering. "Five week old" plants can be produced in less than half the time with this method.

Cucumber seedlings are started under supplemental light intensities of 3,000 to 5,000 lux (280 to 465 fc) from November to February. As much as 7,500 lux (700 fc) of light is added to the natural daylight for growing lettuce. Ten days of continuous supplemental lighting at about 5,000 lux (465 footcandles) can have the effect of about six weeks of growth under natural winter conditions.

Some chrysanthemum growers light their plants for two weeks beginning at the start of short day treatment. The plants receive 7,200 lux (670 footcandles) of supplementary light 12 hours per day, including the natural daylight hours, during this period. Up to two weeks is saved in the flowering time of the crop.

Growth Rooms

It has been pointed out that supplemental lighting is more often used for starting plants than for growing the crop on to maturity. The former application logically leads to the use of a growth room (Figure 10-7). A growth room is a well insulated room, which greatly reduces the heating bill. Benches are generally built in tiers to conserve space. Each bench has a bank of lamps above it which provides the sole source of light. While supplemental lighting in the greenhouse finds more application in Europe than in the United States, growth rooms are popular on both continents.

The growth room can be constructed in a variety of buildings. It may be a room in the headhouse or a building itself such as a shed, barn, or garage. It also may be constructed within a greenhouse. If it is in a building other than a greenhouse, the walls should have an insulation layer such as polyurethane board. The moisture-tight side of the board should be inward.

Benches may be built in tiers, usually two feet apart, although they can be as close as 18 inches. Attached to the bottom of the bench above are the lamps. Fluorescent lamps are best for growth rooms because of the uniform light intensity they emit over a wide area. High intensity lamps would be difficult to use in such close proximity to the plants. Cool white fluorescent lamps are commonly used. A light intensity of 8,000 to 15,000 lux (750 to 1,400 fc) is used depending on the crop. The lower light intensity can be achieved in benches 3.5 feet wide by installing seven tubes 2 feet above the surface of the bench and each running along the length of the bench (Figure 10-8). Thirteen tubes will provide 1,400 fc of light. Tubes can be obtained in lengths up to 8 feet and have a power of 125 watts. A sheet of aluminum foil or a coat of aluminum paint should be provided above the tubes to maximize light intensity below even if reflectorized tubes are used.

Light is generally applied for 16 hours per day; however, some crops such as many of the bedding plants and lettuce will respond to 24 hours of illumination. During the illumination period the temperature is held between

Figure 10-7. A growth room for starting seedlings. Plants are grown on tiered shelves to conserve space. Light is supplied entirely by fluorescent lamps above each shelf. *(Photo courtesy of George J. Ball, Inc., W. Chicago, IL 60185)*

70 and 75°F (21 to 24°C) and in the dark period it is permitted to drop to 65°F (18°C).

The lamps will provide most of the heat needed. Only under exceptionally cold periods is it necessary to provide supplemental heat. A thermostatically controlled heater can be installed for this purpose. The greatest requirement regarding temperature is that of maintaining a uniform temperature. Hot and cold spots will form if the air within the room is not circulated. The two walls running the length of the room should be constructed of perforated material such as pegboard. The pegboard should be set six to eight inches in from the outer wall of the room to provide a chamber for air movement behind the pegboard (Figure 10-9). A false ceiling provides a chamber

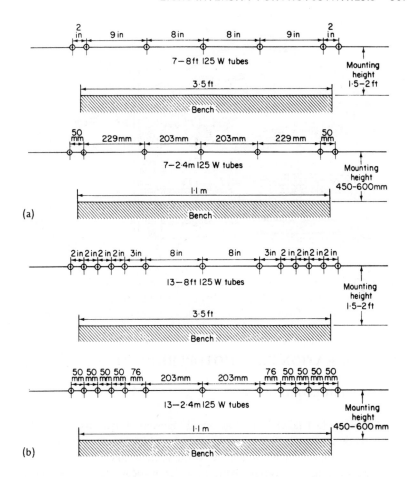

Figure 10-8. Fluorescent tube spacing for 3.5-feet wide tiered benches in a growing room (a) to provide 8,000 lux (750 fc) and (b) to provide 15,000 lux (1400 fc). *(From Growelectric Handbook No. 1: Growing Rooms. The Electricity Council, 30 Millbank, London SW1P 4RD, England)*

overhead which is connected to the wall chambers. A fan is placed overhead which will cause air to be drawn in one wall and expelled through the other, thus setting up an air flow pattern across the growth room. The heater can be installed in the space over the ceiling in front of the fan. Should the room become too hot, a thermostatically activated motorized ventilator is used in the air duct behind the wall or over the ceiling. Very fine details for a number of growth room designs can be found in The Electricity Council, Growelectric Handbook No. 1.

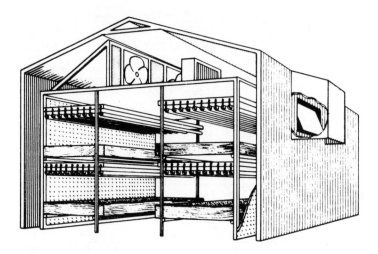

Figure 10-9. Arrangement of benches, fluorescent tubes, air circulation system, heater, and ventilator in a six-bench growing room. *(From Growelectric Handbook No. 1: Growing Rooms. The Electricity Council, 30 Millbank, London SW1P 4RD, England)*

LIGHT DURATION FOR PHOTOPERIODISM

What is Photoperiodism?

We have just taken a look at one dimension of light, its intensity. Now we focus on a second dimension, its duration. Living organisms are innately aware of rhythmic forces in their environment. Fiddler crabs at Cape Cod, Massachusetts, like any other of their species in the world will feed when the tide is low. It is then that food is trapped in small pools in which they can maneuver. When the tide comes in, it is time to sleep. If these crabs are placed in a tank of seawater in the darkness on Cape Cod they will continue to feed when the tide goes out and sleep when it comes in on the beaches outside the tank. Upon moving them to Chicago, they eventually change their feeding time to the time when the tide would be low if there were an ocean in Chicago. Clearly the crab is responding to the gravitational forces of the moon which regulates the tides.

Plants and animals respond to many such rhythmic forces. The rate of metabolism of an earthworm has predictable peaks and valleys in accordance with the lunar month and the 24-hour solar day. Japanese industries have gone so far as to plot efficient and inefficient days in the lives of some of their key employees. There emerges from these data a recognizable rhythm such that one can be assured that on certain days an individual will perform at peak potential while on other days it might be better that he or she is not around.

There is a mechanism in plants which tracks time. It is highly precise and can discern a five-minute difference within a 24-hour cycle. It is called *photoperiodism* because it is locked into the 24-hour solar day and is based upon the light-dark cycle. Photoperiodism is the response of a plant to the day-night cycle. Response can mean many things, including rosette growth of lettuce versus bolting, bulb formation in onions versus leaf and stem formation, tuber formation in dahlia, flowering of chrysanthemum, downward flagging of leaves of bean, a change in the shape of newly forming leaves, red pigmentation in bracts (leaves) of poinsettia, the formation of plantlets along the margins of bryophyllum leaves (*Kalanchoe daigremontiana*), etc.

Plants are customarily classified in regard to photoperiodism as long-day plants, short-day plants, and day-neutral plants. I have chosen in this book to call the long-day plant a short-night plant and the short-day plant a long-night plant because the mechanism which permits plants to track time actually measures the dark period. This avoids the need for reciprocal thinking and corrects two long-standing misnomers.

The long-night plant is one which will undergo a response such as flowering only when the night length becomes more than a critical length. Poinsettias require about 12 hours of darkness to flower. This length of night occurs in the latter part of September. Prior to September 15 the nights are too short to afford a 12-hour dark period, so plants grow vegetatively. In the latter part of September and on later dates the nights are long enough that at least 12 hours of dark period exists, thus the poinsettia buds will change from vegetative buds forming leaves and stems to reproductive buds which form flower parts. Of course several weeks will pass before these flower parts become large enough to be seen. Chrysanthemum, kalanchoe, azalea, and Rieger and Lorraine begonias are all long-night plants in terms of the flowering response. Tuber formation in dahlia and tuberous begonia is a long night response.

Short-night plants undergo a response when the nights are shorter than a critical length. Asters will form a rosette type of growth when nights are longer than a critical length and will develop tall stems and initiate flower buds under shorter nights. Short-night conditions prevent tuber formation in dahlia and tuberous begonia and thereby encourage flowering. Calceolaria and cineraria initiate flower buds at low temperatures. After that point short nights hasten flowering. Short nights increase the height of Easter lily. Plantlets form along the margins of some bryophyllum leaves under short night conditions.

Day-neutral plants, such as the rose, do not respond to the relative length of the light and dark periods. There are other forces which determine when a response will occur in these plants. Some require a certain level of maturity before they flower, while others must accumulate a specific quantity of solar energy. Some varieties of chrysanthemums as well as stock, calceolaria, and cineraria initiate flower buds when a sufficient length of time at a cool temperature has passed. Calceolaria and cineraria require four to six weeks at 50°F (10°C) for flower initiation. In terms of the length of the night and these particular responses, these are all day-neutral plants.

Some plants will flower at any night length but do so faster at a particular night length. Carnations flower at any night length, but fastest under short-night conditions. Rieger begonias will flower at any night length, but fastest under long-night lengths. These are called *facultative short-night* and *facultative long-night* plants respectively.

The critical night length is not any set figure. It is different for each plant species and can be different for cultivars within a plant species. Take the single species of chrysanthemum which is classified as *Chrysanthemum morifolium* Ramat, as an example. The hardy garden varieties can have a critical night length of 8 hours while many greenhouse forcing varieties have a critical night length of 9.5 hours. A night length of 9 hours is below the critical length for the greenhouse varieties so they remain vegetative, while it is more than the critical length for the garden varieties so they initiate flower buds and proceed to flower. Kalanchoe have a critical night length of about 11.5 hours and poinsettia of about 12 hours. Flowering occurs in each case at night lengths greater than these critical lengths.

The critical night length is also dependent upon temperature. The night temperature is more important than the day temperature. Table 10-2 shows the effect of night temperature on the critical night length of chrysanthemum. As the night temperature goes up, the critical night length gets shorter. From this it can be seen that a garden chrysanthemum will initiate flower buds sooner during a hot summer than during a cold summer.

The Mechanism of Photoperiodism

There is a pigment in photoperiodic plants known as *phytochrome* which serves as the light receptor. When the plant is in daylight or artificial light, phytochrome exists in a form known as Pfr which is sensitive to light

Table 10-2
Critical Night Length for the Chrysanthemum Variety Encore
at Each of Three Night Temperatures

NIGHT TEMPERATURE (°F)	CRITICAL NIGHT LENGTH (HR.)
50	10.25
60	9.5
80	8.75

in the far-red region with a peak response at 735 nm. If the plant is exposed to far-red light, Pfr phytochrome will quickly change to Pr phytochrome which is sensitive to red light with a peak response at 660 nm. This same response will occur when the plant is placed in darkness, but it occurs very slowly under this condition. The Pr form developed in darkness or under far-red light rapidly returns to the Pfr form when the plant is exposed to daylight again. Levels of Pfr might look like those proposed in Figure 10-10 during summer and winter daily cycles.

The important point is that the Pfr form is rapidly produced in the light and the Pr form is slowly produced in the dark. The Pfr form is the active form which inhibits flowering in long-night plants and promotes flowering in short-night plants. During the summer when nights are short the level of Pfr in a long-night plant such as chrysanthemum does not get low enough to permit flowering. During a long winter night the level of Pfr does become low enough to permit flowering.

Methods of Photoperiodic Control

Day-length control for the greenhouse chrysanthemum is typical of the long-night crops as a whole. Chrysanthemums are grown for an initial period under short-night conditions to develop a plant of suitable size which will support large blooms and tall stems. Then, the plants are grown under long-night conditions to induce flower bud initiation and subsequent development.

SHORT-NIGHT TREATMENT. Depending on the season of the year and the variety of chrysanthemum the short-night treatment can last from two to eight weeks. If this stage occurs during the summer, there is no need to do anything but grow the plants under the natural short nights. On the other hand, if the crop is planted during the winter when nights are long it will then be necessary to shorten the dark period. This is done by turning lights on during the night. Lights may be turned on in the late afternoon to extend the day into the evening or they may be turned on during the middle of the night to break the dark period. It requires fewer hours of lighting if the dark period is interrupted in the middle of the night, and this is the procedure commonly used. The light break in the middle of the night restores the Pfr phytochrome level, and since neither of the two dark periods before or after the light break are very long, the Pfr level does not diminish sufficiently to permit flowering.

Since the dark period becomes longer as December 21 approaches, the number of hours of supplemental light required increases. The number of hours of light to apply for any given month at 40° latitude N is presented in Table 10-3. A word of caution is needed here. The night length, and consequently the amount of light to apply, depends upon the latitude at which one is located on the earth. The shortest night of the year for the northern

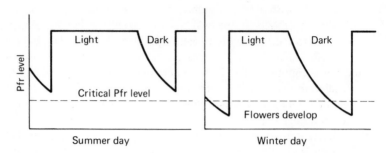

Summer day   Winter day

Figure 10-10. The effects of a summer and winter day-night cycle on the Pfr phytochrome level in a plant. Pfr quickly builds up in the light period and slowly diminishes in the dark period. A long-night plant will flower only when the Pfr level falls below the critical level, as shown, for the long winter night. *(Adopted from The Electric Council, Growelectric Handbook No. 2: Lighting In Greenhouses, 30 Millbank, London SW1P 4RD, England)*

Table 10-3
Duration of Light to Apply During Night for Different Months
to Insure Short-night Conditions at a Latitude of 40°N

MONTH	HOURS OF LIGHT
June–July	0
May–August	2
March–April and September–October	3
November–February	4

hemisphere occurs on June 21. On this day the dark period is 12 hours long near the equator while no darkness occurs at the North Pole. Thus, the farther north one is located, the shorter is the night. The longest night of the year occurs on December 21. There are 24 hours of darkness at the North Pole on that day and 12 hours of darkness near the equator. The farther north one goes, the longer is the night. Thus northern latitudes have shorter summer nights and longer winter nights than points further south. The light period near the equator is always 12 hours long. All places in the world reach a midway point on March 21 and September 21 when the light period is 12 hours everywhere. These relationships can be seen in Figure 10-11.

From this discussion it should be apparent that the period of the year in which light must be applied and the duration needed on any given night will depend upon the latitude where one is located. Some companies providing chrysanthemum cuttings make available excellent catalogues presenting cultural techniques as well as lighting and shading schedules for this crop. The schedules are given according to the zone in which one lives.

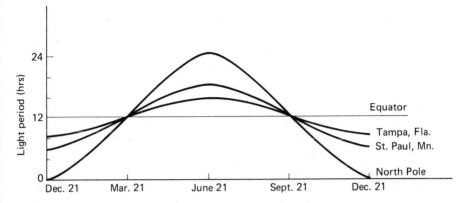

Figure 10-11. The length of the light period throughout the year at different latitudes of the Northern Hemisphere.

Incandescent lamps work best for extending the day-length or reducing the night-length because a large percentage of the light emitted is in the red zone which is required by Pr phytochrome. The required light intensity is very low, most plants responding to 11 to 22 lux (one or two footcandles). A minimum intensity of 108 lux (10 fc) should be provided, however, to avoid any failure. The most important parts of the plant to illuminate are the recently mature leaves.

To provide the required intensity of light for a four-foot wide bed, one string of 60 watt bulbs four feet apart should be installed not more than five feet above the soil along the middle of the bed. Two beds can be lighted by installing a row of 100 watt bulbs six feet apart and not more than six feet above the soil between the beds. Larger incandescent floodlight bulbs can be installed along the center ridge of the greenhouse to light the entire width. A minimum of 1-1/2 watts is required for each square foot of ground lighted. Occasionally the larger lights are installed in clusters to reduce the cost of wiring.

The cost of lighting a crop can be reduced by *flashlighting* or *cyclic lighting*. As little as one second of light at 108 lux (10 fc) intensity every five seconds will keep phytochrome in the Pfr form and cause some chrysanthemum cultivars to remain vegetative. This frequency requires heavy duty switches, thus longer light periods are generally used.

If the standard program calls for four hours of light in the middle of the night, from perhaps 10 PM to 2 AM, one can divide this duration into 30-minute periods and apply light for 20 percent of each period. In this way one would apply light for six minutes out of each 30 minutes between 10 PM and 2 AM. Shorter periods will work as well as long as light is applied 20 percent of the time. It is essential that a minimum light intensity of 108 lux (10 fc) be applied in this system.

A greenhouse range using cyclic lighting could be divided into five zones and all could receive their light requirement during one four-hour period. This would reduce the consumption of electricity by 70 to 75 percent and would permit the use of lighter main wiring which would reduce the initial wiring cost. Timeclocks are available which can control such a system.

LONG-NIGHT TREATMENT. After a period of short nights has been provided to establish the plant, a period of long nights must be provided to bring about flower bud initiation and development. During the winter, the nights are naturally long enough so nothing is done. When this stage of growth occurs in the summer, however, it is necessary to pull black cloth over the plants in late afternoon and off again in the morning. Shade should be applied from 7 PM to 7 AM. Some growers apply it at 5 PM before their work force leaves. This can have harmful effects during the summer if heat builds up underneath. Flowering will be delayed and at higher temperatures flower buds will abort. If it must be pulled at 5 PM, leave the sides up for air circulation and have someone return at 7 PM to lower them. It is necessary to pull black cloth until color shows in the buds. Beyond that time it need not be applied. Black cloth should be applied every day of the week. For each day that is skipped every week, the crop will flower a day or so later.

A good grade of sateen cloth works well. It should be dense enough to reduce the light intensity beneath to 2 fc when the intensity outside is 5,000 fc. Sateen cloth is sufficiently porous to permit water to penetrate which is important in a leaky greenhouse and in field applications. Black polyethylene also may be used as long as water is not a problem. Tears in the cover should be immediately repaired to prevent light leaks. Wherever light leaks in, there will be plants which develop incomplete or hollow flower buds called *crown buds.*

Black cloth which is pulled manually is pulled over frames as pictured in Figure 10-12. The expenditure in labor is considerable for this operation. Larger growers are now gravitating toward power-operated black cloth shading (Figure 10-13). Some make this apparatus themselves. An electric motor turns a pipe shaft along one side of the greenhouse. Cables attached to the shaft run across the greenhouse to a shaft on the other side and back again. Cloth is attached to the cables enabling it to be drawn across the greenhouse and back again.

Power-operated shading equipment is available commercially as well. One very effective system uses extruded aluminum channels the length of the greenhouse above the plants. In each channel is a magnetic power capsule. When activated these run along the channel pulling the leading edge of the cloth across the greenhouse. The cloth hangs down on either side, sealing the sides off from light. A special shade fabric composed of polyvinyl chloride film laminated on woven nylon mesh is used in the system. The fabric carries

Figure 10-12. Manual pulling of black cloth in the early evening during the summer to establish long-night conditions for photoperiodic control of flowering. The light bulbs are used during the middle of winter nights to give a short-night effect. *(Photo courtesy of J. W. Love, Department of Horticultural Science, North Carolina State University, Raleigh, NC 27607)*

a five-year guarantee. It is aluminized on the outer side to reflect light and thereby reduce heat beneath.

A system such as this can be purchased for $1.25 to $1.50 per square foot of ground covered. This seems like a high figure but the advantages which go with it tend to sell these systems. One person at the flip of a switch can cover an acre of greenhouse in a few minutes, alleviating perhaps as much as two to three hours of manual labor. The system can be further controlled by an automatic timeclock, eliminating the need for any person. This savings occurs twice a day. Because a single sheet of fabric is suspended overhead, it is possible to operate the fan and pad cooling system pulling the cool air beneath the cover. This prevents excess buildup of heat, which can occur even at 7 PM in the summer, and in turn prevents reduction in plant quality and delays in flowering.

TEMPERATURE

We have already taken a long look at heat in terms of providing it in the greenhouse, removing it from the greenhouse, and controlling it at the desired level. Now we look briefly at its influence on crops.

Figure 10-13. A commercially available, power-operated system for shading plants to create long-night conditions for photoperiodic control of flowering. *(Photo courtesy of Simtrac, Inc., 8243 N. Christiana Avenue, Skokie, IL 60076)*

Temperature is a measure of the level of heat present. All crops have a temperature range in which they can grow. Below this range processes necessary for life stop, ice forms within the tissue tying up water necessary for life processes, and cells are possibly punctured by ice crystals. At the upper extreme, enzymes become inactive and again processes essential to life stop.

All biochemical reactions in the plant are controlled by enzymes. Enzymes are heat sensitive. The rate of reactions controlled by them will usually double each time the temperature is increased by 18°F (10°C) until an optimum temperature is reached. Further increases in temperature begin to suppress the reaction until finally it stops.

Numerous biochemical reactions are involved in the process of photosynthesis. These all have the net effect of building carbohydrate and storing energy. Photosynthesis occurs during the daylight hours because of its dependence on light. Another extensive set of biochemical reactions are involved in the overall process of respiration. The net effect here is a breakdown of carbohydrate and a release of energy. Respiration occurs in all living cells at all times.

When photosynthesis exceeds respiration, net growth occurs. When they equal each other, net growth stops, and if respiration exceeds photosynthesis the plant declines in vigor and will eventually die. To insure that photosynthesis exceeds respiration, plants are grown cool at night to keep the respiration rate down and warmer by day to enhance photosynthesis.

As a general rule greenhouse crops are grown at a day temperature 5 to 10°F higher than the night temperature on cloudy days and 15°F higher on clear days. With CO_2 enrichment, the day temperatures may be an additional 5°F higher. The night temperature of greenhouse crops ranges mostly from 45 to 70°F (4 to 21°C). Primula, stock, and calceolaria grow best at 45°F, carnation and cineraria at 50°F, rose at 60°F, chrysanthemum and poinsettia at 62 to 64°F and African violet at 70 to 72°F.

There is a rule by F. F. Blackman which in essence states that the rate of any process which is governed by two or more factors will be limited by the factor in least supply. Photosynthesis is a good case in point. It is dependent upon heat, light, CO_2, and other factors. On cloudy days it is futile to raise the temperature more than 5 to 10°F above the night temperature because the low light intensity will limit the rate of photosynthesis and any additional heat applied will be without beneficial effect. On bright days light does not limit photosynthesis; thus, if the temperature is not raised, heat may become the limiting factor for photosynthesis. Even on dark days, the rate of photosynthesis will increase with CO_2 enrichment of the greenhouse atmosphere.

Light intensity is higher in the summer than in the winter and photosynthetic rates can be expected to be higher in the summer. This is very fortunate since it calls for higher daytime temperatures in the summer than in the winter to prevent heat from becoming the limiting factor. The cooling fans can be set at a higher temperature in the summer, as high as 80 to 85°F (26 to 29°C). This saves considerable electrical energy.

Blackman's Law is well illustrated in the curves of Figure 10-14 developed by P. Gaastra. In the lower curve the rate of photosynthesis began to plateau at about 40,000 lux (3,800 fc) of light intensity regardless of whether the temperature was at 68 or 86°F. The 300 ppm level of CO_2 became a limiting factor at that point. When the temperature was held at 68°F and the CO_2 level was increased to 1,300 ppm, the rate of photosynthesis increased. Now the 68°F temperature became the limiting factor because increase in temperature to 86°F at the same 1,300 ppm CO_2 level brought about another increase in photosynthesis.

This interaction of CO_2, light intensity, and temperature is reminiscent of observations in Chapter 9. It was stated at that time that increases in the CO_2 level in the greenhouse brought about beneficial effects from raising the daytime temperature above that normally maintained for many crops. When CO_2 is eliminated as a limiting factor for photosynthesis, a daytime temperature increase of 5°F can often be profitable.

One must be careful when determining how high to raise the temperature because it affects processes in addition to photosynthesis. Generally higher temperatures result in faster growth but with it can occur a reduction in quality. Longer stems, thinner stems, and smaller flowers may occur. Quality and quantity must always be weighed in such a decision. In the

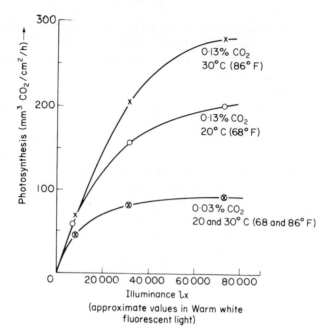

Figure 10-14. Effects of CO_2 concentration, light intensity, and leaf temperature on photosynthesis in cucumber. *(From P. Gaastra, Photosynthesis of Leaves and Field Crops. Netherlands J. Agricultural Science 10(5):311–324, 1962)*

former discussion about raising the temperature 5°F along with an increase in the CO_2 level, no adverse loss in quality is to be expected.

In short, any consideration of light must take into account a consideration of temperature as well as other factors governing growth.

SUMMARY

1. Light plays two general roles in the growth and development of plants. Light is a source of energy for the process of photosynthesis in which carbon is fixed into carbohydrates and ultimately all organic compounds of the plant. A relatively high intensity of light in the energy spectrum of 400 to about 750 nm is required. Light also regulates the developmental form of plants, e.g., vegetative versus reproductive growth. It is the duration of light and not so much its intensity which is important in this process.

2. Light is often a limiting factor to photosynthesis and growth during the winter at northern latitudes. Single greenhouses can be oriented with the ridge east to west and ridge-and-furrow greenhouses north to south in

order to maximize interior light intensity. The glass or FRP covering can be washed. Plants should be spaced further apart in the winter to increase the amount of light per plant.

3. Supplemental lighting during the daylight hours to enhance photosynthesis is highly effective but the economics are questionable. There are situations of high density plantings such as rooting and seedling beds and the production of young plants where it is a profitable operation. Research is actively underway to develop more efficient lamps and to adapt these to greenhouse situations. Fluorescent lamps have been most commonly used, however, there are commercial installations of high intensity discharge (HID) lamps. Continued research is needed to reduce the electrical costs through lamps of increased efficiency and to minimize the size of the fixture for reasons of shading.

4. A number of seedling producers construct growth rooms. Plants are grown on tiered shelves with a bank of fluorescent lights above each shelf. This is the sole source of light for photosynthesis. A growth room can be better insulated than a greenhouse. Often the heat from the lamps is sufficient to meet the heat requirement of the room.

5. Light plays its second role in photoperiodism which is the response of an organism to the day-night cycle. The relative length of the light and dark periods governs a number of responses including flowering, leaf shape, stem elongation, bulb formation, and pigmentation. In terms of flowering, long-night plants are those which initiate and develop flower buds when the nights are longer than a critical length. Conversely, short-night plants are those which initiate and develop flower buds when the night is shorter than a critical length. The critical night length varies among plant species and even among cultivars within a species. Not all plants are photoperiod. Those which do not respond to the day-night cycle are day-neutral plants.

6. Long nights are established in the greenhouse during the summer by covering the plants with a plastic or cloth fabric in the early evening (about 7 PM) and removing it in the morning (7 to 8 AM). The cover should be capable of reducing the light intensity beneath to 22 lux (2 fc) when the outside intensity is 5,000 fc. Automatic equipment is available for this operation. Short-night conditions can be established in the winter by providing 108 lux (10 fc) of illumination for a period of one to four hours during the middle of the night. Incandescent lights serve this purpose best.

7. Phytochrome is the receptor pigment in young tissue which responds to the light-dark cycle. The Pfr form of phytochrome rapidly builds up during the light period and is slowly converted to the Pr form during the dark period. The Pfr form is the active form which inhibits flowering in

long-night plants and promotes flowering in short-night plants. A long night is required to lower the level of Pfr photochrome to the point where flowering can occur in a long-night plant.

8. Heat is a form of energy and a factor essential to growth. Deleterious effects occur from levels too high or too low. Heat is just one factor governing growth. The rate of growth is limited by the factor in shortest supply. It is not always economically feasible to optimize all factors affecting growth in a greenhouse, thus, the best temperature for a crop will depend upon the following factors.

Light is often limiting in the winter. On low-light intensity days (cloudy) a day temperature 5 to 10°F above the night temperature is maintained while on brighter winter days a 15°F higher day temperature is beneficial to growth. Although even higher temperatures would not be beneficial to growth in the winter, they are beneficial in the summer when light intensity is higher and not limiting to growth.

The CO_2 level inside greenhouses often limits growth. When it is raised, growth increases to a point where previously adequate temperatures become the limiting factor. A 5°F rise in day temperature is often beneficial when the greenhouse atmosphere is enriched with CO_2.

SUGGESTED READINGS

Bickford, E. D., and S. Dunn. *Lighting for Plant Growth.* The Kent State University Press, Kent, OH, 1972.

Campbell, L. E., R. W. Thimijan, and H. M. Cathey. "Spectral Radiant Power of Lamps Used in Horticulture." Transactions of the American Society of Agricultural Engineers 18(5):952–956, 1975.

Cathey, H. M., and L. E. Campbell. "Plant Productivity: New Approaches to Efficient Light Sources and Environmental Control." American Society of Agricultural Engineers. Paper No. 75-7501. P. O. Box 229, St. Joseph, MO 49805, 1975.

Downs, R. J. *Controlled Environments for Plant Research.* Columbia University Press, New York, NY, 1975.

Fundamentals of Light and Lighting. General Electric Co., Large Lamps Dept., Nela Park, Cleveland, OH 44112, 1960.

Garner, W. W., and H. A. Allard. "Effect of the Relative Length of Day and Night and Other Factors of the Environment on Growth and Reproduction in Plants." *Journal of Agricultural Research* 18:553–607, 1920.

Growelectric Handbook No. 1: Growing Rooms. The Electricity Council. 30 Millbank. London SW1P 4RD, 1972.

Growelectric Handbook No. 2: Lighting in Greenhouses. The Electricity Council. 30 Millbank. London SW1P 4RD, 1973.

IES Lighting Handbook. 5th ed. Illuminating Engineering Society, 345 E. 47th St., New York, NY, 1972.

Mastalerz, J. W. "Environmental Factors: Light, Temperature, Carbon Dioxide." *In:* Mastalerz and Langhans (eds.). *Roses: A Manual on the Culture, Management, Diseases, Insects, Economics and Breeding of Greenhouse Roses.* Pennsylvania Flower Growers, New York State Flower Growers Association, Inc. and Roses Inc., 1969. pp. 95–108. (Available from: R. W. Langhans, Department of Floriculture and Ornamental Horticulture, Cornell University, Ithaca, NY 14850. $4.)

Plant Growth and Lighting. General Electric Co., Large Lamps Dept., Nela Park, Cleveland, OH 44112, 1964.

Van der Veen, R., and G. Meijer. *Light and Plant Growth.* The Macmillian Co., New York, 1959.

Chapter 11

Chemical
Growth Regulation

Floriculture is unlike other areas of agriculture in that the entire plant, or at least a major portion of the plant, is appraised according to its aesthetic value. While minor insect damage, leaf blemishes, or unusually tall height may not affect the yield or value of a bean crop, it does reduce the value of a potted plant. Several chemicals are used by greenhouse growers to control growth in one or another of its many forms to give the desired aesthetic effect. Final height can be shorter than natural, terminal buds can be pinched (destroyed), the cold requirement of crops such as azalea can be chemically substituted, rooting can be promoted, and hopefully lateral shoots will soon be chemically disbudded (removed).

CLASSIFICATION

Hormones

Chemicals used for stimulating growth are derived from a group known as hormones. Hormones are compounds produced in the plant in one site and then transported to a different part of the plant where they affect growth. *Auxins* and *gibberellins* are two groups of hormones used by the greenhouse grower.

AUXINS. Auxins are chemicals that promote growth in length. The major auxin produced in plants is indole-3-acetic acid (IAA). Auxins are produced in developing buds and young leaves and are transported downward (toward the crown of the plant). IAA and a few related, synthetically produced chemicals are used for promoting rooting of cuttings.

Auxins are involved in *tropistic* growth movements. Such movements include the downward growth of roots, upward growth of shoots, and the

323

growth of shoots and leaves toward the light. Shoots grow toward the light source because auxin is believed to be inactivated by light. This occurs more on the bright side of the stem, thus there is greater growth promotion of the darker side.

Auxins also inhibit lateral shoot development. When the top of the main shoot of a plant is removed, the source of auxin is lost from that shoot and lateral shoots are free to develop. This is why pinching (the removal of shoot tips) is practiced on some floral crops; multiple lateral shoots are promoted. A plant is said to display *apical dominance* when only one shoot predominates. When apical dominance is lost, several lateral shoots usually develop simultaneously.

GIBBERELLINS. Various gibberellins have been isolated from species of the fungus *Gibberella.* This fungus attacks rice plants and causes them to grow tall and threadlike. Gibberellins promote growth, but unlike auxins the promotion is uniform throughout the plant tissue. Growth stimulation occurs through increased cell elongation.

Forms of gibberellic acid (GA) have been researched in floriculture. For instance, gibberellic acid sprayed on geranium flowers at the time of first color appearance (at a concentration of 5 ppm) stimulates a 25 to 50 percent increase in flower size. The number of petals remains constant, but the size of each is larger. When greater concentrations are applied, however, increased responses carry an adverse effect. Stems and flower stalks elongate and become thinner. Stems may become adversely weak, flowers normally flat may become undesirably spikelike.

Gibberellic acid inhibits root formation on leaves and stems; thus is not found in root-promoting products. Gibberellic acid is used by hobbyists for enlarging the size of gardenia blooms. It has been used successfully in research for full or partial substitution of the cold requirement of azalea and hydrangea. Researchers have sprayed budded cyclamen plants with a solution of 10–50 ppm concentration to hasten flowering. The resulting flower stalks are taller.

GROWTH SUPPRESSANTS

Since the late 1940s, several synthetic chemicals have been developed for various forms of growth suppression. The most widely used are those which retard overall plant height. Potted plants must be grown to a height sympathetic with the environment in which they will be used. Many plants grow too tall if not checked. In past years water and nutrients were withheld to reduce height, resulting in bad side effects in the appearance of the foliage and size of the bloom. Poinsettia stems were sometimes folded (Figure 11–1) to reduce height. This was an effective but labor-expensive process. Chemical height retardants are used today.

Figure 11-1. Years ago poinsettia stems were often folded to reduce their height, as shown above. It was a time-consuming process which has been replaced by chemical height retardants applied either as a soil drench or a foliar spray. Chemically treated plants have the same number of leaves on shorter, thicker stems with deeper green foliage. *(Photo courtesy of J. W. Love, Department of Horticultural Science, North Carolina State University, Raleigh, NC 27607)*

Height retardants result in shorter stem internodes but do not affect the number of leaves formed. Stems are thicker and leaves are deeper green because chlorophyll is more dense in the smaller cells. As a result plants have a very pleasing appearance.

Another class of growth suppressants are the chemical pinching agents. These, when sprayed on azaleas, chrysanthemums, or certain woody ornamental plants cause death of the shoot tip within approximately 30 minutes after application. Membranes are destroyed in the plant cells when the chemical Off-Shoot-O® is used. This treatment replaces the need to manually cut the top off each shoot in order to induce branching. Dikegulac® is another pinching agent that affects internal processes rather than physically damaging the apex.

A third group of growth suppressants which are under study today, and show promise of commercial application, are the chemical disbudding agents (Figure 11-2). Standard chrysanthemums and most potted chrysanthemum cultivars require disbudding. This is a very time-consuming process in which all but the terminal flower bud are removed from each main stem. There are chemicals under test which when sprayed on the plant will inhibit lateral bud

Figure 11-2. Various chemicals are under study to find a safe disbudding agent. Buds in each leaf axil of the Wildfire chrysanthemum stem on the right were removed by hand. Buds were removed from the stem on the left by spraying it with an experimental disbudding agent. *(Photo courtesy of R. A. Larson, Department of Horticultural Science, North Carolina State University, Raleigh, NC 27607)*

development and leave the terminal bud unharmed. They are not ready for commercial use since there is still too close a margin of safety in timing and too much variation within cultivars. If applied too early, the terminal bud is injured; if too late, the effectiveness is reduced.

ROOT PROMOTION

Auxins are effectively used for promoting root formation on cuttings. Materials commercially used include indolebutyric acid (IBA), indolepropionic acid (IPA), and naphthalene acetic acid (NAA). IBA and NAA are often found in combination. Many types of cuttings benefit from the use of rooting substances. Root formation occurs faster and in the end the root system is unusually more extensive. The benefit is least on plant species which normally root fast, and there are a few species where no benefit is seen.

Rooting compounds are very concentrated and so are always diluted.

Talc powder is a customary diluent. Active ingredient concentrations of 0.1 to 1.0 percent are used; the lower concentrations for easy-to-root soft cuttings and the higher concentrations for slower to root, woody cuttings. The base of the cutting is dipped into the powder and then tapped to remove all but a thin film of powder. To reduce the possibility of disease transfer, a duster is often used.

Rooting compounds can be diluted by another method for use on woody cuttings where penetration is difficult. A concentrated stock solution of the rooting compound is made by dissolving it in alcohol. The stock solution is further diluted with water to a final concentration in the range of 500 to 5,000 ppm, (0.05 to 0.5%). The cut end of cuttings is dipped in this solution for a short time and then "stuck" into propagation media in a propagation bed. The concentration of the solution and the length of dipping time (five seconds to a few minutes) is determined by the ease of rooting and the penetrability into the woody stem of the cutting.

Rooting compounds are a very common and valuable aid to the propagators of greenhouse crops since so many crops are propagated by cuttings. Chrysanthemum, carnation, African violet, azalea, begonia, geranium, hydrangea, kalanchoe, poinsettia, and many green plants are examples of plants that benefit from rooting compounds.

COLD TREATMENT SUBSTITUTION

Azalea

Researchers have used a group of hormones, the gibberellins, to replace the need for cold treatment. A period of cold treatment is required in the greenhouse forcing program of the azalea. When the plant has reached sufficient size it is pinched for the last time. New shoots are allowed to develop for about six weeks and then flower bud initiation is induced by about six weeks of long-night treatment. Once flower buds are established, a period of six weeks at a temperature of 45°F (7°C) or lower is required for development of flower buds. Plants can be held outside in cold frames in milder climates when winter and spring flowering are desired. More often they are placed in coolers for the cold treatment. After this treatment plants are moved to the greenhouse and are forced into bloom in four to six weeks.

The cool temperature treatment is an expensive one requiring costly moving of plants and also cooler facilities (Figure 11-3). Considerable efforts have been made to reduce or eliminate the cool temperature treatment. Weekly sprays of gibberellic acid at a concentration of 1000 ppm has proven effective (Figure 11-4).

There are various forms of gibberellic acid (GA). When the entire six week cold requirement of azaleas was replaced by chemical treatment in

Figure 11-3. A cooler is required for the growth of certain crops that need a cold period for flower bud development. Such crops include azalea, flowering bulbs, hydrangea, and Easter lily.

Figure 11-4. Azalea "Dogwood" plants during greenhouse forcing. The plant on the left received the standard cold treatment for flower bud development. It is fully budded and will bloom in a few weeks. The plant on the right, rather than being placed in a cooler, was left in the greenhouse and sprayed six times at weekly intervals with gibberellic acid at a concentration of 1,000 ppm. In addition to replacing the cold treatment, this chemical hastened flowering and resulted in larger flowers. *(Photo courtesy of R. A. Larson, Department of Horticultural Science, North Carolina State University, Raleigh, NC 27607)*

research studies, GA_{4+7} for the first three weekly sprays and GA_3 for the last two weekly sprays proved best. The five consecutive weekly sprays begin when flower buds are well developed after the short day treatment. Plants treated in this manner usually flower earlier and have larger blossoms than plants given cold temperature treatment. Most cultivars respond well; however, there can be some variation. For instance, flower pedicels may become too long, causing flowers to droop.

There have also been studies on the partial replacement of the cold treatment. After three weeks of cold treatment, plants were moved to the greenhouse for forcing and three weekly sprays of GA_3 at 250 ppm were made. Half of the cold treatment was eliminated, thereby permitting twice the volume of plants to be moved through the cooler facilities.

Hydrangea

Hydrangeas are also subjected to a period of cold storage. On occasion they are removed prematurely and slow development, small flowers, and short stems ensue. Research studies show promise of eliminating this situation by a spray of gibberellic acid at a concentration of 5 to 50 ppm. Gibberellic acid has not been labeled for use on azalea or hydrangea. Hopefully it will be so that these applications can be made.

HEIGHT RETARDATION

The role of height retardants has already been described. Several are available and more are in the experimental stage (Figure 11-5). Presented in Table 11-1 are crops treated chemically for height control as well as cold treatment substitution and pinching. Growth regulator recommendations and methods of application are included.

Phosfon®

Phosfon® (tributyl 2,4-dichlorobenzylphosphonium chloride) was one of the first growth retardants to be marketed. It is produced by the Virginia-Carolina Chemical Corporation of Richmond, Va. and is labeled for use on chrysanthemum and Easter lily to retard height. Either a dust formulation can be mixed into the potting medium prior to planting or a 10 percent liquid formulation can be diluted in water and applied to established plants as a root medium drench. Phosfon® is toxic to foliage and is never applied as a spray. It has a long residual life. Treated clay pots have been known to exert a dwarfing effect on several successive crops.

Phosfon® has been successfully used to reduce growth of greenhouse forcing azaleas resulting in increased flower bud set. This is a response which can be obtained with B-Nine® and Cycocel® as well.

Figure 11-5. Chrysanthemum 'Nob Hill' treated with the chemical height retardant A-Rest_® at increasing concentrations from left to right. The plant on the extreme left received no chemical treatment. Those to the right have the same number of leaves but shorter internodes, thicker stems, and deeper green foliage. *(Photo courtesy of V. P. Bonaminio, Phytotron, North Carolina State University, Raleigh, NC 27607)*

Phosfon_® is not used to a large extent by greenhouse growers today. Other growth retardants have appeared which are effective on a wider range of plants and which can be applied as foliar sprays.

Cycocel_®

Cycocel_® [(2-chloroethyl) trimethylammonium chloride] is available in a liquid formulation containing 11.8 percent active ingredient. It was formerly known as CCC and is produced by American Cyanamid Company, P.O. Box 400, Princeton, NJ 08540. It is an effective height control agent for azalea and poinsettia.

Cycocel_® is applied as a spray to azaleas at the rate of two to three ounces per gal of water six to eight weeks after the plants have been pinched for the last time. This checks growth and prompts early flower bud initiation. Quite often a larger number of flower buds develop. The retardant helps further by reducing the formation of vegetative shoots at the time of flower bud development. These undesirable sideshoots give the plant an unbalanced appearance.

Table 11-1
Growth Regulator Recommendations for Floricultural Crops*

PLANT	GROWTH REGULATOR	CONCENTRATION	METHOD OF APPLICATION	MIXING RATES English	MIXING RATES Metric	TIME OF APPLICATION	COMMENTS
Azaleas	B-Nine (SADH) Height control	2500 to 3500 ppm (.25–.35%)	Spray to run-off	0.4 to 0.6 oz B-Nine SP/gal	3 to 4.5g B-Nine SP/ℓ	4–6 weeks after last pinch Apply early morning Increases short day response and early bud formation	Apply alone—not in combinations Don't let solution drip on medium
	Cycocel (Chlormequat) Height control	2500 ppm (.25%)	Spray to run-off	2.5 oz Cycocel/gal	20 ml Cycocel/ℓ	Apply after last pinch and again one week later to control height	Can produce medium hard plants, slight chlorosis, and/or late uneven flowering No S.D./early bud response
	Off-Shoot-O Chemical disbudding	2.5% to 6.3%	Spray following label instructions	2 to 5 oz/qt	3 to 6g B-Nine SP/ℓ	Apply any time the plant is actively growing to chemically pinch Use a very fine mist to be most effective	Apply only when have good air movement Follow label instructions carefully

(Table 11–1 continued)

Table 11-1 continued

PLANT	GROWTH REGULATOR	CONCENTRATION	METHOD OF APPLICATION	MIXING RATES English	Metric	TIME OF APPLICATION	COMMENTS
Bedding Plants	B–Nine (SADH) Height control	2500 ppm to 5000 ppm (.25%–.5%)	Spray	0.4 to 0.8 oz/gal B–Nine SP	3 to 6g B–Nine SP/ℓ	3–4 weeks after transplanting to control height May need repeated applications	Spray only turgid plants Don't apply water to foliage for 24 hrs Not effective on snapdragons, celosia, and coleus
Bromelliads	Ethrel (Ethephon) Induction of flowering	25 mg/plant	Pour in "vase" of plant	1 tbsp Ethrel (21.3%)/ 1 qt H$_2$O Apply 2 tsp/plant	12 ml Eth. (21.3%)/ℓ Apply 10 ml/plant	Apply when plants 1½ to 2 yrs old to induce flowering	Plants should flower in 2 months
Chrysanthe-mums (pot)	B–Nine (SADH) Height control	2500 ppm to 5000 ppm (0.25% to 0.5%)	Spray to wet foliage	0.4 to 0.8 oz B–Nine SP/gal	3 to 6g B–Nine SP/ℓ	Apply 10–14 days after pinch, or after shoots are 1–1½" long Second applica-tion 3 weeks later	Do not mix B–Nine with other chemicals

332

Crop	Chemical / Purpose	Concentration	Application	Rate (English)	Rate (metric)	Timing	Remarks
	A-Rest (Ancymidol) Height control	25 to 100 ppm (0.0025 to 0.01%)	Spray ultra low volume fog to just wet foliage	12–48 oz A-Rest + H_2O to make 1 gal	55–380 ml A-Rest + H_2O to make 1 ℓ	Apply immediately after pinch and start of short days	Varieties requiring 2500 ppm B–Nine require 25 ppm A-Rest 5000 ppm B-Nine need 50 ppm A-Rest
	A-Rest (Ancymidol) Height control	0.125 mg to 0.5 mg/6" pot	Drench 6 oz 180 ml/6" pot	1/2 to 2 oz A-Rest + H_2O to make 1.5 gal	25–100 ml A-Rest + H_2O to make 10 ℓ	Apply just as root system spreads over outside of soil ball	Minimum 180 ml (6 oz) of H_2O/6" pot when applying Entire soil must receive uniform application
Easter Lilies	A-Rest (Ancymidol) Height control	1.32 ppm 0.25 mg/6" pot	Drench 6 oz (180 ml)/6" pot	1 oz A-Rest/1.5 gal water	50 ml A-Rest/10ℓ water	Apply when lilies are 3–6" tall to control height. Do not apply Jan. 23 to Feb. 7 as may reduce bud count	Not effective if bark medium is used
Hydrangea	B–Nine SP (SADH) Height control during forcing	5000–7500 ppm (0.5% to 0.75%)	Spray to wet foliage	0.8 to 1.2 oz B-Nine SP/gal	6 to 9g B-Nine SP/ℓ	During the growth period apply 4 weeks after pinch but not after Aug. 5	

(Table 11–1 continued)

Table 11-1 continued

PLANT	GROWTH REGULATOR	CONCENTRATION	METHOD OF APPLICATION	MIXING RATES English	MIXING RATES Metric	TIME OF APPLICATION	COMMENTS
						Repeat applications may be needed	
	B-Nine SP (SADH) Height control during forcing	2500 ppm (0.25%)	Spray to wet foliage	0.4 oz B-Nine SP/ gal	3 g B-Nine SP/ℓ	During the forcing period apply 1st spray between 2nd and 3rd week (4-5 leaf stage) 2nd spray one week later	Can apply after buds visible if necessary
Poinsettia	Cycocel (Chlormequat) Height control—August	3000 to 6000 ppm (0.3% to 0.6%) dilute 1:20-1:40	Drench 6 oz (180 ml)/ 6" pot	3 to 6½ oz Cycocel/ gal	25 to 50 ml Cycocel/ℓ	Apply in August on a cool and cloudy day after plants are established in the pot to control height	Apply about 2 weeks after pinching
	Cycocel (Chlormequat) Height control Sept.– early Oct.	3000 ppm (0.3%) (dilute 1:40)	Drench 6 oz (180 ml)/6" pot	3 oz/gal	25 ml/ℓ	Apply this rate if second application in Sept. or Oct. is needed	Late application may reduce bract size

Cycocel (Chlormequat) Height control late Oct.	1500 ppm (0.15%) (dilute 1:80)	Drench 6 oz (180 ml)/6" pot	1.5 oz/gal 13 ml/ℓ	Apply between Oct. 15–30 if unusually bright, hot fall	Late application may reduce bract size
A-Rest (Ancymidol) Height control Sept.–Oct.	2.6 ppm 0.5 mg/6" pot	Drench 6 oz (180 ml/6") pot	2 oz A-Rest + H_2O to make 1.5 gal 50 ml A-Rest + H_2O to make 5 ℓ	Apply 3 weeks after pinch or when breaks are 2–4" long or 8–12 weeks before crop finishes	
Tulip A-Rest (Ancymidol) Height control	0.125 mg to 0.5 mg/pot	Drench 4 oz (120 ml/6") pot	1–4 oz A-Rest + H_2O to make 2 gal 40–160 ml A-Rest + H_2O to make 10 ℓ	Apply 1–4 days after bringing into greenhouse	Response varies with cultivars; not effective if applied after 4 days in greenhouse

*Adapted from R. D. Heins, R. E. Widmer, and H. F. Wilkins, Department of Horticultural Science and Landscape Architecture, University of Minnesota

Cycocel® is recommended only as a drench for poinsettia height retardation. Sprays can result in blotchy yellowing of foliage about 24 hours after application. This is a temporary situation and is not noticed at flowering time. Research results indicate that Cycocel® shows promise for height control of geranium seedlings and cuttings.

B-Nine SP®

B-Nine SP® (N-dimethylaminosuccinamic acid) was formerly called B-995 and is produced by Uniroyal Chemical, Division of Uniroyal, Inc., Naugatuck, CT 06770. It is an effective height retardant for potted chrysanthemums, cut chrysanthemums, azaleas, hydrangeas, bedding plants, poinsettias, and gardenias. B-Nine SP® is sold as a soluble powder containing 85 percent active ingredient plus a wetting agent and is applied as a foliar spray to the upper leaf surfaces generally at concentrations of 0.25 to 0.50 percent active ingredient.

Azaleas are treated with B-Nine SP® for the same reasons Cycocel® and Phosfon® are used—to promote early and more extensive flower bud set and to retard vegetative shoot development. Some cultivars of standard chrysanthemum develop a long pedicel (flower stem) which is unattractive. A compact flower with a short pedicel can be produced by spraying the upper third of the foliage to the point of runoff two days after disbudding with a 0.25 percent concentration of B-Nine SP®. Pot mums are sprayed when new shoots are 1½ inches long, about two weeks after the pinch. No delay in flowering occurs as is experienced from the use of Phosfon®. B-Nine SP® is particularly useful in producing compact bedding plants. It is effective on petunias, marigolds, zinnias, asters, cosmos, and salvia, but not on celosia, coleus, or snapdragons.

A-Rest®

A-Rest® [α-cyclopropyl-α-(ρ-methoxyphenyl)-5-pyrimidinemethanol] is the most recent addition to the growth regulator line and is produced by Elanco Products Company, Division of Eli Lilly and Company, Indianapolis, IN 46206. A-Rest® effectively controls height of chrysanthemums, poinsettias, Easter lilies, and tulips. It is purchased as a solution containing 250 mg of active ingredient per quart (264 ppm). A-Rest® can be applied as a spray or as a drench.

Cost of Materials

It is difficult to make cost comparisons for height retardants. All are not effective on each crop. Some are applied as a drench while others are applied as a spray. The number of pots that can be sprayed with a gallon of

Table 11-2

Approximate Costs of Various Height Retardants and Methods of Application
for Treating a Single Plant in a 6-Inch Pot

REGULANT	COST OF PRODUCT	METHOD OF APPLICATION	RATE OF PRODUCT DILUTION	RATE OF DILUTED PRODUCT APPLICATION	COST PER 6-INCH POT
Phosfon L®	$21.95/pt (liquid)	drench	1 oz/54 qt	6 oz/pot	0.5¢
Cycocel®	$16.25/qt (liquid)	drench	1 qt/10 gal (.3%)	6 oz/pot	7.5¢
		spray	1 qt/10 gal (.3%)	1 gal/100 sq ft	2.5¢
B-Nine SP®	$22.20/lb (powder)	spray	0.4 oz/gal (.25%)	1 gal/100 sq ft	0.8¢
A-Rest®	$35.75 qt (liquid)	drench	0.75 oz/gal	6 oz/pot (0.25 mg/pot)	3.5¢
		spray	2 oz/gal	1 gal/100 sq ft (0.25 mg/pot)	3.5¢

retardant depends upon the spray equipment, with the high-pressure, fine-droplet spray covering more area. The concentration of retardant varies, depending upon the crop and its stage of growth. Calculations presented in Table 11–2 are intended to give a rough idea of the cost of using height retardants.

The assumptions are made that six-inch pots of a crop such as poinsettia or chrysanthemum are being treated and that one gallon of spray will treat 100 square feet of bench or 67 plants. The resulting figures indicate that chemical height control is inexpensive considering the improved quality of the crop that is achieved.

CHEMICAL PINCHING

Off-Shoot-O$_{®}$ (primarily methyl octanoate and methyl decanoate in combination with an emulsifying agent) is produced by Procter and Gamble Company, Cincinnati, OH 45201. It is termed a chemical pinching agent because it causes death of the terminal bud on shoots which in turn results in the development of side shoots (Figure 11–6). Often more side shoots are produced from a chemical pinch than from a manual pinch. Off-Shoot-O$_{®}$ is applied in a very fine spray to wet the shoot tips. The remainder of the plant need not be treated and spraying is stopped before the point of runoff. Runoff increases the possibility of injury to lateral buds and leaves.

Azaleas are effectively pinched with this chemical. Considerable labor is saved since azaleas must be pinched many times in order to produce a large plant with numerous shoots. Concentrations of 3 to 6 percent are used depending upon the cultivar. A 4.5 percent concentration is common. Chrysanthemums can be chemically pinched but there is an element of risk. Solution running down the stem often causes girdling of the stem at the soil level, and ultimately death of the plant. Cultivars vary in their susceptibility. The spray must be applied in a very fine mist to avoid runoff. Growers generally do not use chemical pinching for chrysanthemums. Several species of woody ornamentals can also be chemically pinched.

SUMMARY

1. The speed and extent of root formation of cuttings can be enhanced by the auxin IAA (indole-3-acetic acid). Related compounds IBA (indolebutyric acid), IPA (indolepropionic acid), and NAA (naphthalene acetic acid) are used alone and in combination in commercial rooting products.

2. Azaleas and hydrangeas require a cold treatment for flower bud development. Often coolers are used for treating azaleas. This is an expensive process which one day may be totally replaced in most cultivars of azaleas,

Figure 11-6. A greenhouse forcing azalea plant sprayed with the chemical pinching agent, Off-Shoot-O®. Note the dead terminal buds and the resulting side shoots. This process is repeated several times over a 12 to 18 month period to develop a highly branched plant of suitable size for forcing into bloom. *(Photo courtesy of J. W. Love, Department of Horticultural Science, North Carolina State University, Raleigh, NC 27607)*

and partially replaced in the others, by sprays of gibberellic acid. Five sprays of 1,000 ppm at weekly intervals during the normal time of cold storage permit flower buds to develop without cold temperatures. Hydrangeas having received too little cold storage might be sprayed with gibberellic acid during subsequent forcing to restore their normal rate of growth and flower size.

3. Many greenhouse potted plants grow taller than desired. Plants with short internodes can be produced by treatment with chemical height retardants including Phosfon® (for azaleas, chrysanthemums, and Easter lilies), Cycocel® (for azaleas and poinsettias), B-Nine® (for azaleas, bedding plants, chrysanthemums, hydrangeas and poinsettias), and A-Rest® (for bedding plants, chrysanthemums, Easter lilies, poinsettias, and tulips). Height retardation in azalea fosters more rapid flower bud initiation and sometimes a greater number of flower buds.

4. The terminal end of each shoot of azalea plants must be pinched (removed) several times to produce large, bushy plants. This is a time-consuming and expensive procedure which can be accomplished with a

chemical pinching agent, Off-Shoot-O$_®$. When sprayed on the plant the terminal buds die, leaving lateral buds unharmed and free to develop.

5. Several chemicals are currently under study for a wide variety of applications. New height retardants with greater effectiveness on a wider range of plant species are being investigated. Chemical disbudding agents are being sought which will kill side buds and leave the terminal bud. This is presently a very tedious hand procedure for chrysanthemums. Chemicals which will increase the number of side shoots developing after a pinch appear feasible. Many other labor saving and crop improvement chemical treatments may one day be available to the grower.

6. There are several other uses for which the commercial growth regulants have been proven effective in research studies. However, they have not been labeled through EPA for these uses and, as a result, it is illegal to use them for these purposes. It is the intent of this book to recommend only those chemicals and uses that are cleared by EPA.

SUGGESTED READINGS

The manufacturers of growth regulators have technical literature available covering crop responses, methods of application, modes of action and other background information.

Kiplinger, D. C., R. O. Miller, and H. K. Tayama. *Plant Growth Regulators.* Cooperative Extension Service, The Ohio State University, Bulletin 486, 1967.

Mitchell, J. W. and G. A. Livingston. *Methods of Studying Plant Hormones and Growth-Regulating Substances.* USDA ARS Agriculture Handbook No. 336, 1968.

Plant Growth Substances. A series of conferences have been held on the topic of plant growth substances and proceedings have been printed. The eighth conference was held in Tokyo in 1973 and the proceedings were published in 1974 by Hirokawa Publishing Company.

Sachs, R. M. and W. P. Hackett. "Chemical Inhibition of Plant Height." *HortScience* 7:440–447, 1972.

Shanks, J. B., "Chemical Growth Regulation for Floricultural Crops." *Florists' Review* 147:34–35, 1970, 50–58.

VanOverbeek, J., "The Control of Plant Growth." *Scientific American* 219:75–81, 1968.

Chapter 12

Insect Control

Insects, mites, and other related animal pests constitute an ever present threat to the quality of greenhouse crops. Aside from the damage done to the crop, the presence of insects on the final product is disconcerting to the consumer. Most greenhouse crops are sold for aesthetic value and insects cannot be tolerated. The greenhouse environment is well suited to insects. A careful plan of prevention and control of insects must be developed for any greenhouse range.

INSECT PREVENTION

Weed Control

Insects abound in our world. During the warmer seasons they live in the soil and on vegetation outside the greenhouse. They crawl or fly into the greenhouse, or they may be carried in on clothing. Smaller insects such as thrips are carried in the airstream entering the greenhouse through the pads of the cooling system. Weeds harbor insects and diseases. They give the establishment an unsightly appearance which discourages customers and weakens the morale of employees. You can rest assured that weeds reduce your profitability. Weeds should be cleared away from the area surrounding the greenhouse and should also be eliminated in the greenhouse because they provide a hiding place and a source of food for insects. It does no good to spray crop plants in the bench if weeds under the bench are not sprayed; yet, to spray these weeds is a waste of time and money. Some growers keep the area bare around their greenhouses while others maintain mowed grass. Thrips develop in grass flowers, hence, mowing is important. This greatly reduces the types and numbers of insects invading the greenhouse.

Be very careful when selecting a herbicide (weed killer) for use adjacent to a greenhouse. Any herbicide which volatizes is potentially dangerous.

Plant Entry

Insects can be brought into the greenhouse on plants. Purchased seedlings and cuttings should be inspected carefully for insects. If they are present, these plants should be isolated and treated with pesticides. Common sources of insect and disease problems are established plants brought to the greenhouse by customers. You will often be approached by friends and customers who want you to rejuvenate a plant for them. This often leads to more trouble than the plant is worth. Do not allow the entry of such plants in your production area.

If you find it expedient to treat occasional plants or isolated areas, keep a window cleaner sprayer filled with pesticides in alcohol. Use 95 percent ethanol diluted 1:1 with water or 70 percent rubbing alcohol diluted 2:1. Add 1/8 teaspoon all-purpose E. C. pesticide spray per pint (or other recommendation). The alcohol acts as a surfactant and increases efficacy. This may be too expensive for widespread use, but is excellent for spot treatment.

Early Detection

It is inevitable that insects are going to get into the greenhouse. If they can be detected early, they can be eliminated before any significant damage is done and before any drastic pesticide applications are required. For one reason or another insects often will establish themselves in a particular location in the greenhouse. It may be a warmer temperature zone or an air current that carries them there, or perhaps it is an area that is difficult to spray and thus not well protected. The grower should identify such spots and check them regularly. As a matter of fact, the whole range should be checked daily by the manager when making rounds to determine which areas to water.

Insects often exhibit plant preferences. Some varieties of a crop are more attractive to them than others. These should be watched carefully. Most insects seek the undersides of leaves. An inspection of plants from above may not reveal their presence. Other pests, such as slugs, hide beneath pots or pieces of bark or leaves on the surface of the root medium during the day and come out to feed at night. One must be aware of these habits and look in the proper place for the pest or know the signs of the pest.

Preventative Spray Program

It is a good insurance measure to spray periodically to stop insect and disease problems before they begin. Many growers spray every seven to ten days with a combination of a miticide, insecticide, and a fungicide. Dr. H. T.

Streu of Rutgers University recommended three general spray mixture alternatives in the thirteenth edition of the *Ball Red Book* for a preventative program. These are:

SPRAY NO. 1

---

24 ozs. Omite$_®$ 30% WP
 8 ozs. lindane 25% WP
 8 ozs. Benlate$_®$ 50% WP
24 ozs. zineb, ferbam or maneb plus spreader-sticker, if necessary

---

SPRAY NO. 2

---

16 ozs. Diazinon$_®$ (AG500) 50% EC
 8 ozs. Pentac$_®$ 50% WP
 8 ozs. Benlate$_®$ 50% WP
24 ozs. zineb, ferbam or maneb plus spreader-sticker, if necessary

---

SPRAY NO. 3

Meta Systox-R$_®$ (see label for directions)
24 ozs. Kelthane$_®$ 50% WP
 8 ozs. Benlate$_®$ 50% WP
24 ozs. zineb, ferbam or maneb plus spreader-sticker, if necessary

---

INSECT AND OTHER ANIMAL PESTS
IN THE GREENHOUSE

There are numerous insects and related pests that attack plants in the greenhouse. In order to effectively control these pests their nature must be understood. The majority of infestations are due to ten types of pests. Before any control measures can be planned, the pest must be identified. While a few pesticides kill pests in general, most are made specifically for one or a few pests. Spider mites, for instance, are controlled by a specific group of pesticides known at miticides.

Feeding habits are very important. A pest such as the cyclamen mite which feeds in the small scales of buds is likely to escape injury unless a surfactant is added to the spray to insure penetration into the bud. White flies which feed on the lower sides of leaves point out the importance of spraying from beneath as well as from above. Knowledge of feeding habits also serves to tell the manager where to check for early detection of a problem.

The method of feeding by a pest will permit detection of those which are too small to be seen with the unaided eye or those which hide beneath clods of soil or under pots during the day. Slime trails are indicative of slugs, distorted growth of new leaves can indicate cyclamen mites, light brown tracks in a leaf signify the presence of leaf miners, and patches of sandy colored pinpoint spots on leaves are the result of a pest with piercing-sucking mouth parts such as aphids and spider mites.

Many pesticides do not kill eggs, thus the life cycle of a pest must be known. An insect such as the aphid, which can reproduce at seven to ten days of age, requires a more frequent spray program than one such as the mealybug which takes six to eight weeks to mature.

Some of the more important greenhouse pests are described in this section. Pertinent features about their identity and habits are presented to aid in an understanding of their control. For additional information see *Floricultural Insects and Related Pests—Biology and Control* by A. G. Gentile and D. T. Scanlon.

Aphids

Aphids attack a wide variety of greenhouse crops. There are several types of aphids differentiated by color. The most prevalent greenhouse species is known as the green peach aphid, *Myzus persicae* Sulzer (Figure 12-1). The wingless forms of green peach aphid are yellowish green in summer and pink to red in the fall and spring. The winged forms are brown. Aphids are 1/8 inch or less in length. They feed by inserting a tubelike piercing mouth part into the leaf and sucking out the sap. Feeding usually occurs in buds and undersides of leaves. Feeding on young bud leaves results in distorted leaves as they continue to grow. Older leaves may display patches of chlorotic pinpoint spots where cell contents have been drawn out.

Aphids excrete honeydew which is rich in sugar. A black sooty mold often grows on the honeydew, marring the appearance of the plant. Ants collect the honeydew and sometimes go so far as to farm aphids by moving them to suitable host plants and protecting them.

Aphids usually give birth to living female nymphs. The nymphs give birth to successive generations of female nymphs in as short a time as 7 to 10 days. Each aphid reproduces for a period of 20 to 30 days. One aphid can give birth to 60 to 100 nymphs. The entire process takes place without mating. When the food supply becomes short or the colony overcrowded, winged females appear and migrate. Male and female forms appear outdoors with advancing winter in the northern but not in the southern United States. These mate and eggs are laid which constitute an overwintering stage.

Fungus Gnats. (Bradysia species and Sciara species)

Fungus gnats (Figure 12-2) are thin, grey colored flies with long legs and antennae. They reside mainly on soil and will fly short distances when disturbed. The adult is about 1/8-inch long and has one pair of clear wings.

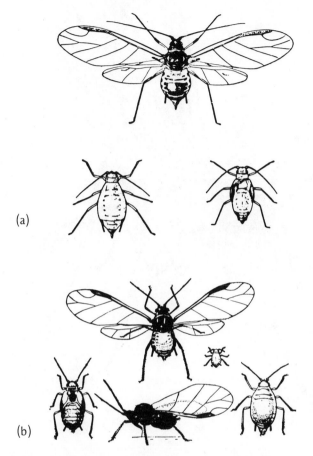

Figure 12-1. Winged and wingless forms of aphids: (a) green peach aphids; (b) melon aphids. (*USDA sketch*)

The body ranges in color from a black head to brownish yellow legs and abdomen.

Damage is caused by the larvae which are legless white worms with a black head which grow to about 1/4-inch in length. These larvae normally feed on soil fungi and decaying organic matter. When population densities increase fleshy storage organs such as bulbs and roots may be attached. Delicate seedlings may be killed. A wide variety of crops are injured. Infected plants may turn yellow, lack vigor, or wilt.

The female lays eggs in clusters of 20 to 30 on moist soil surfaces. Soil rich in organic matter is preferred. As many as 300 eggs are laid during the ten-day life span of the adult. The egg hatches in about six days into a larva. The larva feeds for 12 to 14 days and then changes into a pupa in the soil. After five to six days an adult fly emerges from the pupal stage. The life cycle from egg to adult requires about four weeks.

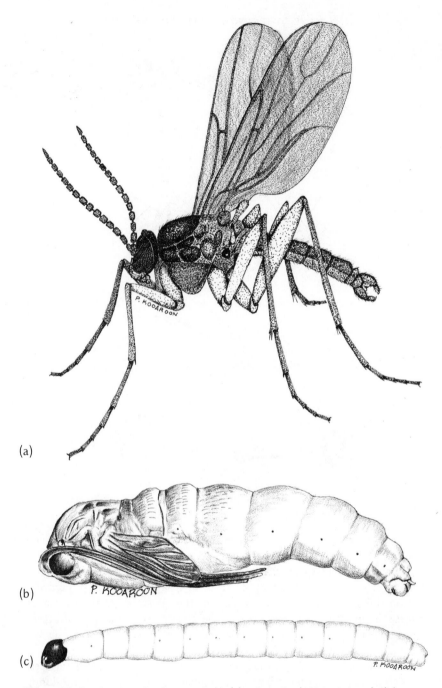

(a)

(b)

(c)

Figure 12-2. Stages of a fungus gnat: (a) adjult fly (1/8-inch long); (b) pupa (1/8-inch long); (c) larva (up to 3/16-inch long). *(Sketch courtesy of J. R. Baker, North Carolina Agricultural Extension Service, Raleigh, NC 27607)*

346

Leaf Miners

Leaf miners, when in the larval (worm) stage, tunnel between the outer layers of leaves making unsightly tunnels (Figure 12-3). A heavy infestation renders the plant useless for sale.

The adult female is a stocky fly about 1/12-inch long which punctures the leaf surface with a tubelike appendage on the abdomen known as an *ovipositor* and inserts eggs through it. This activity leaves small white spots on the leaf. A larger number of punctures are made than the number of eggs deposited. Males and females feed on the sap which oozes from the punctures. Each female lays about 100 eggs in its two to three week life span. The egg hatches in five to six days into a soft white maggot which reaches 1/10-inch long when mature. The maggot can tunnel for up to two weeks at which time it turns into a pupa. After about two weeks an adult fly emerges from the pupa, flys to a new leaf, and the life cycle begins again. About five weeks is required for the life cycle from egg to adult.

There are numerous species of leaf miners but two are most prevalent in the greenhouse. A serpentine leaf miner adult [*Liriomyza trifolii* Burgess] has a blackish body with yellow markings, a yellow head, and brown eyes. It makes serpentine mines. The chrysanthemum leaf miner (*Phytomyza atricornis* Meigen) adult is larger and black in color. Blotchy as well as serpentine mines are formed by these maggots.

Mealybugs

Mealybugs (*Pseudococcus*) are oval-shaped insects that appear white because of a waxlike powder which covers their body (Figure 12-4). The waxy deposit on their body includes filaments extending out around the periphery of the body as well as some longer filaments up to ½-inch long extending from the back to give the appearance of a tail in the long-tailed mealybug. The actual insect is 1/5- to 1/3-inch long.

Mealybugs feed by means of a piercing, sucking mouth part. During feeding citrus mealybugs inject a toxic substance into the plant. The plant becomes chlorotic and malformed. Like aphids, these insects also excrete honeydew which provides a substrate for a black sooty mold to grow upon further disfiguring the plant. Ants sometimes farm these insects much as they do aphids.

Long-tailed mealybugs give birth to living nymphs. Citrus mealybugs lay eggs which are deposited in a cottony sac. Several hundred yellowish or orange eggs are contained in a sac. The eggs can hatch in five to ten days into nymphs. The nymphs move about feeding for six to eight weeks when they finally become adults. The life cycle from egg to adult takes seven to ten weeks under favorable conditions.

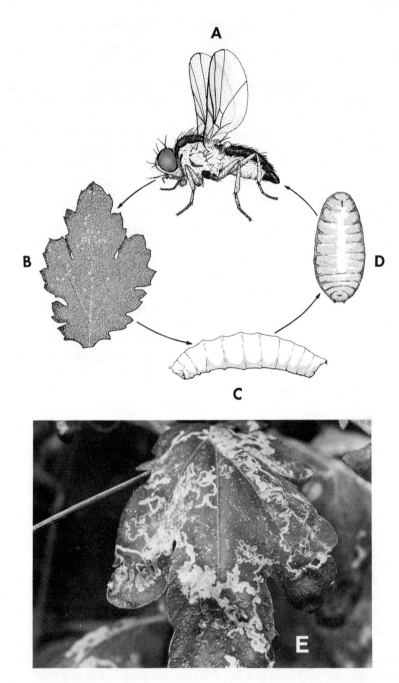

Figure 12-3. Stages of the leaf miner fly: (a) adult; (b) egg and feeding punctures; (c) larva; (d) pupa; (e) damage to chrysanthemum in a commercial greenhouse. *(Sketch courtesy of J. R. Baker, North Carolina Agricultural Extension Service, Raleigh, NC 27607)*

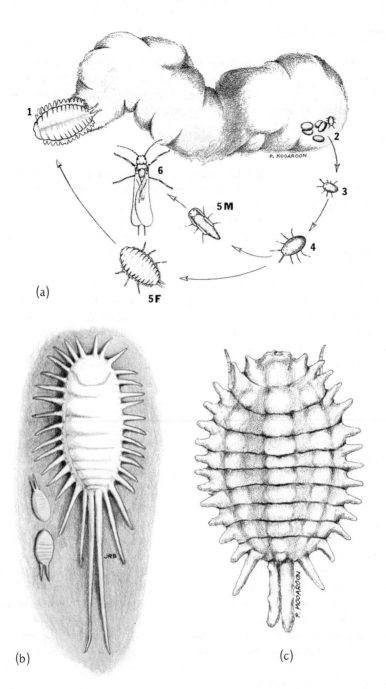

Figure 12-4. Various stages of mealybugs: (a) citrus mealybugs in all stages; (b) adult long-tailed mealybug; (c) Mexican mealybug. *(Sketch courtesy of J. R. Baker, North Carolina Agricultural Extension Service, Raleigh, NC 27607)*

349

The waxy protective layer makes it difficult to control mealybugs. Surfactants help wettable powder formulations of pesticides stick better. Aerosols play a useful role here as well. The nymphs, having a thinner protective ccoating, are easier to kill than the adults.

Mites

Mites are not insects; they belong to the class *Arachnida* which includes spiders and scorpions. In the adult form they have four pairs of legs. There are many species of mites, including several that attack crops.

Cyclamen mites (*Steneotarsonemus pallidus* Banks) are very small, about 1/100-inch long when full grown. They cannot be seen with the unaided eye. These mites are semitransparent with a brownish tinge. Their development is favored by a high humidity (80 percent or more) and a low temperature (60°F). The life cycle from egg to adult can occur in two weeks, but the adult female lives on for three to four weeks, laying up to 100 eggs.

Cyclamen mites affect a broad range of plants, many of them green plants. The mite lives and feeds in the bud and small adjacent leaves. It feeds with piercing, sucking mouth parts. Symptoms (Figure 12-5) are curling of leaflets from outside inward and distortion of young leaves such that small depressions are formed. Flowers may also be distorted or fail to open altogether.

Two-spotted mites, also known as red spiders (*Tetranychus urticae* Koch), are perhaps the most troublesome of all greenhouses pests (Figure 12-6) These mites may be greenish, yellowish, or red in color and have two dark spots on their bodies. They are about 1/50-inch in length.

Two-spotted mites cause chlorotic stippling of leaves as though a very fine tan to yellow sand had been sprinkled on them when populations increase. However, on mums and other plants with thick leaves, chlorotic stippling may not be noticed. The spiders spin a silk strand which forms a web over leaves and flowers. Leaves and flowers soon begin to desiccate and consequently turn brown. These mites are most prevalent on undersides of leaves and in flowers. They are difficult to control in the flower. The time span from egg to adult is 10 days at 80°F (26°C), 20 days at 70°F (21°C) or may be several months at lower temperatures. Low relative humidity favors development of this mite. Eggs hatch in four to five days into six-legged nymphs which feed for a short time. Next comes an inactive resting stage, a nympho-chrysalis, of about a 1-½-day duration. This sequence is repeated for a total of three resting stages. The eight-legged adult emerges from the last resting stage.

During the egg stage and the resting stages most miticides are ineffective, whether applied as an aerosol, smoke, or nonresidual spray. Since all stages are usually present simultaneously, several miticide applications are

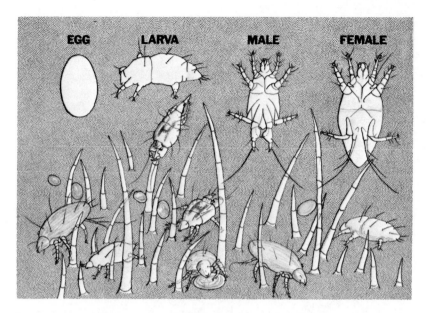

Figure 12-5. All stages of the cyclamen mite shown to scale with the trichomes (leaf hairs) on a gloxinia leaf. *(Sketch courtesy of J. R. Baker, North Carolina Agricultural Extension Service, Raleigh, NC 27607)*

necessary. At high temperatures it may be necessary to apply these as often as two days apart.

Scale Insects

There are several genera of scale insects all belonging to the superfamily Coccoidea (Figure 12-7). They vary in overall shell size up to ¼-inch. Scale insects are similar to mealybugs and are included in the same superfamily. There are unarmored types of scale insects (coccids) which have a rubbery outer coating that cannot be detached. Some secrete wax. They may be flat, oval, or globular. The unarmored scale insects secrete honeydew which encourages development of the black sooty mold.

The many other types of scale insects are armored (diaspidids). The scale is not attached to the body and is composed of a wax secretion and castoff skins of the immature stages of the insect. The scale covering can take on several shapes from round to oyster-shell shaped, can be several colors, and can be smooth or rough. Armored scale insects do not secrete honeydew.

The female armored scale insect does not move about as does the mealybug. She is saclike, wingless, usually legless, and feeds through a piercing, sucking mouth part injecting toxic saliva as she does. Some scale insect

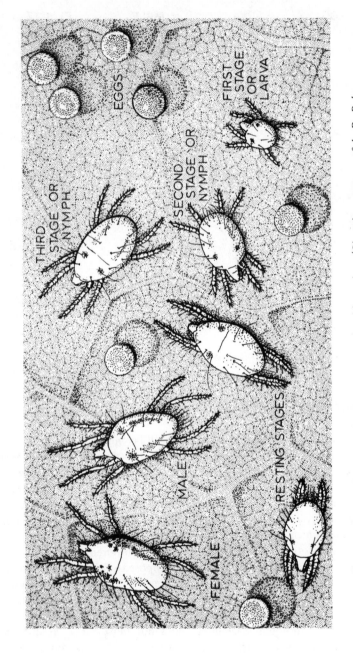

Figure 12-6. All stages of the two-spotted spider mite. (*Sketch courtesy of J. R. Baker, North Carolina Agricultural Extension Service, Raleigh, NC 27607*)

352

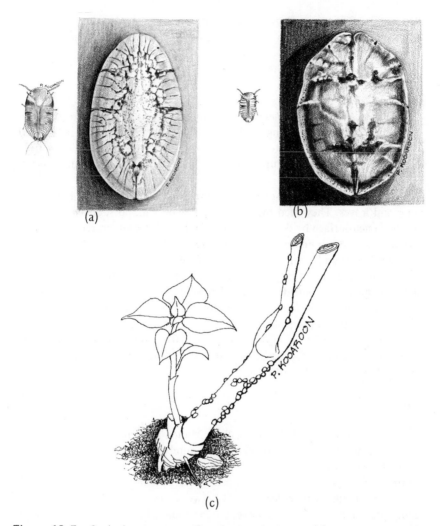

Figure 12-7. Scale insect pests of ornamental plants: (a) brown soft scale *(right)* with its crawler; (b) hemispherical scale *(right)* with its crawler; (c) bloodleaf plant infested with hemispherical scale. *(Sketch courtesy of J. R. Baker, North Carolina Agricultural Extension Service, Raleigh, NC 27607)*

species give birth to living young while others lay eggs. The male has legs and one pair of wings, but no mouth parts (it does not feed). In some species males are rare or absent, and virgin females give birth to young or lay eggs.

The first nymph (crawler) has legs and can travel about for two days in search of a suitable feeding area. It then inserts its mouth parts into the leaf and begins forming a shell. It remains here through several molts, losing its legs on the first molt. Eggs or young are produced under the body of the female and under the armor of the scales. Three to seven generations can develop in a year.

Slugs and Snails

Slugs and snails (Figure 12-8) are not insects. They are mollusks (a group of animals including snails, sea snails, clams, oysters, and octopuses). The slug lacks a shell, whereas the snail has a hard shell similar to some of its counterparts in the sea. Slugs range in size from one-half to four inches in length.

Slugs and snails have chewing mouth parts which they use to eat seedlings and leaves. They feed by night and hide beneath pots, benches, or litter on the bench surface by day. Dark, moist hiding places are preferred. The slug exudes a slippery liquid as it moves along. When it dries, a shiny track can be seen which easily identifies the presence of slugs.

Slugs and snails may crawl into the greenhouse from vegetation or debris immediately outside the greenhouse. This is one more reason to keep the greenhouse surroundings clear or mowed. They are also easily transported in on pots, flats, soil, or plants.

Slugs and snails lay eggs in clusters of 20 to 100 in moist crevices along the soil or containers. Eggs can hatch in 10 days or less at temperatures above 50°F (10°C). Maturity occurs in three months to a year.

Thrips

Thrips (Figure 12-9) are small (1/25-inch long) insects with two pairs of fringed wings. They build up in large numbers outdoors and swarm into greenhouses during the warmer months. Many are carried in air currents. Thrips feed on a broad range of crops. They are commonly found in buds, on flower petals, in axils of leaves, and between the scales of some bulbs. The adults are visible to the unaided eye, but are usually hidden in buds or flowers. They can be detected by tapping buds or flowers over a sheet of white paper. Thrips will fall onto the paper and can be seen. The adults can be yellow, tan, brown, or black depending on the species encountered.

The adult thrips cuts holes in leaves with a sawlike ovipositor on her abdomen and inserts eggs in them. Eggs hatch into nymphs in two to seven days and begin feeding. They have a rasping mouth part which is used to scrape the tender leaf or petal surface. They then suck the exuding plant sap. This causes a white, sometimes silver, discoloration. The injury occurs in streaks rather than a stippling pattern as is the case with mites or aphids. Later the whitish areas will turn tan or brown as the cells dry. The entire life cycle can occur in two weeks. Longer times are required at lower temper-

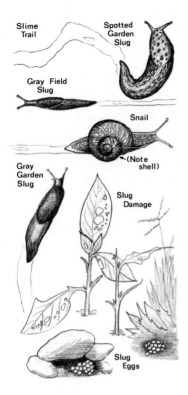

Figure 12-8. Various slugs and a snail. (*Sketch courtesy of J. R. Baker, North Carolina Agricultural Extension Service, Raleigh, NC 27607*)

atures. The feeding nymphs and adults excrete brown droplets which turn black. These can be detected on petals and leaves.

Whiteflies

Greenhouse whiteflies (*Trialeurodes vaporariorum* Westwood) are small insects (about 1/16-inch long) with four wings (Figure 12-10). They are covered with a white waxy powder and resemble miniature moths. They fly short distances when plant foliage is disturbed. They are found mainly on the undersides of young leaves. The host plant is broad. Crops on which whiteflies are particularly troublesome are ageratum, chrysanthemum, fuchsia, lantana, petunia, poinsettia, salvia, and tomato.

Although whiteflies are tropical insects, they are always present in one greenhouse or another during the winter. This is a testimony to their ability to tolerate pesticides. During the summer they fly into the greenhouse from numerous host plants outside and in the winter they spread from one greenhouse range to another on plant material or on clothing of workers. Yellow clothing is especially attractive to whiteflies.

Whiteflies feed through a piercing, sucking mouth part sometimes

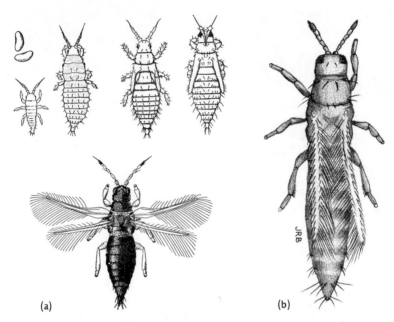

Figure 12-9. Thrips (greatly enlarged: both species about 1/16-inch maximum). (a) Stages of the greenhouse thrips; (b) an adult flower thrips. *(Sketch courtesy of J. R. Baker, North Carolina Agricultural Extension Service, Raleigh, NC 27607)*

causing yellow stippling of leaves. They excrete honeydew which supports growth of black sooty mold.

The adult whitefly lays a few to 20 eggs often in a circle. Up to 250 eggs are laid by each female. Each is attached to the leaf in an upright fashion by a thin stalk. The eggs are creamy at first but eventually become dark. Newly hatched crawlers emerge from eggs in five to ten days and seek a feeding place. They insert their mouth into the leaf tissue and remain stationary for three weeks or so undergoing three molts. During these stages they are flat, scalelike insects and are transparent to greenish yellow in color. At the end of this period they transform into a nonfeeding yellowish green pupa with two conspicuous eyes. A week later the winged adult can emerge. Females begin laying eggs two to seven days later. Depending upon temperature, the whole life cycle can take four to five weeks.

Eggs, pupae, and to a degree the scalelike larvae, are not susceptible to pesticides. The adults are readily killed. Aerosols and smokes do a good job of knocking down adults but a day later new adults may emerge. At warm temperatures pesticides may need to be applied as often as three times per week for a total of 10 to 15 applications. Sprays, because of their residual activity are much more effective, but a continual program must be main-

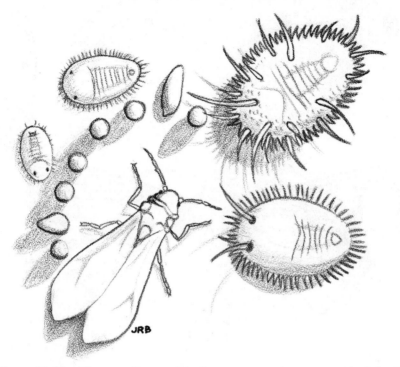

Figure 12-10. The greenhouse whitefly: eggs, nymphs, pupa, and adult all found on lower leaf surface. *(Sketch courtesy of J. R. Baker, North Carolina Agricultural Extension Service, Raleigh, NC 27607)*

tained throughout the period of one life cycle. If one application is missed such that adults are afforded an opportunity to lay eggs, the whole program must be started again. Two pesticides, resmethrin (SBP 1382$_{®}$) and kinoprene (Enstar$_{®}$) have revolutionized whitefly control. Both are toxic to all stages of greenhouse whiteflies and will usually give complete control after two or three applications.

Worms

Worms, the immature stages of several types of moths, attack crops in a variety of ways (Figure 12-11). Worms are a problem particularly during the warmer months when moths abound outdoors. They randomly fly into the greenhouse or are attracted by lights. Once inside, moths lay eggs from which worms hatch.

Beet armyworms eat leaves of carnation, chrysanthemum, cyclamen, geranium, snapdragon, and other crops. Corn earworms eat succulent plant parts, preferably the buds, of chrysanthemum, gladioli, roses, etc. European

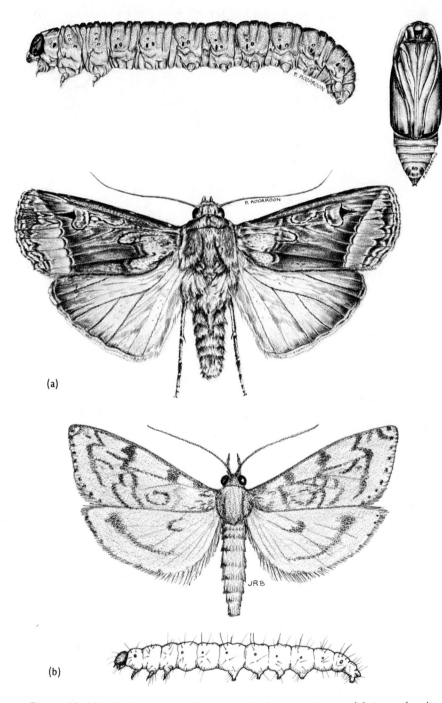

Figure 12-11. Various caterpillar pests in the greenhouse: (a) larva *(top)*, pupa, and adult of the black cutworm; (b) larva and adult of the greenhouse

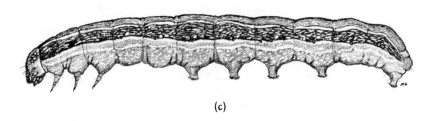

(c)

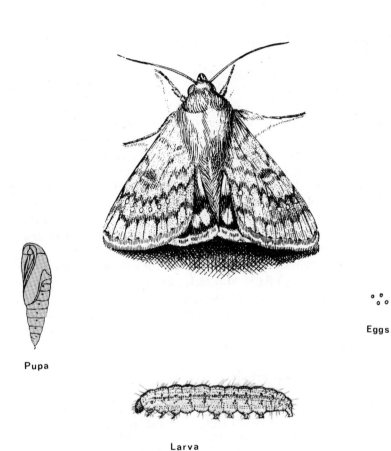

Pupa

Eggs

Larva

(d)

leaf tier; (c) beet armyworm; (d) corn earworm adult, eggs, larva, and pupa. *(Sketch courtesy of J. R. Baker, North Carolina Agricultural Extension Service, Raleigh, NC 27607)*

359

corn borers tunnel into the stems of plants, particularly chrysanthemums. Cutworms feed on aerial plant parts. Leaf tiers and leaf rollers tie young leaves together or into a nest and feed on them from within.

Many other kinds of worms are occasionally encountered, but the control for all is similar. Stomach poisons with long residual lives are most effective. Biological control is available through sprays of *Bacillus thuringiensis* Berliner (Biotrol BTB_{®}, Dipel_{®} or Thuricide_{®}). This is a bacterium which attacks worms. Plants must be sprayed as new growth occurs to keep all surfaces protected. Once inside the stem, bud, or nest of webbed leaves control of these insects is almost impossible.

METHODS OF PESTICIDE APPLICATION

Seven methods for bringing pesticides into contact with insects on plants are widely used. For a given pest problem there are generally two or more methods of control available. Existing equipment, weather conditions, the type and stage of development of a crop or pest, susceptibility of a particular crop to injury, and economics will dictate which to use.

Sprays, dusts, and mists require more effort to apply but leave a residue on the plant which continues to kill after the application. Aerosols, fogs, and smokes propel fine droplets of the insecticide into the air so that any existing insects, whether they be on the crop, beneath the bench, or elsewhere are killed. An effective residue is not left by these methods of application; repeated application is necessary or else these systems must be used in conjunction with spraying or dusting. While aerosols, fogs, and smokes are very simple to apply, the materials tend to be expensive and only a limited number of insecticides are available in such forms. Systemic insecticides in granules are not the easiest to apply but they offer a long residual period. A rather broad spectrum of insects and mites can be killed with a material such as aldicarb (Temik_{®}) for a period of about six weeks. On some crops systemic pesticides eliminate the need for a tedious spray program.

Spray Application of Pesticide

Spraying is the most common method of pesticide application in the greenhouse. Numerous pesticides are formulated for mixing with water and spraying on the plant. Emulsifiable concentrates (EC) are pesticides in an oily preparation with an emulsifying agent which renders the oil miscible in water. Without the emulsifying agent the oil (which dissolves the pesticide) would not mix with water.

Wettable powder (WP) pesticides are solid particles, usually clays, which are dispersed in water. The spray tank should have an agitator in it to prevent the particles from settling out. WP formulations tend to be less toxic to plants than EC formulations of the same pesticide.

Leaf and stem surfaces have a waxy cuticle covering them. This surface has a tendency to repel water to varying degrees depending upon the plant species. When spray droplets bead up on the leaf surface, a considerable area is left unprotected and small insects are able to continue feeding. The problem can be remedied by the addition of a surfactant to the spray. Surfactants are also known as spreaders, wetters, or spreader-stickers. The surfactant lowers the surface tension which increases the ability of the spray to spread out over the plant surface. A number of surfactants are on the market for this purpose and among them are such materials as DuPont Spreader-Sticker®, Triton B-1956®, and Plyac®. Use the recommended rate because too much surfactant can cause plant distortion. Mild liquid household detergents can also be used at the rate of 1 pint/100 gallons (one-half teaspoon/gallon). Incomplete wetting is mainly a problem of wettable powders since EC formulations already contain an emulsifying agent which is itself a surfactant.

WP formulations should be mixed first in a bucket and then poured into the sprayer tank. This is done to avoid solid deposits which might plug the nozzle or result in an error in the concentration.

Sprayers can range from 1- to 4-gallon hand-pumped units to electric or gasoline motor-powered sprayers of 10- to 200-gallon capacity (Figure 12-12a). Sprayers up to 30 gallons are on wheels and are brought into the end

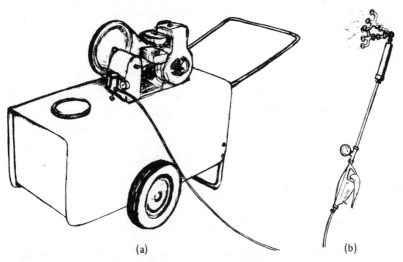

(a)   (b)

Figure 12-12(a). A gasoline motor-powered pesticide sprayer with a 30-gallon tank capacity typical of many used for greenhouse pest control. Such sprayers commonly operate at 200 psi; (b) a Cornell nozzle used for spraying greenhouse crops. Six nozzles spray at a variety of angles to insure complete coverage of upper and lower leaf surfaces. A gauge indicates spray pressure and a lever gives the operator on-off control of the spray. *(Sketch courtesy of J. R. Baker, North Carolina Agricultural Extension Service, Raleigh, NC 27607)*

or main aisles of the greenhouse. A hose attached to the sprayer is dragged along each aisle to permit spraying of the entire bench. A nozzle at the end of the hose is used to break the spray into fine droplets and direct the spray in a full pattern for maximum coverage of plants sprayed. Pressures up to several hundred pounds per square inch (psi) are used to insure a small droplet. A pressure of 200 psi is very common. Install a pressure gauge at the sprayer or near the nozzle to assure the correct pressure for even coverage.

It is very important that the undersides of leaves be sprayed. To do this the nozzles should be at a 45° to 90° angle to the axis of the nozzle handle or a sprayer with several nozzles, such as the Cornell nozzle (Figure 12-12b), at different angles should be used. The nozzle should be handled in a sweeping action to insure that all of the plant is covered. Particular attention should be paid to reach plants in the interior of a bench; otherwise, a point of reinfestation is left.

Some larger greenhouse ranges make use of a permanently installed plumbing system which brings spray from the mixing tank to any given section in the range. A single spray hose is attached at whichever point spraying is desired.

Many sprays are corrosive to the spray equipment. They can be dangerous to workers if left in the hose or sprayer. With time, solid deposits can occur in the tank, lines, or nozzles. For these reasons the sprayer should be emptied after use and rinsed out. Clear water then should be pumped through the entire system to clean it.

Dust

A few pesticides can be obtained in a dust form. The active pesticide is mixed with talc, clay, diatomaceous earth, or similar filler. Dusters are used to apply dusts. These range from hand-cranked units for small greenhouse uses to large motorized dusters. Dusts, being lightweight, remain in the air for a period of time. Respirators or gas masks, depending on the toxicity of the pesticide, should be used to avoid inhaling them. Dusting is not a common method of pest control because of the visible residue left on the plants.

Mist Application of Pesticide

Mist application of pesticides is similar to spraying and dusting in that a residue is applied to the plant surfaces which continues to kill after the application is made. Pesticides are used at 10 to 20 times the concentration used in a spray. They are applied through a mist blower by injecting the pesticide into a high-velocity airstream. Equipment used for mist is often used for dust as well.

The pesticide is mostly diluted by air rather than water. Because of its high concentration, a small amount is applied to any given area and the whole operation must go very quickly. This is a more complex method of application than most of the others. A skill is required to avoid application of too large a quantity at any one spot. Plant injuries are likely to result from over-application.

Aerosol Application of Pesticide

A few insecticides (no fungicides) can be obtained in cylinders under pressure (Figure 12-13). These are sometimes referred to as bombs (see Table 12-1 for a list of available aerosols). A propellant such as freon is also contained in the cylinder. Under pressure the propellant is a liquid, but when released into the lower pressure of the atmosphere it expands into a gas and

Figure 12-13. A cylinder of aerosol pesticide. A pressurized liquid propellant such as freon expands to gas when released, carrying the pesticide with it into the greenhouse atmosphere. The applicator is wearing proper attire for handling restricted use pesticides. It includes rubber boots and gloves, a gas mask, and a nylon suit over all remaining parts of the body.

moves at a high velocity carrying small droplets (50 to 150 microns) of insecticide with it.

The small liquid pesticide droplets are small enough to drift on the air currents, quickly dispersing throughout the entire greenhouse atmosphere. With time they settle out mostly onto the upper surfaces of plants. Since little residue accumulates on lower leaves and undersurfaces, this form of pesticide application is used for immediate killing of existing insects and is very often used in combination with a spray, dust, or mist application which leaves a residue.

The quantity of insecticide released is determined by the length of time the valve on the cylinder is open. The total length of time required is determined by the volume of air in the greenhouse. It is usually sufficient to make one pass through the center aisle of narrower greenhouses (up to 35 feet wide) and two passes through wider greenhouses.

The volume of the greenhouse can easily be determined by multiplying the floor area by the average height (Figure 12-14). The average height can be determined by adding the height at the side wall to the height at the ridge and dividing by 2.

$$\text{length} \times \text{width} = \text{floor area}$$

$$(40 \text{ ft} \times 100 \text{ ft} = 4000 \text{ sq ft})$$

$$\frac{\text{wall height} + \text{ridge height}}{2} = \text{average height}$$

$$\left(\frac{8 \text{ ft} + 14 \text{ ft}}{2} = 11 \text{ ft} \right)$$

$$\text{floor area} \times \text{average height} = \text{greenhouse volume}$$

$$(4000 \text{ sq ft} \times 11 \text{ ft} = 44,000 \text{ cu ft})$$

There are some very critical temperature requirements for the use of aerosol bombs. The temperature should be preferably 70°F (21°C) or above. Below 60°F (15°C) improper distribution and reduced pest kill occurs. At temperatures above 85°F (30°C) injury often occurs to the plants. One temperature should be selected and maintained as closely as possible since dosage rate is dependent upon it. This temperature range is best held during the evening in the summer or late afternoon in the winter.

It is also important that the aerosol be applied on a calm day so that it is not drawn out of the greenhouse or caused to distribute unevenly. The greenhouse must remain closed for several hours (at least three) during treatment.

Moisture on the foliage during application usually leads to injury. The plants should be well watered and the foliage dry at the time of application.

Table 12-1
Pesticides Available in Aerosol, Fog, and Smoke Formulations

PESTICIDE	FORMULATION		
	Aerosol	Fog	Smoke
DDVP (Vapona$_®$)	X	X	X
diazinon		X	
dicofol (Kelthane$_®$)		X	
dinocap (Karathane$_®$)		X	
dithio (sulfotepp)	X	X	X
endosulfan (Thiodan$_®$)			X
lindane			X
malathion	X	X	
malathion-lindane-ovicide		X	
mevinphos (Phosdrin$_®$)	X		
naled (Dibrom$_®$)		X	
nicotine		X	X
parathion	X	X	X
Pentac$_®$		X	
tedion			X
tedion-dithio			X

Fog Application of Pesticide

A limited number of insecticides and fungicides are available in oil-base carrier preparations for use in fogging equipment (Table 12-1). Most are prepared at 10 percent insecticidal strength. This method of application is very similar to that of aerosols. The same precautions must be followed. The pesticide is heated by a device to form small droplets (10 to 60 microns) which are propelled into the greenhouse atmosphere. Unlike the aerosol which cannot be seen, a white fog forms in this case which makes it easier to know if all areas are treated equally.

Various foggers may have gasoline motors or propane burners and may be carried on the back or pulled through the greenhouse on wheels. The pesticide formulation is either injected into a hot pipe, the exhaust, or a hot air stream to cause vaporization. For narrow greenhouses one pass through the center aisle is sufficient while in wider greenhouses the fogger should be moved through two or more aisles. Protective clothing and masks should be worn in accordance with the toxicity of the pesticide since it is very difficult to avoid contact in this method of application.

The fog should not be directed toward the plants because heavy deposits as well as hot exhaust scales can be injurious to the plant. The oils used

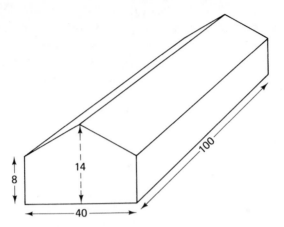

Figure 12-14. Sketch of a greenhouse with dimensions for calculating the volume used to determine the quantity of aerosol pesticide required.

are injurious to some plant species. Flowers tend to be more susceptible than foliage. The fog should be aimed into the aisles.

Air leaks in the greenhouse and windy conditions outside make it difficult to do a uniform job with fogging. Carbon buildup in the machine may also impair the effectiveness. The fogger should be cleaned periodically with wood alcohol or with a cleaner provided by the manufacturer.

Smoke Application of Pesticide

Smokes are the simplest forms of pesticides to use. No special equipment is needed. Small containers of a combustible formulation containing the pesticide are placed along the center aisle of the greenhouse and ignited, usually with a sparkler. The pesticide is carried in the smoke throughout the greenhouse. Pesticides which can be used in smoke are limited to those few which can withstand the intense heat (Table 12-1).

Smokes are generally less phytotoxic to plant foliage and flowers than aerosols and fogs, but the dose rate is as important. The volume of the greenhouse must be calculated and divided by the volume one can will treat to determine how many cans to use.

Further precautions are the same as for aerosols and fogs. Do not use at temperatures above 85°F or below 60°F. Close ventilators on the greenhouse and turn off fans. Avoid using these methods on a windy day. Be sure the plants are well watered and the foliage is dry. Once the pesticide is applied, place warning signs on all doors indicating that the greenhouse is under fumigation.

Root Media Application

For various reasons insecticides may be applied to the root medium. Troublesome insects in the root medium may be killed by drenching with a water formulation. Some insecticides are available as granules which are applied dry to the root medium, sometimes worked into the root medium, and are finally watered to activate a release of the insecticide. In addition to killing insects in the root medium, systemic insecticides may be applied to the medium to kill insects on the plant. Such insecticides are taken up through the plant roots to the stems and leaves; insects then feeding on the plant are killed.

One particular granular insecticide which bears special mention is aldicarb (Temik$_®$). This is a highly toxic systemic insecticide which is registered for the control of spider mites, aphids, thrips, mealybugs, whiteflies, and leaf miners. Temik 10G$_®$ is applied at the rate of 18.4 to 36.7 ounces per 1,000 square foot of plant bed or closely packed pots. One eighth of a teaspoon per pot is used for spaced six-inch pots. Temik$_®$ must be applied uniformly since it is toxic to plants at moderately low levels. The injury occurs as burning of leaf tips and margins.

Application to individual pots can be made with a small spoon or for large numbers of pots through an EZ Feeder Measure Master$_®$ applicator which has been modified for metering out small quantities. Broadcast application can be made to pots placed rim to rim or for fresh flower beds. Holes are punched in the cap of plastic or metal cans with an ice pick. Temik$_®$ is placed in the can and is shaken from it over the plants. The plants should be dry so that the granules will settle on the root medium.

Temik$_®$ is very toxic to humans. The applicant should wear protective clothing, a respirator, and goggles. Care should be taken to avoid spilling granules on nongrowing areas. Equipment which grinds granules should be avoided since safety rests in the entrapment of Temik$_®$ in the granules. Once applied, Temik$_®$ should be watered in well. This begins the release process. For a period of one week the root medium should not be handled. Temik$_®$ should not be applied to media prior to planting and should not be used on edible crops or in media to be used for growing edible crops for a period of one year.

Systemic granular insecticides in general are highly toxic to humans. They should not be used in root media prior to planting because this will cause stunting of transplants and bring the workers into needless contact with them. Granules should not be applied prior to steam pasteurization since this can cause a hazardous release.

Table 12-2

Commercial Greenhouse Ornamental Insect Control*

NOTE: Always follow label directions when handling or applying bracts and chrysanthemum blossoms. Do not add surfactant when applied pesticides. *Aldicarb* is extremely toxic. Apply after plants are established to roses. *TEPP* is extremely toxic. *Tetradifon* may injure roses especially and as pests appear. Repeat in 6 to 8 weeks if necessary. *Demeton* is extremely toxic and also may damage roots of chrysanthemum. *Dichlorvos* tremely toxic and also may damage roots of chrysanthemum. *Dichlorvos* may damage chrysanthemum varieties Shasta, Pink Champagne and Nightingale. *Dicofol* is not compatible with sulfur. *Dimethoate* will damage chrysanthemums, Easter lily. Use on trial basis on each variety of azalea, fern, gloxinia, hydrangea, schefflera, and Saintpaulia. *Endosulfan* will damage some geraniums and chrysanthemum varieties. *Malathion* may injure begonia, crassula, fern, petunia, orchids, violet, Saintpaulia, gloxinia, some red carnations and some rose varieties. Metaldehyde will injure Cattleya and Phalaenopsis orchids. *Naled* may damage chrysanthemum variety Pink Champagne, dutchman's pipe, wandering jew, poinsettias, rose varieties White Butterfly, Golden Rapture. *Nicotine sulfate* will damage young chrysanthemum and lily. *Parathion* is extremely toxic. Will injure aster, crassula, gladiolus, kalanchoe, fern, gardenia and hydrangea. *Pentac*® will damage foliage of chrysanthemum. *Plictran*® may injure poinsettia

Aerosols are available containing combinations of many of the above materials. Be sure to follow manufacturers' recommendations as to rates of use and precautions for the operator. Treated houses should be ventilated for one hour before re-entering. As a rule, aerosols are used at a rate of 1 lb per 50,000 cu ft of house, however, for thrips control, 1 lb per 100,000 cu ft may be sufficient. For best results, bomb temperature should be 80 to 90°F. and greenhouse air temperature 75 to 70°F. May bleach open mums or cause leaf drop on roses (if sulfur present).

Some of the insecticides above are extremely toxic. All instructions on the label regarding handling, protective clothing, etc. should be followed. They are recommended for use by experienced operators. Learn symptoms of poisoning. Call a doctor. Take the label or pesticide container to the hospital with the victim.

● Restricted use pesticide.

FLOWER	INSECT OR MITE	INSECTICIDE AND FORMULATION	AMOUNT OF FORMULATION TO USE PER GALLON	MINIMUM INTERVAL BETWEEN APPLICATION AND REENTRY	PRECAUTIONS AND REMARKS
ANY	Aphid	SPRAY			Apply as needed. Repeated application usually needed.
		endosulfan (Thiodan)			
		24.2 EC	1 tsp	24 hours	
		50 WP	1 tbsp	24 hours	

			Slight to moderate injury to some blooms. Try to control in pre-bloom stage.
kinoprene (Enstar) 65.3 EC	½ to 1 tsp	When dry	
lindane 25 WP	1 tbsp	When dry	
malathion 57 EC	2 tsp	When dry	
nicotine sulfate 40 EC	1½ tsp		
oxydemetonmethyl (meta-systox®) 25 EC	1 tsp	When dry	
AEROSOL • dichlorvos (Vapona) 10 A endosulfan (Thiodan) 10 A malathion 15 A • parathion 10 A propyl thiopyrophosphate (Dithiono) 5 A • TEPP 10 A		After house ventilated for 1 hour	

(Table 12–2 continued)

Table 12-2 continued

FLOWER	INSECT OR MITE	INSECTICIDE AND FORMULATION	AMOUNT OF FORMULATION TO USE PER GALLON	MINIMUM INTERVAL BETWEEN APPLICATION AND REENTRY	PRECAUTIONS AND REMARKS
		VAPOR naled (Dibrom) 60 EC		After house ventilated for 1 hour	Apply on steam pipes at rate of 1 oz per 10,000 cu ft. Have pipes at 160° F. Will corrode pipes with continued use.
	Brown soft scale	propyl thiopyrophosphate (Dithiono) 5 A		After house ventilated for 1 hour	
	Cabbage looper	naled (Dibrom) 60 EC	1½		Treat as needed.
		● dichlorvos (Vapona) 10 A ● mevinphos (Phosdrin) 10 A		After house ventilated for 1 hour	
	Cutworms	carbaryl (Sevin) 50 WP	2 tbsp	When dry	Apply to soil surface beneath plants.

Leaf miner	• dichlorvos (Vapona) 10 A, malathion 15 A		After house ventilated for 1 hour	
	• parathion 10 A			
	malathion 57 EC	2 tsp	When dry	
Leaf roller	naled (Dibrom) 60 EC		After house ventilated for 1 hour	Apply as vapor as for aphid.
Mealybug	• dichlorvos (Vapona) 10 A		After house ventilated 1 hour	Apply aerosols as for aphid.
	• parathion 10A, propyl thiopyrophosphate (Dithiono) 5 A			
	malathion 57 EC	2 tsp	When dry	
	naled (Dibrom) 60 EC		After house ventilated for 1 hour	Apply as vapor as for aphid.

(Table 12–2 continued)

Table 12-2 continued

FLOWER	INSECT OR MITE	INSECTICIDE AND FORMULATION	AMOUNT OF FORMULATION TO USE PER GALLON	MINIMUM INTERVAL BETWEEN APPLICATION AND REENTRY	PRECAUTIONS AND REMARKS
	Millipede	● ethion 8 lb gal EC	5 fl oz	When dry	75 gal for 2500 sq ft bench space.
		malathion 57 EC	1 tsp	When dry	150 sq ft per gal each 7 to 10 day.
	Plant bug	● parathion 10A		After house ventilated for 1 hour	
	Rose chafer	endosulfan (Thiodan) 24.2 EC 50 WP	2 tsp 2 tsp	24 hours 24 hours	
	Scales	See mealy bug.			Same as mealy bug.
	Slugs and snails	metaldehyde B 15 D			More than one application usually necessary. Follow label directions.
	Sowbug	lindane 25 WP malathion 4 D	1 tbsp 1 lb	When dry	150 sq ft each 7 to 10 days.

Spider mite	AEROSOL		After house ventilated for 1 hour	
	• dichlorvos (Vapona) 10 A			
	propyl thiopyrophosphate (Dithiono) 5 A			
	SPRAY			
	carbophenothion (Trithion) 25 WP	2 tbsp		
	dicofol (Kelthane) 35 WP	2 tbsp	When dry	
	Pentac 50 WP	1 tsp	When dry	
	Plictran 50 WP	1/2 to 2/3 tsp	When dry	
	tetradifon (Tedion) 25 WP	1 tbsp		
	VAPOR		After house ventilated for 1 hour	Apply naled as for aphid. Apply pentac as slurry on steam pipes at rate of 1 lb active per 450,000 cu ft every 5 days until control obtained. Apply tetradifon as slurry on steam pipes at rate of 1 lb per 200,000 cu ft.
	naled (Dibrom) 60 EC			
	Pentac 50 WP		When dry	
	tetradifon (Tedion) 90 P			

(Table 12–2 continued)

Table 12-2 continued

FLOWER	INSECT OR MITE	INSECTICIDE AND FORMULATION	AMOUNT OF FORMULATION TO USE PER GALLON	MINIMUM INTERVAL BETWEEN APPLICATION AND REENTRY	PRECAUTIONS AND REMARKS
	Thrips	lindane 25 WP malathion 25 WP	1 tbsp 2 tbsp	When dry	Extra sticker may be needed with most sprays. Aerosols may also be used as for aphid.
	Whitefly	AEROSOL ● dichlorvos (Vapona) 10 A endosulfan (Thiodan) 10 A ● parathion 10 A propyl thiopyrophosphate (Dithiono) 5 A		After house ventilated for 1 hour	
		resmethrin (SBP 1382) 1A			5 to 10 seconds per 100 sq ft. Apply in late evening or at night.

	SPRAY			
	endosulfan (Thiodan) 24.2 EC	1 tbsp	24 hours	
	50 WP	1 tbsp	24 hours	
	malathion 25 WP	2 tbsp	When dry	Slight to moderate injury to some blooms. Try to control in pre-bloom stage.
	kinoprene (Enstar) 65.3 EC	½ to 1 tsp	When dry	Apply in late evening or at night.
	resmethrin (SBP 1382) 24.3 EC	2 tsp	When dry	Apply as for aphid.
	VAPOR			
	naled (Dibrom) 60 EC		After house ventilated for 1 hour	
Cyclamen mite	dicofol (Kelthane) 35 WP	1 tbsp	When dry	Use 65–70°F water when spraying.
	endosulfan (Thiodan) 24.2 EC	2 tbsp	24 hours	
	25 EC	1 tbsp	24 hours	
AFRICAN VIOLET	endosulfan (Thiodan) 10 A		After house ventilated for 1 hour	Follow label directions.

(Table 12–2 continued)

Table 12-2 continued

FLOWER	INSECT OR MITE	INSECTICIDE AND FORMULATION	AMOUNT OF FORMULATION TO USE PER GALLON	MINIMUM INTERVAL BETWEEN APPLICATION AND REENTRY	PRECAUTIONS AND REMARKS
	Mealybug	malathion 57 EC	1½ tsp	When dry	
		• dichlorvos (Vapona) 81 EC			Vaporize 1 fl oz per 10,000 cu ft. Ventilate after 2 hours.
ASTER	Aphid	endosulfan (Thiodan) 24.2 EC	1 tbsp	24 hours	
		25 WP	2 tbsp	24 hours	
		malathion 25 WP	2 tbsp	When dry	
	Cyclamen mite	dicofol (Kelthane) 18.5 EC endosulfan—as aphid on aster	2 tsp	When dry	
	Leafhopper	malathion 25 WP	2 tbsp	When dry	Spray every 10 days.

	Pest	Insecticide	Amount	Re-entry	Remarks
	Mealybug	malathion 25 WP	2 tbsp	When dry	Several applications may be necessary
	Plant bug	Same as mealybug on aster.			
	Spider mite	Same as mealybug on aster. • TEPP 25 WP	1 tbsp		
	Thrips	Same as mealybug on aster.			
AZALEA	Aphid	AEROSOL • dichlorvos (Vapona) 10 A malathion 15A • parathion 10A		After house ventilated for 1 hour	
		SPRAY endosulfan (Thiodan) 24.2 EC 50 WP malathion 57 EC	1 tbsp 1 tbsp 2 tsp	24 hours 24 hours When dry	

(Table 12–2 continued)

377

Table 12-2 continued

FLOWER	INSECT OR MITE	INSECTICIDE AND FORMULATION	AMOUNT OF FORMULATION TO USE PER GALLON	MINIMUM INTERVAL BETWEEN APPLICATION AND REENTRY	PRECAUTIONS AND REMARKS
	Cyclamen mite	dicofol (Kelthane) 18.5 EC 35 WP endosulfan (Thiodan) 24.2 EC 50 WP	1 tsp 1 to 1½ tbsp 1 tbsp 1 tbsp	When dry When dry 24 hours 24 hours	
	Lace bug	● parathion 10A		After house thoroughly ventilated for 1 hour	A problem in late spring or early summer.
	Leaf roller	malathion 57 EC 25 WP	1½ tbsp 2 tbsp	When dry When dry	
		● dichlorvos (Vapona) 81 EC		After house ventilated thoroughly 1 hour	Apply dichlorvos as vapor at 1 fl oz 81 EC per 10,000 cu ft. Ventilate after 2 hours.

Spider mite	malathion 57 EC 1½ tsp 25 WP 2 tbsp tetradifon (Tedion) 25 WP 1 tbsp ● TEPP 5 A	When dry When dry When dry	Apply at 1 lb per 100,000 cu ft unless otherwise noted on label. Sprays are preferred for certain mite species, especially those which are dark red.
Whitefly	● dichlorvos (Vapona) 10 A ● parathion 10A ● TEPP 5 A	After house ventilated for 1 hour	Use 3 applications of azinphosmethyl and parathion aerosols 8 days apart. Use 6 applications of dichlorvos or TEPP 4 days apart.
BEGONIA Aphid	Same as for aphid on azalea		
Cyclamen mite	Same as for cyclamen mite on azalea.		

(Table 12-2 continued)

Table 12-2 continued

FLOWER	INSECT OR MITE	INSECTICIDE AND FORMULATION	AMOUNT OF FORMULATION TO USE PER GALLON	MINIMUM INTERVAL BETWEEN APPLICATION AND REENTRY	PRECAUTIONS AND REMARKS
	Mealybug	Same as for mealybug on African violet and aster.			
	Spider mite	Same as for spider mite on aster.			
	Thrips	malathion 50 EC 25 WP	1½ tsp 2 tbsp	When dry When dry	
	Whitefly	Same as for white fly on azalea.			
BULB CROPS	Aphid	endosulfan (Thiodan) 24.2 EC 50 WP	1 tbsp 1 tbsp	24 hours 24 hours	
		● dichlorvos (Vapona) 10 A		After house ventilated for 1 hour	
CALCEOLARIA	Aphid	● dichlorvos (Vapona) 10 A		After house ventilated for 1 hour	

Plant	Pest	Material	Amount	Timing
	Thrips	endosulfan (Thiodan) 24.2 EC 50 WP	1 tbsp 1 tbsp	24 hours 24 hours
		• dichlorvos (Vapona) 10 A		After house ventilated for 1 hour
		malathion 50 EC 25 WP	2 tsp 2 tbsp	When dry When dry
	Whitefly	Same as whitefly on azalea.		
	Mealybug	Same as thrips on calceolaria.		
CALLA	Spider mite	• dichlorvos (Vapona) 10 A		After house ventilated for 1 hour
		malathion 57 EC 25 WP • TEPP 20 EC	2 tsp 2 tbsp ½ tsp	When dry When dry
	Thrips	Same as thrips on calceolaria.		

(Table 12-2 continued)

Table 12-2 continued

FLOWER	INSECT OR MITE	INSECTICIDE AND FORMULATION	AMOUNT OF FORMULATION TO USE PER GALLON	MINIMUM INTERVAL BETWEEN APPLICATION AND REENTRY	PRECAUTIONS AND REMARKS
CARNATION	Aphid	• aldicarb (Temik) 10 G		After watered in with ½ inch water. Do not market potted plants for 28 days.	20–30 (or 40 for carnations, rose, snapdragon) oz per 1,000 sq ft bench space or closely packed pots. Apply after plants are established and as pests appear. Repeat in 6 to 8 weeks if necessary.
		• dichlorvos (Vapona) 10 A		After house ventilated for 1 hour	
		malathion 15 A • mevinphos (Phosdrin) 10 A		After house ventilated for 1 hour	
		endosulfan (Thiodan) 24.2 EC	1 tbsp	24 hours	
		50 WP	1 tbsp	24 hours	
		malathion 57 EC	1½ tsp	When dry	
		25 WP	2 tbsp	When dry	

Pest	Pesticide	Amount	Re-entry	Remarks
Bud mites				Sanitation important; cut and destroy infested buds.
Mealybug	malathion 15 A		After house ventilated for 1 hour	
Spider mite	•aldicarb (Temik) 10 G		Re-enter after watered in with ½ inch water. Do not market potted plants for 28 days.	30 to 40 oz per 1,000 sq ft bench space or closely packed pots. Apply after plants are established and as pests appear. Repeat in 6 to 8 weeks if necessary.
	•demeton (Systox) 6 EC		After watered in thoroughly	Applied week after benching; gives 4 to 6 weeks protection.
	malathion 15 A		After house ventilated for 1 hour	
	•mevinphos (Phosdrin) 10 A			
	carbophenothion (Trithion) 45 EC	1½ tsp		
	dicofol (Kelthane) 18.5 EC	1 tsp	When dry	
	35 WP	2 tbsp	When dry	

(Table 12–2 continued)

Table 12-2 continued

FLOWER	INSECT OR MITE	INSECTICIDE AND FORMULATION	AMOUNT OF FORMULATION TO USE PER GALLON	MINIMUM INTERVAL BETWEEN APPLICATION AND REENTRY	PRECAUTIONS AND REMARKS
		dimethoate (Cygon, De-Fend) 2.67 EC	1½ tsp		
		malathion 57 EC	1½ tsp	When dry	
		25 WP	2 tbsp	When dry	
		oxydemeton methyl (Meta-Systox R) 25 EC	1 tsp		
	Thrips	● dichlorvos (Vapona) 10 A		After house ventilated for 1 hour	
		malathion 15 A			
		malathion 57 EC	2 tsp	When dry	
		25 WP	2 tbsp	When dry	
	Whitefly	malathion 15 A			
		● mevinphos (Phosdrin) 10 A		After house ventilated for 1 hour	

CHRYSANTHEMUM	Aphid	• aldicarb (Temik) 10 G		Re-enter after watered in with ½ inch water. Do not market potted plants for 28 days.	20 to 30 oz per 1,000 sq ft of bench or closely packed pots.
		pirimor 50 WP	Premeasured package		Safe for blossoms. Try to control aphids before blossoms open to avoid dead aphids in petals.
		• mevinphos (Phosdrin) 10 A		After house ventilated for 1 hour	
	Cabbage looper	Bacillus thuringiensis (Dipel) 3.2	1 to 2 tsp	When dry	Cover thoroughly.
	Chrysanthemum gall midge	lindane 25 WP	1 tbsp		Weekly applications as needed.
	Corn earworm	carbaryl (Sevin) 50 WP	2 tbsp	When dry	Repeat as needed. Dusts also effective.
	Leaf miner	• aldicarb—as for aphid on chrysanthemum			
	Mealybug	malathion 15 A		After house ventilated for 1 hour	

(Table 12–2 continued)

385

Table 12-2 continued

FLOWER	INSECT OR MITE	INSECTICIDE AND FORMULATION	AMOUNT OF FORMULATION TO USE PER GALLON	MINIMUM INTERVAL BETWEEN APPLICATION AND REENTRY	PRECAUTIONS AND REMARKS
	Spider mite	● aldicarb–as for spider mite on carnation			
		malathion 15 A ● mevinphos (Phosdrin) 10 A		After house ventilated for 1 hour	
	Thrips	aldicarb–as for aphid on carnation			
	Whitefly	malathion 15 A ● mevinphos (Phosdrin) 10 A		After house ventilated for 1 hour	
		● aldicarb–as for spider mites on carnation			

CYCLAMEN	Cyclamen mite	dicofol (Kelthane) 35 WP endosulfan (Thiodan) 24.2 EC 25 EC	1 tbsp 2 tbsp 1 tbsp	When dry 24 hours 24 hours	Repeat as needed.
		endosulfan (Thiodan) 10 A		After house ventilated for 1 hour	Follow label directions.
EASTER LILY	Aphid	● aldicarb—as for aphid on carnation			
GERBERA	Aphid	● aldicarb—as for aphid on chrysanthemum			
	Leaf miner	● aldicarb—as for aphid on carnation			
	Spider mite	● aldicarb—as for aphid on carnation			
	Whitefly	● aldicarb—as for spider mite on carnation			
ORCHID	Spider mite	● aldicarb (Temik) 10 G		Re-enter after watered in with ½ inch water. Do not market potted plants for 28 days.	30 to 40 oz per 1,000 sq ft of bench or closely packed pots. Apply just prior to emergence of flower spikes. Repeat in 6 to 8 weeks if needed.

(Table 12–2 continued)

Table 12-2 continued

FLOWER	INSECT OR MITE	INSECTICIDE AND FORMULATION	AMOUNT OF FORMULATION TO USE PER GALLON	MINIMUM INTERVAL BETWEEN APPLICATION AND REENTRY	PRECAUTIONS AND REMARKS
POINSETTIA	Mealybug	• aldicarb–as for spider mite on carnation			
	Spider mite	• aldicarb–as for spider mite on carnation			
	Whitefly	• aldicarb–as for spider mite on carnation			
ROSE	Aphid	• aldicarb–as for aphid on chrysanthemum			
		• mevinphos (Phosdrin) 10 A		After house ventilated for 1 hour	
	Mealybug	malathion 15 A		After house ventilated for 1 hour	
	Rose chafer	endosulfan (Thiodan) 24.2 EC 50 WP	1 tbsp 1 tbsp		

388

			After house ventilated for 1 hour
	Spider mite	• aldicarb—as for spider mite on carnation	
		malathion 15 A • mevinphos (Phosdrin) 10 A	After house ventilated for 1 hour
	Whitefly	malathion 15 A • mevinphos (Phosdrin) 10 A	
SNAP-DRAGON	Aphid	• aldicarb—as for aphid on chrysanthemum	
	Cyclamen mite	same as for cyclamen mite on cyclamen	
	Spider mite	• aldicarb—as for spider mite on carnation	

*From J. R. Baker, In *North Carolina Agricultural Chemicals Manual.* School of Agriculture and Life Sciences, North Carolina State University, Raleigh, NC 27607, 1977.

PESTICIDE RECOMMENDATIONS

Pesticide recommendations can be obtained from a number of sources, and some are listed at the end of this chapter. All recommend only the pest and crop for which they are registered with the federal Environmental Protection Agency (EPA). The use of a pesticide for another crop or pest constitutes a violation of the law, even though it may be safe to the crop and an effective control measure for the pest.

Some materials are designated RESTRICTED USE PESTICIDE. The label of these pesticides will carry the words DANGER, POISON, and will have a skull and crossbones on them. In most states they can only be sold to and applied by a certified applicator. This is a person who has passed a course on pesticide handling and safety and who has been licensed by the state. Check with your Cooperative Extension Service for further information in this regard.

Pest Control Table

Table 12-2 was developed by J. R. Baker (North Carolina Agricultural Extension Service, Raleigh, NC 27607). The first entries list control measures for specific greenhouse pests without reference to crops. Then the crops are listed alphabetically and after each the pests that bother the crop and the control measures to be taken against the pest. The minimum interval of time between application and re-entry is quite important for safety of personnel.

Spider Mite Control

The philosophy of controlling spider mites is somewhat different from that of controlling other pests because of the resistance which mites can develop toward pesticides. Any given population of mites is a rather heterogeneous mixture. Often there will be a few mites in the population which are resistant to whichever miticide is used. The others will be killed while these will survive and multiply. Fortunately the resistant strains are less prolific than the susceptible strains, but occasionally they can build up to a serious level.

One miticide should be selected in a mite control program and used repeatedly. If mites become resistant to it, a second miticide from another chemical group (Table 12-3) should be substituted for it and used until such time as resistance is developed to it. The second miticide is then replaced by one from a third chemical group. When all groups have been used, one can return to the first group. Generally by then, the resistance to the first group has been lost.

Care should be taken not to alternate miticides since simultaneous resistance to a number of miticides can occur, thus reducing one's ability to

Table 12-3
Miticides by Chemical Class and Category of Animal Toxicity

MITICIDE	CHEMICAL GROUP	TOXICITY CATEGORY
Dithione®	Organophosphate	I (highly toxic)
Phosdrin®	Organophosphate	I
Systox®	Organophosphate	I
TEPP	Organophosphate	I
Trithion®	Organophosphate	I
Cygon®, DeFend®	Organophosphate	II (moderately toxic)
Meta-Systox R®	Organophosphate	II
Dibrom®	Organophosphate	III (slightly toxic)
malathion	Organophosphate	III
Temik®	Carbamate	I
Pentax®	Chlorinated hydrocarbon	II
Thiodan®	Chlorinated hydrocarbon	II
Kelthane®	Chlorinated hydrocarbon	III
tedion	Chlorinated hydrocarbon	III
Plictran®	Organo-tin	III
Morestan®	Miscellaneous	III

control the pest. The concentration of miticide should not be raised above the recommended level since plant damage may occur and legally, pesticides must be used in accordance with the label.

FURTHER PESTICIDE CONSIDERATIONS

Timing

The length of time between insecticide applications is very important. It depends upon (1) the residual life of the pesticide, (2) the life cycle of the pest, and (3) the method of kill of the insecticide.

When killing insects with a seven-day life cycle by aerosol or smoke insecticides which kill adults but not eggs, it is necessary to treat at six-day intervals until the insect is eliminated. Usually, three treatments are sufficient. Figure 12-15 shows this sequence of action. The first application (day 1) kills most of the insects but not the eggs. The eggs begin hatching immediately after treatment because no insecticidal residue is left by aerosols or smokes. Six days later, before these insects have matured to the stage when they can lay eggs, a second application of insecticide kills them. Insects which escaped the first application are also killed, but they have had a chance to lay

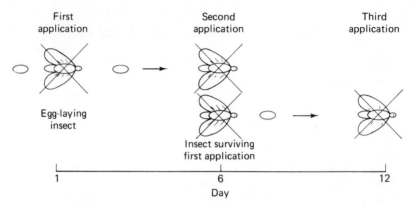

Figure 12-15. An illustration of the destruction of a population of insects having a seven-day life cycle by means of aerosol or smoke with no residual effect.

a few eggs. These eggs hatch after day 6 and on day 12, before the new insects have laid eggs, they are killed by the third insecticide application, thus ending the population of insects.

If a spraying interval longer than the life cycle of the insect is used, eggs will always be present and the insect population will not be eliminated. Generally life cycles increase in length with decreasing temperatures.

An insecticide which leaves a residue capable of killing may be applied less frequently because it continues to kill for part of the interval between applications.

Pesticide application frequencies of five to seven days are common for the eradication of many types of insects and mites. Even a frequency as short as three days may be necessary for eradicating spider mites and whiteflies during hot weather. Systemic insecticides such as Temik® are to be considered separately since their long residual effectiveness eliminates the need for periodic application.

Pesticide Compatibility

Do not mix pesticides until you are certain they are safe together. Sometimes two pesticides which are safe to use on a crop individually, become toxic to the crop when mixed. Other times mixing two pesticides reduces their effectiveness because of precipitation or clumping. The compatibility chart in Figure 12-16 indicates which pesticides should not be mixed. Further mixing precautions are to be found on the actual pesticide labels.

As a general rule, avoid mixing different kinds of formulations such as wettable powders and emulsifiable concentrates. Avoid mixing most pesticides in alkaline solutions (pH above 7.0) such as the alkaline fertilizers.

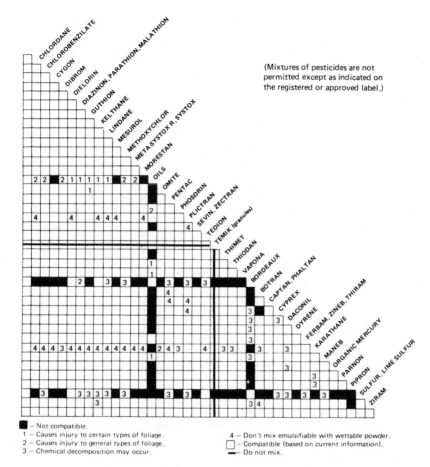

Figure 12-16. Compatibility chart for mixing insecticides, miticides, and fungicides. *(From L. K. Cutkomp, Minnesota State Florists' Recommendations for Greenhouse and Floriculture Pest Control, 1973)*

Never mix herbicides (weed killers) with any other pesticides. Use separate equipment for herbicides. A herbicide residue in an insecticide spray could cause extensive damage to a crop.

Plant Toxicity

When a pesticide is injurious to a plant species as a whole, recommendations will not be found on the label for that crop. There are, however, pesticides labeled for use on crops where there are a few cultivars that are injured by the pesticide. Lists of cultivars injured by specific pesticides can be found in some of the pest control manuals recommended at the end of this chapter for further reading and also at the beginning of Table 12-2. Whenever you are not certain about the plant toxicity of a pesticide, you should apply it to a small number of plants and wait one week to determine whether or not it is safe.

Shelf Life

Some pesticides are dated as to their effective life, many are not. Generally after one year they should be inspected for symptoms of deterioration. The effectiveness of some pesticides is reduced or lost, while others may become toxic to plants. Emulsifying agents in EC formulations often become toxic. To help guard against this problem, pesticides should be dated when purchased and properly inventoried to insure use of the older materials first. The visual symptoms listed in Table 12-4 indicate the need to dispose of the material.

PESTICIDE SAFETY

Handling of pesticides is a very serious matter. Many of the materials are highly toxic to man. Even where the immediate toxicity is not great, there is the risk of a long-term effect. Often the long-range effects are not known. All pesticides should be handled with an urgency of caution.

Pesticides serve an invaluable role in the greenhouse. The subtropical environment of the greenhouse and unlimited host plant supply provides an ideal setting for insect development. Competition within the industry necessitates high quality standards and precludes insect damage. A pest control program is necessary. While one should not fear pesticides, a healthy respect for them is essential.

The pesticide program should be in the hands of one or more employees who are carefully trained for the job. It should not be an orphan job passed weekly to different personnel, often those least familiar and qualified. Human life is at stake.

There are a number of common sense rules to follow which will now be taken up in logical order.

Storage Area

Store pesticides in a well ventilated, locked closet or room to which children and other unauthorized people have no access. Be sure the temperature remains between 40° and 90°F (4 to 32°C). Place a warning sign on the door indicating that the room contains pesticides. It is a good idea to keep a list of the contents of the room posted as well. A floor plan of the building showing the location of the pesticide room and its contents should be pro-

Table 12-4
Visual Symptoms of Various Pesticide Formulations that Indicate It Is
Time to Stop Using and Dispose of Pesticide

FORMULATION	VISUAL EVIDENCE OF DETERIORATION
Emulsifiable concentrates	When milky coloration does not occur with the addition of water and when sludge is present or any separation of components is evident in the container
Oil sprays	When milky coloration does not occur with the addition of water
Wettable powders	When lumping occurs and the powder will not suspend in water
Dusts	Excessive lumping
Granulars	Excessive lumping
Aerosols	Generally effective until the opening of the aerosol dispenser becomes obstructed

vided for the local fire department. This will give them a better chance to protect themselves in the event of a fire.

Labels

Be sure that labels remain on all containers. Tape or glue them on if they become loose. Read the label before using any pesticide. It contains valuable information as to which insects and crops it can be used on. To use it for any other purpose is illegal. The toxicity rating, symptoms of poisoning, and antidote also are generally included. Rates and methods of application are listed as well. Failure to comply with them could lead to ineffectiveness on the one hand or injury to the crop on the other.

Poison Information Centers

Throughout the nation there are poison information centers. These centers have personnel who can advise your physician as to action to take in the event of poisoning. Obtain the address and phone number of your local center and post it on the outside of your pesticide room. Collect a set of labels of the pesticides you use and keep them handy. In the event of poisoning, take the appropriate label and the address and phone number of your local poison information center with you to the physician. Since such poisonings are not common, valuable time is often lost in a hospital looking up the proper chemical identity of a pesticide and its antidote. The label and poison information center can provide this information.

Pesticide Containers

Keep pesticides in their original containers. Never transfer them to another container. If the label is lost from a container and there is any uncertainty about the contents, dispose of the material. *Don't guess!* Do not reuse pesticide containers. The slightest residue is potentially dangerous. Most people killed by pesticides are children. Several cases have occurred where pesticides were transferred to household containers such as soda bottles only to be found and drunk by a child.

LD$_{50}$

Categories of toxicity of pesticides have been set forth in the Federal Insecticide, Fungicide, and Rodenticide Act. The toxicity of pesticides is quantitatively expressed as an LD$_{50}$ value either for oral or dermal entry into the body. The former refers to ingestion through the mouth and the latter to absorption through the skin. In either event, LD$_{50}$ refers to the amount of pesticide, expressed in milligrams (mg) per kilogram (kg) of body weight, which will kill 50 percent of a group of animals tested within 14 days of poisoning. These figures are fairly well applicable to the human. The lower the LD$_{50}$ value, the more poisonous is the pesticide because less of it is required to kill. Listed in Table 12-5 are most of the available pesticides by toxicity category and their LD$_{50}$ values. Note that packages in the *highly toxic* category must bear the words DANGER and POISON as well as a picture of a skull and crossbones. Any time this is seen exercise the ultimate in precaution. Note the LD$_{50}$ values of pesticides you use and be sure your application personnel are aware of them.

Protective Clothing

When applying pesticides wear unlined elbow-length rubber gloves and rubber boots. It is important that they not be lined since cloth linings will absorb pesticides and are difficult to wash. Waterproof coveralls extending from the neck to wrists and ankles should be worn. Do not wear absorbent coveralls since they will absorb spills and hold the pesticide in contact with the body. It is well to keep the coveralls buttoned at the neck and outside the gloves and boots so that pesticides cannot enter them. A rubberized hat with brim should be worn since pesticides are readily absorbed through the scalp.

Table 12-5

Toxicity of Pesticides, Including Many Not Registered for Greenhouse Use*

COMMON NAME OF CHEMICAL[a]	TRADE NAME	TYPE OF COMPOUND	ACUTE[b] ORAL (mg/kg)	ACUTE[b] DERMAL (mg/kg)
		Highly Toxic		

(Acute oral LD50 (to rats) from 0–50 mg/kg. The label of the majority of these pesticides shows the signal words "Danger—Poison" (printed in red) and the skull and crossbones. (From a taste to 7 drops could be lethal to a 150 lb man.))

COMMON NAME OF CHEMICAL[a]	TRADE NAME	TYPE OF COMPOUND	ACUTE[b] ORAL (mg/kg)	ACUTE[b] DERMAL (mg/kg)
Cyanides (Fum)	Cyanogas	calcium cyanide	extremely toxic	extremely toxic
Chloropicrin (Fum)			LC50.8 mg/liter	severe irritation
Methyl bromide (Fum)			LC50–1 mg/liter	extremely toxic
Aldicarb (I)	Temik	carbamate	0.93	2.5
TEPP (I)		phosphate	1.05	2.4
Phorate (I)	Thimet	phosphate	1–3	3.6
Cyclohexamide (F)	Acti-dione PM		2	extremely toxic
Demeton (I)	Systox	phosphate	2–6	8–14
Disulfoton (I)	Di Syston	phosphate	2–7	6–15
Fensulfothion (I)	Dasanit	phosphate	2–11	3–30
Mevinphos (I)	Phosdrin	phosphate	4–6	4–5
Parathion (I)		phosphate	4–13	7–21
Sulfotepp (I)	Dithio	phosphate	5	8
Carbofuran (I)	Furadan	carbamate	5	885
Fonofos (I)	Dyfonate	phosphate	8–17.5	25
EPN (I)	EPN-300	phosphate	8–36	25–230
Carbophenothion (I)	Trithion	phosphate	10–30	27–54
Arsenic compounds (I)			10–50	Toxic

(Table 12-5 continued)

Table 12-5 continued

COMMON NAME OF CHEMICAL[a]	TRADE NAME	TYPE OF COMPOUND	ACUTE[b] ORAL (mg/kg)	ACUTE[b] DERMAL (mg/kg)
Azinphosmethyl (I)	Guthion	phosphate	11–13	220
Methyl parathion (I)		phosphate	14–24	67
Methomyl (I)	Lannate	carbamate	17–24	1500
Endosulfan (I)	Thiodan	hydrocarbon	18–43	74–130
Methamidophos (I)	Monitor	phosphate	18.9–21	118
Monocrotophos (I)	Azodrin	phosphate	20	342
Phosphamidon (I)	Dimecron	phosphate	20–22.4	107–143
Dioxathion (I)	Delnav	phosphate	23–43	63–235
Mexacarbate (I)	Zectran	carbamate	25–37	1500–2500
Methidathion (I)	Supracide	phosphate	25–48	375
Ethion (I)	Nialate	phosphate	27–65	62–245
Dinitro compounds (F,I,H)	DNOC	dinitro phenol	30	150–600 (guinea pig)
Oxamyl (I,N,A)	Vydate		37	2960 (rabbit)
Dieldrin (I)		hydrocarbon	46–60	60–100
Coumaphos (I)	Co-Ral	phosphate	56	860
Nicotine sulfate (I)		alkaloid	83	285
Paraquat (H)			120	480

Moderately Toxic

(Acute oral LD50 (to rats) from 50–500 mg/kg. The label of these pesticides shows the signal word "Warning".)

Kerosene		solvent	50 for comparison	
Rotenone (I)		botanical	50–75	950 + rabbit

398

Pentachlorophenol (H,I)	PCP	phosphate	50–140	mild reaction
Dichlorvos (I)	Vapona	phosphate	56–80	75–107
Oxydemeton-methyl (I)	Meta-Systox-R	phosphate	65–76	250
Bux (I)	Bux-Ten	carbamate	87–170	400 rabbit
Lindane (I)		hydrocarbon	88–125	1000
Arprocarb (I)	Baygon	carbamate	95–100	1000
Crotoxyphos (I)	Ciodrin	phosphate	125	385 rabbit
Pirimicarb (I)	Pirimor	carbamate	147	—
Chlorpyrifos (I)	Dursban	phosphate	163	—
Chlordimeform (I)	Fundal & Galecron		162–170	255
Aromatic solvents		solvent	170	—
dimethoate (I)	Cygon	phosphate	215	400–610
Fenthion (I)	Baytex	phosphate	215–245	330
Chlordimeform hydrochloride (I)	Fundal & Galecron	phosphate	225–280	4000+
Naled (I)	Dibrom	phosphate	250	800
Dichlonfenthion (N,I)	VP-13 Nemacid	phosphate	250–270	6,000
Metaldehyde (M)		hydrocarbon	250–1000	—
Phosmet (I)	Imidan	phosphate	300	3160
Vorlex (Fum)	Vorlex		305	—
Diazinon (I)	Diazinon	phosphate	300–400	455–500
Chlordane (I)		hydrocarbon	335–430	690–840
Diquat (H)			400–440	500+
2,4,5-T (H)			481–500	mild reaction
Fenithrothion (I)	Sumithion	phosphate	500	1300
Plictran (A)			540	2000+

(Table 12-5 continued)

Table 12-5 continued

COMMON NAME OF CHEMICAL[a]	TRADE NAME	TYPE OF COMPOUND	ACUTE[b] ORAL (mg/kg)	ACUTE[b] DERMAL *mg/kg
		Low Toxicity		
(Acute oral LD50 above 500 mg/kg. The label of these pesticides shows the signal word "Caution".)				
Carbaryl (I)	Sevin	carbamate	500–850	4000+
Petroleum solvents		solvent	about 510	–
Crufomate (I)	Ruelene	phosphate	548	3000
Trichlorfon (I)	Dylox-Dipterex	phosphate	560–630	2000+
Ethylene dichloride (Fum)			670–890	3890 rabbit
Formaldehyde	Formalin		800	mild reaction
Metam-Sodium (Fum)	Vapam	carbamate	820	800
Dicofol (A)	Kelthane	hydrocarbon	809–1100	1000
Acephate (I)	Orthene	phosphate	945	–
Chlorobenzilate (A)	Acaraben	hydrocarbon	960–1220	5000+
Morestan (A,F)		carbonate	1100–1800	2000+
Ryania (I)		botanical	1200	4000+ rabbit
Pyrethrum (I)		botanical	1345	2060 rabbit
Ammonium sulfamate (H)	Ammate X		1600–3900	mild reaction
Ronnel (I)	Korlan	phosphate	1940	5000+

Common name (class)	Trade name	Chemical class	Oral	Dermal
Temophos (I)	Abate	phosphate	2000	2000
Kinoprene (I)	Enstar	insect growth regulator	2330	9000 rabbit
Propargite (A)	Omite	sulfite	2500	—
Pentac (A)		hydrocarbon	3160	3160+ rabbit
Trifluralin (H)	Treflan E		3700–10,000	5000
Tetrachlorvinphos (I)	Gardona, Rabon	phosphate	4000–5000	5000+ rabbit
Resmethrin (I)	SBP 1382	synthetic pyrethroid	4240	3040+
Chloropropylate (A)	Acaralate	hydrocarbon	5000	10,200+ rabbit
Methoxychlor (I)	Marlate	hydrocarbon	5000	6000+
Perthane (I)		hydrocarbon	8170	—
Benomyl (F)	Benlate	carbamate	9590	little reaction
Tetradifon	Tedion	hydrocarbon	14,700	10,000
Bacillus thuringiensis	Dipel, Biotrol, Thuricide	bacteria	harmless	harmless

*From: A. G. Gentile and D. T. Scanlon. "Floricultural Insects and Related Pests—Biology and Control." Section I. Florogram—Specialty Manual Issue for Commercial Greenhouse Growers, Massachusetts Coop. Ext. Ser., Suburban Exp. Sta., Waltham, MA 02154, 1976.

[a]Letters in parentheses indicate the class of pesticide as follows: (A)-acaracide, (F)-fungicide, (FUM)-fumigant, (H)-herbicide, (I)-insecticide, and (M)-molluscicide.

[b]Acute poisoning—Severe poisoning which occurs after a single exposure to the pesticide.

Chronic poisoning—Poisoning which occurs as a result of repeated exposures to small doses of the pesticide over a long period of time.

When Category III (*Slightly Toxic*) pesticides are used which bear the word CAUTION on the label you should use goggles and a respirator. The respirator has two cartridges which filter out pesticide fumes and particles in the air being breathed. Respirators cover just the nose and mouth. Generally the cartridges are good for eight hours of use. If the odor of pesticides is detected when the respirator is tightly fastened to the face, the cartridges should be immediately replaced.

Category I and II pesticides, bearing on the label DANGER-POISON plus a skull and crossbones or WARNING, warrant the use of a gas mask covering the entire face (Figure 12-13). Air entering it passes through a large cannister in which fumes and particles are filtered out. The manufacturer will indicate the number of hours that the cannister can be safely used. It should be replaced after that. If the odor of a pesticide is detected, it should be replaced immediately.

After application of pesticides, the outside of the gloves should be washed in a warm detergent solution before removing. This prevents contamination of the hands in the process of removing the gloves. The boots, hat, mask, and goggles should be washed next in a detergent solution. The coveralls need to be laundered after each use. Disposable waterproof coveralls and hats are now available which can be discarded after each use. Finally, the employee should take a thorough shower using plenty of soap. It is for this latter reason that it is best to spray at the end of the day. If pesticide application is done early in the day, there is the temptation to wait until the end of the day to clean up. This prolongs exposure of the individual to any contamination there might be on him or her, particularly if it is a warm day and the pores of the body are open.

Respirators and gas masks have covers or tape to place over the inlet when not in use. This prevents the absorption of gases and solids during storage which might use up the absorbant contained within. Masks, respirators, and clothing should never be stored in the pesticide room since they would be prone to absorb pesticide vapors.

Equipment

Manufacturers of equipment will provide safety check lists. They are mostly common sense rules and should be followed. A number of accidents have occurred as a result of improperly maintained equipment. Old spray hoses in particular should be replaced before they burst and douse the operator.

Eating and Smoking

Never smoke, eat, or drink while preparing or applying pesticides. This provides a very likely avenue of entry for the pesticide into your body. Keep all foods and beverages out of and away from the pesticide storage room. Do not eat in the greenhouse where plants are routinely treated with pesticides. Set up a lunch and coffee break area in a safe part of the work building where there is no chance of pesticide contamination.

Signs and Locks

At the time you begin to apply pesticides, place signs at the greenhouse entries forbidding entrance and indicating that pesticides have been applied. The signs should remain until it is safe to work on the plants again (see Table 12-2). Signs are particularly necessary when aerosols, fogs, and smokes are used. These signs should indicate that fumigation is occurring. Because of the nature of some people, the greenhouse should be locked.

Disposal

Empty pesticide containers are potentially dangerous because of the difficulty of removing all residue from them. Each state has a set of rules for disposing of them. Contact your Cooperative Extension Service to learn what these rules are. This is especially important when disposing of pesticides which have deteriorated.

SUMMARY

1. Insects can constitute a major problem for greenhouse crops. It is easier to prevent insect populations from building up than to eradicate them. Weeds harbor insects and diseases, thus, they should be eliminated inside and around the outside of greenhouses. New plants introduced into the greenhouse should be checked for insects and treated if any are found. A constant vigil should be kept for the appearance of insects in the greenhouse and immediate action taken when they appear.

2. The major insects and related pests in greenhouses include aphids, fungus gnats, leaf miners, mealybugs, mites, scale insects, slugs, snails, thrips, whiteflies, and worms.

3. There are seven methods of pesticide application in the greenhouse. Aqueous spray application of pesticides is the most popular method. Mist application is similar and involves liquid preparations 10 to 20 times more concentrated than sprays but applied in considerably less volume. Application of dust formulations of pesticides is practiced to a limited degree.

    Spray, mist, and dust applications leave a residue on the plant surface which has a residual effectiveness. Other methods of application including aerosol, fog, and smoke disperse the pesticides throughout the greenhouse atmosphere killing insects in hard-to-reach crevices, under benches, etc., but have little or no residual activity. Systemic insecticides can be applied to the root medium. They are taken up into the plant and result in death of insects and related pests feeding on the plant. These pesticides have long residual activities and can replace the need for other methods of application.

4. Greenhouse managers are legally bound to follow the approved uses for pesticides set forth on their labels. Since these are constantly prone to change, the manager must keep all literature up-to-date. Greenhouse pest control recommendations are continually updated by a number of state universities and state flower grower organizations.

5. Pesticides must be properly selected to insure effectiveness and prevent plant injuries. Some combinations of pesticides are toxic to plants while others become ineffective. A compatibility chart should be consulted. Many pesticides used alone are safe on one plant species but not on another. Some are safe for most cultivars of a crop but may injure a few other cultivars.

6. Proper timing of pesticide applications is important. Pesticides may be effective in some stages of an insect's life cycle but not in others, such as the egg or pupa stages. A simple application, therefore, does not eliminate the insect population. Additional treatments must be made at the correct time to catch the remaining insects in a vulnerable stage and before they progress to another resident stage.

7. Human safety should be the major concern on each manager's mind. Safety precautions should include: (a) a labeled, well-ventilated, locked storage area for pesticides, (b) labels on all pesticide containers and use of appropriate containers, (c) posted address and telephone number of the nearest poison information center, (d) familiarity of each pesticide applicator with the toxicity of each pesticide he or she handles, (e) use of protective clothing during pesticide application, (f) application equipment in a good state of repair, (g) no eating or smoking in areas where pesticides are being or have been applied, (h) signs and possibly locks on all access doors to recently sprayed areas, and (i) proper disposal of pesticide containers and old pesticides.

SUGGESTED READINGS

Ball, V. *The Ball Red Book. 13th ed.* Geo. J. Ball, Inc., W. Chicago, IL, 1975. pp. 118–26.

Becker, P. "Pests of Ornamental Plants." Ministry of Agriculture, Fisheries and Food. Bul. 97. Her Majesty's Stationery Office, 49 High Holborn, London, WC1V 6HB, England, 1974.

Bing, A., et al. *Cornell Recommendations for Commercial Floriculture Crops, Part II. Disease, Pest, and Weed Contol.* New York State College of Agriculture and Life Science, Cornell University, Ithaca, NY 14853, 1975.

Cutkomp, L. K. "Recommendations for Greenhouse and Floricultural Pest Control–1973." MN State Florists' Bul. (special issue). Department Entomology, Fisheries, and Wildlife, University of Minnesota, St. Paul, MN 55108, 1973.

Gentile, A. G. and D. T. Scanlon. *Floricultural Insects and Related Pests– Biology and Control.* Sec. I. Specialty Manual Issue of the Florogram. Massachusetts Cooperative Extension Service, Suburban Experimental Station, Waltham, MA 02154, 1976.

1975-76 Pesticide Recommendations for Greenhouse Flower Crops. Pub. 381. Ontario Ministry of Agriculture and Food, Toronto, Ontario, Canada, 1975.

North Carolina Agricultural Chemicals Manual. School of Agriculture and Life Science, North Carolina State University, Raleigh, NC 27607, 1977. Published annually.

Powell, C. C. and R. K. Lindquist. "Insect, Mite and Disease Control on Commercial Floral Crops." Cooperative Extension Service. The Ohio State University, Columbus, OH 43210, 1975.

Chapter 13

Disease Control

Infectious diseases are the downfall of the careless grower. Many diseases cannot be eradicated. At best they can only be contained. Others cannot be contained, which means that the infected portion of the crop must be quickly identified and removed. As a whole, fungicides and bactericides are not nearly as effective as are insecticides and miticides.

Prevention plays a very important role in disease control. But even with the best of preventative programs disease organisms will get a foothold in the greenhouse. There are disease organisms transmitted in soil or ground water which can be carried in on the bottom of a pot or the sole of a shoe. Some fungi such as the rusts and *Botrytis* produce windblown spores. If host plants are growing near the greenhouse, these spores can be blown into it. Your disease prevention program depends upon that of other greenhouse ranges if you are purchasing seedlings or cuttings or, in some cases, even seed. Numerous pathogens are readily transported on these plant parts.

Knowing the inevitability of disease, the manager must be careful to check daily for its presence in the same manner that he or she watches for insects and checks the need for water.

Much of what has been discussed for pest control is apropos to this discussion on control of disease organisms. The same application equipment is used including sprayers, dusters, foggers, and smokes. Surfactants are important in WP formulations. LD_{50} values are assigned to fungicides, bactericides, and nematicides as well. These chemicals are to be found in the compatibility chart presented in Chapter 12. In general all of the safety rules governing insecticides and miticides pertain equally well to fungicides, bactericides, and nematicides.

DISEASES OF GREENHOUSE CROPS

There are numerous pathogenic diseases of greenhouse crops. They come under four general categories—virus, bacteria, fungi, and nematode (Figure 13-1). It is important to know the characteristics of each as well as the life cycles of specific pathogens in order to determine how to control them. Some require free water on the plant foliage in order to develop. Others require a very wet root medium. Yet others appear exclusively on purchased

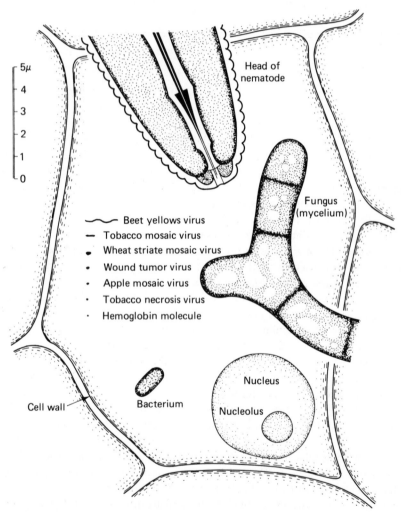

Figure 13-1. Schematic diagram of the shapes and sizes of certain plant pathogens in relation to a plant cell. *(From G. N. Agrios, Plant Pathology. Academic Press. New York, 1969)*

cuttings. Each of these requirements suggests a very effective way of controlling the pathogen.

Aside from introductory paragraphs, the following accounts of viruses, fungi, and nematodes are taken verbatim from the writing of Drs. R. K. Horst and B. E. Williamson of the Department of Plant Pathology at Cornell University as presented in Cornell recommendations for commercial floriculture crops.

Viruses

Viruses are minute organisms similar in size and chemistry to the genetic material (DNA) within plant and animal cells. Viruses live within cells causing numerous abnormalities (Figure 13-2). Virus diseases are generally eliminated by removing and destroying the infected plants. Pesticides do not exist for combating these diseases.

Despite a lack of agreement on a definition of virus, much is known about plant response to them. Because plants do not produce antibodies, they neither recover from a virus infection nor become immune. Once a plant is infected, it may remain infected for life, even though symptoms of disease may become masked

Figure 13-2. Mosaic virus of rose with its characteristic symptoms of leaf puckering and yellow discoloration. *(From R. K. Jones, Department of Plant Pathology, North Carolina State University, Raleigh, NC 27607)*

or the plants "grow out of it" under certain conditions. Thus, perennial plants and vegetatively propagated greenhouse plants carry the virus from one crop to the next with continuing loss to the disease.

SYMPTOMS. Although the most common symptom of virus infection is stunting or dwarfing, it is more often the leaves that show the first and most evident signs. Most common are color changes: leaves show spots, streaks, blotches, and rings of light green, yellow, white, brown, or black or develop rather uniform yellow or orange coloration. Leaves can also be changed in size or shape; they can pucker or have rolled margins. Flowers can be dwarfed, deformed, streaked, faded, green instead of the usual color, or even changed into leafy structures. These are only a few of the more obvious symptoms of virus infection in plants.

SPREAD. In general, viruses are not transmitted through seed. A crop grown from seed can suffer serious loss if a virus disease appears early and has an efficient means of spread. However, the next year the crop will again start clean. Although viruses can spread unaided from cell to cell in one plant, they require active assistance to spread from one growing plant to another and a wound through which to enter the plant. Most frequently, viruses are spread by insects feeding on a healthy plant after feeding on an infected one or by grafting with a scion from an infected plant or by using infected stock plants as a source of cuttings.

INDEXING PROGRAM. The use of pathogen-free propagating material is extremely important in any disease control program. Culture-indexing and virus-indexing are probably the best known methods of eliminating certain pathogens from propagative material. These methods are particularly important in controlling internal pathogens which affect chrysanthemums, carnations, and geraniums, that is, viruses and vascular wilt pathogens. Programs using these procedures have been developed by several propagating specialists. Culture- and virus-indexed plant material is free of the pathogens for which the index is set up to check; however, such plant material *is not disease resistant* and naturally requires a growing medium free of the designated pathogens and good cultural practices if the full potential of healthy plants is to be realized.

Culture-indexing is performed by removing thin slices obtained aseptically from the base of a cutting and placing the slices in a nutrient medium. Nutrient medium cultures showing any fungus or bacterial growth are discarded along with the cuttings from which the slices were removed.

Virus-indexing makes use of indicator plants for each specific virus since many cultivars can act as "sleepers," that is, virus carriers that show no external symptoms. "Sleeper varieties or cultivars" are a tremendous threat since they can be responsible for a large amount of virus spread before the grower realizes he has a serious problem. When the plants are about to flower, the seriousness of the problem is realized in uneven plant growth and flowering time along with reduction in flower quality.

Diseases of crops for which indexing programs have been developed follow.

Chrysanthemum

Viruses
Chrysanthemum stunt
Chrysanthemum mosaics
Chrysanthemum aspermy
Chrysanthemum chlorotic mottle
Vascular wilts
Verticillium wilt
Bacterial blight

Geranium

Vascular wilts
Bacterial blight
Verticillium wilt

Carnation

Viruses
Carnation mottle
Carnation ringspot
Carnation mosaic
Carnation streak
Carnation etch-ring
Vascular wilts
Fusarium wilt
Phialophora wilt
Bacterial wilt
Slow wilt

Bacteria

Bacteria are single-celled microorganisms. Bacterial diseases are difficult to control. A few bactericides exist. Control is primarily through prevention and elimination of infected plants. There are not as many bacterial diseases as fungal diseases (Figure 13-3). Some of the more common bacterial diseases are bacterial wilt of carnation (*Pseudomonas caryophylli*); bacterial blight (stem rot and leaf spot) of geranium (*Xanthomonas pelargoni*); soft rot of cuttings, corms, bulbs, etc. (*Erwinia chrysanthemi*); bacterial leaf spots such as on geranium and English ivy (*Xanthomonas hederae*); fasciation on crops including carnation, chrysanthemum, geranium, and petunia (*Corynebacterium fascians*); and crown gall on rose, chrysanthemum, geranium, etc. (*Agrobacterium tumefasciens*).

Fungi

The fungal diseases are the most numerous and lend themselves best to control measures (Figure 13-4). Fungal organisms are much more complex than bacteria. They are multicellular organisms often comprising several

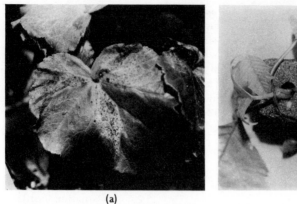
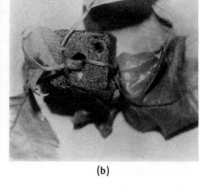

(a)   (b)

Figure 13-3. Bacterial diseases: (a) bacterial leaf spot on Rieger begonia; (b) bacterial soft rot of the stem of a poinsettia cutting. *(From D. L. Strider, Department of Plant Pathology, North Carolina State University, Raleigh, NC 27607)*

tissues. Some of the more important categories as described by Doctors Horst and Williamson follow.

Powdery Mildew

Powdery mildew, one of the most easily recognized of all plant diseases, is characterized by the presence of the whitish, powdery mildew growth on surfaces of leaves, stems, and sometimes petals. The fungal threads (hyphae) and the spores (conidia) that develop on short, erect branches, known as sporophores (conidiophores), are visible under a strong lens. Under some conditions, however, the threads are so sparse that the mildew can be detected only by examination under strong light, with the use of a good lens or dissecting microscope. In some cases the mildew development is limited to small areas in which the leaf cells are killed and turn black.

The mildew spores are easily detached from the sporophores and carried by air currents to surrounding plants where they initiate new infections. On some host plants, such as dahlia, zinnia and phlox, infection commonly is limited to older foliage late in the season, and damage is chiefly the unsightliness of the mildew growth itself. On other plants, such as rose and delphinium, the young foliage and stems often become severely distorted in addition to being covered by the whitish mildew growth. Seriously affected plants may be of little value as cut flowers or potted plants.

(a)   (b)

(c)   (d)

Figure 13-4. Fungal diseases: (a) powdery mildew on rose; (b) *Botrytis* blight in the spore-forming stage on a poinsettia leaf under mist propagation; (c) damping off of salvia seedlings; (d) *Pythium* root rot of chrysanthemum *(left)* normal plant *(right)*. *(From R. K. Jones and D. L. Strider, Department of Plant Pathology, North Carolina State University, Raleigh, NC 27607)*

CONTROL. Unlike the spores of nearly all other fungi, powdery mildew spores can germinate and initiate infections at humidity levels far below those commonly encountered in field or greenhouse. Development of mildew following infection, however, may be more rapid and luxurious at higher humidities. As a deterrent to mildew in greenhouses, ventilation and heating should be adjusted to avoid high-humidity conditions.

Under some conditions, fungicides for mildew control are essential both outdoors and under glass. Recommendations are almost certain to change, but one fungicide, sulfur, will always be on the list. Fungicidal dusting sulfurs can be applied quickly and easily with either hand or power dusters. Wettable sulfur sprays can be applied with standard spray equipment. In greenhouses sulfur can be "vaporized" by painting a slurry of sulfur in water on steam heating pipes or by heating pure sulfur in commercially available vaporizers. Regular use of sulfur as a preventive will usually keep powdery mildew from becoming a serious problem. Other fungicides that have been found effective as mildew control sprays include: benomyl, Karathane®, Parnon®, and Pipron®.

Botrytis Blight

The common grey-mold fungus, *Botrytis cinerea*, attacks a wide variety of ornamental plants, probably causing more losses than any other single pathogen. The fungus causes a brown rotting and blighting of affected tissues. Very small seedling asters can be rotted; stems of geraniums are commonly attacked, snapdragon stems can be invaded and the upper part of the stem killed; petal tissues of many plants, including carnations, chysanthemums, roses, azaleas, geraniums, can be spotted and ruined; begonia stems can be rotted and the plant rendered unsalable. The fungus is usually identified by the development of fuzzy, greyish spore masses over the surface of the rotted tissues, although such sporulation will not develop under dry conditions.

Spores of *Botrytis* are produced on distinctive dark-colored hairlike sporophores and are readily dislodged and carried by air currents to new plant surfaces. The spores will not germinate and produce new infections, however, except in contact with water, whether from splashing, condensation, or exudation. Furthermore, with some possible exceptions, only tender tissues (seedlings, petals), weakened tissues (stubs left in taking cuttings, tissues infected by powdery mildew), injured tissues (bases of cuttings), or old and dead tissues are attacked. Active, healthy tissues, other than petal tissues, seldom are invaded.

CONTROL. Because of the requirement of high humidity for spore production and of actual condensation for spore germination and infection, *Botrytis* can usually be controlled under glass by avoiding splashing and by heating and ventilating to prevent any condensation on the plant surfaces. Because the fungus readily attacks old or dead tissues and produces tremendous quantities of airborne spores, the importance of strict sanitation cannot be overemphasized. All old blossoms and dead leaves should be removed, and all fallen leaves and plant debris on or under the benches should be gathered and burned.

Fungicides may be required under some greenhouse conditions and on field-grown or clothhouse crops of carnations and chrysanthemums. Captan sprays have been used with fair success and a minimum of plant injury. The degree of control, however, has not been as high as desired, and the spray residue is quite noticeable.

Botran$_®$ has been used very effectively on chrysanthemums and other ornamentals, and it leaves no conspicuous residue; but there have been some reports of minor plant injury. Chlorothalonil also has been used successfully as a spray (Bravo$_®$ or Daconil 2787$_®$ wettable powder) but occasionally has damaged open blooms of azaleas and some rose varieties. The material has also been effective when "volatilized" by heat and is available as Exotherm Termil,$_®$ a smoke generator. There have been reports of pronounced skin reaction (dermatitis) on arms and faces of some workers who have handled plants soon after treatment with any one of the formulations. See label for crops for which chlorothalonil is cleared. Phytotoxicity has been reported with chlorothalonil where free water is present on blossoms at time of treatment. Benomyl is reported effective in control of *Botrytis*.

Root Rot Diseases

Rhizoctonia and *Pythium* not only cause damping-off of seedlings, but together with *Thielaviopsis* are very important in causing root and basal stem rots of older plants. These three fungi are common inhabitants of soil and attack a very wide range of plants. Each is dependent for spread on mechanical transfer of mycelia, sclerotia, or resting spores in infested soil particles (on flats, tools, pots, baskets, or in the end of the watering hose) or infected plant tissue. Basic control measures effective against 1 are also effective against the other 2. Most important control measures are (1) use of a light, well-drained soil mix; (2) thorough pasteurization of the mix, containers, tools, benches, and so forth, that come into contact with the plants; (3) clean plants; (4) a sound sanitation program; and (5) supplementary soil treatments with chemicals to minimize recontamination problems.

Pythium causes a rather black, wet rot that makes roots look hollow and collapsed. It is favored by cool, wet, poorly drained soils. If *Pythium* is present, the soil should never be watered excessively. Dexon$_®$ mixed into the medium prior to potting or applied as a soil drench is highly effective in controlling it. Drench applications of Dexon$_®$ can be repeated every 6 to 8 weeks as necessary.

Rhizoctonia causes a drier brown rot. It is favored by an intermediate range of moisture, neither too wet nor too dry. *Rhizoctonia* disease is frequently thought to be favored by high temperature, but this is not always so. Terraclor$_®$ or benomyl applied as a soil drench is highly effective in control.

Thielaviopsis causes a drier lesion than *Rhizoctonia,* one that soon turns black because of the large number of black spores of the fungus produced in the lesion. The disease is not a problem in soil adjusted to pH 4.5 to 5.0. Benomyl as a soil drench at label rates effectively controls *Thielaviopsis*. Mertect® applied experimentally to the soil as a postplant drench has effectively controlled this disease.

Damping-off Disease

Damping-off of seedlings, which is caused mostly by fungi, can be a complex of several diseases occurring separately or simultaneously. Usually *Rhizoctonia* or *Pythium* is involved.

PREEMERGENCE INFECTION. Seed decay prior to germination or rot of seedling before emergence is commonly caused by a watermold, usually *Pythium* or sometimes *Phytophthora*, although other fungi, possibly seed-borne, can be involved. Poor seed can be blamed.

POSTEMERGENCE INFECTION. Rot developing at the soil line after emergence, which causes the seedling to topple, is commonly caused by *Rhizoctonia;* but occasionally it is caused by watermolds. This is the conspicuous type of damping-off most frequently reported by growers. Seedlings grown under very adverse conditions may only be girdled at the soil surface and remain upright. Transplanted, such seedlings remain hard and stunted and eventually die. This condition is usually caused by *Rhizoctonia.* In some cases, the watermolds can invade the rootlets at the tips and progress upward to the stem; thereupon the plant dies.

Rhizoctonia is the most frequent cause of seedling damping-off as determined by culturing.

For all practical purposes, *Rhizoctonia* and *Pythium* do not have an air-borne stage. Therefore, spread of both fungi depends upon mechanical transfer of mycelia, sclerotia, or resting spores in infested soil particles (on flats, tools, baskets, or in the end of the watering hose) or infected plant tissue. This is important in control. If soil or other medium is steamed or chemically treated, and care is taken to prevent recontamination, damping-off should be of little significance. Sowing seed in a layer of screened sphagnum moss, vermiculite, perlite, peat-lite mix, or other presumably sterilized material also helps.

If damping-off appears in the seed flats or the seed bed, Dexon® applied as a soil drench gives excellent control of *Pythium,* and Terraclor® or benomyl soil drench provides excellent control of *Rhizoctonia.* Truban® can also be used for controlling *Pythium,* but does not appear to be as effective as Dexon® in our experience. If necessary, a combined Dexon®-Terraclor® drench can be applied. Do not apply Terraclor® more than once in the seed flat or seed bed. Buy treated seed, or before sowing, treat seeds with ferbam or other fungicide to help prevent damping-off of seeds.

Dust soil lightly with ferbam after seeding to help prevent recontamination. If, in spite of treatment, damping-off starts after seedlings are up, try Terraclor₍ᵣ₎ as above.

Verticillium Diseases

Verticillium is a fungus capable of infecting a very wide variety of ornamental plants, some of the more important being chrysanthemums, China asters, snapdragons, roses, geraniums, and begonias. Symptoms vary with the host. Snapdragons can appear completely healthy until blossoms develop, when the foliage can suddenly wilt completely. The conductive tissues of some varieties can turn brown or purple, particularly the woody stem tissues. With chrysanthemums and some others there is usually a marginal wilting of the leaves, followed by chlorosis and eventually death and browning of the leaves, which remain attached and hang down against the stem. These symptoms commonly develop at first on only one side of the plant and only after blossom buds have formed. Young, vigorous plants usually remain symptomless. The buds on 1 or 2 branches of plants of red-flowered varieties of greenhouse roses turn blue and fail to open; the leaves and the green stem tissues can become mottled; and when the stem is shaken, the leaves can fall from the plant, and the stem dies. Additional shoots can develop from basal buds and go through the same sequence, though eventually a shoot may remain healthy. Usually there is no vascular discoloration. With semituberous-rooted begonias some yellowing of leaf margins can occur, but the most distinctive symptom is development of an extremely shiny lower leaf surface. The symptoms thus are quite variable, but the most characteristic are the one-sided development, the wilting and yellowing of leaf margins progressing upward from the lowest leaves, the lack of any leaf or stem lesions, and normal-appearing roots.

The fungus causing the disease invades the soil and may persist there for many years. Initial infection usually occurs through normal roots, and the fungus grows upward through the water-conducting (xylem) tissues. Infected plants of some types (for example, chrysanthemums) are usually not killed by the fungus and, during periods of rapid vegetative growth, can appear symptomless. Cuttings taken from such plants can, however, carry the fungus internally and serve to introduce the disease to new areas.

CONTROL. Plant only in soils that have been steamed or treated with chloropicrin to eliminate *Verticillium*. Obtain planting stock only from a reliable dealer, and purchase chrysanthemums and geraniums from propagators who culture-index all nucleus stock.

Nematode Diseases

Nematodes are very small round worms sometimes called eelworms. For the most part they cannot be seen by the unaided eye. Nematodes are present in essentially all soils but many of the numerous types are not harmful. Nematode assays of soil samples will quite often reveal the presence of harmful types. It is not until a large population of these types builds up that crop injury occurs (Figure 13-5). Often this does not occur because of natural predators in the soil. Soil pasteurization is the most effective method of eradicating nematodes. There are chemicals which work to varying degrees of success. The following description of nematodes is by Drs. Horst and Williamson.

ROOT KNOT NEMATODE is the most common of the nematode diseases. Infected plants usually appear stunted and unthrifty and tend to wilt on warmer days. When such plants are dug, the root galls are generally conspicuous and easily recognized. The presence of galls does not necessarily indicate crop loss, for with adequate moisture and fertility, infected plants may still grow and produce almost normally.

Six kinds of root knot nematodes are recognized in the United States today. The host ranges and host-parasite relationships may vary, but all have essentially the same life history.

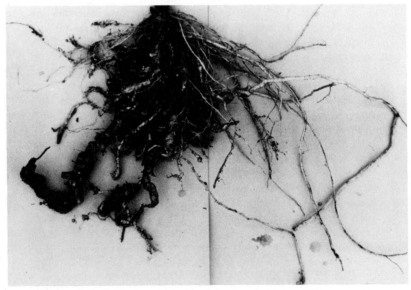

Figure 13-5 Symptoms of root knot nematode on tomato roots. *(From R. K. Jones, Department of Plant Pathology, North Carolina State University, Raleigh, NC 27607)*

LIFE CYCLE. Eggs of root knot nematode (*Meloidogyne*) are about twice as long as wide. These are usually found in a gelatinous mass about the posterior end of the female. Eggs hatch into small, slender worms (larvae) about 1/50 inch long. The larvae migrate through the soil seeking new roots which they enter near the tip. Once inside the root, with its head located in what will become the vascular cylinder, the nematode does not change position. Stimulated by the nematode's saliva, nearby root cells develop into "giant cells" which provide nourishment. Other cells adjacent to the nematode enlarge and increase in number so that the familiar gall or "knot" develops. After the "giant cells" are functioning, the nematode goes through 3 moults (shedding of cuticle), becomes an adult female, and starts the cycle over. A female can lay as many as 2000 eggs during her life, but the average is probably 200 to 500.

The temperature of the soil is critical in the development of the nematode. It takes about 17 days at 85°F for females to develop from infective larvae to egg-laying adults, 21 to 30 days at 76°F, and 57 days at 60°F. Females fail to reach maturity at temperatures above 92°F or below 59°F.

Spread within a greenhouse or a field occurs through movement of infested soil or plant debris by man, water, and possibly wind. Migration of larvae through the soil is limited to perhaps a few feet per year.

CONTROL. There is no known cure for root knot nematodes. With continued care, infected bed or bench plants can produce a good crop. Discard infected potted plants carefully to prevent spreading the nematode. Preplanting treatments of steam or chemicals effectively eliminate nematodes from soil, but be sure that infested crop residues are thoroughly decomposed.

OTHER ROOT-ATTACKING NEMATODES can cause chlorosis, stunted and unthrifty growth of above-ground parts of the plant. Roots can be shortened, thickened, excessively branched to the point of becoming matted, and occasionally killed. Root galls are generally absent except on plants such as those attacked by *Xiphinema*.

Generally these nematodes can be controlled effectively, even after above-ground symptoms are evident, by post-planting chemical treatment with Nemagon®, Fumazone®, and Dasanit® as well as with several other chemicals currently on the market. These have provided safe, effective control on a number of horticultural crops. Although these chemicals have been reported as safe on certain test plants, prudence suggests treating a small number of plants to determine safety before treating the entire crop. Apply only to crops for which use is registered and stated on the labels.

LEAF (FOLIAR) NEMATODES cause leaf spots and defoliation. The spots are first discernable on the lower leaf surface as yellowish or brownish areas that turn eventually almost to black. Although the lesions are small at first, with favorable conditions of temperature and moisture, they may spread until much of the leaf is destroyed. On chrysanthemum the leaf veins retard the spread of the nematodes through the leaf, causing the lesions to be V-shaped or angular. Infection begins on the lower leaves and progresses upward. On *Peperomia,* gloxinia, African violet, and Rieger begonias the lesions are less definite in outline; and infection may occur on any leaf. Unlike other nematodes, foliar nematodes do not persist in the soil in the absence of living host-crop tissues.

DISEASE PREVENTION

The value of root media pasteurization discussed earlier in this book can readily be seen. It also should be apparent that no resistance to pathogen reinfection is imparted to the root medium by pasteurization. A total program of sanitation is needed. Learn to integrate disease control into all of the cultural operations of your business.

Sterilize Pots and Other Containers

All materials which have contacted another crop must be sterilized before coming into contact with the newly pasteurized root medium. In this list of materials are tools, flats, pots, wire or plastic supports for plants, and watering systems. Presented in Table 13-1 are a number of useful disinfectants and items which can be sterilized with each. Care should be taken in using formaldehyde because it burns the skin. Wear gloves and an apron. The bleaches will discolor clothing so again an apron should be worn.

Sterilize Potting Benches

Too often potting benches are used as work and storage benches. Tools, motors, supplies, etc. accumulate. Dirt begins to settle between all this and soon it is impossible to sterilize the bench. Keep the potting bench clear. Sweep it off after each use with a broom maintained just for that purpose. Don't use a broom which is also used on the floor. At the end of each week it is a good idea to swab the bench off with a disinfectant such as LF-10® or bleach.

Isolate Root Media Storage

Bins for holding root media components should be high enough so that ground water does not flow into them. If they are in a location where dust from crop areas can blow into them, they should be covered.

Table 13-1
Common Disinfectants Used in the Greenhouse for
Sterilizing Tools, Containers, and Other Materials That Come
into Contact with Pasteurized Root Media

DISINFECTANT	RATE	APPLICATION
LF-10® or	1 part LF-10 to 100 parts water	Plastic pots—soak for 30 minutes and rinse in water if LF-10® is used
sodium hypochlorite (household bleach)	1 part bleach (5.25% sodium hypochlorite) to 9 parts water	Tools—same as above
		Water system pipes— thoroughly wet with a sponge or rag
		Flexible water tubes—soak for 30 minutes and rinse with water
		Plastic or wire plant supports—syringe (a proportioner may be used)
formaldehyde (formalin)	1 part formalin (40% formaldehyde) to 50 parts water	Flats—soak in solution 30 minutes, rinse and aerate until fumes are gone
		Pots (plastic and clay)— same as above
Copper naphthenate	2% solution in Stoddard solvent (VarSol®)	Wooden benches, wooden flats—paint or dip and wait until dry to use

Avoid Foreign Soil

People will naturally gravitate toward putting one foot on the side wall of a bench when talking or surveying a greenhouse. This should not be done because soil on the bottom of the shoe is scraped off into the bench. Such soil may have originated in another greenhouse range or in someone's garden. The chance of a disease organism being in it is quite high.

Foreign soil will undoubtedly be deposited on the greenhouse floor. One easy way in which it is spread to the bench is by the end of the watering hose. It is a natural impulse to drop the hose on the ground when one is done with it. A hose on the ground picks up soil which is later flushed off all along the bench during watering. If the floor soil is contaminated the whole crop may quickly become infected. A simple inexpensive broom handle clip can be nailed to the side of the bench near the water faucet or a hook can be fashioned out of heavy wire. When turning off the water, the hose end is hung up.

Clean Up Debris

Sometimes a crop may become its own worst enemy. In a weakened state it is more susceptible to a number of pathogens. Plant parts should never be cast where a disease organism can grow and produce inoculum. Poorly rooted cuttings should never be thrown under the bench. When pinching the tops from plants or removing the lateral flower buds (disbudding) never throw these plant parts on the floor. Strap a cloth pouch around your waist for holding plant tissue. Disbud pot mums over a container into which the buds can fall (Figure 13-6). Do not expect employees to always go the extra yard for disease prevention. Devise systems whereby they can operate in accordance with sound principles of sanitation with little or no extra effort.

At the end of each crop there is usually a percentage of plants or flowers left which did not meet the market standards. If another crop is not coming in directly behind that one, it is tempting to leave the reject plants in the bench until all hope of sale is gone. Clean these plants out immediately! They are weak and will become even weaker as they are neglected. They constitute likely tissue to be infected and, once infected, an excellent source of infection for other crops. During spring and fall when evening condensation is common on plants, old flowers invariably become infected with *Botrytis*. It is nearly impossible to eradicate in old flowers.

Plant debris should be placed in a compost pile or dump far enough away from the greenhouse so that soil-borne microorganisms, windblown spores, and insects contained in it cannot make their way back to the greenhouse.

Clean Stock

When you purchase seedlings or cuttings you are relying on the sanitation program of another business. Select your plant sources by their reputation. An occasional pathogen or pest problem can come along with plants from the best of propagators. Inspect each lot of plants. If disease is present, isolate these plants and discard or treat them immediately.

If you propagate your own cuttings maintain a careful preventative disease program on the stock plants. Carefully inspect stock plants before taking cuttings to avoid cuttings from any infected plants. If a knife is used for removing cuttings, periodically dip it in rubbing alcohol to sterilize it. Transport the cuttings in clean containers and work on a sterilized surface. If there is any doubt, keep the cuttings on clean newspaper.

Figure 13-6. A disbudding stand holds the pot mum at working height. As disbuds are removed and dropped, a funnel directs them into a basket. Plant tissue discarded on the floor provides a good host for disease organisms.

Environmental Control

The life cycles of pathogens as discussed earlier suggest cultural procedures for reducing their incidence. Diseases such as *Botrytis* blight depend upon free water on the plant surface for spores to germinate. Free water often occurs as condensation. Warm air holds more water than cold air. During warm fall and spring days the air picks up moisture. Evenings at these times of year are generally cold. As the air cools, its moisture-holding capacity drops until the dew point is reached and water begins to condense on any solid surface.

Condensation can be combated by two methods. Many growers keep the ventilators open an inch or so (or exhaust fans on at low capacity) when the heat comes on in the late afternoon. Cold air enters the greenhouse while warm moist air leaves. The cold, drier air entering is heated and further dried. Then, after 15 or 20 minutes, the ventilators are closed or fans turned off. A warm, dry air now exists in the greenhouse. Moving air in the closed greenhouse is a second step in eliminating water on plant surfaces. The horizontal air flow system or the overhead polyethylene ventilation tube system will minimize temperature differentials and cold spots where condensation is likely to occur.

Mildew is encouraged by high humidity. Ventilating during the early stages of heating and maintaining good air circulation will help control it. Humidity can further be reduced by watering early in the day when the warm air can absorb moisture from wet surfaces.

Spread of root rot and damping off pathogens depends upon mechanical transfer of the root medium in which they reside. Automatic watering helps out here because it minimizes the splashing and lateral transfer of soil associated with hand watering. It also eliminates the use of a nozzle which may periodically touch the root medium along the bench.

A number of the root rot and damping off pathogens are enhanced by high root media moisture levels. A well drained root medium should always be used. Water should be applied only as needed. Too high a frequency encourages development of these diseases.

Weed Control

Weeds harbor insects and disease. The importance of eliminating weeds in and around the greenhouse has already been stressed in Chapter 12. Various weeds can serve as a host for several pathogens which infect greenhouse crops.

FUNGICIDE AND BACTERICIDE RECOMMENDATIONS

Most greenhouse ranges have a regular spray program which in addition to an insecticide and miticide includes a fungicide. By maintaining a fungicidal residue on the plant, establishment of many disease organisms is prevented.

Other crops which are particularly susceptible to soil-borne root rot and damping off diseases and which are grown in an area where such diseases have been a problem can be protected by the use of fungicidal drenches. Dexon® is effective against *Pythium,* Truban® against *Pythium* and *Phytophthora,* benomyl against *Rhizoctonia* and *Thielaviopsis,* and Terraclor® against *Rhizoctonia.* These fungicides are mixed in water and are applied to the root medium in the fashion of a normal watering. Combinations are often used to give a broader spectrum of protection. Benomyl plus Truban$_®$ or Dexon$_®$ plus Terraclor$_®$ are popular combinations. Banrot$_®$ is a commercially available combination. Upon planting, a new crop is drenched with one of these. Bedding plants, poinsettia, and Easter lily are some crops for which this practice is popular.

Listed in Table 13-2 are the more common types of greenhouse diseases and the chemicals which can be used for their control. Diseases attacking specific crops and their control recommendations are listed by crop in Table 13-3.

SUMMARY

1. Categories of pathogens causing plant diseases are viruses, bacteria, fungi, and nematodes.

2. Viruses are the smallest of the pathogenic organisms infecting plants and are similar in size and chemistry to the genetic material (DNA) contained in the nuclei of plant and animal cells. There are no pesticides for controlling viruses and plants neither recover nor become immune to them. Control depends upon procurement of virus-free plants, insect control, and disposal of infected plants. The more common symptoms include: stunting, distortion of leaves or flowers, and spots, streaks, blotches, or rings on leaves with yellow, white, brown, black, or orange discolorations. Viruses are most commonly spread by specific insects or through vegetative propagation by such means as grafting and cuttings.

3. Bacteria are single-celled microorganisms. Bacterial diseases are difficult to control since only a few bactericides exist. Again, control is mainly through elimination of infected plants as well as pasteurization of root media and sterilization of containers and tools. The number of bacterial diseases on greenhouse crops is small in relation to the number of fungal diseases. The more common symptoms of various bacterial diseases are wilting, stem rot, leaf spot, soft rot of cuttings, corms or bulbs, fasciation, and crown gall.

4. Fungal pathogens comprise a large group of multicellular organisms. They are more successfully controlled than other categories of pathogens due to a larger number of effective chemicals known as fungicides. Pasteurization of root media and sterilization of containers and tools also play an important part in control. Some of the most common fungal diseases of greenhouse crops are powdery mildew, *Botrytis* blight, verticillium wilt, and root rots including *Pythium, Rhizoctonia,* and *Thielaviopsis.* Control measures range from the application of fungicides (both topical and systemic) to reduction of free moisture on plants and reduction of high humidity around plants.

Table 13-2
Common Floral Crop Diseases and Chemicals Effective in Their Control*

DISEASE	CHEMICALS FOR CONTROL	REMARKS
Damping Off and Cutting Rots	(1) PCNB (Terraclor®) (2) Benomyl (Benlate®) (3) Diazoben (Dexon®) (4) Ethazol (Truban®, Terrazole®) (5) Captan (6) Ethazol and thiophanate-methyl (Banrot®)	(1) and (2) for *Rhizoctonia* only. (3), (4), and (5) for *Pythium* and *Pythophthora* only. (1) and (5) for pre-plant use. (2) for *Botrytis* rot.
Water Mold Root Rots	(1) Diazoben (Dexon®) (2) Ethazol (Truban®, Terrazole®) (3) Captan (4) Ethazol and thiophanate-methyl (Banrot®)	(3) for preplant use.
Other Root and Stem Rotting Fungi	(1) PCNB (Terraclor®) (2) Ethazol and thiophanate-methyl (Banrot®) (3) Benomyl (Benlate®)	(1) for pre-plant use. (3) for *Botrytis* stem rot.
Wilts	None	Control with good sanitation and clean cuttings.
Leaf and Flower Spotting Fungi	(1) Benomyl (Benlate®) (2) Chlorothalonil (Daconil®, Exotherm Termil®) (3) Captan (4) Maneb (5) Mancozeb (FORE®) (6) Ferbam (7) Zineb	(1) and (2) for *Botrytis* control; (3) through (10) for other diseases; check labels for specific information. Copper may cause plant injury.

	(8) Folpet (Phaltan₎)	(1) For carnation rust only. Check labels for crop
	(9) Ziram	registrations. Frequent application generally neces-
	(10) Fixed coppers	sary with all these materials.
Rusts	(1) Oxycarboxin (Plantvax®)	
	(2) Zineb	
	(3) Ferbam	
	(4) Mancozeb (FORE®)	
Powdery Mildews	(1) Benomyl (Benlate®)	Frequent applications and good coverage essential.
	(2) Cycloheximide (Actidione PM®)	Cycloheximide and sulfur may cause plant injury.
	(3) Piperalin (Pipron®)	
	(4) Parinol (Parnon®)	
	(5) Dinocap (Karathane®)	
	(6) Sulfur	
Bacterial Diseases	(1) Streptomycin (Agri-strep®)	Both materials may cause plant injury.
	(2) Fixed coppers	
Nematodes, Soil	(1) Aldicarb (Temik®)	See description for (1) under insecticide chapter.
	(2) DBCP (Nemagon®)	
	(3) Oxamyl (Vydate®)	
Nematodes, Foliar	(1) Demeton (Systox®)	See description under insecticide chapter.
Viruses	None	Control insects. Rogue infected plants.

*From: C. C. Powell and R. K. Lindquist. "Insect, Mite and Disease Control on Commercial Floral Crops." Cooperative Extension Service. The Ohio State University Bul 538, 1975.

Before purchasing and using any pesticide, check all labels for registered use, rates, and frequency of application.

Table 13-3
Chemical Control Recommendations for Diseases of Floral Crops*

CROP	DISEASE	PESTICIDE & FORMULATION	RATE OF FORMULATION	SCHEDULE & REMARKS
AZALEA	Ovulinia petal blight	zineb 75 W	1 lb/100 gal of water 2 tsp/1 gal of water	Spray 3 times each week during bloom.
		zineb 6 dust	Dust	
		thiram 65 W	1 lb/100 gal of water 2 tsp/1 gal of water	
	Leaf gall	zineb 75 W ferbam 76 W	2 tsp/1 gal 2 tsp/1 gal	Spray just before leaves unroll in spring.
	Phytophthora root rot	ethazole (Truban®, Terrazole®) 30% WP	10 oz/100 gal/400 sq ft or ½ pt/6" pot	Water in immediately after application. Repeat at 4- to 12-week intervals. Effective for disease prevention.
	Parasitic nematodes	DBCP 70.7 EC (Nemagon®, Fumazone®)	2 tsp/sq yd	Drench, follow with additional water to allow penetration to 3 to 5 inches. Repeat every 2 years.
BEGONIA	Powdery mildew	benomyl 50 W (Benlate®)	½ lb/100 gal of water 1 tsp/1 gal of water	Spray every 7 to 14 days.

CARNATION	Botrytis blight	Benlate 50 WP	½ lb/gal or 1 tsp/1 gal	Spray every 7 to 14 days (2 or 3 times per week during wet periods).
	Alternaria blight	zineb 75 W	1½ lb/100 gal water + spreader 2½ tsp/1 gal of water	Spray every 7 days.
		captan 50 W	2 lb/100 gal of water	Spray every 10 days.
	Gray mold (Botrytis)	zineb 75 W	1 lb/100 gal of water 2 tsp/1 gal of water	Spray every 7 to 14 days.
		Daconil 2787 75 W	1 lb/100 gal of water 2 tsp/1 gal of water	
		benlate 50 W	½ lb/100 gal of water 1 tsp/1 gal of water	
		Exotherm Termil	3½ oz/10,000 cu ft	Fumigate every 7 to 14 days.
	Fusarium wilt	steam	180°F for 30 min under tarp	Use disease free plants.
	Fusarium stem rot	benomyl 50 W (Benlate®)	½–1 lb/100 gal water 1–2 tsp/1 gal water	Use disease free plants; spray every 7–14 days; keep humidity low.

(Table 13-3 continued)

429

Table 13-3 continued

CROP	DISEASE	PESTICIDE & FORMULATION	RATE OF FORMULATION	SCHEDULE & REMARKS
CHRYSANTHEMUM	Leaf rust	ferbam 76 W	1½ lb/100 gal water 3 tsp/gal of water	Spray every 7 days beginning when disease first appears.
	Ascochyta ray blight	zineb 75 W	1 tsp/1 gal of water ½ lb/100 gal of water	Spray 2 to 3 times per week as flowers begin to open
	Stemphylium ray speck	Daconil 2787 75 W	1 lb/100 gal of water 2 tsp/1 gal of water	Spray every 7 to 14 days
		Exotherm Termil	3½ oz/10,000 cu ft	Fumigate every 7 to 14 days.
	Gray mold	zineb 75 W	1 lb/100 gal of water 2 tsp/1 gal of water	Spray two to three times per week as flowers begin to open.
		Daconil 2787 75 W	1 lb/100 gal of water 2 tsp/1 gal of water	Spray every 7 to 14 days after disease first appears.
		benomyl (Benlate®) 50 W	½ lb/100 gal of water 1 tsp/1 gal of water	Spray every 7 to 14 days after disease first appears.
		Exotherm Termil	3½ oz/10,000 cu ft	Fumigate every 7 to 14 days after disease first appears.

	Disease	Chemical	Rate	Remarks
	Pythium root rot	Dexon 35 W	1 tsp/4 gal of water	Drench at 10 to 14 day intervals.
	Pythium and root parasitic nematodes	methyl bromide	1 to 2 lb/100 sq ft.	Apply under cover 10 to 14 days prior to planting.
	Rhizoctonia root rot			See Greenhouse Flowering Crops.
GERANIUM	Botrytis blight	benomyl (Benlate®) 50 W	1 tsp/gal	Spray every 7 to 10 days.
	Pythium blackleg	Dexon 35 W	1 tsp/4 gal water	Drench for 20 sq ft; use additional water for penetration 3 to 5 inches. Repeat 10 to 14 days.
	Rust	zineb 75 W	2 tsp/gal water	Spray every 7 to 10 days.
GLADIOLUS	Botrytis foliage blight	zineb 75 W	1½–2 lb/100 gal water 2½–3 tsp/1 gal water	Spray every 7 to 10 days (during wet periods 2–3 days). Add spreader.
	Curvularia leaf spot	zineb 75 W maneb 80 W mancozeb 80 W	1½–2 lb/100 gal water 2½–3 tsp/1 gal water	Same as for Botrytis.
	Fusarium corm rot	Busan 72 EC (10.2 lb/gal)	1 pt/100 gal of water	Soak corms 15 min. Prestorage plus preplant
		benomyl (Benlate®) 50 W	1 lb/100 gal of water	

(Table 13-3 continued)

Table 13-3 continued

CROP	DISEASE	PESTICIDE & FORMULATION	RATE OF FORMULATION	SCHEDULE & REMARKS
		captan 50 W	1 lb/10 gal of water	For homeowners soak corms 20 to 30 min. Prestorage plus pre-plant.
KALANCHOE	Powdery mildew	benomyl (Benlate®) 50 W	½ lb/100 gal water 1 tsp/1 gal water	Spray every 7 to 14 days.
LILY EASTER	Botrytis blight	benomyl (Benlate®) 50 W	½ lb/100 gal water 1 tsp/1 gal water	Spray every 7 to 14 days.
	Rhizoctonia root rot	benomyl (Benlate®) 50 W	½–1 lb/100 gal water 1 tsp/1 gal water ½ pt/6" pot	Drench immediately after planting.
	Pythium root rot	ethazole (Truban®, Terrazole®) 30 W	3–10 oz/100 gal water ½ pt/6" pot	Drench immediately after planting.
		Dexon 35 W	½ lb/100 gal water 1 tsp/1 gal water	
NARCISSUS	Basal rot (Prestorage and/or preplanting)	Mertect 60 W	1½ lb/100 gal water	Soak 15 to 30 min.

POINSETTIA	Botrytis	benomyl (Benlate₍®₎) 50 W	½ lb/100 gal or 1 tsp/1 gal	Spray every 7 to 14 days
	Rhizoctonia root rot and Thielaviopsis root rot	benomyl (Benlate₍®₎) 50 W	½–1 lb/100 gal water 1 tsp/1 gal water ½ pt/6″ pot	Drench immediately after planting.
	Pythium root rot	ethazole (Truban₍®₎, Terrazole₍®₎) 30 W	3–10 oz/100 gal water ½ pt/6″ pot	Drench immediately after planting.
		Dexon 35 W	½ lb/100 gal water 1 tsp/1 gal water	
RHODODENDRON	Phytophthora root rot	ethazole (Truban₍®₎, Terrazole₍®₎) 30 W		See Azalea.
ROSE	Black spot	benomyl (Benlate₍®₎) 50 W folpet 75 W (Phaltan₍®₎) Daconil 2787 75 W Topsin M 70 W	¾ tbsp/2 gal 1 tbsp/gal ¾ tbsp/2 gal ¾ tbsp/2 gal	Every 7 days and twice each week during rainy periods.
	Powdery mildew	benomyl (Benlate₍®₎) 50 W	0.5 lb/100 gal 1 tbsp/2 gal	
		Karathane 75 W	0.5 to 0.75 tsp/2 gal water	

(Table 13–3 continued)

Table 13-3 continued

CROP	DISEASE	PESTICIDE & FORMULATION	RATE OF FORMULATION	SCHEDULE & REMARKS
SNAPDRAGON	Parasitic nematodes	DBCP 70.7 (Nemagon®; Fumazone®)	1 tsp/sq yd	See Azalea.
	Rust or Cercospora leafspot	mancozeb 80 W	1½ lb/100 gal water 1½ tsp/1 gal of water	Spray every 10 to 14 days beginning at first appearance of disease. If severe disease develops spray every 7 days.
ZINNIA	Alternaria leaf spot	captan 50 W maneb 80 W	3 tsp/1 gal of water	Spray every 7 to 10 days after disease appears.
	Powdery mildew	See under Rose		
Greenhouse flowering crops such as CHRYSANTHEMUM GERANIUM POINSETTIA SNAPDRAGON ANNUALS	Damping-off after planting Pythium	Dexon 35 W	1 lb/100 gal for 400 sq ft (8 oz/100 gal at 8 oz/6-inch pot)	Drench as disease appears. Use good soil fertilization before planting and disease free seeds. Sanitation and prevention are most important.
	Rhizoctonia	benomyl (Benlate®) 50 W	1 lb/100 gal	

Plant	Disease	Chemical	Rate	Remarks
Flowering Annuals except SALVIA and CARNATION	Damping-off	methyl bromide	2 lb/100 sq ft	10 to 14 days before planting. Follow cautions on label.
Flowering Annuals	Botrytis blight or gray mold	captan 50 W zineb 75 W Phaltan 75 W benomyl (Benlate®) 50 W	1 tsp/1 gal of water	Spray every 4 to 7 days after disease appears and during wet periods.
	Powdery mildew	benomyl (Benlate®) 50 W	½ lb/100 gal or 1 tsp/1 gal	Spray at first appearance and at 10- to 14-day intervals.

*From: R. K. Jones, D. M. Benson, D. L. Strider, and J. C. Wells. In: North Carolina Agricultural Chemical Manual. School of Agr. & Life Sci., North Carolina State Univ., Raleigh, N.C. 27607, 1977. p. 224–227.

5. Nematode diseases are caused by small round worms generally not visible to the eye. Nematodes abound in all soils with most being harmless. These pests penetrate plant roots causing lack of vigor and stunting of the plant, shortened and thickened roots, and chlorosis of the foliage. Root knot nematodes stimulate the development of giant root cells which develop into galls or knots. Foliar nematodes infect leaves causing yellowish or brownish spots and areas which enlarge and turn darker. Leaf death and sometimes abscission follows. Root knot nematode can only be controlled by discarding infected plants and pasteurizing the root medium. Other root-attacking nematodes can be controlled by post-planting root media applications of such chemicals as Nemagon$_{®}$, Fumazone$_{®}$, and Dasanit$_{®}$.

6. The first, and very often the only, line of defense against diseases is prevention. Purchase disease-free plants by dealing with reputable propagators. Periodically pasteurize all root media and sterilize growing containers and tools. Prevent weed establishment in and around the outside of greenhouses. Clean up plant debris such as pinched-off plant tops and disbuds. Maintain proper air circulating equipment, heating and ventilating practices and watering practices to minimize the occurrence of free water on plants. Above all, keep a constant watch for initial disease development and take appropriate action when it occurs.

7. When disease does get a foothold, follow proper label recommendations for the use of an appropriate bactericide, fungicide, or nematocide. These pesticides fall under the same laws of usage as insecticides and one must adhere strictly to instructions on the label. The same rules of safety apply and similar methods of application are used. Insecticides, miticides, and disease-control chemicals are often applied together.

SUGGESTED READINGS

[In addition to the references listed at the end of Chapter 12, the following are suggested.]

Baker, K. F. "The U. C. System for Producing Healthy Container-Grown Plants." California Agriculture Experiment Station and Extension Service Manual 23. Berkeley, CA 1957. pp. 28–51, 197–216.

Horst, R. K. and P. E. Nelson. "Diseases of Chrysanthemum." N.Y. State College of Agriculture, Cornell University Information Bulletin 85. Ithaca, NY, 1975.

Manning, W. J. *Disease Control for Commercial Plants in Massachusetts.* Florogram 7(2):1–29, 1974.

Nichols, L. P. and O. D. Burke. "Diseases of Commercial Florist Crops." The Penn. State Univ., Col. of Agr., Ext. Ser. Cir. 517, 1963.

Nichols, L. P. and P. E. Nelson. *Diseases. In* Mastalerz, J. W. (ed.) "Bedding plants: a Manual on the Culture of Bedding Plants as a Greenhouse Crop." Pennsylvania Flower Growers, 103 Tyson Bldg., University Park, PA 16802, 1976. pp. 406–422.

Pirone, P. P. *Diseases and Pests of Ornamental Plants.* The Ronald Press Co., New York, 1970.

Chapter 14

Post-Harvest Handling

Unlike potted plants, fresh flowers present a special problem. A fresh flower is still a living specimen even though it has been cut from the plant. Its maximum potential vase life, although acceptable in the marketplace, is short. There are many impinging forces that can interact to reduce fresh flower vase life, that is, the period of time during which fresh flowers possess aesthetic value. As an industry, we have not been highly successful in preserving the potential life of fresh flowers. As mentioned earlier, some 20 percent of harvested fresh flowers become unmarketable as they move through the market channel (harvesting, packaging, transporting, and selling). A very significant proportion of the remaining flowers are sold in a weakened condition which leads to consumer dissatisfaction. Something must be done about poor quality flowers if the fresh flower industry is going to be progressive. Fortunately there are well-known solutions for the bulk of this problem. First, we need to take a look at why there is such a decline in the vase life of fresh flowers.

VASE LIFE

Cultural Influences

Basically, those forces which improve crop quality before and after harvest usually improve vase life. Light intensity is very important. A crop grown under dirty glass or during a period of inclement winter weather, such that light is a limiting factor for photosynthesis, will be low in carbohydrate content. Respiration continues after the flower is harvested but little photosynthesis occurs because light is limited in the packing house, florist shop, and consumer's home. When carbohydrates are low, respiration is very low

439

and flower *senescence* (deterioration) occurs. Optimum light intensity during growth of the crop is very important to vase life.

The time of the day when flowers are harvested can be very important for some crops, for instance, roses. Carbohydrates build up during the day through photosynthesis and reach a peak in late afternoon. During the night carbohydrates are utilized during respiration. Roses cut at 4:30 in the afternoon were found by Howland to last longer than those cut at 8:00 A.M.

Temperature also enters into the picture because it influences photosynthesis and respiration, which in turn influence carbohydrate accumulation. During hot periods of the year, crops sensitive to high temperatures, such as carnations and roses, have shorter vase lives because flowers contain low carbohydrate levels. When the temperature is raised to an adversely high level to force earlier flowering, the same problem occurs.

The nutrition of the crop likewise has an effect on flower longevity. Shortages or toxicities of nutrients that retard photosynthesis will reduce vase life. Deficiencies in a number of nutrients, including nitrogen, calcium, magnesium, iron, and manganese, result in a reduction in the chlorophyll content, which in turn reduces photosynthesis. The net result is a low carbohydrate supply for the flower. On the other hand, high levels of nitrogen at flowering time can have an adverse effect on keeping quality, particularly for carnations and roses.

Diseases and insects reduce the vigor of the plant, directly reducing vase life. Diseases also reduce vase life indirectly: injured tissue releases large quantities of ethylene gas, which hastens senescence or deterioration of the flower.

Cause of Vase Life Decline

Fresh flowers deteriorate for one or more reasons. Five of the most common reasons for early senescence are:

1. Inability of stems to absorb water due to blockage.

2. Excessive water loss from the cut flower.

3. A short supply of carbohydrate to support respiration.

4. Diseases.

5. Ethylene gas.

Inability to absorb water is a very common reason for premature wilting. The water-conducting tubes in the stem (*xylem*) become plugged. Bacteria, yeast, and/or fungi living in the water or on the flower foliage proliferate in the containers holding the flowers. These microorganisms and their chemical products plug the stem ends, restricting water absorption. They continue to multiply inside and eventually block the xylem tubes (Figure 14-1). Chemical blockage also can occur. Chemicals present in some stems, upon cutting, change into a gum-like material which blocks the end of the stem. This material is suspected to be composed of oxidized tannins in some plants and in others it is unidentified.

Excessive water loss from flowers can lead to wilting and reduction in quality and vase life. After harvest, flowers should be removed from the field or greenhouse and refrigerated as soon as possible. Leaving the flowers out of water, in warm air or in warm drafts such as from a heater, causes considerable damage. Flowers should be in water and under cool temperatures as much as possible from the time they are cut until they reach the final consumer.

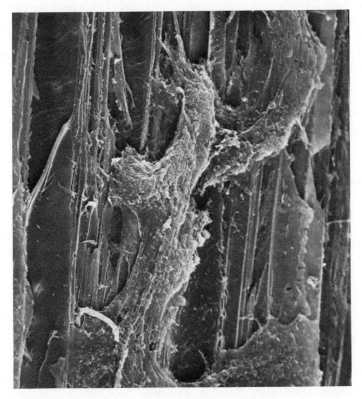

Figure 14-1. A longitudinal section (1,500 X magnification) of a rose stem showing the interior of water-conducting cells and a slime plug blocking some of the cells. Such slime plugs can be composed of microorganisms, particularly bacteria, and solidified compounds from the flower itself. *(Photo courtesy of H. P. Rasmussen, Department of Horticulture, Michigan State University, E. Lansing, MI 48824)*

Low carbohydrates are another reason for flower deterioration. A low carbohydrate supply can occur as a result of improper storage temperatures and handling. Respiration continues to be governed by temperature after harvest. Low temperatures reduce respiration and conserve carbohydrates, thereby prolonging quality and vase life. Each of the many stages in the marketing channel must be watched. Flowers should be placed in cold storage as soon after harvesting as possible. They should be refrigerated during surface transport and during holding periods at the wholesaler and retailer. Serious damage occurs when flowers are left on a heated loading dock at the motor or air freight terminal or when they are left sitting in a hot warehouse for a day or so.

The harmful effects of disease and pests, as well as the effect of ethylene, have already been pointed out. Fruits, especially apples, give off large quantities of ethylene gas, making it inadvisable to store lunches containing fruits in coolers. It has already been mentioned that ethylene is evolved from plant tissue, particularly injured and old plant tissue. The cooler should be kept clean of plant debris such as cut stems and leaves that might accumulate on the floor. Old unsalable flowers should be discarded.

Ethylene gas has many deleterious effects. Generally it causes premature deterioration of flowers. It also causes sleepiness (the upward cupping of petals) of carnation flowers; this gives the flower an appearance of wilting, but the phenomenon is not reversible.

Preservatives for Extending Vase Life

Considerable research has been conducted over the past 25 years to find a preservative solution which will combat some of the causes of deterioration and reduction of vase life. One of the earliest home remedies called for table sugar (sucrose) plus aspirin, and sometimes a penny was added to the vase to provide copper as a bactericide. Another remedy used carbonated lemon soft drinks containing sugar. There is some value in these remedies, but aspirin is not readily soluble and the penny is essentially insoluble. Hence, the remedies supply sugar but do not control microbial growth.

Floral preservatives perform three functions: (1) they provide sugar (carbohydrate), (2) they supply a bactericide to prevent microbial growth and blockage of the water conductive cells in the stem, and (3) they acidify the solution. The latter function suppresses bacterial development and, through some unknown process, prevents wilting of flowers. It is suspected that the acidity helps prevent chemical blockage.

Various universities and the U.S. Department of Agriculture have developed successful preservatives (Figure 14-2). The most popular preservatives today contain 8-hydroxquinoline citrate (8-HQC) and sucrose (common table sugar). Listed in Table 14-1 are preservative formulas for five fresh

Figure 14-2. Floral preservative trials on gladiolus flowers. The flower on the left is in water and the one on the right is in a preservative containing 600 ppm 8-hydroxyquinaline citrate plus 4 percent sucrose. *(Photo courtesy of F. J. Marousky, U.S. Department of Agriculture, Agricultural Research Service, Bradenton, FL 33505)*

flowers. The 8-HQC is a bactericide and an acidifying agent. In addition to suppressing bacterial development and lowering the pH, 8-HQC also prevents chemical blockage, thus aiding in the absorption of water. Sucrose taken up by the stem maintains quality and turgidity and extends vase life by supplementing the carbohydrate supply.

There are a number of commercial preservatives on the market, including such products as Floralife®, Petalife®, Oasis®, Rogard®, and Everbloom®. These work well. One can also purchase 8-HQC under the name oxine citrate from florist supply companies and add sucrose to make the preservatives listed in Table 14-1.

Floral preservatives are very effective in maintaining quality and extending longevity. On the average, they can double the vase life of cut flowers when compared to water. Snapdragons with a life expectancy of five to six days last up to twelve days in preservative. The life expectancy of roses can be extended from three to five days to seven to ten days. Carnations with a vase life expectancy of five days, after extensive shipping, have been shown to last twelve days in preservatives.

REFRIGERATED STORAGE

The most common system for handling harvested flowers is refrigerated storage, which involves the following sequential steps:

1. Flower stems should be cut with a sharp knife or shears to prevent crushing of stem and water-conduction cells.

2. The cut flowers should be placed in a preservative solution as soon as possible to prevent wilting. The flowers should not be allowed to be out of water while they are waiting to be transferred to the storage or grading rooms. If cut in the field, buckets containing solution can be brought out on trailers to hold the harvested flowers. Flowers cut in the greenhouse should not be left in the sun or out of water for more than a few minutes. One person should be assigned to carry these flowers to the grading room or storage cooler immediately. One chrysanthemum grower has installed a conveyor system to carry cut flowers to the grading room.

Table 14-1.
Floral Preservative Formulas for Five Fresh Flowers.

FLOWER	8-HQC		SUCROSE	
	Oz/10 Gal	ppm	Oz/10 Gal	%
Gladiolus	0.80	600	54	4
Carnation	0.27	200	27	2
Chrysanthemum*	0.27	200	27	2
Rose	0.27	200	27–42	2–3
Snapdragon	0.41	300	20	1.5

*Use this formula for other flowers in general.

3. As soon as flowers arrive at the storage room they should be placed in preservative solution inside the refrigerated storage room. If wilted, they should be placed in a warm preservative solution at room temperature until turgid. They should then be placed in the cooler.

4. The temperature of the refrigerated room should be 33-40°F. The lower the temperature, the better, because the respiration rate falls off with diminishing temperature. Low respiration rates have an effect similar to that resulting from adding sucrose to the preservative solution in that they conserve carbohydrates within the flower. A temperature range of 35-40°F is usually encountered in flower coolers. Special attention should be paid to some flowers, such as orchids and gardenias, which cannot withstand low temperatures. If Catteleya orchids are stored below 50°F, they will show signs similar to frost injury (petal browning).

5. Air should be gently circulated inside the cooler only to the extent necessary to insure uniform temperatures in all areas. Unprotected flowers placed in a direct air stream will be desiccated. Flowers immediately adjacent to a cooling coil may freeze even though the air temperature is above freezing. Since the coil itself is below the freezing point, radiant heat is lost from the flower to the coil, and the flower can be colder than the surrounding air.

6. Potential sources of ethylene gas should be avoided by keeping fruit and vegetables out of the cooler. Discard old flowers. Wash the inside of the cooler periodically.

7. Replace the preservative solution at two to seven day intervals. The preservative should be checked periodically for bacterial growth, which is apparent when the solution becomes cloudy. In spite of the bactericides in preservatives, microorganisms will develop and need to be eliminated periodically. To accomplish this, wash the buckets with a disinfectant such as bleach or LF-10®.

Refrigerated storage goes beyond this point, but from here on it becomes difficult to insure that it is carried out properly. The flowers are now sold to a wholesaler who in turn sells them to a retail shop. These people should continue to preserve the quality you have worked hard to maintain. The wholesaler and retailer should hold the flowers under refrigeration as you have. Whenever possible flowers should be transported under refrigeration. Needless delays at shipping terminals should be avoided. Instruct the wholesaler and retailer to cut one-half inch from the base of the stems whenever it has been necessary to leave the flowers out of water for a period of time and then to place them in warm water at a cool air temperature to avoid the ends of the stems drying out and restricting water movement.

Many growers, wholesalers, and retailers are of the opinion that these procedures, particularly the use of floral preservatives, are not necessary. Undoubtedly they have partial evidence to support their view. However, if they could look at the whole market channel they would realize they are wrong. It is too late for the retailer to get maximum effectiveness from a preservative if the grower or the wholesaler has failed to use one. Flowers left to wilt in the greenhouse while others are cut have already lost a significant portion of their quality and longevity. Precautions taken after that time will have diminished effects and at times may appear to be without effect. Very often, abusive handling is the main culprit to flower deterioration.

DRY STORAGE

Flowers can be held in refrigerated storage for one to three weeks depending on the species. Refrigerated storage is more generally used as an aid for maintaining quality as flowers pass through the market channel. Dry storage is used when flowers must be held for periods longer than one to five days. Roses may be held in dry storage up to 18 days, chrysanthemums and carnations up to three weeks, and rooted cuttings of chrysanthemums and carnations for as long as six weeks. Gladioluses do not store well.

Flower prices depend to a great degree upon market demand. Prices are high at holidays, but flowers cannot always be scheduled to bloom at each holiday. Dry storage offers a means of holding flowers without deterioration for a high priced holiday market.

Only the best quality flowers should be dry stored. Those of poor quality will have a short vase life if any at all when they are removed from storage. Flowers should be cut and packaged for storage immediately without placing them in water. Standard cardboard flower boxes are suitable, but a lining of polyethylene film should be placed in it to cover the flowers and seal in moisture (Figure 14-3). Desiccation can be a problem in long-term storage, especially when an absorbent container such as cardboard is used.

A common problem of dry storage is the presence of free water on the flowers which encourages the development of disease. While flowers freeze only at temperatures below 29°F, the free water will freeze at 32°F. Resulting ice crystals on the petals can be injurious. Boxes and flowers packed at warm temperatures develop condensation (free water) as the plants and air inside are cooled. Because of the polyethylene barrier, the water cannot escape. Disease, enhanced by this moisture, is a common cause of failure in dry storage. Boxes of flowers should be cooled open in a 38-40°F cooler, then sealed and placed in a 31°F cooler.

Most flowers freeze at 27-29°F, so it is essential that the temperature stay above this point. Flower life expectancy is lessened at 33°F and drops rapidly at temperatures above that point. Many of the failures of this system have been due to high temperatures or fluctuating temperatures. Since the

Figure 14-3. Bunches of pompon chrysanthemums being packed in a poly-ethylene cardboard carton. The polyethylene will be placed over the flowers, the lid placed on the box, and then it will be stored at 31°F for a period up to three weeks. *(Photo courtesy of F. J. Marousky, U.S. Department of Agriculture, Agricultural Research Service, Bradenton, FL 33505)*

dry storage cooler should not be opened too often, another cooler is needed for regular refrigerated storage. The 31°F cooler is often built inside the 35-40°F cooler to provide for a more uniform temperature.

Space should be left between boxes of flowers when they are placed in storage initially. Respiration is occurring, and this produces heat. A large stack of boxes can generate enough heat and provide sufficient insulation to prevent thorough cooling of the inner flowers. Leave space between each stack of boxes and between every other box in a stack to permit the absorption of heat by circulating cool air.

Flowers removed from dry storage need to be hardened. Cut one-half inch from the bottom of each stem. Place the flower in a preservative solution inside a 38-40°F cooler. Allow the flowers to become fully turgid before marketing them; this will take 12 to 24 hours. When properly handled, dry stored flowers should have reasonable quality and the same longevity as fresh flowers. Poor temperature control or disease will decrease quality and longevity.

Dry storage is used only to a limited degree by the industry and works best with chrysanthemums. Chrysanthemums, carnations, and roses are the crops to which it is primarily applied. Much more potential exists here than is being realized. The main reason for its low level of acceptance has probably been failures due to inept handling of the system.

BUD HARVESTING

Bud harvesting is a procedure that is used infrequently but is fairly well proven and has a tremendous potential. Carnations and chrysanthemums can be harvested and shipped in the bud stage, which cuts down greatly on their volume and hence lowers the cost of shipping. The wholesaler may then store the buds or open them immediately for resale. Once open, the flower has at the least the same vase life potential as a flower cut mature.

Bud harvesting enables a grower to produce more crops per year in his greenhouse space. He must, of course, either provide space for opening these buds himself or pass along part of his production savings to the wholesaler or retailer, who now must provide facilities and time for opening the buds. In any event, there is a significant increase in net return to the grower.

There are other advantages to this system. Buds are more immune to handling injuries and ethylene toxicity, making a higher quality final product possible. As in the case of mature harvested flowers, buds will dry store very well, enabling one to build up his inventory for higher-priced market dates. Bud harvesting is not a new concept for all crops, since roses, gladiolus, iris, tulips, peony, etc., have always been cut in the bud stage.

Carnations are cut when one-half to one inch of petal color is showing (Figure 14-4). Standard chrysanthemums are cut when the buds are two inches in diameter. Buds at this stage can be placed directly into dry storage or they can first be shipped dry under ice or refrigeration in a box and then be put into dry storage. When needed, buds are removed from the storage box, one-half inch of stem is cut off, and they are placed in a floral preservative solution. The buckets of buds are held in an opening room at 70-75°F until the buds are fully open. A low light intensity is provided in the opening room. Carnation buds open in two to three days and chrysanthemum buds in seven to nine days. The open flowers may be held under refrigeration in the preservative solution or they may be sold directly. The quality and longevity of these flowers has been reported to be superior to those harvested at maturity.

Bud harvesting will become important in the future. Growers who ship flowers great distances, across North America or from other countries, will recognize the value and find it necessary to use this system. Greater cooperation among growers, wholesalers, and retailers will be needed.

THE FUTURE

We can look for some very fascinating developments in the future with regard to post-harvest handling. For some time now, fruit has been stored in "controlled atmosphere" (CA) systems. Crisp, fresh apples stored from

(b)

Figure 14-4. (a) Carnation buds cut at three stages of maturity: (left) petals just showing, (center) one-quarter inch of petals showing, and (right) three-quarters inch of petals showing. (b) The same buds after three days in an opening solution. The youngest buds will require seven to eight days total opening time, the intermediate buds four to five days, and the oldest buds three days. The oldest buds are ready for retail use after three days in the opening solution. For greatest efficiency of growing and post-harvest handling time, the buds should be harvested when three-quarters inch of petals is showing. *(Photos courtesy of F. J. Marousky, U.S. Department of Agriculture, Agricultural Research Service, Bradenton, FL 33505)*

September to June are the products of this system. The merits of the system in relation to flower storage are being tested. In such a system flowers would be stored at low temperatures in an atmosphere very low in oxygen (1–3 percent) and high in CO_2 (2–5 percent). The low oxygen and high CO_2 levels further reduce the rate of respiration.

Hypobaric (low pressure) storage is a much newer idea. Fruits, vegetables, or flowers are placed in a sealed chamber and a vacuum is established in the chamber down to a pressure of about 50 mm of mercury. The chamber is constructed to maintain a vacuum, yet allow fresh air to be swept through it. The chamber is also cooled to a low temperature. As the chamber is evacuated, the oxygen content is reduced to a level which sharply reduces respiration. Ethylene gas evolved by the plant tissue is quickly removed by the flowing air.

Controlled atmosphere and hypobaric storage have not proven themselves to be practical in the floriculture industry yet, but there is tentative evidence that these systems might play a role in the future of floriculture. More testing is needed before low pressure storage is realized.

SUMMARY

1. The five common factors which reduce vase life of harvested fresh flowers are: (1) the inability of stems to absorb water due to blockage by microbial organisms or solidified chemicals; (2) excessive water loss from the cut flower; (3) a low supply of carbohydrate to support respiration; (4) the presence of pathogenic diseases; and (5) ethylene gas derived particularly from fruit or from injured and deteriorating plant material.

2. Maximum vase life potential is achieved by producing high quality flowers rich in carbohydrate; preventing the occurrence of diseases before and after harvest; harvesting at the proper stage; placing flowers in a floral preservative immediately upon cutting and maintaining them in such a preservative throughout the marketing channel; keeping cut flowers at a low temperature (33–40°F) whenever possible during handling and marketing; and preventing the build-up of ethylene gas around stored flowers by removing injured and old plant material and keeping fruit out of the storage cooler.

3. Floral preservatives can double the vase life of fresh flowers when compared to water. Generally they provide sugar to supplement the carbohydrate supply in the flower, a bactericide, and an acidifying agent which suppresses bacterial development in the storage water. Sucrose (table sugar) is a common source of sugar and 8-hydroxyquinoline citrate is often used as the bactericide and acidifying agent.

4. Refrigerated storage of flowers in preservative solution works well for periods of a few days, as is often necessary during the marketing period.

Dry storage of flowers can be used when they must be held for longer periods—up to 18 days for roses and three weeks for chrysanthemums and carnations. Freshly cut, turgid flowers are placed in polyethylene-lined cartons without water, and the cartons are held in a 31°F cooler. Flowers stored in this manner have essentially the same longevity after removal as flowers handled in the more conventional manner.

5. Some flowers such as roses, iris, and tulips have traditionally been cut in the bud stage, while others such as carnation and chrysanthemum are customarily harvested in an open stage. These latter crops can also be harvested in the bud stage with a considerable reduction in the culture time required in the greenhouse. Harvested buds may be shipped and/or stored at this stage. Ultimately, they are placed in an opening solution, similar to a floral preservative, at room temperature. Carnation buds open in two to three days, and chrysanthemum buds open in seven to nine days. A savings in production expense and shipping cost can be realized and less injury is sustained during shipping.

SUGGESTED READINGS

Ball, V. *The Ball Red Book.* George J. Ball, Inc. W. Chicago, IL, 1975.

Carpenter, W. J., and D. R. Dilley. *Investigations to Extend Cut Flower Longevity.* Michigan Agricultural Experiment Station Research Report 263, 1975.

Kofranek, A. M., and A. H. Halevy. "Conditions for Opening Cut Chrysanthemum Flower Buds." *Journal of American Society Horticultural Science* 97(5):578–584, 1972.

Marousky, F. J. "New Methods for Improving Keeping Quality for Gladiolus, Roses and Chrysanthemums." *Florists' Review.* 145(3770) 67, 116–119, 1970.

Mastalerz, J. W., and R. W. Langhans. Roses: A Manual on the Culture, Management, Diseases, Insects, Economics and Breeding of Greenhouse Roses. (See Chapter 19, Post-Harvest Life, by J. W. Boodley and Chapter 20, Low Temperature Dry Storage, by J. W. Mastalerz.) Pennsylvania Flower Growers, New York State Flower Growers' Association, Inc., and Roses Inc, 1969. Available from: R. W. Langhans, Department of Floriculture and Ornamental Horticulture, Cornell University, Ithaca, NY 14850.

Robertson, J. L., and G. L. Staby. "Economic Feasibility of Once-over Bud Harvest of Standard Chrysanthemums." *HortScience* 11(2):159–160, 1976.

Staby, G. L., J. L. Robertson, D. C. Kiplinger, and C. A. Conover. Procedures of National Floricultural Conference on Commodity Handling. Ohio Florists' Association, 2001 Fyffe Ct., Columbus, OH 43210, 1976.

Chapter 15

Marketing

There is as much science, technology, and art applied to floral crops after harvest as before. Storage, packaging, transportation, design, advertising, marketing, and servicing can all be involved in flower or plant handling after harvest. The input can be sufficiently great to justifiably raise the final retail price to as much as several times the level of the wholesale price. Failure to properly market a crop can negate the efforts which have gone into producing a quality crop.

Marketing actually begins with the planning of the crop. It entails a market demand evaluation to insure that the correct crops, sizes, colors, and so forth are grown to meet market needs. Cultural schedules are developed to finish the crop at a potentially profitable time. All too often growers become concerned entirely with maximizing the use of bench space and lose sight of the market demand and selling price of the crop. Once a crop is properly planned, the more obvious steps of marketing begin at harvest time.

PACKAGING

It requires skill to harvest fresh flowers at the proper stage of maturity. This is a topic covered in detail in books on flower crop production and it will not be discussed here. It is sufficient to note that, with the exception of roses, there is a degree of latitude in the stage of development at which the flower must be cut. The exact stage depends upon the length of time and type of handling in the market channel. European and Colombian carnations are often harvested in a tight stage (with guard petals upright) to facilitate shipping and lengthen home life. Carnations grown for local consumption are generally harvested open (guard petals horizontal or lower) to minimize handling time. Standard chrysanthemums can be similarly harvested in the bud stage, as described in the previous chapter.

453

Floral products are packaged in conventional unit sizes. Roses and carnations are packaged in bunches of 25 while the number is 10 for standard chrysanthemums, snapdragons, gladioli, tulip, daffodil, iris, and most other fresh flowers. Pompon chrysanthemums are bunched according to weight with 9 ounces being common. Generally the stems are 30 inches long and not less than 5 stems are included in a bunch. The weight of the bunch varies with different growers. Bunches of fresh flowers are often placed in a plastic sleeve to protect the blooms and the stem ends are bound with an elastic or string. Bunches so wrapped are placed in cardboard containers for refrigerated storage or shipping. Colors are not mixed in individual bunches nor are the types of flowers mixed within a carton. Different colored bunches are conventionally mixed within the carton in whatever proportion they are produced. The wholesaler and retailer are expected to take them in this ratio to guarantee a market for all. Communication is required between grower and wholesaler for the system to work.

Potted plants are usually sold individually to full service florists. Some of the larger suppliers of mass markets package pot plants in cardboard cartons in varietal proportion so they can be more easily stacked in trucks, handled, and inventoried, especially if distributed from the central warehouse of a chain store.

Potted plants are often placed in a plastic or paper sleeve just prior to shipping. The sleeve compacts the foliage reducing the amount of valuable shipping space required by the plant. It also protects the plant from damage during handling. Some growers take advantage of the sleeve as a strategic place to advertise their company and to offer cultural suggestions.

Packaging will play a very important role in the future, particularly for those growers servicing the mass market. Plants are already being marketed in complete enclosures which nearly eliminate evaporation and the need to water them during the period of marketing. The container consists of clear plastic for viewing the plant and for transmission of light for photosynthesis. Some make use of cardboard for the frame, a handle, and a place to advertise. Fresh flowers also may be packaged to prolong shelf life. Such packaging enables control of the atmosphere within and extends life. The location of packaging (grower, wholesaler, retailer) will depend upon comparative costs and returns of the alternatives. This is a fertile area the grower should look into.

GRADES AND STANDARDS

There has been considerable controversy over grading. Opponents cite hidden factors such as the increased cost of handling. Proponents see grading as a means of discouraging poor quality in the marketplace and achieving financial remuneration for quality. It could also go a long way toward nurturing consumer satisfaction.

Most fresh flower producers use a grading system. But one problem is the diversification of grading systems among growers and even the shifting of standards by an individual grower as average flower sizes change throughout the year. If grades could be standardized for all growers it would be a great benefit for wholesalers and retailers. Ultimately, that which benefits the market system and consumer usually brings benefits to the grower.

As discussed earlier, fresh flower production is in a slump. The problem is one of quality and price. Standardized grading could give both the marketer and consumer a means for judging and demanding the quality they are willing to pay for. It would give the grower a tangible objective and measuring stick for achieving a better product. Greater consumer satisfaction should lead to increased product demand. Higher quality production and handling would help reduce flower loss in the market channel, which could be helpful in reducing the final selling price of flowers. Obviously, marketers must get involved in this aspect also.

Grading standards thus far developed are for fresh flowers. Although a single national set of standards has not been established for roses, nearly all growers grade by stem length. Increments of two, three, or four inches are used to separate grades, with the most common being three inches beginning at a minimum length of nine inches. Flowers with weak stems, blemished foliage, off-color blooms, or bullhead blooms are sold as a utility grade. The Society of American Florists has been instrumental in developing grades for carnations (Table 15-1).

Grades and standards have not been developed for potted plants in either the flowering or green plant categories. Green plants in particular should be graded to protect the consumer as well as the grower of quality plants. Green plants are grown in a favorable environment relatively rich in nutrients and sunlight. They are then utilized, hopefully for many years, in a rather marginal indoor environment. A period of acclimatization must be provided by the grower for these plants to make the transition successfully. Acclimatization can be costly since it entails a period of slow growth when nutrients and light are reduced. Growers who do not acclimatize their crops may realize a profit in the short run, but in the long run the industry is hurt by consumer dissatisfaction. Standards for green plants should take into account such handling so that it is encouraged and rewarded.

When the grower has finished grading and packing his fresh flowers or potted plants it is generally his task to ship them to the wholesaler or retailer. Green plants are an exception as they are often shipped by the grower at the retailer's expense or are picked up directly by the wholesaler or retailer.

Table 15-1.
Society of American Florists' Standards for Carnation Grades[a]

	BLUE GRADE (FANCY) (1)	RED GRADE (STANDARD) (2)	GREEN GRADE (SHORT) (3)
Minimum length[b] (in)	22	17	12
Minimum flower[c] diameter (in)	Tight[d] 2	1-3/4	No requirement
	Fairly Tight 2-1/2	2-1/4	
	Open 3	2-3/4	

[a]Flowers in the blue, red and green grades should be full, symmetrical, free of insect, disease, mechanical injury, and free of bloom defects such as slab side, bullhead, blow heads, singles, sleepy appearance, splits, and discoloration. The stems should be of sufficient strength so that they do not deviate more than thirty degrees from the horizontal plane when held one inch above the minimum length of the grade with the natural curvature down. Any flowers with these defects are either sold at a lower price or are discarded.

[b]Length measured from top of bloom to cut end of stem.

[c]The flower diameter is the greatest dimension of the petals measured through the center of the bloom. The guard petals of open blooms are held horizontal when determining size.

[d]*Tight*—guard petals up, center petals up but fluffed. *Fairly Tight*—guard petals horizontal, center petals up and fluffed. *Open*—guard petals are horizontal or lower, center petals are out or down.

THE MARKET SYSTEM

Consumers exist wherever people live—in the cities, towns, and villages scattered throughout the states and provinces of this continent. Floral production, on the other hand, is more centralized. This is particularly true of the fresh flower industry. The heaviest concentration of gladiolus comes from Florida, carnations from Colorado and California, spray-type chrysanthemums from Florida and California. The trend is not as well established for flowering plants, but the vast majority of green plants come from Florida and California. Under such circumstances a complex marketing system is necessary (Figure 15-1).

The marketing system serves the functions of gathering together the various floral products of many diverse growers, of bringing these within reach of consumers both close and distant to the producers, and of developing a consumer awareness and desire to purchase the floral products.

Fresh Flowers

The floral marketing system has several components to it. There are a number of possible channels within the system. Fresh flowers pass through

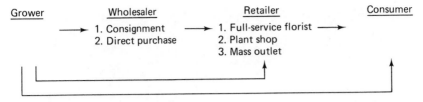

Figure 15-1. Channels through which fresh flowers flow from the grower to the final consumer.

the most extensive channel, thus providing us with a good overview of the whole system. Customarily, fresh flowers pass from the grower to a wholesaler. Often the wholesaler is a *commission* wholesaler, one who takes flowers on consignment. This means that the grower is paid for those which the wholesaler sells but not for those which he fails to market. The commission wholesaler sells the flowers at a wholesale price and then takes his commission of about 25 percent from this price, returning the remainder to the grower.

More recently a trend has been developing for wholesalers to buy flowers outright from the grower. This system is more expedient where flowers are produced in mass in an area and wholesaled at a great distance away. Although the wholesaler appears to assume all the risk, this is not the case. Flower losses can be reflected in lower prices for the grower or higher prices to the consumer. The latter affects consumer demand, which hurts the grower.

Wholesalers sell flowers to retailers. Some retailers travel to the wholesale house to make their purchases while others are serviced by trucks operated by the wholesaler. Wholesale florists quite often stock supplies needed by retail florists. Included are such items as ribbon, net, vases, wreaths, etc. which are used in the daily operation of a full-service retail flower shop. The inventory may be larger, including plastic flower arrangements and giftwares to be sold directly by the retail florist.

Most of the sales are made over the phone by salespeople employed by the wholesale florist. When the orders are filled, the remaining space on the truck is filled with flowers and merchandise which will probably be sold along the route (Figure 15-2). Each florist is generally serviced twice a week, often by more than one wholesaler. These truck routes serve a very valuable role for retail florists who are located in remote areas. The wholesale florist likewise plays a valuable role for the retail florist near transportation facilities. The wholesaler brings together hundreds of items from numerous sources for the retailer's use. This saves the retailer considerable time and expense as well as the problem of overstocking on items which must be purchased in case lots and soon become outdated. The wholesaler makes it his business to keep abreast of changing tastes in supplies which further benefits the retailer.

Figure 15-2. The interior of a wholesaler's truck used for delivering fresh flowers and potted plants to full-service retail florists. Although not common, a small refrigerated room for fresh flowers is located at the forward part of this truck.

There are various types of retailers as anyone who purchases flowers or plants is well aware. Traditionally we think of the full-service florist where there is a designer to arrange flowers and an available delivery service. Plant shops and flower boutiques are becoming more numerous. These are cash-and-carry outlets where plants and flowers may be purchased. Sometimes simple arrangements of flowers are offered, mainly for home decoration, but delivery service is not provided. A number of full-service florists operate such shops as well. Mass market retail outlets have become a very large business. Close to half of the production of the United States passes through these outlets. These are the cash-and-carry stands, wagons, mini shops, etc. which are located in high traffic areas within supermarkets, department stores, discount stores, shopping malls, airports, and on street corners. The markup is generally 30 to 40 percent. Therefore, when a plant sells for $1.00, the mass market outlet retains $0.30 to $0.40 while the grower receives $0.60 to $0.70.

An often misunderstood subtlety exists between two systems for setting the retail price. *Mark-up* refers to a percentage of the retail price while *mark-on* relates to a percentage of the wholesale price. To illustrate the difference, assume that you as a grower receive $1.00 each for your potted plants. One retail outlet using a 33 percent mark-up charges its customers $1.50 per plant. $1.00 (wholesale price) $\div$ (1 − 0.33) = $1.49. A second outlet using a 33 percent mark-on charges $1.33 per plant. (1.33 × $1.00 (wholesale price) = $1.33.)

FLOWERING PLANTS

Flowering plants, as a rule, are sold directly to retail outlets by growers. Flowering plant growers are generally situated near population centers. Long distance transportation does not enter into the picture as extensively as in the fresh flower case. The typical flowering plant grower would operate one or more trucks for delivery purposes. He operates his own sales department. Plants are generally delivered within 100 miles. There has been a feeling in the past that potted plants are too heavy to transport the distances fresh flowers are shipped. To a degree this is true in that potted plants cannot be shipped by air as many of the fresh flowers are. However, in recent years some very large pot plant ranges have developed to supply the mass market. Such ranges successfully deliver plants 500 miles and more by truck. Insulated trucks are used which are heated in winter and cooled in summer.

Green Plants

Green plants are produced mainly in Florida and California which dictates the need for a marketing system as described for fresh flowers. Often, the wholesaler turns out to be a grower operating in close proximity to the retail market. While the basic line of green plants are tropicals which in spite of transportation are most economically produced in subtropical regions, there are some that can be produced economically in close proximity to the market. The local grower-wholesaler business combination allows the flexibility needed to develop this potential.

The wholesaler trucks the plants from Florida or California to his greenhouse range where he holds them until he can market them to retailers along his truck routes. The greenhouse is necessary for holding these plants since a considerable length of time may pass before some are sold. The greenhouse also affords an opportunity to supplement the line of plants with some which can be produced more profitably than bought. There are yet other plants which are purchased in early stages of growth and finished locally. The grower-wholesaler business combination is working out well for the green plant industry.

Direct Sales

Locally produced fresh flowers are in high demand when produced continuously throughout the year and at a high level of quality. There is some effort on the part of retailers to trade directly with such sources. With a modest effort, a grower can establish his market without passing through the wholesaler. This system is used particularly by smaller growers.

New growers of fresh flowers and more often of potted plants sometimes sell directly to the final consumer. This allows them to enter into two businesses for little more overhead than that of the growing operation. Funds are generated faster this way. This system works well when the extra labor can be provided by the owner assuming that there is not a more profitable use for his labor at the time. This is at best a temporary system and soon a decision must be made as to whether to operate one or both businesses.

There are a number of large full-service retail outlets operating their own production ranges. This is becoming even more popular among some of the mass market retailers. Care must be taken to keep separate records on each business, lest one should exist at the expense of the other. Quite often the retail outlet is the more successful of the two, in which case it might be better to purchase flowers and plants from elsewhere.

Flower Auctions

Flower auctions exist where there is concentrated production some distance away from the retail market. The Dutch flower auctions are perhaps the most famous (Figure 15-3). Flower production, concentrated in a few regions of an already small nation of The Netherlands, supplies retail markets throughout Europe. To make the distribution system efficient, growers send fresh flowers and plants to an auction where they are purchased by wholesalers who in turn distribute them to retailers throughout Europe. This adds an extra link between the grower and the wholesaler in the distribution chain illustrated in Figure 15-1 but in so doing it brings wholesalers into contact with hundreds of growers who would otherwise be unreachable.

Figure 15-3. The exterior and interior views of the United Flower Auctions in Aalsmeer, The Netherlands. This is the largest flower auction in the world with approximately 3,600 members. Such auctions serve as a distribution channel between growers and wholesalers. *(Photos courtesy of United Flower Auction Aalsmeer, Aalsmeer, The Netherlands)*

461

A second strong motivation for forming auctions in The Netherlands and Canada were the questionable practices of some wholesalers who played growers off against each other. Growers by definition are in a weak market position because of the perishability of their product. By uniting in a producers cooperative, an individual's weak market position is strengthened.

Dutch auctions charge the growers/members a commission of about 5 percent. The buyer pays about 0.3% service costs. This does not necessarily increase the retail price over that in a system without a flower auction since the job of the wholesaler is made more efficient by the auction.

A typical auction functions as follows. Flowers or plants are delivered by the grower to the auction where they are set out on display. Early in the day wholesalers peruse each lot to assess quality and condition. In so doing they decide which they wish to purchase and how much they are willing to pay. Later in the morning, wholesalers take their assigned seats in the auction room as pictured in Figure 15-4.

Each lot of plants is brought before the wholesalers, one at a time. The clock at the front of the room indicates the identification number of the grower of the plants and the lot number of the plants. An auction employee holds the plants for all to see and the auctioneer gives a brief assessment of the plants. The sale begins when the clock pointer, set on 100, is released and begins its descent in price. The value of each unit on the clock's scale of 0 to 100 is denoted on the clock, whether it be 1, 5, 10, 25 or 100 Dutch cents. When the pointer comes down to the price a wholesaler is intending to pay he presses a button at his desk which stops the clock and electrically records his identification number and the price on the clock at that point. The wholesaler finalizes the sale by indicating the quantity of the lot he wishes to purchase. In a matter of a few hours all of the day's sales are made.

This system works rapidly. As many as 700 transactions can be made per clock per hour. The interests of both seller and buyer are served. If the buyer waits for an exceptionally low price he may lose the chance to purchase the plants he desires. If on the other hand he bids too soon, he pays a needlessly high price. Each lot of plants is judged independently and its price is established accordingly. The principle of supply and demand expresses itself in this system.

When sales are finished, flowers or plants are moved from their display areas to loading docks where the trucks of the various wholesalers are waiting. Even this process is often mechanized. Carts are loaded according to purchaser and are moved automatically along tracks to the loading area. When the day ends, the auction house is ready to repeat its cycle.

Two auctions have opened in Canada in recent years, one in Toronto and the other in Vancouver. Concentrated production at a distance from scattered markets played a role in the establishment of these auctions, particularly the Toronto auction. Wholesalers and retailers alike make purchases in these auctions.

Figure 15-4. One of five auction rooms in the United Flower Auctions Aalsmeer, The Netherlands, where over two billion flowers and plants are sold each year. *(Photo courtesy of United Flower Auctions Aalsmeer, Aalsmeer, The Netherlands)*

The auction system has not yet found application in the United States. In earlier days this was due to the close proximity of growers and markets which facilitated direct purchases. When concentrated fresh flower production areas emerged, growers formed cooperatives to handle marketing or assumed the responsibility directly. It would appear that the auction system would serve well in the concentrated green plant production industry of Florida and California where many growers are producing products sold to numerous wholesalers throughout North America.

ADVERTISING

The need for advertising varies. A grower who sells to one or to a few wholesalers will probably find no need to advertise. The grower of a centralized crop such as green plants in Florida or fresh flowers in California will probably be interested in new wholesale outlets. This grower often advertises in the various florist trade papers.

The retailer has the greatest need for advertising. Unfortunately, cost has been a deterrent. Those who do advertise generally find it profitable. Newspaper ads are most commonly used. Radio spots are also valuable, particularly toward the weekend and in connection with a gardener's program. Television has been used by some and can have a far-reaching effect when done properly. Mailing lists have provided a very successful avenue of communication with the consuming public for many retailers.

It is not the intent of this book to take more than a cursory look at retail marketing. While the major burden of advertising rests on the retailer, the grower is not without obligation. The allied supply industry—growers, wholesalers, and retailers—are all parts of one system which culminates in the sale of floral products to the consumer. It has been demonstrated in the floral industry that advertising effectively increases the demand for these products. This ultimately benefits all segments of the industry; thus all should share in the advertising program.

Shared advertising is often practiced in other businesses. The Coca Cola® sign so often used to display the name of a restaurant is paid in part by the Coca Cola Company. Advertisements for a given product, regardless of the retail outlet, will carry the same logo (sketch, picture, etc.). The logo is developed and provided at the expense of the producer. The advertising cost for many items presented by the local supermarket in its newspaper ads are borne by the producer of the products.

There are national and international advertising programs in the floral industry. The floral wire services collect a percentage of the gross wire sales of their member retail florists and use these funds for wide-range advertisement. The individual retail florists expend additional funds for local advertising. Through the centralized program of the wire houses expensive but highly effective advertising media can be used. National television and major magazine ads are procured. Billboard space is contracted. Consumer information literature is underwritten, such as the booklet, *Professional Guide to Green Plants* sponsored by Florists' Transworld Delivery Association.

The closest the floral industry comes to a properly shared advertising program is seen in the efforts of the American Florists' Marketing Council (AFMC) of the Society of American Florists (SAF). This organization carries on a national advertising program with funds derived from all segments of the floral industry on a voluntary basis. The AFMC is running advertisements in national magazines and newspapers such as *U.S. News and World Report, Redbook, Sports Illustrated,* and the *Wall Street Journal,* as well as radio spot ads on the ABC, CBS, and NBC networks. In addition they prepare and offer at cost in-store display banners, newspaper advertisement mats ready to submit to the newspaper once the retailer's name and address are inserted, radio spot scripts, and truck and billboard signs. The overall program is having a positive effect on increasing the floral market but needs to be much larger in light of the potential market.

Floral growers have an obligation to share the overall marketing responsibility of the industry. There are several things they can do.

1. Financially support cooperative advertising programs such as the AFMC

2. Explore the possibility of and, when warranted, work with wholesalers and retailers in local promotional programs

3. Establish communications with the wholesale and retail segments of the industry through membership in their organizations, attendance at their conventions, and reading of their literature

Much of the potential of the floral industry is dependent upon a greater degree of cooperation among the diverse businesses making up the floriculture industry. A major problem in the industry today is lack of unity as seen in separate grower, wholesaler, and retailer organizations, meetings, literature, and attitudes. Such disunity can hurt even at the individual growers level. Wire services periodically feature specific fresh flowers and plants in their promotional programs. Grower alerts are issued long in advance of the promotional date but many growers are not tuned in. This has a bad effect in the marketplace since the promotional item falls into short supply and prices rise adversely. It can be disadvantageous to the growers who find themselves heavy on nonpromotional items and short on those in demand. Through interindustry communication it should be possible to use promotional programs as a means for coping with inadvertant overproduction, periods of low market demand, and establishing consumer demand for products and product forms rendering larger profit to the grower, greater ease of handling in the market channel, and increased consumer satisfaction.

There are other ways the grower can play a role in the overall promotional or advertising program.

4. They must concern themselves with consumer satisfaction. This can be done by selecting plant varieties which stand up best in the region in which they are marketed. Fuchsias are beautiful most anywhere in the spring but are a disappointment to consumers in hot climates when the heat of summer arrives. Such sales should be discouraged and in their place crops adapted to the situation should be promoted. The grower has a responsibility to make such decisions and to educate the retailer. It is the further responsibility of the grower to produce plants of quality and free of insects and disease. Whether the consumer relates plant failure to the grower or to himself the main effect is the erosion of his or her desire to make a subsequent purchase.

The consuming public has an underlying desire for information. This is often as important as the product itself.

5. The grower should provide identification and cultural information

with each unit sold. Plastic stakes are available with such information for many types of pot plants. If not available, one could have such stakes made or could attach an information sheet to the plant or could have the information printed on the plastic sleeve if used.

The grower's responsibility to educate does not stop here.

6. The grower must pass information along to the retailer as to how the product is to be handled during marketing. He or she should also supply information which the retailer can pass along to the consumer. This responsibility is particularly important in the mass market channels where merchandisers often have little experience in handling plants. Some larger growers supplying mass markets have found it advantageous to work with the management in chain stores in training their produce managers to properly handle floral products.

There are no binding laws forcing a grower to participate in advertising or promotional programs. Advertising as discussed thus far falls under two categories: *brand name advertising* in which the advertising firm is directly promoting its own products, and *generic advertising.* In brand name advertising, for example; Nelson the Florist advertises poinsettias for Christmas so that the townspeople will buy from him rather than from the supermarket. The effects of such advertising are relatively easy to evaluate. The fact that most retailers and wholesalers engage in it is testimony to its success.

Generic advertising promotes flowers and plants in general without reference to any brand names. Its purpose is to expand the total market. The AFMC program is an example of this type of advertising or promotion. It is difficult to evaluate the usefulness of such advertising, since the effects are indirect. A large producer servicing the mass market over an expansive region will probably sense an effect and feel that the expenditure returns a profit. A smaller grower, particularly one selling to full-service retail florists, may not feel that it is profitable. This is a business decision which must be made by each firm; however too few businesses have realistically considered generic advertising. It would be better for the floriculture industry as a whole if more businesses were involved.

SUMMARY

1. Packaging of fresh flowers has been standardized by convention. A set number or weight of flowers constitute a bunch. Bunches are shipped in cardboard cartons, the number contained within depending upon the grade. Potted plants were customarily sold individually and often in plastic sleeves. It is common today for potted plants to be shipped in cardboard cartons and to be sold in the multiple contained within a

carton. The number in a carton depends on the pot size, type of plant, and the grower. Pot plant packaging is new and not standardized.

2. Grades and standards exist for some fresh flowers but not for potted plants. Grading is a voluntary program which is practiced by many growers. It would be advantageous to the floral industry and the consumer if all growers adhered to a single grading system. Today there are many systems in use. Grades and standards are needed for potted plants as well.

3. Fresh flowers are usually purchased from growers on consignment by wholesalers who in turn sell them to retailers. The wholesaler retains about 25 percent of the wholesale price to cover expenses and profit.

4. Potted flowering plants are generally sold directly by growers to retailers. Potted green plants often pass through a wholesaler on route to the retailer.

5. Flower auctions are popular in Europe and have recently opened in Canada. They serve well as a channel between growers and wholesalers when production is concentrated and located at a considerable distance from the retail market.

6. Advertising, as in any other business, is crucial to the floral industry. Any increase in consumer demand has the potential to benefit all segments of this industry. While the heaviest investment in advertising is made by the retailers, the burden is shared by wholesalers, growers, and allied trades as well. The American Florists' Marketing Council (AFMC) of the Society of American Florists (SAF) carries out a promotional program financed by voluntary contributions from all of the industry. Considerably more promotional effort must be made by the floriculture industry before it comes up to the standards of most other industries. Growers can do their part by supporting existing national promotional programs, by joining in local promotional programs with wholesalers and retailers, by communicating more extensively with the wholesaling and retailing groups, by supplying technical information to retailers to aid them in handling floral products and better advising the consumer, and by producing high quality plants well acclimated to the consumer's environment so that satisfaction is guaranteed.

SUGGESTED READINGS

Berninger, L. M. *Managing a Garden Center.* Reston Publishing Co., Reston, VA, 1978.

Laurie, A., D. C. Kiplinger and K. S. Nelson. *Commercial Flower Forcing.* 7th ed. Chapter 14. McGraw-Hill Book Co., New York, 1968.

Pfahl, P. B. *The Retail Florist Business.* 2nd ed. Interstate Printers & Pub., Inc., Danville, IL, 1973.

Staby, G. L., J. L. Robertson, D. C. Kiplinger and C. A. Conover. *Proceedings National Floriculture Conference on Commodity Handling.* Ohio Florists' Assoc., 2001 Fyffe Ct., Columbus, OH 43210. 1976.

Society of American Florists' Grades and Standards Committee, 901 N. Washington St., Alexandria, VA 22314. This committee is responsible for developing flower grades and standards.

Numerous popular and academic books exist on marketing. As a student, one should consider a course in marketing essential.

Chapter 16

Business Management

Management and labor are distinctly different activities. Management is the directing of labor, time, and materials. Labor is the execution of plans developed. The owner of smaller greenhouses often finds it necessary to be a laborer as well as a manager. This is all right as long as he or she never loses sight of the need to manage. Without proper management an owner–manager expends a great deal of effort with little return, the attitude of the labor force deteriorates, and the business fails to meet its goals. This situation is unstable and ultimately leads to failure.

Management efforts must be applied to planning the expenditure of labor, time, and materials and must allocate these expenditures properly to crop production and to marketing. As the greenhouse range grows in size, the integration of production and the subsequent marketing of this production becomes complex and responsibilities such as purchasing materials, handling billing and payments, bookkeeping and even correspondence in general become great enough to distract the manager from production and marketing operations. At this point, a business affairs office with its own staff is warranted, as well as additional managerial personnel.

BUSINESS STRUCTURE

Managers themselves must be properly organized and managed in order for a business to suceed. It is important that each manager be held responsible for his or her assignment and the work of employees below him or her. At the same time each employee should answer to one person only.

The labor of a greenhouse production business falls into four general categories (Figure 16-1). The efforts directly involved in producing crops come under the production department. The marketing department solicits orders, packages the crop, delivers and performs whatever other services

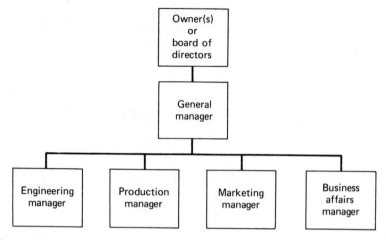

Figure 16-1. A typical managerial structure of a greenhouse business. The owner(s), in the case of a single proprietorship or partnership, or the board of directors of a corporation, carry the full responsibility for the business. The manager of each of four departments takes orders directly from a general manager, who takes orders from the owner. All labor within a department answers directly to the management of that department. The four common departments are engineering (repairs and construction), production, marketing, and business affairs.

might be required at the point of sale. A third department, engineering, maintains the physical plant and equipment. It has the further task of custom building facilities and equipment such as benches in the greenhouse, racks for the trucks, etc. The business affairs department handles such affairs as record-keeping for tax and cost accounting purposes, billing, purchasing, and payroll administration.

Full responsibility for the business is held by the owner. The owner of a small business often fills the various management roles as well. If such is the case, he or she serves two roles and is entitled to the manager's salary and whatever profits are left over. The small business has few employees and direct communication can be maintained between each employee and the owner. Although the functions of the four departments exist, separate managers are not required. The owner handles all management.

When the business grows in size, it becomes impractical for the owner to manage all functions. The owner assesses his or her talents and interests and continues to manage one or more departments. Personnel are employed to manage the other departments. For example, the general manager of the company might continue to serve as manager of the engineering and marketing departments. The general manager hires a business affairs manager who at first manages and carries out the tasks of that department alone and later supervises a number of clerks subsequently hired. The general manager also hires a production manager to manage the labor force involved in growing the crops. The two new managers take their orders directly from the general manager who is the owner in this case. Each employee receives his or her orders from his or her department manager and not from the general manager.

Further expansions may increase the workload of the general manager to the point where the owner serves only in that capacity. Engineering and marketing managers may then be hired. Perhaps at that time the size of the production department has become too great for a single manager to effectively handle it. Submanagers might be hired to manage production sections. The submanagers take orders from the production manager and in turn the employees under them take orders only from them. Production sections are defined by logic. If the greenhouse business is situated in two locations, each might constitute a section. If potted plants and fresh flowers are grown, it is logical to place each in its own section since the physical facilities (bench type and arrangement, planting area, etc.) differ.

The owner may enter into other business ventures such as wholesale marketing, retailing, or even an unrelated business. The establishment of another business may possibly require all of his or her attention; in which case the role of general manager of the greenhouse business should be relinquished. At that point he or she no longer draws a managerial salary, but does receive the profits.

Two or more owners in partnership must organize in such a manner that the business is commanded with a single voice. Duality of command is constantly open to discrepancy and undermines productivity. One partner might serve as general manager, while the other serves below him or her as manager of one or more departments. In another arrangement one owner may be a silent partner while the other is general manager. Both partners share in the profits according to their initial agreement but the managing partner generally draws in addition a salary in accordance with his or her managerial input. There are many ways to organize a partnership, but the important point is that a unified line of command is established and that the agreement between partners be in writing.

The owners of a corporation are the stockholders. A number of greenhouse businesses are corporations. Obviously each owner cannot be allowed to give orders. Stockholders' meetings are periodically convened to decide the objectives and methods of operation of the corporation. A board of directors is set up to represent all of the stockholders. The board of directors communicates in a single voice with the general manager of the company.

A proper balance of management and labor must be achieved. Management is costly, as the students of floriculture well know since it is these positions they ultimately seek. But indiscriminate reduction of the management force can be even more costly as it leads to a breakdown in communications and inefficiency of resource utilization. The owner must watch the profit and loss statement and weigh it against the operational efficiency of his or her business to determine when it is the proper time to adjust the management force.

LABOR MANAGEMENT

Personal Management

Labor management begins with management of oneself. To manage others one must manage one's own life in such a way as to develop traits of leadership. Leadership, coupled with financial and other personal inducements, should provide the motivation needed for workers to carry out their job assignments.

Leadership

A leader is one who through practice comfortably wears traits of self-motivation and perseverance for he or she will have to provide the impetus to stimulate activity when there is a resistance to move ahead. He or she must provide the motivation when the task becomes wearying and success seems out of reach. A leader must naturally emanate traits of integrity and justice. These qualities gain respect, without which leadership cannot exist. A just system gives the worker a sense of security and an inducement to render an honest day's service for an honest day's wage. Justice calls for setting aside personal prejudices and relationships to see that each individual is judged on his or her own merits. It calls for a just reward where earned and constructive criticism or assistance where needed. A leader must have empathy, for it is only through compassion and understanding that the myriad of gaps in personality and position of the workers can be bridged. Unless some common ground can be found, communication is not possible.

Elements of Success

The manager who has the qualities of leadership must organize his or her efforts in such a way as to achieve success. Success depends upon a goal, a plan, faith, and perseverance.

Goal

The manager must establish the success of the business as his or her primary goal. This can be spelled out in many ways. It may be a monetary figure that the business should achieve by some point in time, a volume of production for the existing greenhouse area, a prespecified lower level of crop loss, a projected level of quality, an expansion in business size, or the adoption of new crops into the production scheme. If the manager is not the owner, it is important that his or her goals coincide with those of the owner. A business in the free enterprise system can only afford to financially reimburse employees in proportion to their contribution toward the financial gain of the business.

When the manager sets a goal, it must be explicit, e.g., dollar value of income, a certain number of pots, a definite percentage of flowers in the premium grade. When a specific quantity is set as the goal, the manager is able to determine where he or she is in relation to the goal. With this knowledge, all efforts can be apportioned to reach the goal.

The goal is very important. Without it a course of action cannot be plotted. Some years ago, contestants of quiz shows were interviewed some ten years after they had won large sums of money. Each was asked to show the positive achievements they had made as a result of the unexpected sum of money which had entered his or her life. More than nine out of ten failed to show any lasting value derived from the money. On the contrary, many found themselves in a poorer lot of life as a result. Loss of initiative, complacency, inability to adapt back to a lower material level of life when the funds were depleted, and other such problems took their toll. Divorce was a common result. The problem stemmed from acquisition of money without a goal to direct its proper use. It is unusual when one can properly manage that which he or she is incapable of earning. If the contestants had had a realistic goal and a plan for attaining the required money, it is very likely it would have been used to improve their lot in life.

Plan

A goal alone is not enough to bring success. Just as one does not drive to an unfamiliar destination without a road map, a goal is not attained without a plan. Plans are sometimes demanded of us, as in the case of arranging a loan. Lending agencies demand a pro-forma as part of the application to see how the money is to be used and what the chances of success and repayment are. This same planning should enter into all operations of the greenhouse range.

Before drafting a plan, the objective should be researched. The manager should obtain literature in order to establish a background. He or she should communicate with other firms that have successfully undertaken this objective. Suppliers of materials required for the objective are another good source of information. Finally the manager integrates this knowledge into his or her own past experience and logic and sits down to formulate a plan.

The plan must encompass a timetable. A reasonable timetable is a weapon against procrastination. The plan should earmark primary objectives within the goal for periodic review and secondary objectives for setting up daily work plans. Each objective must have a stated date of accomplishment.

Crop production depends upon a number of straightforward operations performed on a precise schedule. A good program has the misleading appearance of monotony. A chrysanthemum range, for instance, has its reoccurring three-month cycle of planting, pinching, lighting, shading, disbudding, watering, fertilizing, spraying, and harvesting. A new manager can quickly settle into a state of boredom and, in the absence of a plan, can begin to perform operations late or miss them altogether. Monotony is quickly replaced with an almost impossible task of saving the crop. The astute manager seeks to establish a simple plan of culture that meets all of the needs of the plant on schedule. He or she then satisfies the need for adventure and creative outlet through an empathy for the plant and an attention to detail. Even the best plans do not hold up forever. Most change begins subtly. The keen manager develops a feel for where insects or disease might first appear and develops a recognition of the infinitesimal changes in plant appearance signaling encroaching disorder. In short, he or she heads off conflict before the need arises to fight a battle. It is an ever-changing challenge which can only be met when the gross physical requirements of the crop are guaranteed in a plan.

Faith

Goals and plans require a degree of faith on the part of the manager. If he or she harbors doubt in his or her ability to accomplish the plan, it tends to feed on itself and grow in his or her mind. The feeling is inadvertently transmitted to the workers who will further magnify it and reflect it back. Doubt is self-destructive and can only be countered by faith.

Everyone has doubts at one time or another. Doubt can be minimized by practicing an attitude of positive thinking. Those doubts which still exist can be disposed of through a process of autosuggestion.

We form impressions from everything we do, see, hear, or feel. These impressions may be negative or positive. There is no middle ground. Information received by our conscious facilities feeds into our subconscious. Our minds are at work day and night gathering evidence to support conclusions we have drawn.

When we entertain the idea of failure, we begin to see evidence around us that would suggest failure. When we anticipate success, our minds tend to blank out evidence which would suggest failure and recognize mainly evidence supporting impending success. Our faith in success is thereby strengthened. This in turn causes us to gravitate toward an environment in which answers exist for the needs of our goal; thus it facilitates our ability to draft a plan.

Our attitudes are readily communicated even without speech. An attitude of direction and self-confidence attracts other positive thinking people. This is important because one rarely solves all of his or her problems independently. Each member of a group contributes a different perspective and additional information. The greenhouse manager should never "go it alone." He or she should seek a relationship with positive thinking people at his state university, among the management of other greenhouses, allied tradespeople, community business people, and civic groups. All conceivable types of information and perspectives eventually come to bear on greenhouse management.

Perseverance

Perseverance, in addition to a goal, a plan, and faith, is essential to success. Very often our first plan will fail. If you give up at this point, then you will not be a successful manager. Each apparent failure has a lesson contained in it which points the way to an improved plan. People who press on after repeated failures invariably succeed.

The effective manager comes to learn that success is a journey and not a destination. While a plan for the culture of a crop must be simple and precise, it must also be continuously altered to accommodate changing cultivars, climate, market dates, automation, etc. Maintenance of faith requires constant practice of positive thinking. Above all, to realize viable goals, a manager must continuously develop a perspective of the business firm he or she serves, the floriculture industry, the labor force, and the needs of society as a whole.

Manager-Employee Relationship

Assuming that the labor force has an adequate level of skill and motivational potential, its accomplishments will depend upon the manager. The labor force must be aware of the managerial structure, know the goals toward which they work, be delegated sufficient authority to accomplish their jobs, understand the system by which they are to be evaluated, and be assured of recognition for their efforts.

MANAGEMENT STRUCTURE. As previously discussed, each employee must answer to only one superior. Such a system gives continuity to the chain of command so that the firm's goals are not altered or diluted. It also minimizes confusion in the mind of each employee so that he or she can more fully apply himself or herself to the task. To maintain such a system each employee should be made aware of the overall structure of management. Although the structure demands that each employee take orders from his or her immediate superior, there should also be a system for higher appeal in the event that an employee feels he or she is not treated fairly by his or her superior. Such a system guards the employee against unfair treatment and at the same time allows the firm to identify improper management.

GOALS. People seek to improve their self-esteem. Some attain self-esteem by serving in a managerial role and others by implementing plans of the firm which they deem to be of value. In either event the employee seeks to have a part in a goal of value. Despite the role, no matter how mundane it may be, each employee can relate to the overall mission if properly motivated.

Each individual, therefore, should be made aware of the goals in which he or she participates, their value to the firm or to society, and the importance of his or her part in the plan. This is an easy task for the manager in floriculture because the product is one which brings pleasure to mankind. It enriches personal lives, improves the human environment, helps to heal wounds, adds to the pitch of emotional experiences, and expresses sentiments more aptly than words. Flowers, like their artistic and recreational counterparts, bring added meaning to life beyond that of survival.

The manager should point out the goals of the firm. The properly motivated employee takes pride in the growth of the firm for which he or she works. Greenhouse owners have found to their surprise a spirit of exhiliration among employees during periods of greenhouse expansion. One would think that in such a period of added stress just the opposite mood would take over; however, a feeling of accomplishment prevails because workers are participating in goal setting. The firm which is living off its depreciation, i.e., running into the ground, is one in which management of the labor force is difficult, if not impossible.

Finally, the manager must clearly inform each employee of the task he or she is to achieve as part of the overall goal. The task should be spelled out in detail and a deadline should be given. It is important that the manager have the employee repeat the work assignment to eliminate any misconceptions. No doubt should exist in the employee's mind as to what is expected. This puts the employee in a position to apply all his or her resources directly to accomplishing the task. Any doubt in the objective will dilute an employee's efforts.

Where the chain of command is long, involving perhaps owner, general manager, production manager, and several subproduction managers, it is wise to post a long-range set of production plans for periodic reference by all concerned. Some growers have devised graphical ways of doing this as seen in Figure 16-2. Such a visible plan aids the managers in maintaining their responsibilities and in briefing their employees.

DELEGATION OF AUTHORITY. Without some level of authority, an employee cannot organize his or her own activity. The manager must

Figure 16-2. A production schedule chart in the management office of the Royal Carnations Co. in Bogota, Colombia. Each row represents a production area and has holes for each week of the year. Numbered pegs are inserted in holes for the weeks when an operation is to be executed for that production area. The number refers to the operation and a detailed set of instructions for the operation can be found in the pages at the left side of the board.

always assume full responsibility for the tasks performed by those under his or her command. On the other hand, he must delegate authority to his subordinates. Such authority may cover decisions of priority, purchases, and labor assistance. This authority permits the employee to organize his efforts for greater efficiency and to proceed without the minute to minute supervision of the manager.

Delegation of authority becomes more important as the number of employees answering to a manager increases. It often turns out to be one of the most difficult roles for the manager to perform. It can be difficult to relinquish authority over applications of growth regulators or pesticides when the stakes are so high and the responsibility of error still rests on the manager. If such authority is not relinquished, however, the manager may not be able to attend to responsibilities of higher priority.

EVALUATION. The employee should know at the outset how performance will be evaluated. Such a system gives him or her a chance to gauge his or her performance. The employee has a chance to improve performance before being reprimanded and to pace himself or herself. The evaluation system is equally valuable for the manager because it provides a means for guiding the professional development of the employee and thereby further assuring that his or her responsibilities as manager are met.

A set of standards for the employee's work should be established. This might include, in the case of disbudding pot mums, the loss of not more than one terminal bud for each three pots, a time allocation of three minutes per pot, no unnecessary breakage of foliage, placement of all disbuds in a receptacle, and orderly replacement of the pot and watering system after disbudding.

The method of evaluation should be set. The person planting cuttings might be given a set of labels bearing his or her name so that one can be placed in each section which he plants. Periodically the manager checks the planting operation, complimenting those who have performed well and correcting those who have not performed so well.

It is well to set up a periodic meeting with each employee to review performance. This serves as a reminder to the employee to give some attention to his or her efforts and it gives the manager an easy means to communicate a judgement without unduly alarming the employee.

There are those managers who reserve these comments for times when job performance is poor. Some employees may understand that no comment is a vote of confidence, but most are unable to respond to this system. A periodic evaluation system circumvents the problem of lack of recognition.

Sometimes it helps to provide an overall record of accomplishment. One grower has posted a chart in the center of his carnation production area. Data is added weekly to graphs showing the total production for the week, the proportion of the total represented in each flower grade, and the quantity of loss due to neglect on the part of labor. This system provides all employees with a continuous evaluation of the range as a whole and tends to encourage higher performance.

REWARD. The employee works foremost for pay. One rarely feels he or she has enough. Increased pay is a stimulus for improved performance, but must be handled equitably. If poor evaluation of performance or favoritism enters into the system of pay raises, it has a negative effect on performance.

At times financial recognition of superior service is not possible. This does not nullify the need for an evaluation and reward system. People are social beings and as such are very concerned about recognition. The manager must make it his or her business to notice good performance and to express appropriate appreciation. At the same time the manager must be certain to notice and help correct poor performance. Both are an integral part of the system for encouraging performance.

Working Conditions

Working conditions are as important as the manager-employee relationship for encouraging good performance. Consider your own feelings when (a) walking along a street in a town with no trees or plantings and with noisy traffic passing a few feet away versus (b) walking along a pedestrian mall landscaped with lawn and planters and overhung by trees. Without realizing it, many greenhouse ranges develop into a harsh, repelling environment which brings about negative feelings in the employees. How much stimulation is there to plant seedlings neatly and at the precise depth when all around are weeds, trash, and unrepaired greenhouses?

FACILITIES. The greenhouses, headhouse, rest rooms and the surroundings should be orderly and clean. It was pointed out earlier that this is an important part of insect and disease control. It is also important to proper management.A harmonious environment suggests a state of finesse, which with a little encouragement by the manager can be achieved.

A job is not finished until it is cleaned up. Tools, empty cartons, etc., should always be in their proper places. Greenhouse aisles, headhouse, and areas around the greenhouse should be clear. Aside from the negative messages that such messes impart, they also present hazards and a physical barrier to efficient operation.

There should be a program of preventive maintenance for all equipment to insure that jobs will always be done on schedule. A little paint on a tank before it rusts, grease on a bearing before it freezes, or a tune-up on a rototiller before it stops will prevent breakdowns which could snowball into a stoppage of many other operations.

Each human has an internal rhythm. When the pace of his or her work is geared to this rhythm, efforts are minimized and productivity is maximized. Disruptions in the form of ambiguous orders, undue changes in orders, and equipment breakdown break the work momentum. It is fatiguing and depressing to the employee.

Respectable work facilities should be provided. Human dignity dictates that bathroom facilities be provided. If the sole being of an individual does not command respect, why should his or her productivity be any different? A pleasant area for eating and taking breaks also should be provided. A brief repose at mid-morning, noon, and mid-afternoon is as much for the benefit of the firm as for the employee. A tired employee is not productive.

There are many other aspects of the physical facilities that warrant attention if the manager simply puts himself in the position of the employee. Worthwhile improvements are those which prevent needless fatigue and facilitate work efficiency. Rubber mats on the floor and, under some circumstances, chairs are an asset to progress. Convenient centralization of tools and supplies also increases efficiency.

The range layout as a whole should be formulated with efficiency in mind. A flat site and ridge-and-furrow greenhouses rather than separate structures permits automation and minimizes walking effort. Service buildings on the north side, midway along the greenhouses, minimize travel distances. Service approaches to the final location where supplies are stored eliminate needless relocations. Permanently plumbed pesticide lines, local steam outlets for pasteurization, and central fertilizer proportioning equipment improve efficiency. Conveyor systems for moving flowers, potted plants, and supplies to or from production areas should be considered.

PRODUCT QUALITY. The demand for low quality products is small. The profitability of such production is low at best. Some years ago it was stated in the Florist and Nursery Exchange that Mr. Larry Taylor of Denver Wholesale Florist found on a year-around average it took 1.8 standard grade (second) carnations or 3.5 short grade or 7.5 design grade or 11 split calyx blooms to equal the profit of one fancy grade (first) bloom.

Aside from market price, product quality is important to personnel management. It affects the same principle of the employee relating to the firm. When one knows that he or she is part of a quality production scheme, the incentive is there to try to meet these standards in his or her own work.

EDUCATION. Most people take pleasure in learning. It is flattering to an employee when the firm thinks enough of him or her to provide an education along with the job. Actually, there is a mutual advantage since the employee who understands the why and what of his tasks has the potential to make a better worker. It puts him or her in a position to reason out better ways of doing the job and how to solve his or her problem when the job doesn't go right.

Education in a small firm need not consist of anything more than the manager talking with employees as they work. The employee should be given an appreciation of the various cultural procedures involved in a crop and how they interrelate. He or she should be aware of the quality standards required by the market. He or she should know the problems which can arise from such mistakes as insect or disease establishment, excessively high or low temperatures, improper photoperiod control, the wrong planting depth, nutritional disorders, and overwatering.

A worthwhile employee welcomes such knowledge. Equipped with such, one is in a position to better himself within the firm and a knowledgeable employee assists the manager in meeting his or her responsibilities.

Larger firms, in addition to the procedure just discussed, sometimes make use of training sessions for their employees. These may be held on the premises of the firm and be conducted by management within the firm or by instructors hired from outside. Outside services are available for such topics as management and marketing. Visits from university personnel, allied trade representatives, or competitive greenhouse operators can be a very valuable source of information. If possible, the general manager should arrange an opportunity for key personnel to meet with such an individual. One cannot help but be impressed by the professional manner in which the Colombian growers receive such visitors. Preparation is apparent in the complete involvement of the management staff and the organized quest for information by each staff member.

Numerous meetings are sponsored each year by industry organizations, state universities, and by other state and federal agencies. Again, this is an excellent educational opportunity for the owner and his or her key employees. Many state universities with a horticulture or plant science department conduct annual or semiannual floricultural short courses of one to three days duration. Commodity groups such as Roses, Inc., The American Carnation Society, and Bedding Plants, Inc. sponsor meetings. The Society of American Florists, The Produce Marketing Association, and various wire services hold meetings with topics ranging in scope from the grower to the wholesaler to the retailer. There are yet other wholesaler and retailer associations sponsoring meetings.

Most of the organizations mentioned publish newsletters containing current floral news items as well as technical subjects. One should definitely get on the mailing list of the horticulture department at his local state university. He or she should join his or her local flower growers' association as well as a national growers' association. Many growers join grower associations in other states as a means of expanding their sources of information and ideas. Information derived from these organizations should be passed down through the firm by one or another of the methods discussed earlier.

PRODUCTION MANAGEMENT

Record-Keeping

The grower who does not keep records is committed to repeat the same errors over and over. Every business must keep records for income tax purposes. With a little more thought and effort a set of records can be developed for cost accounting purposes. Cost accounting is a system for assessing the costs of conducting a business. The costs of each input—labor, utilities, materials—are determined and compared to a reasonable proposal of costs. The overall profitability of the business is determined.

To know at the end of a year that a business made a profit is not enough. Some crops may have been profitable while others were marketed at a loss. Given grades of fresh flowers or sizes of pot plants may have contributed little or nothing to the profit. It could be that one market channel was more profitable than another. These differences must be known or else the poorer alternatives may be allowed to increase out of proportion to the better alternatives. Cost accounting provides a tool for comparing the cost of producing units. The units may be different crops, different sizes of a given crop (bedding plants in 1¾-inch versus 3-inch pots), different market dates for a given crop, or different methods for producing and marketing a crop.

CULTURAL RECORDS. Before growing a crop one should decide which records to keep. One set will be financial, including costs of such items as plants, containers, root media, labor, utilities, etc. The other set of records are cultural in nature. Cultural records are maintained for the purpose of (a) providing a plan for duplicating successful crops, and (b) giving an accounting from which the cause of errors in the culture of the crop can be determined and then corrected in the next crop.

CULTURAL SCHEDULE RECORD. Long before a crop is planted, a cultural schedule should be written listing dates and labor budgets for such operations as root medium preparation, planting, syringing, fertilization, pesticide application, pinching, pruning, chemical growth regulation, disbudding, anticipated harvest period, and clean-up. This cultural schedule should be maintained in the general manager's office. The information should be duplicated on a cultural schedule record sheet which is hung in the greenhouse at the location of the crop being grown (Figure 16-3). The cultural schedule record sheet serves as a daily reminder to the production manager as to the various operations that must be performed.

When each operation is performed, the date is entered on the cultural schedule record sheet in the greenhouse and the name of the performing employee is entered. Should an unscheduled operation or an alteration in a scheduled operation be necessary, a description of the operation is entered in the record. At the end of each day the entries are verified and initialed by the manager overseeing the operations.

PLANT ENVIRONMENT RECORD. A second set of culture-related records contains the plant environment records, including temperatures inside and outside the greenhouse, solar radiation, root media nutrient analyses, foliar analyses, insect and disease occurrence, and visual observations. Temperature should be recorded in the greenhouse to determine if the desired temperatures have been maintained. Deviations from both low-temperature and high-temperature phases have an adverse effect on plant growth and prevent efficient use of energy. Such records give an assessment of the quality of the heating and cooling equipment and indicate breakdowns. They can prevent the erroneous conclusion, when the crop matures at the wrong time, that the schedule is incorrect. To change the cultural schedule in that case would only lead to a second mistimed crop. Recording thermometers with a seven-day record are available for this purpose (priced around $125). One should be placed in the aspirated control box in each zone of the greenhouse range. The seven-day graphs should be kept chronologically in a notebook.

Inside temperatures give an indication of the condition of the temperature control equipment while outside temperatures are a reflection of fuel and electrical consumption. A record of outside temperatures can be ob-

Greenhouse section		Benches	Crop	Cultivar	
IV		9–15	Cut Mums	Nob Hill	
Date scheduled	Date accomplished	Operation		Employee	Mgr. initials
3-7-78		Plant 7" x 8"			
3-7		Fertilize, half strength			
3-7		Start lighting at night			
3-14		Fertilize and spray			
3-21		Fertilize and spray			
3-28		Pinch			
3-28		Fertilize and spray			
4-4		Fertilize and spray			
4-11		Fertilize and spray			
4-18		Fertilize and spray			
4-18		Start shading			
4-19		Prune plants back to 2 or 3 shoots			
4-25		Fertilize and spray			
5-2		Fertilize and spray			
5-9		Fertilize and spray			
5-16		Fertilize and spray			
5-23		Fertilize and spray			
5-30		Fertilize and spray			
5-30		Disbud			
6-6		Fertilize and spray			
6-13		Spray			
6-20		Spray			
6-24		Harvest			

Figure 16-3. A typical cultural schedule record placed at the end of a bench in the greenhouse. All planned cultural operations are entered on the record prior to planting the crop. As the operations are performed, the actual dates, any changes in descriptions, and the names of employees performing the operations are entered. The manager verifies the record with his or her initials.

tained from your local branch of the National Weather Service. Data are gathered at several points in each state and are published. The grower should keep a record of daily minimum and maximum temperatures, heating degree days, and solar radiation. The winter temperatures and heating degree days data are useful in determining if the fuel bill of one winter will be representative of successive years. It also can be used to determine what proportion of the total fuel bill to allot to each crop grown during the heating season. This is important information for cost accounting. Summer temperature data can be used in a like manner. Summer temperature extremes result in crop delay and poor quality. Such records permit proper assessment of the blame.

Solar radiation values indicate the amount of light reaching the earth's surface and thereby indicate when light is a limiting factor. When growth is limited by insufficient light, increases in temperature, fertilization, or CO_2 level are ineffective and a waste of money. Records such as those for solar radiation give the grower an indication of which factor is limiting to growth, thereby enabling him or her to decide whether or not the alteration of environmental factors will be profitable.

The periodic root media tests and foliar analysis reports should be saved chronologically by crop. These are also valuable in determining the limiting factors to growth and thereby explaining exceptionally good or poor growth. As mentioned in Chapter 8, these records are also used for establishing the fertilization program itself.

All states have agricultural extension agents who can identify insect and disease problems. Some states have insect and disease clinics where samples can be sent for identification. Whenever an insect or disease problem is identified, it should be reported in the plant environment records. These factors again explain poor quality and yield.

PRODUCTION RECORD. The third set of culture-related records needed by the general manager are the production records. These records are gathered throughout the growth period of the crop. The production manager should assess the condition of each crop weekly and enter this into the production record. For a crop such as gloxinia, the width of a dozen typical plants might be measured and the average value entered into the record. The average height of a chrysanthemum crop could be measured and recorded. Visual observations also should be recorded, considering such factors as form, leaf color, leaf size, stem thickness, and appearance of chlorosis or necrosis.

These types of information allow for the comparison of the present crop with previous crops. A problem such as phosphorus deficiency, which is not apparent to the eye in early stages, can be identified through the smaller than normal growth measurements. Looking at a poor crop in retrospect, the stage of growth when trouble first occurred can be identified. The cultural record and plant environment records can then be checked to find the cause of the problem. In most cases, when the cause can be found it can be corrected in subsequent crops.

The production record should also include the number of blooms or pots harvested, the date, and the grade or quality. These records are needed for cost accounting and are used in the same manner as the earlier growth measurements just described.

FINANCIAL RECORDS. Just as cultural records must be gathered so that cultural mistakes can be identified, assessed, and corrected, financial records must be collected for improving the procedures for conducting business.

Income. Income should be recorded by crop. It is important to further subdivide income by date of sale, market outlet, and grade of product. Such a breakdown allows for comparison of relative profitability of season, market outlets, and grades.

Expenses. All inputs into the production and marketing of each crop must be identified. Each input is then quantitized in a monetary value and entered as an expense. Some expenses are easily identified with a given crop such as cuttings, pots, planting labor, disbudding labor, and trucking to market. These are known as *variable costs* because their magnitude varies with the size of the crop and from one crop to another. Other costs are known as *fixed costs* because they will continue even when production stops. Examples are interest on the loan for buildings and equipment, taxes, insurance, and management salaries. There are yet other costs which appear to fall between fixed and variable. These are *semi-fixed costs* which increase as production increases but are not directly related to the number of units produced. Secretarial and bookkeeping labor and greenhouse repairs are examples of semi-fixed costs. They increase with increasing production but are not directly related to a pot of mums or a bunch of roses.

Variable costs permit the most sensitive cost analysis. The method of record collecting sometimes determines whether an expense can be treated as variable, fixed, or semi-fixed. Labor will be at best a semi-fixed cost if only the total number of hours worked per week are recorded. When the number of hours expended on each crop is recorded, it can be treated as a variable cost, since the labor per unit of production can be determined.

Labor in the former case would be divided by the total area in production, regardless of whether the crop was pot mums or poinsettias. Since each square foot of production area carries the same expense, a comparison of the cost of production or the profitability of pot mums and poinsettias would not take into account labor, one of the largest expenses. A comparison in the latter case, where labor was accurately related to each crop, would permit an accurate comparison of the crops.

Labor could be even further identified by operation. W. W. Grimmer, in his booklet *Greenhouse Cost Accounting,* breaks labor down into 49 categories (Table 16-1). Each employee is required to fill out a time sheet at the end of each day in which he or she identifies the quantity of time spent, the crop, and the labor operation category (Figure 16-4). The manager verifies these sheets. From these sheets the total labor input for each operation of each crop can be calculated.

Table 16-1.

Code of Labor Operations in a Greenhouse Business*

PRODUCTION LABOR (BY CROP AND OPERATOR NUMBER)	NONPRODUCTION LABOR (BY OPERATOR NUMBER ONLY)
1 Propagation	50 R & M Buildings
2 Seeding	51 R & M Greenhouses
3 Grafting	52 R & M Benches
4 Transplanting	53 R & M Steam & Water
5 Mixing Soil	54 R & M Electrical
6 Potting	55 R & M Boiler Room
7 Moving Plants	56 R & M Machinery
8 Jeep Operation	57 R & M Trucks & Tractors
9 Weeding	58 Shade—Remove Shade
10 Pinching	59 Sales—Pick Orders
11 Disbudding	60 Sales—Wrap
12 Water and Syringe	61 Sales—Pack
13 Cultivate Soil	62 Sales—Load Trucks
14 Mulch	63 Trucking—Delivery
15 Stake and Tie	64 Trucking—Around Plant
16 Black Cloth Shading	65 Fire Boilers
17 Pruning	66 Temperature Control
18 Grade Pot Plants	67 Stock Room
19 Cutting Flowers	68 Laboratory
20 Grading Cut Flowers	69 General Miscellaneous Labor
21 Fertilizing	70 Supervision
22 Fumigating	71 Office
23 Spraying	72 New Construction
24 Dusting	73 Grounds Maintenance
25 Sterilizing	
26 Cleaning up	

*From W. W. Grimmer. *Greenhouse Cost Accounting.* Gateway Technical Inst., 3520 30th Ave., Kenosha, WI, 1975.

This type of variable expense record permits comparisons within a crop. Alternative methods may be studied such as manual pinching of azalea versus chemical pinching. Such a record also indicates where the greatest expenses lie so that the possibilities for their reduction can be studied.

Fixed Expenses. Detailed expense records by crop are very important but not always possible. The first letters of each of the five common fixed expenses spell DIRTI; they are known as the "DIRTI Five." These are depreciation, interest, repairs, taxes, and insurance.

Depreciation is the decline in value of an asset due to such causes as wear or obsolescence. Depreciation rates must be determined for tax purposes for the buildings and each item of equipment. The anticipated salvage value

Daily Time Sheet

Name _____

Clock number _____

Date _____

Operator no.	Crop	Hours	For office use only

Approved by: _____   Checked by: _____

Figure 16-4. A daily time sheet to be filled out by each employee and verified by the manager for the purpose of assessing labor as to crop and type of operation. *(From W. W. Grimmer, Greenhouse Cost Accounting, Gateway Technical Institute, 3520 30th Ave., Kenosha, WI, 1975)*

of the item at the end of its useful life is subtracted from its initial purchase value. The resulting value is divided by the number of useful years anticipated for the item. The resulting figure is the annual decline in value, known as depreciation. Depreciation for structures and equipment is a tax deduction. Theoretically the owner applies this money toward the replacement of facilities and equipment; however, in actuality he or she is free to dispose of it in any manner seen fit. Depreciation is a true expense and must be added into the production costs.

Interest is the cost to the business for using someone else's money to set up and run the business. The interest cost exists whether the money was borrowed from a commercial lending institution or was provided by the owner. If the owner puts up the money to establish the business, he or she must expect to receive interest for that money from the business. If he or she does not, then the interest which could have been made by investing the money elsewhere is lost. To get an accurate picture of the profitability, interest on all borrowed money must be entered as an expense, even though it must be declared by the owner as income if supplied by him.

Repairs to facilities and equipment will be required periodically. Maintenance also falls into this category since it is a logical expense for keeping repairs realistic.

Property taxes are a fixed expense including those paid to municipal, county, and state governments.

Insurance on facilities and equipment is a fixed expense. Labor-related insurance is not included here but comes under the expense category of labor.

Semi-Fixed Expenses. This set of expenses is difficult to categorize. At times it may be possible to treat them as variable expenses. Office expenses include supplies, labor, and the telephone bill. All are expended for the whole range of crops and for the facilities as a whole; however, their magnitude will increase with rising production.

Outside services of accountants and attorneys, travel to technical meetings or to business appointments relating to the business in general, and organizational dues are also semi-fixed expenses.

Management salaries are another semi-fixed expense. Under some conditions they come very close to a variable expense. When the owner is the manager there is a temptation to consider management salary as profit. This should not be done, since it interferes with cost accounting. An unrealistically low cost of production emerges, which cannot be maintained as the range expands beyond the size which the owner can manage alone. The manager should consider what he or she would pay a hired manager to do the job he himself is doing and enter it as an expense. The owner should realize that an employee could be hired to replace him or her thereby freeing him to derive income from another endeavor. This type of thinking might set the stage for a more profitable use of time.

Variable Expenses. These are the easiest expenses to identify. Each increases as the number of units produced increases. In this category are labor, plants, seeds, and growing supplies such as pots, root media, labels, pesticides, growth regulators, and fertilizers.

Fuel can be a variable expense if some measure of consumption is kept relative to crops. The weekly number of heating degree days could be used to determine the fuel consumption attributed to each week of the heating season. Within each week the fuel cost could be proportioned to each crop according to area occupied and inside temperature maintained. This is too large a bill to be treated as a fixed expense.

Electricity could be treated in the same manner. During the summer cooling may account for the greater part of total consumption and during the winter photoperiodic lighting may constitute the heaviest consumption.

Sales expenses should take into account packaging materials (sleeves, labels, and cartons), packaging labor, delivery labor, and sales labor. In a large operation where separate office personnel and telephones are used for sales, these expenses can also be listed under sales and can possibly be relegated to crops.

Labor has already been discussed. As indicated, labor of production and marketing should be treated as a variable expense as much as possible.

Expense Comparison. It is difficult to state a general cost of production or marketing. There is a different set of figures for each crop. There are also great differences among categories of growers. A small business may have a relatively high labor bill but low equipment expense compared to a large automated business. Taking a large range of crops and businesses into account the total expenses per square foot of bench area would probably be about $0.14 per week. In 1964 it was considered to be about $0.07. This includes all expenses of production and marketing except plants, seeds, bulbs, pots, and root media.

The relative relationship of each expense to the total can be seen in the circle graph by W. W. Grimmer in Figure 16-5. This is a composite of a study of several categories of fresh flower and pot plant growers in Wisconsin and

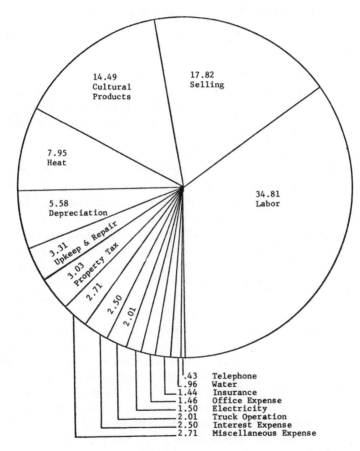

Figure 16-5. The relationship of each production and marketing expense to the total expense. *(From W. W. Grimmer. Greenhouse Cost Accounting. Gateway Technical Institute, 3520 30th Ave., Kenosha, WI, 1975)*

Michigan. Mr. Grimmer indicated that the sales expense for the growers surveyed is low and would probably run at least 25 percent for the industry as a whole.

Cost Accounting

The records thus far gathered are in two general categories, cultural and financial. The cultural records can serve to set a consideration of the financial records into perspective. Before the accounting office settles down to a cost analysis of a crop which has shown no profit, the cultural records should be studied. Failure may be due to one of such diverse factors as managerial error in executing the cultural schedule, uncontrolled disease, or boiler failure. In any case, assessment and correction of the problem is a cultural consideration. An analysis of expenses and revenue will do little to shed light on the problem.

PROFIT OR LOSS ASSESSMENT. After the cultural records have been studied, and barring any unduly large cultural problem, cost accounting becomes an important operation. A cost analysis statement as pictured in Table 16-2 is developed for each crop. Its main purpose is to determine the profitability of the crop. The statement further serves to pinpoint the causes of expense and sources of revenue.

The fixed expenses are commonly determined on a per square foot of bench basis and the crop is assessed according to the area it occupies. Variable expenses are assigned directly to the crop. Revenue may be identified by flower grade for fresh flower crops. If more than one market channel is used, and pricing differs, revenue is entered according to market channel.

Cost analysis by crop permits the grower to determine which crops are most profitable at various times of the year. It gives him or her an opportunity to determine the more profitable market dates in spite of seasonal changes in expenses such as fuel. It can be a difficult task to determine workable combinations and rotations of crops for greenhouse culture. Without this type of cost analysis serious error may be made.

When determining the profitability of a crop one must add in the fixed costs associated with vacant bench space that is associated with the crop. This may occur during the early culture of a crop such as bedding plants when plants are in the seedling or cutting stages. Vacant space is held for spacing of plants as they develop. The rotation in which bedding plants and poinsettias are grown makes use of greenhouse space in the spring and fall but leaves considerable space open in the summer. Often this space cannot be fully utilized because the market demand for floral products is low at that time and the length of time between the bedding plant and poinsettia crops is too short to grow many crops. Fixed expenses continue and must be met for the empty space during this period.

Table 16-2.

Cost Analysis Sheet for an Individual Crop Listing Expenses, Revenues,
and Profit or Loss

Crop_____ Greenhouse Section _____ Date _____

EXPENSES
  Fixed and Semi-Fixed
    Depreciation (facilities and
                  equipment)   _____
    Interest   _____
    Repairs and maintenance
      (facilities and equipment)   _____
    Taxes   _____
    Insurance   _____
    Office expenses   _____
    Telephone   _____
    Accounting and legal fees   _____
    Travel and dues   _____
    Management salaries   _____
    Automotive   _____
    Miscellaneous   _____
  Variable
    Seed   _____
    Cultural supplies   _____
    Labor   _____
    Fuel   _____
    Electricity   _____
    Sales costs   _____
                              Total Expenses   _____

REVENUES

Grade	Units	Unit Price	Total

                              Total Revenues   _____

PROFIT OR LOSS   _____

PLANNING FOR PROFIT INCREASE. Profit depends on the management of expenses and the production of revenue. There are many things which can be done to increase revenue. Many methods have already been introduced in reference to various greenhouse operations.

The market price of fresh flowers varies with supply and demand; however, there are well established annual patterns. A price curve can be developed from market reports given in weekly trade papers. Quite often land grant university libraries maintain some of these. The firm should subscribe to such literature and develop a record of its own. Flowering pot plant prices are fairly stable but demand varies considerably. There are times when part of the crop cannot be sold. Even if this were not the case, the percentage of pots not sold due to form or condition would tend to decrease during a period of peak demand. Whether the increased demand affects price, or the percentage of the crop sold, the result is an increase in revenue.

Crop rotations should be designed to maximize bench utilization as long as they do not result in crops of low profitability. The grower with a bedding plant-poinsettia rotation might look into propagating poinsettia cuttings during the summer. If this were not profitable for his or her own use alone, the selling of cuttings might be considered. Even though this is the same plant that he or she grows in the fall, the grower must consider it as a separate crop for cost accounting purposes. The sales price of the cuttings used within the business is the price the business would normally pay for these. Profits for the propagation business are then calculated from that point.

Greenhouse productivity also can be maximized by the physical arrangement of the growing space. Benches running the length of the greenhouse will occupy about 67 percent of the floor space, while peninsular benches may cover 75 percent of available space. The former benches are often more practical for fresh flowers, but a pot plant grower will benefit more from the latter arrangement. Movable benches which make use of some of the aisles also should be considered. The system of growing pot plants on a paved floor offers even a greater advantage for increasing revenue. Hanging baskets grown over aisles permit nearly 100 percent utilization of greenhouse space. Increased use of greenhouse space is important because it reduces the fixed costs per unit of growing space. This concept should be pursued as long as it is not offset by another input such as labor. Conceivably, the aisles could become too narrow or the blocks of plants too wide to allow for efficient use of labor. Such relationships can be established through cost analysis of trial crops.

Revenue can be increased by producing higher quality products. *There is always a demand for the highest quality.* Low quality produce is generally dumped first. Even for flowering pot plants there is a range in prices. The grower of high quality can usually command a higher price for his or her products. This is most pronounced for fresh flowers which are priced according to grade. The cultural records should suggest factors in the greenhouse environment which are limiting growth as well as errors in the cultural schedule. A fresh coat of paint, reflective material on the north wall, clean glass, and proper plant spacing can improve light intensity which is often limiting in the winter. Repair or replacement of heating and cooling equipment, the injection of CO_2 into the greenhouse atmosphere, better sanitation, improved drainage of the root medium, and many other factors discussed in this book should be considered for increasing quality. There is little profit in the floriculture industry for low quality producers.

Cutting fresh flowers in the bud stage shortens the length of time the crop is in the bench, permitting a higher volume of production. Greenhouse space is replaced by opening room space in the grower's service building or, even more preferably, the marketplace. The substitution of space and gain in time has been shown to be profitable.

Revenue is tied into the choice of a market channel. Prices can vary among the different outlets. The speed of payment is quite variable. Most large mass market chains have a reputation for prompt payment; uncollected debts are not common. A rapid cash flow permits the grower to minimize the amount of money to be borrowed and thereby minimizes interest expense. Slow receipt of payment and bad debts are a real problem for some growers.

A final alternative the grower has for increasing revenue is to raise prices. Within reason, this can be and is done. Prices tend to reflect the average grower's expenses and the market demand. Where there is competition, price increases are inadequate to offset poor business management.

A second step in improving profits is that of managing (reducing) expenses. This can be a very evasive challenge. Growers tend to react to sudden changes and overlook other more important subtle changes. A good system of cost accounting can prevent this problem.

Professor A. O. Voigt of Penn State University presented an interesting analysis of a grower's situation. The fuel cost for producing a six-inch poinsettia rose $0.065 from a cost of $0.06 in 1972 to a cost of $0.125 in 1974. The industry as a whole was deeply alarmed at the doubling in fuel costs and many felt that such prices might eventually put them out of business. Strong support developed for research into methods of energy conservation and alternative energy sources, and justifiably so. But what about the other expenses? While the cost of fuel doubled by rising $0.065, the grower's total production and marketing costs rose $0.54. The cost of cuttings alone increased by a larger amount than did the fuel and his total labor bill increased $0.07 per pot.

Fuel prices are a real challenge for the grower, but they are not the only problem. Considerable attention should be given to labor, marketing expenses, and cultural supplies which are larger expenses that are also rising rapidly (see Figure 16-5).

An empirical profitability study was made by P. J. Kirschling and F. E. Jensen at Rutgers University for four-inch pot mums in a model double-layer polyethylene greenhouse range. The range encompassed 17,664 square feet of bench space and was situated on a one-acre lot of land. Three crops of pot mums were considered per year with no production in the summer. Production costs were developed for this model. The effect of changes in the wage rate and the marketable percentage of the crop on profitability were calculated as shown in Table 16-3. From such a table the market price necessary to yield a specified profit can be readily ascertained.

Kirschling and Jensen further calculated the effect which a one percent increase in various factors would have on profit (Table 16-4). Considering the 100 percent rise in fuel cost mentioned earlier, a profit drop of 218 percent would be anticipated, based on the 2.18 percent reduction in profit per one percent rise in fuel cost reported in Table 16-4. This could be offset by an 8.1 percent rise in the price received per plant which would raise the price from $0.60 to $0.649. (218 percent profit decline ÷ 26.90 percent profit rise per one percent increase in price per plant = 8.1 percent required increase in price per plant).

The figures presented in Table 16-4 apply only to its specific model and are not to be used by other firms. Each firm must develop its own change sensitivity chart. The progressive grower will invariably develop detailed expense records. These will provide the data needed to calculate the effect which an increase or decrease in an expense factor will have on profit. Armed with this information, the progressive grower is in a position to pinpoint production operations most critical to profits and then to do something about improving the condition of that operation.

The point cannot be emphasized too strongly that successful ownership or management of a greenhouse business for someone else depends as much upon a knowledge of business principles as it does upon a technical knowledge of crop production. A person entering or already in the greenhouse business should consider supplementing his or her knowledge with courses in accounting, personnel management, business law, and marketing.

SUMMARY

1. There are four general categories of operations within the greenhouse business: crop production, marketing, engineering, and business affairs. Each department has a manager and over all four is a single general manager. The general manager answers to the owners. In a large business there may be submanagers in each department. In a small business the owner may serve as general manager as well as manager of each department.

2. A manager's ability to govern the affairs of others depends upon his or her ability to manage himself or herself. He or she must conduct himself

Table 16-3

Estimated Annual Entrepreneurial Profits* from a Plastic Greenhouse
Operation Model Producing 3 Crops of 4-inch Chrysanthemums.†

WAGE RATE	PERCENTAGE OF CROP MARKETABLE				
	80	85	90	95	100
$2.00	$11,117	$16,505	$21,913	$27,311	$32,709
2.50	6,103	11,502	16,900	22,298	27,696
3.00	1,090	6,488	11,887	17,285	22,811
3.50	- 3,923	1,475	6,873	12,271	17,670
4.00	- 8,936	- 3,538	1,860	7,258	12,656

*Entrepreneurial profits are defined as total revenues less total expenses except management cost. Sales price per pot is $0.65.

†Adapted from P. J. Kirschling and F. E. Jensen. *Profitability of Pot Chrysanthemum Production under Plastic Greenhouses.* N.J. Agricultural Experiment Station A.E. 351, 1974.

Table 16-4.

Sensitivity* of Changes in Economic Profit to One-Percent Increases
in Some Factors of Production of Chrysanthemums in 4-inch Pots in a
Plastic Greenhouse Operation Model.†

FACTOR (INCREASED BY 1 PERCENT)	ECONOMIC PROFIT (CHANGE IN PERCENT)
Price received per plant ($)	+26.90
Yield, percent of crop marketable	+24.63
Production materials expense ($)	- 7.17
Production labor (man-hours)	- 5.25
Labor wage rate ($)	- 5.25
Equipment investment ($)	- 4.18
Management cost ($)	- 3.93
Cuttings ($)	- 3.81
Packaging costs ($)	- 2.28
Fuel ($)	- 2.18
Interest rate on money (%)	- 0.97

*Levels of 60¢ per plant, $2 per hour, 95% yield, and $15,000 management cost were assumed for the sensitivity analysis.

†From P. J. Kirschling and F. E. Jensen. *Profitability of Pot Chrysanthemum Production under Plastic Greenhouses.* N.J. Agricultural Experiment Station A.E. 351, 1974.

or herself in a manner which fosters leadership. This includes self-motivation, perseverance, integrity, and a sense of justice. Further, he or she must operate according to the rules of success. These entail establishment of worthwhile goals, development of precise plans, unaltering faith in his or her ability to achieve the goals, and relentless perseverance.

3. An effective manager-employee relationship calls for several situations. The employee must be aware of the management structure so that he or she knows clearly the source of orders and to whom he or she is to answer. The employee must know the goals of the firm and the specific portion of each that he or she is to perform. The employee must have sufficient authority to work out the accomplishment of assignments. Finally there must be a system of evaluation by which the employee's performance is appraised and there must be a just system of reward or constructive criticism.

4. Working conditions have a bearing on labor management. The physical facilities should be neat to encourage orderly work. Proper bathroom and eating facilities demonstrate respect for the employee and increases the chance that such respect is transferred by the employee to his or her job. Preventive maintenance and timely repair of equipment and facilities reduces discord in the employees' efforts. Efficient arrangement of work areas, supplies, and equipment averts needless expenditures of energy. Production of quality crops evokes a spirit of pride which the employee transfers into his or her work. Most employees look upon an educational experience provided by the employer as a desirable benefit. Such provision also has great benefit to the firm because it improves the employee's ability to carry out his or her mission.

5. Production management is absolutely dependent upon record-keeping, for without it one is destined to repeat errors. Cultural records serve to identify causes of cultural errors and are used as the framework for improved crop production plans. Financial records, including sources of revenue and expense, provide the tools for an analysis of marketing and business affairs in general.

6. The use of records goes well beyond the realm of income tax returns and the analysis of past performance. Records are used for profit planning. Profits depend upon management of expense and production of revenue. Records provide the basis for cost analysis of alternative production operations, which in turn has a bearing on expenses. They provide the basis for assessing the effect of increases in selling price on profits. Most important, such analyses identify the relative effects of various expenses and revenues on profit, thereby providing a system of priorities in the effort to obtain increased profits.

SUGGESTED READINGS

Bange, G. A., F. E. Bender, and G. A. Stevens. *Planning and Accounting for Profit in Floriculture.* University of Maryland Agricultural Experiment Station. MP 806, 1972.

Griffith, H. V. and R. N. Payne. "An Analysis of Pot Chrysanthemum Production Methods, Direct Costs and Space Use." *Oklahoma State University Agricultural Research Bulletin B-670,* 1969.

Grimmer, W. W. *Greenhouse Cost Accounting.* Gateway Technical Institute, 3520 30th Ave., Kenosha, WI, 1975.

Hill, N. *Think and Grow Rich.* Fawcett Publications, Inc., Greenwich, CT, 1960.

Kirschling, P. J. and F. E. Jensen. "Profitability of Pot Chrysanthemum Production Under Plastic Greenhouses." *New Jersey Agricultural Experiment Station. AE 351,* 1974.

____. "Profitability of pot Chrysanthemum Production Under Plastic Greenhouses." *New Jersey Agricultural Experiment Station Bulletin 835,* 1974.

Mueller, F. J. and G. I, Prater. *Greenhouse Management: Cost Control and Profit Planning.* Proceedings of the 1968 WSU Greenhouse Management Institute, University of Washington, Seattle, WA, 1969.

Nelson, K. S. *Greenhouse Management for Flower and Plant Production.* The Interstate Printers and Publishers, Inc., Danville, IL, 1973.

Peale, N. V. *You Can If You Think You Can.* Fawcett Publications, Inc., Greenwich, CT, 1974.

Schwartz, D. J. *The Magic of Thinking Big.* Prentice-Hall, Inc., Englewood Cliffs, NJ, 1965.

Glossary

Abortion The partial or complete arrest of a developing tissue, as in embryos, buds, etc.

Abscission The separation of leaves, flowers, fruits, or other plant parts from the plant, generally following the formation of a separation layer of cells.

Actinomycetes A group of microorganisms apparently intermediate between bacteria and fungi, and classified as either.

Apical dominance The suppression of lateral shoot development by the apical bud (shoot tip).

Asset Any item of value or resource. Assets of a business include cash, amounts owed to the business by its customers for goods and services sold to them on credit, merchandise held for sale by the business, supplies, equipment, buildings, and land.

Auxin A group of hormones that induce growth through cell elongation.

Bactericide An agent or preparation used for killing bacteria.

Bacterium (plural *bacteria*) A unicellular microscopic plant that lacks chlorophyll and multiplies by fission.

Bedding plants A wide range of plants that are propagated and cultured through the initial stages of growth by commercial growers and are then sold for use in outdoor flower and vegetable gardens.

Blindness The condition of a plant stem evidenced when the bud stops developing. It is a frequent problem of roses during low light periods.

Blown head A bloom that is excessively open.

Bluing The objectionable development of blue pigment in flower petals, usually after harvest.

Boiler horsepower A quantity of heat equal to 33,475 Btu.

Btu (British Thermal Unit) The amount of heat required to raise the temperature of one pound of water one degree Fahrenheit at or near its point of maximum density.

Bulk density The mass per unit bulk volume; e.g., the bulk density of a soil-based medium in a dry state might be 70 pounds per cubic foot.

Bullhead A flower whose short petals, particularly at the center, give it a blunt, broad appearance. Also, a flower whose excess number of petals gives it a blunt, broad appearance.

Calyx A term referring to the sepals collectively. It is the first of the series of floral parts and is usually green and leaflike, but may be colored like the petals.

Cambium A zone or cylinder of meristematic (dividing) cells located between xylem and phloem tissues in plants. The cambium cells divide to form new xylem and phloem cells.

Cation exchange capacity (CEC) A measure of the ability of an absorbing material such as root medium to hold exchangeable cations such as various fertilizer nutrients including ammonium-nitrogen, potassium, calcium, magnesium, iron, manganese, zinc, and copper. It is generally measured in milliequivalents per 100 grams of dry absorbing material (me/100 g), and a value of 10–30 me/100 g is considered ample for greenhouse root media. A root medium with low CEC does not retain nutrients well and consequently must be fertilized often.

Chloropicrin Tear gas. A chemical used for pasteurizing greenhouse root media. It is not as popular as methylbromide but can be used in carnation root media.

Chloroplast A specialized body (organelle) in the cytoplasm of some plant cells which contains chlorophyll.

Chlorosis The process by which normally green plant tissue turns lighter green and eventually yellow due to the loss of chlorophyll or the failure of chlorophyll to form.

Clay A mineral component of soils consisting of particles less than 0.002 mm in diameter.

CO_2 The chemical formula for the gas carbon dioxide.

Conidiophore A specialized hypha on which one or more conidia are produced.

Conidium (plural *conidia*) An asexual fungus spore formed from the end of a conidiophore.

Convection heat loss Loss of heat from the greenhouse as it moves in air convection currents to the greenhouse covering, then through the covering by conduction, and finally away from the outside of the covering.

Convection heater A heater that does not contain a heat exchanger. Heat leaves the heater in the smoke. The smoke is carried the length of the greenhouse in a pipe which serves as an exchanger as heat passes through its walls to the greenhouse air.

Corporation A legal entity, separate and distinct from the persons (stockholders or shareholders) who own it. The corporation has all the rights and responsibilities of a person and may buy, own, and sell property; sue and be sued; and enter into contracts with both outsiders and its own shareholders. The most important advantage of the corporate form is its responsibility for its own acts and debts and the freedom of its owners from liability for either.

Cost accounting The use of the cost data of producing a given product for the purpose of assessing and controlling those costs. Since a knowledge of costs and controlling costs is vital to good management, a large greenhouse firm often engages the services of a cost accountant.

Critial night length The length of darkness less than which a short night plant, or more than which a long night plant, will undergo a photoperiodic response. The critical night length varies with plant species and even sometimes with cultivars within a species.

Crown bud A flower bud whose development has ceased. It sometimes develops the appearance of a crown. Generally this cessation of development breaks apical dominance, resulting in the development of side shoots. Crown buds may be caused by excessively low or high temperatures or in long night plants by a series of short nights while the flower bud is developing.

Curtain wall The nontransparent lower portion of the sidewalls of a greenhouse.

Cuticle A nonliving waxy layer covering all plant cells that are in contact with air. Although this layer protects plant cells from drying, water and nutrients can slowly penetrate it as in the case of foliar fertilization.

Cutting The portion of a plant removed for the purpose of asexual propagation. It may be part of a stem, a leaf, or part of a root depending on the species of plant to be propagated. Commercial cultivars of chrysanthemums, for example, are propagated by removing terminal stem pieces and placing the lower inch of them in a rooting medium in a moist environment to induce new root formation.

Cyclic lighting An alternative method of applying light during the night to achieve the photoperiodic effect of long days. The customary lighting period is divided into a number of subperiods, each comprised of a duration of light followed by darkness. The total duration of light can be reduced by as much as 80 percent. Where three hours of light are customarily applied, six consecutive cycles of five minutes of light and 25 minutes of darkness can be substituted, thereby reducing electrical consumption greatly.

Damping-off A disease caused by a number of fungi, mainly *Pythium, Rhizoctonia,* and *Phytophthora.* The symptoms include decay of seeds prior to germination; rot of seedlings before emergence from the root medium; and development of stem rot at the soil line after emergence, causing seedlings to topple.

Day neutral plant A plant that does not respond to the relative lengths of light and darkness in the daily cycle.

Depreciation Decline in value of an asset due to such factors as wear or obsolescence.

Desiccation The process of drying. Desiccation of plants results from a lack of water. High root medium levels of soluble salts cause desiccation of roots by preventing water from entering the roots.

Detergent *See* surfactant.

Disbudding The process of removing flower buds from a plant stem, generally to improve the size of the remaining bud or buds. In most cases the terminal flower bud is retained and all of the lateral (side) flower buds are removed.

Disease A plant is said to be diseased when it develops a different appearance or changes physiologically from the normally accepted state. These differences are called symptoms. Disease can be caused by such unfavorable environmental conditions as temperature extremes, insects, or pathogenic organisms such as nematodes, fungi, bacteria, or viruses.

Distribution tube A clear plastic tube with holes along either side that is suspended overhead along the length of the greenhouse to provide uniform distribution of air within the greenhouse.

Dry matter That which remains of the plant after water has been driven off. For purposes of foliar analysis, leaves are generally dried for one day at a temperature of 158°F (70°C).

Eave A component of the greenhouse frame to which the side wall and roof are connected.

Employee One who works for wages or salary in the service of an employer.

Employer One who employs another.

Emulsifiable concentrate (EC) A liquid pesticide preparation in which the pesticide is dissolved in oil and which contains an emulsifying agent to render the oil miscible in water.

Emulsifying agent A chemical which when added to two immiscible liquids renders them miscible.

Even span greenhouse A greenhouse both of whose roof slopes are of equal length and angle.

Facultative long and short night plants Plants which do not require a night length longer or shorter than a given critical length for a response to occur, but which will respond faster if the dark period is longer or shorter respectively than a critical length.

Fan and pad cooling A system for cooling greenhouses used during the warmer months of the year. Warm air expelled through exhaust fans in one wall is replaced by air entering through wet pads on the opposite wall. The entering air is cooled by the evaporation of water in the pad.

Fan-tube cooling A system for cooling greenhouses used during the cooler months of the year. Cold air entering through a louver high in the gable of the greenhouse is directed along the length of the greenhouse through a clear plastic distribution tube. Pairs of holes spaced equidistant along the length of the tube's opposite vertical walls permit uniform air distribution throughout the greenhouse.

Fasciation A malformation in plant stems resulting in an enlarged and flattened stem, as if several stems were fused.

Fixed costs Costs of conducting business which are not directly related to the number or type of items produced. Interest on a greenhouse mortgage, for example, is fixed because it remains unchanged if poinsettias are grown rather than azaleas, or even if no crop is grown.

Floramull® A white water-absorbing synthetic urea formaldehyde type resin produced by BASF Corp. It is an amendment used in root media for its high water-holding capacity, since it holds water to the extent of approximately 50 percent of its volume.

Floriculture The art and science of growing those plants valued for their aesthetic characteristics rather than woody plants used in the outdoor landscape.

Flowering plants Greenhouse crop plants grown in a pot and sold in the flowering state.

Footcandle (fc) A unit of illumination equal to the direct illumination on a surface everywhere one foot from a uniform point source of one international candle. It is equivalent to 10.76 lux.

Forced air heater A heater containing a heat source, a heat exchanger, and a fan for expelling the heated air.

Fresh flowers Flowers marketed subsequent to being cut from commercial crops.

FRP (fiberglass reinforced plastic) FRP panels are used as the transparent covering on some greenhouses.

Fungicide An agent or preparation used for killing fungi.

Fungus An undifferentiated plant lacking chlorophyll and conductive tissues.

Gibberellins A category of hormones that stimulate growth through cell division or elongation or both.

Glasshouse A term used more commonly in Europe to designate a structure used for growing plants that has a transparent cover and an artificial heat source. The American equivalent is *greenhouse.*

Greenhouse A structure used for growing plants that has a transparent covering and an artificial heat source.

Greenhouse range A term referring collectively to two or more greenhouses at a single location that belong to the same business entity.

Green plants Commercial crop plants grown in a pot and sold primarily for the aesthetic value of their foliage.

Headhouse A workbuilding in close proximity to or attached to a greenhouse. This facility might be used for such purposes as a workshop, storage area, pesticide room, potting area, eating area, etc.

Herbicide A chemical used for killing weeds.

Hormone An organic substance produced in one part of the plant and translocated to another part where in small concentrations it regulates growth and development.

Horticulture The art and science of growing fruits, vegetables, flowers, and woody ornamentals as well as spice, medicinal, and beverage plants.

Host plant A plant that is invaded by a parasite and from which the parasite obtains its nutrients.

Humus The relatively stable fraction of the soil organic matter remaining after the major portion of added plant and animal residues have decomposed.

Hydroponics A system of growing plants in which water constitutes the root medium.

Hypha (plural *hyphae*) A single branch of the mycelium which makes up the body of a fungus.

IAA (indole-3-acetic acid) A naturally occurring auxin produced in apical meristems of both roots and shoots.

IBA (indole-3-butyric acid) A synthetically produced auxin.

Infiltration heat loss Loss of heated air from the greenhouse through cracks.

Inoculum The pathogen or its parts that can cause disease; that portion of individual pathogens which are brought into contact with the host.

Insecticide An agent or preparation used for killing insects.

Internode The portion of a plant stem between two nodes. The node is the portion of the stem where one or more leaves are attached.

Interveinal Pertaining to the space between the vascular tissue (veins) on a leaf.

Larva The immature, wingless, and often wormlike form in which some insects hatch from the egg, and in which they remain through increase in size and other minor changes, until they assume the pupa or chrysalis stage.

Lean-to greenhouse A greenhouse built against the side of another structure such that it has only one sloping roof.

Loam A textural class name for soils having reasonably balanced amounts of sand, silt, and clay. Loam soils can contain from 7 to 28 percent clay, 28 to 50 percent silt, and less than 52 percent sand.

Logo A word, slogan, or sketch used to convey a thought. A logo is often used in advertising programs, e.g., *Say It With Flowers* or the cougar on a Mercury automobile advertisement.

Long night plant A plant that undergoes a photoperiodic response, such as flowering, only when the night length is greater than a critical length.

Lumen A unit of light equal to the light emitted in a unit solid angle by a uniform point source of one international candle.

Lux The international unit of illumination, being the direct illumination on a surface which is everywhere one meter from a uniform point source of one international candle. It is equal to one lumen per square meter, or 0.0929 footcandles.

Management The making of decisions which affect the profitability of a business.

Mark-on The percentage of the wholesale price added on to the wholesale price to arrive at a retail price; added in order to cover overhead and profit.

Mark-up The percentage of the retail price added on to the wholesale price to cover overhead and profit. An item purchased for $1 and selling for $2 has a mark-up of 50 percent and a mark-on of 100 percent.

Mass marketing In the field of floriculture, the sale of floral products through high-traffic outlets such as supermarkets, discount stores, department stores, sidewalk stands, shops in shopping malls, etc. Generally it entails cash-and-carry sales without delivery and a modest mark-up by full-service florist standards.

Meristem A tissue composed of embryonic, unspecialized cells actively or potentially involved in cell division. An apical meristem is a meristem located at the apex (tip) of a shoot or root.

Methylbromide A chemical commonly used for pasteurizing greenhouse root media. It should not be used in carnation root media.

Microorganism (microbe) A small living organism that requires the aid of a microscope to be seen.

Miticide An agent or preparation used for killing mites.

Mycelium The hypha or hyphae that make up the body of a fungus. Mycelium are the microscopic threadlike strands that make up the body of a fungus.

NAA (naphthalene acetic acid) A synthetically produced auxin.

Necrosis The state of being dead and discolored.

Nematocide An agent or preparation used for killing nematodes.

Organelle One of several types of small structures within plant or animal cells that are bounded by a membrane. The chloroplast is one type of organelle in which photosynthesis occurs.

Ovipositor A prominent structure projecting from the posterior end of females of some insects which is used to deposit eggs.

Pasteurization The selective destruction of some, but not all, living micro-organisms. Root media are pasteurized to eliminate harmful disease organisms and to retain the beneficial microorganisms.

Pathogen An entity (fungus, bacterium, nematode, virus) that can incite disease.

Peat The organic remains of plants that have accumulated in places where decay has been retarded by excessively wet conditions. There are many types of peat, some desirable and others not, used for greenhouse root media.

Peat humus Peat that is at an advanced stage of decomposition in which the original plant remains are not identifiable. It is not generally a desirable form of peat for greenhouse root media because of its rapid rate of decomposition and its occasionally high rate of ammonium nitrogen release.

Peatmoss Peat consisting predominately of slightly humified (decomposed) *Sphagnum* moss species. Horticultural peatmoss contains over 75 percent sphagnum moss.

Pedicel Stem of one flower in a cluster.

Perimeter heating system A row of heating pipe or pipes just inside the perimeter walls of a greenhouse.

Perlite A siliceous volcanic rock that is crushed and heated to 1800°F to cause it to expand into lightweight (about six pounds per cubic foot) particles with closed air-filled cells. Perlite is used as a substitute for sand when a lightweight root medium is desired.

Pesticide An agent or preparation used for killing living organisms which are a nuisance or are harmful to crops.

Petiole The stalk or stemlike portion of a leaf.

Photoperiodism The response of a plant or animal to the relative length of day and night. The response in plants can take on many forms, including flowering, changes in leaf shape or internode length, and bulb or tuber formation.

Photosynthesis The manufacture of carbohydrate from carbon dioxide and water in the presence of chlorophyll, using light energy and releasing oxygen.

Phytotoxic Toxic to plants.

Pinching Removal of the top of a vegetative plant stem in order to cause it to form several branches.

Polyethylene   A plastic material used in the greenhouse industry in the form of thin films for covering greenhouses. It is an inexpensive substitute for glass. Generally two layers are used, the outer being 6 mil (six one-thousandths of an inch) thick and the inner either 4 or 6 mil thick.

Pompon chrysanthemums   A term used in this book to denote the chrysanthemum cultivars grown with several flowers on each stem. The term *spray chrysanthemum* is more commonly used.

Potable   Drinkable.

Pressurizing fan   A fan in the end of the clear plastic greenhouse distribution tube which forces heated air, exterior cold air, or interior warm air through the tube depending on whether the system is being used for heating, cooling, or air circulation respectively.

Proprietorship   A business owned by a single individual.

Pupa   The intermediate, usually quiescent, stage assumed by many insects after the larval stage and maintained until the adult stage.

Purlin   A component of the greenhouse frame running the length of the greenhouse just below the root covering which connects the trusses together.

PVC (polyvinylchloride)   A plastic material available in corrugated sheets. This material was used for covering greenhouses during the 1960s, but due to its rapid deterioration from ultraviolet light it has virtually disappeared from the greenhouse industry.

Radiant heat loss   The radiation of heat from a warm body, such as plants in a greenhouse, to a cooler body, such as the covering on the greenhouse or the sky and earth outside.

Rafter   A frame component spanning the space between the eave and the ridge. Unlike a sashbar, glass is not attached to it.

Reglaze   To replace the glass or the glazing compound which seals the glass on a greenhouse.

Respiration   Those biochemical processes in the plant or animal which result in the consumption of oxygen and carbohydrate, the evolution of carbon dioxide, and the release of energy. Respiration has the reverse effect of photosynthesis.

Revenue   Income; return from investment.

Ridge   A component of the greenhouse frame to which the upper portion of the two roof slopes are connected.

Ridge-and-furrow greenhouses Two or more greenhouses connected to each other along their length at the eave. In this case the eave becomes a gutter otherwise known as the furrow. The common sidewall is eliminated in each greenhouse. Such greenhouses are less expensive to heat and easier to automate than an equivalent area of separate greenhouses.

Root medium (plural *root media*) A suitable substrate in which plant roots can grow; it consists of one or more mineral and/or organic components mixed together. This term is most commonly used in the greenhouse and nursery circles of agriculture.

Sand A soil mineral particle measuring 0.05 to 2.0 mm in diameter.

Sashbar The bar to which glass is attached in a greenhouse.

Senescence The process of growing old; aging.

Sepal One of the components of the calyx.

Short night plant A plant that undergoes a photoperiodic response, such as flowering, only when the night length is less than a critical length.

Sill The portion of the greenhouse which rests on the curtain wall and to which the sidewall sashbars are attached.

Silt A mineral component of soils consisting of particles measuring 0.002 to 0.05 mm in diameter.

Slab-side Also known as *cling-side*. A flower that has failed to open symmetrically. The petals on part of the circumference are still straight up, while the remaining petals have opened in a normal fashion.

Sleepiness A condition in flowers in which petals curve upward, giving the appearance of a wilted condition. It is commonly caused by ethylene gas after harvest.

Soil The upper, heavily weathered layer of the earth's crust which supports plant life. It is a mixture of mineral and organic materials.

Solenoid valve An electrically activated valve which controls the flow of gases or liquids. Such valves can be activated by a time clock or a Moist Scale® to control the flow of water in automated greenhouse watering systems.

Split A flower having a split calyx, in which the petals protrude from the split. It is a common problem of carnations.

Spore The reproductive unit of fungi consisting of one or more cells; analogous to the seed of green plants.

Sporophore   A hypha or fruiting structure bearing spores.

Spreader-sticker   *See* surfactant.

Standard chrysanthemums   Cultivars of chrysanthemum customarily grown with one large flower on each stem.

Sterilization   The destruction of all living organisms. Greenhouse tools and growing containers are periodically sterilized to eliminate harmful organisms including pathogenic diseases, insects, nematodes, and weeds.

Strap-leaves   Leaves whose margins are partially or completely missing such that the leaf is narrower than normal, often resembling a strap.

Structure   The arrangement of soil particles into groups or aggregates.

Surfactant   A chemical used to alter the surface properties of liquids. Surfactants are added to pesticide sprays to reduce the surface tension of the spray liquid, thereby enabling it to spread out more readily over the plant leaf surface. Without a surfactant, complete coverage of the leaf surface often is not achieved. Surfactants used for this purpose include *spreader-stickers, wetting agents,* and *detergents.* Surfactants are also used to enhance the initial wetting of root media containing relatively dry peatmoss, which tends to be waxy and water-repellent.

Symphillid   A small, translucent to white, many-legged arthropod ranging up to one-quarter inch in length which feeds on the roots of plants.

Systemic   Spreading internally throughout the plant body. Some pesticides are systemic, as are some pathogens.

Texture   The relative proportion of various sizes of mineral particles in a given soil or root medium.

Tropism   A growth response or bending toward or away from a stimulus. Geotropism is in response to gravity: roots grow toward, and shoots away from, the center of the earth's gravity. Phototropism is in response to light: shoots tend to grow toward light.

Truss   A compound component of the greenhouse frame spanning the width of the greenhouse and consisting of rafters, chords, and struts which are welded or bolted together.

Uneven span greenhouse   A greenhouse with one roof slope longer than the other, generally for the purpose of adaptation to a hillside.

Unit heater   A forced air heater. Unit heaters are usually mounted overhead in a greenhouse. They may contain a firebox or receive heat in the form of steam or hot water from a boiler elsewhere.

Variable cost A cost that increases proportionately with each additional unit produced and ceases if no units are produced. The cost of pots, root medium, and plants are variable costs in pot mum production; the mortgage on the greenhouse range is not a variable cost, but rather a fixed cost because it continues even if no pot mums are produced.

Vascular tissue Tissue in the root, stem, leaf, or flower stem, including phloem for conducting organic substances throughout the plant, xylem for conducting water and nutrients primarily from the roots to the shoot, and supporting fiber cells. Vascular tissue in leaves is often called veins.

Vase life The length of time that a cut flower retains its aesthetic value after it has been placed on display.

Veinal Pertaining to the vascular tissue (veins) or the tissue immediately above the vascular tissue in a leaf.

Ventilator A glazed panel attached to the greenhouse with hinges that permit opening for ventilation purposes.

Vermiculite A micaceous mineral that exfoliates (expands by separation of the many layers composing it) when heated. It is used in the expanded state as a lightweight component of greenhouse root media. Its desirable properties include a light bulk density of 7–10 pounds per cubic foot, a relatively high cation exchange capacity of 19 to 23 me/100g, and a high water-holding capacity.

Wettable powder In floriculture, an agricultural chemical formulated generally in talc or dry clay. It is suspended in water by continual mixing and is applied as a spray or root medium drench.

Wetting agent *See* surfactant.

Xylem A tissue in the plant that transports water and nutrients upward from the roots to the foliage. Cells connected end-to-end form xylem tubes. Vessels are the predominant xylem cells in flowering plants and have open ends. Tracheids predominate in the conifer (pines, etc.) xylem; rather than having open ends, they have pits along their sides connecting to adjacent tracheid cells. Vessel and tracheid cells are nonliving at the time they carry out the function of water and nutrient transport.

Index